RADICAL WARRIOR

Abby — Hope you enjoy

RADICAL WARRIOR

*August Willich's Journey from German
Revolutionary to Union General*

• • • • • • • • • • • • • • • • • • • •

David T. Dixon

Maps by Hal Jespersen

[signature: David T. Dixon]

THE UNIVERSITY OF TENNESSEE PRESS / *Knoxville*

Frontispiece: Brigadier General August Willich on horseback, c. 1864.
Lithograph by Ehrgott, Forbriger, & Co. Library of Congress.

Library of Congress Control Number: 2020940679

Contents

Illustrations

FIGURES

MAPS

Acknowledgments

Significant barriers prevent stories of obscure but significant German immigrants like August Willich from being told. The greatest challenge is source material that survives only in archaic Fraktur font or barely legible Kurrentschrift handwriting. The worldwide web affords American researchers limited access to some collections, but many other important books and documents require visits to archives in Germany and across Europe.

For non-German speakers, the key to producing comprehensive life stories of German Americans is collaboration with colleagues. Without their help and insight, this book could not have been written. Andrea Herrde deserves first mention for translating numerous passages and an entire pamphlet with the eye of an editor. Her boundless enthusiasm for the American Civil War, combined with a librarian's love for language, made her indispensable. Felix Zimmermann and I formed a successful research partnership that blossomed into a friendship culminating in road trips across Germany, France, and numerous battlefields in the southern United States. His forthcoming German-language dissertation will include new insights on Willich and the history of ideas. Wolfgang Hochbruck of Freiburg University invited us into his home and shared his knowledge and expertise, along with hearty fare and his own compelling stories. A trio of fine scholars of German American history, Peter Lubrecht, Yogi Reppmann, and Don Heinrich Tolzmann, buoyed me with early enthusiasm for this project and helped direct me to innumerable sources and contacts. *Moin-moin*, gentlemen!

I owe a debt to many accomplished historians who wrote articles or book chapters featuring Willich, especially James Barnett, Rolf Dlubek, Loyd Easton, Mischa Honeck, Karen Kloss, Christine Lattek, Boris Nicolaevsky, Kraig Noble, Joseph Reinhart, Charles D. Stewart, and Pat Young. Foremost among these is Mike Peake of Corydon, Indiana. Mike is the expert on the Thirty-Second Indiana Volunteer Infantry and is responsible for preserving America's oldest Civil War monument. He safeguarded and published the priceless drawings of Adolph Metzner. Mike's extensive knowledge of Willich and the Civil War helped me locate important sources and earns him special thanks.

No work on a Civil War subject would be complete without the steward-ship of the men and women of the National Park Service. Staff members at several battlefields were particularly helpful to my efforts: Jim Ogden and Lee White at Chickamauga, Charlie Spearman at Shiloh, and Jim Lewis at Stones River. Tony Patton of the Friends of Resaca Battlefield tramped through the pouring rain to help me understand that engagement.

Advance readers are to an author as skirmish lines are to a regiment. Greg Biggs, Earl Hess, Andrew Houghtaling, Al Mackey, Dave McGuire, Dave Powell, Dan Roper, and Tim Smith added context and probed the work for errors and omissions. Peer readers Aaron Astor and Andrew Zimmerman lent their skills and knowledge to help polish the manuscript.

Editor Thomas Wells and the team at the University of Tennessee Press shepherded the project to completion with outstanding communication and professional éclat. Cartographer Hal Jespersen met each request for custom mapmaking with his usual efficiency and accuracy.

Innumerable archivists, librarians, and curators made the search for manu-scripts and illustrations bearable and occasionally exciting. Kudos to the staff at the city archives of Besançon, France, who endured my halting French and opened the shuttered 1848 exhibit for me. Eva Bissinger of the Reutlingen, Germany town archives provided a stunning image of their Freischar banner from 1849. Johanna Schadel supplied Norwegian language translation.

I owe a huge debt of gratitude to my wife, Jeanne, who allowed a quirky dead bachelor general to occupy the guest room of our home for several years while I juggled my latest history obsession with the demands of our household.

Finally, as I write these acknowledgments, my thoughts are drawn to thou-sands of immigrants who lost their lives fighting for their adopted country in our nation's bloodiest war. May their sacrifice get the recognition it deserves and their names be remembered always.

RADICAL WARRIOR

Introduction

• •

RESURGENT REVOLUTIONS

HUNDREDS OF CINCINNATI GERMANS packed Arbeiter Hall on Sunday, January 29, 1860, then proceeded to the elegant Melodeon Building on the northwest corner of Walnut and Fourth Streets. They climbed stairs to the third floor where they joined a throng of like-minded citizens from all over the city for an annual event. A twenty-five-foot-high ceiling adorned with chandeliers, stuccoes, and ornamental elaboration made Melodeon Hall one of the country's most beautiful public spaces. The crowd heard from several speakers celebrating the 129th birthday of one of America's Founding Fathers. Local labor leader and newspaper editor August Willich gave the German-language address, praising Thomas Paine as the "embodiment of patriotism and free thought."[1]

Paine was America's first and foremost Revolutionary theorist. His direct and simple language appealed to literate colonists of all backgrounds. *Common Sense*, published in January 1776, sold more than one hundred thousand copies, the largest-selling book in American history proportional to population.[2] Paine's treatise helped persuade other founders to pursue independence, rather than merely a redress of grievances endured under their English sovereign. While living in France, Paine helped ignite the French Revolution. He later opposed the execution of Louis XVI on humanitarian grounds, then was imprisoned and barely escaped the guillotine himself. When his appeal to George Washington for help fell on deaf ears, Paine published a scathing denunciation of the American icon. Contempt for both the president and organized religion made Paine a pariah in the same United States he had played such a large role in creating. When he died in 1809, only six people attended his funeral. Two of the mourners were black freedmen.[3]

Abraham Lincoln was a great admirer of Thomas Paine. The twenty-six-year-old attorney and future president wrote a defense of Paine's deism in 1835, but an adviser burned it to save Lincoln's political career.[4] In 1860 some Philadelphians lobbied for Paine's portrait to hang alongside his patriot contemporaries in Independence Hall. Public outcry quashed that idea.[5]

August Willich sympathized with many of Paine's views on universal human rights, and with his opposition to all forms of slavery, animus against organized religion, and belief in the concordance of private interest with public good. Paine's vision included a political system as a compact among citizens, ever evolving toward a more perfect society until the need for government withers and moral virtue triumphs. Willich believed Paine when the Revolutionary patriot claimed, "We have it in our power to begin the world all over again."[6]

Like Paine, Willich derived certainty of purpose from his moral convictions. Paine insisted that liberty of conscience was not a favor bestowed on people by their government but a natural right of mankind. Willich's own conscience was shaped by two key figures in his childhood: the military hero father he never knew, and the famous liberal theologian and foster father who helped raise him. As a young man, Willich struggled to reconcile competing impulses he had inherited from his fathers. Filled with ethnic pride and romantic dreams of German destiny, the Prussian teenager fully embraced his duty to follow in his father's footsteps by serving in the military. Living in the extended family of acclaimed liberal philosopher Friedrich Schleiermacher, the young boy learned to question authority and set his own moral compass.

As he grew to manhood and became an army officer, Willich found his conscience troubled by the stark social divisions that title and privilege reinforced. He made the difficult decision to renounce his nobility and abandon a career in the Prussian Army. Initially seeking reform within existing government and religious frameworks, Willich soon adopted a radical prescription: overthrow the monarchy and replace it with communism.

Revolution in Europe began when the citizens of Paris rose up on February 22, 1848. French radicals, bent on restoring the republic Napoleon had usurped, rioted, and forced their king into exile. Consequently, they ignited a spontaneous conflagration of democratic revolts that swept the Continent. German republicans and liberal democrats mobilized rapidly, staging no fewer than three armed rebellions against the monarchs of several German states.[7]

Willich was a senior military leader in the rebel cause. Insurrections were put down easily in the German Confederation and throughout Europe. Willich eclipsed Karl Marx, becoming the popular leader of German political refugees in London, but enthusiasm for revolution ebbed soon after their arrival. Though European revolutionaries achieved little in the short term, their goals of democracy and republican government on the Continent eventually came to pass. Like Thomas Paine, leading German revolutionists of 1848 became folk heroes in their day only to be chastised later as heretics or dreamers. Most were all but forgotten by succeeding generations.

Willich adapted his political philosophy and tactics to his new home in America. Scorned at first by Karl Marx as a stubborn idealist and dangerous adventurist in a Europe not yet ripe for revolution, Willich matured into a pragmatic and patient radical. He grudgingly acknowledged some of Marx's theories of labor and economy as worthy of consideration while immersing himself in the cause of the American worker. Where better to revise the relationship between labor and capital than in the largest democratic republic on earth? Willich edited one of Cincinnati's German-language newspapers, a handy mouthpiece for advancing his social and political views. Moreover, Willich worked tirelessly to help workers organize while promoting a unique vision of a social republic with trade unions and trade associations replacing traditional legislative structures. Yet he had limited success. Willich's grandiose schemes were discounted by more practical reformers who achieved modest gains in wage increases and reasonable working hours by the early 1860s.

• • • • •

Willich's life offers an intimate glimpse into the international dimension of America's Civil War.[8] In an age of global social, economic, and political upheaval, transatlantic radicals helped affect America's second great revolution.[9] For Willich, the nature and implications of that revolution turned not on Lincoln's conservative goal of maintaining the national Union, but on issues of social justice, including slavery, free labor, and popular self-government. It was a war not simply to heal sectional divides, but to restore the soul of the nation, revive the hopes of democrats worldwide, and, in Willich's own words, "defend the rights of man."[10]

Thousands of rebels from the unsuccessful revolutions of 1848 and 1849 were among a million and a half individuals who emigrated from Germany to America in the decade prior to the Civil War. They became known collectively as "Forty-Eighters."[11] Leaders like Willich were largely responsible for rallying an estimated two hundred thousand men of German birth to enlist in the Union army once the Civil War erupted, a far greater number of recruits than from any other contemporary foreign-born population.[12] Many German American Union officers had fought for freedom in Europe. Their contribution to the Union war effort was significant, even conclusive on some battlefields. Only a handful of German Americans have achieved adequate recognition for these feats in the face of pervasive bias against immigrants that has persisted in America since the mid-nineteenth century.

The destiny of many radicals in Western societies has been consignment to historical obscurity. For example, few memorials to Thomas Paine exist in the United States despite his enormous influence in kindling the revolution that secured American independence. Though Willich's likeness in bronze or stone appears nowhere in Germany or America, monuments to a few contemporaries like Carl Schurz, Franz Sigel, and Friedrich Hecker grace public spaces in cities and towns where large numbers of German immigrants settled. Virtually all were erected before two world wars in the twentieth century dampened enthusiasm for public tributes to German-born Americans. The collective influence of Willich and his Forty-Eighter peers lives on in their contributions to progressive reform in American public education and as part of a rich cultural milieu of music, art, and literature. As Paine suggested, the Forty-Eighters remade their world in a new country, creating communities that stressed Enlightenment values of free thought and self-improvement.[13]

Most midcentury political exiles like Willich were highly educated radicals from middling or upper ranks of European society. They sustained their commitment to democratic revolution by using similar tactics as in 1848. Many entered journalism, doubling the number of US German-language newspapers in the 1850s in just four years. They started German social clubs called Turnverein, which sprung up all over the country. Willich was involved in a handful of the overtly socialist Turner societies. For these revolutionists, survival of the republican experiment in America, however imperfect, was the last and best hope for a new world order based on freedom, equality, and justice. In America, as in the German states of the Vormärz period, the constituency of Forty-Eighter radical activists was heterogeneous—a huge challenge when crafting a persuasive message and forging political unity.[14]

German immigrants in the 1850s were a diverse lot. Lawyers, professors, doctors, and military veterans left their homeland alongside thousands of craftsmen, skilled artisans, farmers, and common laborers making a new start in America. Newcomers ran the gamut in their religious beliefs and political ideology. Their motives for leaving Germany are difficult to discern, but economic opportunity in a free society was frequently mentioned. Although the overwhelming majority of these immigrants to America hailed from a small region in the German Confederation's southwest, they retained strong identities as Badeners and Rhinelanders, Bavarians and Prussians, Württembergers and Hessians. This is not to mention the many thousands of second and third generation German Americans who had established affiliations with churches and political parties in the United States. Radical Forty-Eighters like Willich employed a deliberate, conscious strategy to leverage what some historians call a German penchant for joining to construct a new German American ethnic identity. They formed worker organizations, started social clubs, and conducted festivals promoting German cultural superiority, a "German spirit," as Willich described it. That spirit carried with it a moral obligation. It was the destiny of German Americans to continue the work of revolution in their new home and perfect the American republic as an example for humankind.[15]

Americans had thrown off the oppressive yoke of monarchy, yet they later faced the prospect of losing half the country to a plantation aristocracy that considered slavery integral to Southern society. Slaveholding was a threat to republican government and a moral abomination in the eyes of German American radicals like Willich, who were overwhelmingly antislavery and predominantly abolitionist. Unlike many American-born abolitionists, these revolutionaries' opposition to human bondage was not grounded in religious fundamentalism. Rather, it was based on their moral and political principles; many were freethinkers. Willich and his peers understood the inherent conflicts in American political ideology. US citizens preached freedom and equality while owning slaves. German American radicals pressed newcomers, mostly Democrats, to join the newly formed Republican Party following presidential candidate John C. Frémont's adoption of an antislavery platform. While most northerners came to embrace Lincoln's emancipation policy gradually as a war measure, leading German Forty-Eighters viewed the Civil War as a war of slave liberation from the very beginning.[16]

Willich linked free labor ideology to the crusade against chattel slavery. The plight of African slaves reminded Germans of the long tradition of forced servitude in Europe. Although manorial privilege and serfdom was disappearing, mid-nineteenth-century Western European peasants faced staggering social change. Industrial capitalism threatened to turn all but the owners of the means of production into wage slaves. In America's well-publicized rags-to-riches folklore, a worker might finally get a fair shake or even an equal stake in a more perfect republican Union. Willich and many leading German Forty-Eighters wanted to help refine and reform the New World's capitalist juggernaut into a model society where all people could pursue happiness and true social equality. Demise of the American republic would delight the monarchs of Europe but was unconscionable to those who longed for a better world.[17]

Fifty-year-old August Willich had neither wife nor family, no American forefathers to honor, and no wealth or property to defend. Nevertheless, he rushed to help raise a regiment immediately after hearing of the attack on

Fort Sumter. His men affectionately called him "Papa" and "the Old One." William T. Sherman, a man not known for his effusive praise of immigrants, called Willich's all-German regiment "splendid," marveling that they fought in "beautiful style."[18] Willich's accomplishments rank him among the most successful brigade commanders in the Civil War.

Enlisting as a private but immediately appointed adjutant of the all-German Ninth Ohio Infantry, Willich took responsibility for training the volunteers, drawing on his extensive experience in the Prussian Army. Their dexterity on the drill field became the talk of Ohio, earning him promotion to the rank of major. Willich's coolness under fire in leading his skirmishers paved the way for General George McClellan's victory at the Battle of Rich Mountain in western Virginia. He was rewarded with promotion to colonel and command of a new German regiment, the Thirty-Second Indiana Infantry, in August 1861.

Willich made the most of his new command. He created the first dedicated pioneer company in the Union army and made important technical contributions in pontoon bridge building. At the Battle of Rowlett's Station near Munfordville, Kentucky, in December 1861, a portion of his regiment fended off a much larger force of cavalry by deploying a hollow-square defense, killing Colonel Terry of the Texas Rangers and earning an improbable victory. Willich displayed unmatched bravery while leading five successive charges against Confederate forces at Shiloh, changing front nine times. He paused to calm overanxious troops by drilling them in the manual of arms, his back to the enemy amid a shower of hostile fire. Willich's performance at Shiloh earned him promotion to the rank of brigadier general and command of a brigade in what became the Army of the Cumberland.

Willich led from the front, employing innovative tactics in his new role. He was at the focal point of the initial Confederate assault at Stones River, where his division was outnumbered four to one and overrun. Willich was captured and spent several months in the notorious Libby Prison in Richmond before being exchanged. Rejoining his command, he implemented a novel technique called "advance firing," then used it with devastating effect to capture Liberty Gap in June 1863. In September at the Battle of Chickamauga, Willich employed advance firing brigade-wide and added "retreat firing" to his tactical arsenal. His masterful performance in a losing effort earned his brigade the nickname "Iron Brigade of the Cumberland." He followed the capture of Orchard Knob near Chattanooga in November 1863 by being the first brigade to summit Missionary Ridge in one of the most audacious offensive actions of the war.

Willich's combat service ended at Resaca, Georgia, in May 1864, when a rebel sniper's bullet shattered his right arm, leaving him disabled for life. He subsequently served as post commander at Cincinnati, where he played an instrumental role in limiting arms shipments to Copperheads and Confederate sympathizers in the northwestern border states. Willich led troops from his former brigade through mop-up exercises in Texas shortly after the war ended, but poor health forced him to resign his commission. He received the brevet rank as major general of US volunteers in October 1865.

Willich's military accomplishments helped defeat the slaveholder oligarchy and ensure survival of republican government. It was the great achievement of his life. Just as Paine came on the American scene at the right time and place to inspire British colonists to rebel against their king, Willich and other recent immigrants were well positioned in 1861 to renew the call for freedom through revolution, as they had done in Europe just thirteen years earlier. Willich commanded thousands of ethnic Germans, and many of them, like himself, were committed to nudging the American republic closer to Paine's ideals of human rights and social justice. "Europe, not England, is the parent country of America," Paine insisted. "This new World has been the asylum for persecuted lovers of civil and religious liberty from *every part* of Europe."[19] "The cause of America," the patriot said in 1776, "is in a great measure the cause of all mankind."[20] So it was again in 1861. The Union had to prevail, not just for its own sake, but for the benefit of the Western world. Willich was on the same page with America's radical propagandist when Paine wrote, "My country is the world, and my religion is to do good."[21]

In 2018, the first Turner society in America celebrated its 170th anniversary in Cincinnati. Nineteenth-century Turnvereine were much more than community centers for German Americans. Early Turner mottos included *Frisch, fromm, fröhlich, frei*, which translated from German reads, "Lively, upright, joyous, and free," and *Mens sana in corpore sano*, Latin for "A sound mind in a sound body." In the years leading up to the Civil War, most Turners were unabashedly socialist in their philosophy and radical in their politics. Over time, their clubs remained important gathering places for Americans of German heritage but surrendered their radicalism to a republic committed to capitalism. Freethinkers dwindled and establishment religion flourished.

However, modern Turners still profess to follow radicals like Paine and Willich when they speak of their core values. Turner author and Cincinnati businessman Ernest Weier, writing of the society's philosophy in the twentieth century, stressed that true liberty was impossible "if one is forced to feel, to think or to act differently from the dictates of his own individual conscience."[22] August Willich believed in that creed. He sacrificed nearly everything to obey the command of his conscience to fight social injustice with pen and sword.

GENERALS CARL SCHURZ AND AUGUST WILLICH. CARTE DE VISITE.
CARL SCHURZ HOUSE, FREIBURG, GERMANY.

Chapter One

● ●

WARRIOR

THE NEW AMERICAN REPUBLIC that Thomas Paine had helped to inspire and the political independence that George Washington subsequently won on the battlefield sent shock waves across Europe. French radicals wasted little time in attempting to imitate the success of their young allies, initiating an ambitious, sweeping social revolution in 1789, the same year that Washington was elected president of the United States of America. After observing the early stages of the French Revolution, English philosopher Edmund Burke wondered aloud about the destiny of republics. "The effect of liberty to individuals is," Burke cautioned, "that they may do what they please. We ought to see what it will please them to do, before we risk congratulations."[1]

Leaders of the French Revolution underestimated the scale of social and political challenges that they faced. They overreached in adopting the most radical aims of Enlightenment philosophers. To French revolutionists, perfect equality was the natural order of things, and leaders must impose it on the entire populace, whether they were ready for it or not. Philosopher Jean-Jacques Rousseau described this approach best. "Whoever refuses to obey the general will shall be compelled to it by the whole body, which means nothing if not that he will be forced to be free."[2] Leaders like Maximilien Robespierre judged who was complying with proper revolutionary behavior and guillotined thousands deemed enemies of the revolution. Romantic visions of a new social order devolved into a macabre nightmare.

The American Revolution had more limited aims, had been carefully planned, and was carried through with a conventional army. The French Revolution relied on incohesive gangs of disorderly malcontents, resulting in chaos and terror. American observer Gouverneur Morris described the French: "They have taken genius instead of reason for their guide, adopted experiment instead of experience, and wander in the dark because they prefer lightning to light."[3] The French Republic disintegrated as popular general Napoleon Bonaparte consolidated his power and became emperor of France. Dreams of French revolutionary leaders were abandoned for the time being.

By the end of first quarter of the nineteenth century, the American Revolution had begun to transform the new nation in ways that its founders had not anticipated. Partisan politics created division between Jeffersonians and Hamiltonians, whose visions of democracy diverged. While the American North industrialized, the South remained agrarian. The critical constitutional compromise on slavery became a source of sectional agitation. Whereas the French Revolution remained a troubled child in deep slumber, its North American counterpart grew restless in its adolescence. Europeans wondered whether modern republican government could mature and survive.

• • • • •

In the midst of such uncertainty, Johann August Ernst von Willich entered the world on November 19, 1810, in the town of Braunsberg, in East Prussia. Like most German boys, he was called by his second name, "August." Ethnic Germans had no country of their own. Their homeland was part of the Holy Roman Empire, and in the first half of the eighteenth century, Prussia had emerged as one of the largest states in that domain. When Frederick the Great ascended the Prussian throne in 1740, he inherited a strong centralized government ruling three million subjects and backed by a formidable army. The core of the military, lesser nobility known as Junkers, dominated local affairs, court life, and particularly the army. Willich's grandfather Georg Wilhelm was a local official in the town of Celle. He gained favor with Frederick and was responsible for the family's elevation to noble status in 1766. Wilhelm later repaid his debt to his king by sending sons to serve in the Prussian Army.[4] Military service to the Fatherland was a duty carried through the generations, and it formed a critical part of August von Willich's identity as a proud ethnic German and a loyal Prussian subject.

Early nineteenth-century Europe endured tremendous change and constant war. Napoleon Bonaparte's ambitions knew no bounds; he stormed across the Continent, gobbling up territory at will. Prussia joined other European powers in the "Fourth Coalition," declaring war on France in 1806. Napoleon had already established a French protectorate in the Rhineland

id had troops in place near the Prussian border. Prussia's rash deci-
eclare war before their allies could position themselves in support
ight into the French emperor's hands. Napoleon defeated the Prus-
October 14, 1806, at the twin Battles of Jena and Auerstedt, then
Berlin two weeks later. When visiting the tomb of Frederick the
e asked his officers to remove their hats. "If he were alive," the French
imagined, "we would not be here."[5]

It Willich's father, Johann Georg, served as a captain in the Tenth
a cavalry brigade commanded by Maj. Gen. Friedrich Gideon Wolky.
soldiers were feared and famous. Their audacious uniforms were
.e most elaborate and expensive in the entire army. On parade, horsemen
sported gaudy red-lined panther skins and tight breeches. During campaigns
their uniform was accented with red and crowned with a tall, black shako
cap. The costume reinforced the troops' swashbuckling reputation and was

PRUSSIAN FUSILIER AND HUSSAR IN UNIFORM, C. 1815.
ENGRAVING BY T. GODDARD AND I. BOOTH.
AUTHOR COLLECTION.

designed to terrorize enemies. Officers carried curved sabers and smooth-bore carbine muskets and rode small, agile horses. The Hussars were light cavalry whose primary role was skirmishing and scouting. Young August von Willich was determined to follow in his father's footsteps and to know him by studying his martial deeds.

Captain Willich in his elegant cavalry uniform beside his beautiful wife, Frederika Lisette Michalowska, a Polish stage actress, cut a glamorous figure. When war wounds ended his active service in 1794, Willich was awarded the *Pour Le Mérite*. He was granted several positions in civil administration and became mayor of Braunsberg in 1808 He died in 1814, the same year that Napoleon was forced to return France to its 1792 borders following the re-capture of Berlin by a renewed Russian-Prussian offensive.[6] Captain Willich left his widow with two young boys and a modest military pension that was not enough to support the family, let alone educate the children. Lisette sent her oldest son, Julius, to live with his uncle, who was also an army veteran. August went to live with the family of the former Henriette von Willich, Lisette's widowed sister-in-law. Henrietta had married an eminent man who would provide the boy with a liberal education. For three-year-old August, exposure to one of the Continent's great thinkers would have a profound effect on his future.[7]

Celebrated theologian and philosopher Friedrich Schleiermacher earned his reputation as the father of modern liberal theology for his efforts to rec-oncile Enlightenment ideas with traditional Protestant teachings. In 1810, the year after he married Henriette von Willich, Schleiermacher helped found the University of Berlin. By 1817, his leadership had facilitated the brief reunion of the Reformed and Lutheran divisions of the German Protestant Church. Schleiermacher was a sensitive and sympathetic man who struggled to un-derstand a changing world. His role as August von Willich's foster father left a lasting imprint on the boy as he grew to manhood.[8]

Young August spent much of his childhood years on the Isle of Rügen at the estate of Schleiermacher's sister-in-law Charlotte von Kathen, who became his foster mother. At other times, the family lived in the Schleiermacher resi-dence in Berlin. Willich was tutored along with the Schleiermacher children until he was old enough to attend cadet school. Friedrich Schleiermacher had definite opinions on the value of a public education, reasoning that such instruction in an urban community "is always conducted on a much grander scale than it is possible to attain at home." Schools imposed much stricter order than a tutor could enforce, the division of subjects among several spe-cialist teachers led to a depth of learning superior to the home school model.

Public schools also built character through a feeling of self-dependence and a clear sense of right, according to the philosopher. "It is these two qualities," Schleiermacher assured his family, "that make the man."[9] Young August von Willich grew up in this privileged environment where much opportunity was provided to him. In return, the orphan boy was expected to repay this investment through public service.[10]

Schleiermacher's views on children were progressive for his times. He saw youngsters as full human beings worthy of respect and dignity and capable of teaching adults a few things. "Be converted and become as little children," the famous philosopher once said.[11] Young August von Willich learned to think critically and question everything. His foster father's approach to parenting fostered an independence of mind in Willich that he retained throughout his life.

GERMAN PHILOSOPHER AND THEOLOGIAN FRIEDRICH
SCHLEIERMACHER (1768–1834). LITHOGRAPH BY GENTILI
AFTER DRAWING, C. 1820, BY FRANZ KRÜGER.
AUTHOR COLLECTION.

August had a strained relationship with his birth mother, who remarried and started a second family when he was a young child. Although older brother Julius kept in contact with Lisette, August would have nothing to do with her. He hated his mother for abandoning her children and possibly for a more unforgivable sin.[12] Rumors that August von Willich was actually the illegitimate son of one of the Prussian royal princes persisted throughout his adult life. Willich never denied them; in fact, he himself hinted that they were true. "Look into my eyes and you will see the Kaiser," he often said later in life. Most of his closest friends believed the story. Prince August, the never-married nephew of Frederick the Great, had many children by numerous women and was the frequent lunch companion of Schleiermacher during the time that young Willich resided in Berlin.[13]

During the 1820s, Schleiermacher developed a distrust of the reactionary policies of King Friedrich William III of Prussia. The philosopher's liberal views on society and politics had a profound impact on his youngest foster son. Schleiermacher tiptoed gingerly along a tightrope between Enlightenment reforms and loyalty to his king. He compared the administration of the church to a free-state constitution, likening church members to citizens and clergy to mere servants of the people. Presbyteries and synods answerable to the congregation should regulate order and discipline in the church, Schleiermacher believed. To royal ears these opinions sounded like democracy, and that was something the monarch could not abide.[14]

Attempting to bring the church under direct royal control, the king proposed a commission to regulate ecclesiastical matters and composed his own compulsory liturgy. Schleiermacher argued strongly against such measures. If they were designed merely to transfer the authority of a pope to a prince, he reasoned, then the time was ripe for another Reformation. Schleiermacher's insistence that congregations manage their own affairs led royal authorities to suspect that the professor was a closet republican. He was ultimately charged with "demagogic agitation" by the Prussian government. "My outward position is very precarious," he wrote Charlotte von Kathen in 1824. Only Schleiermacher's wide popular appeal allowed him to retain his chair at the University of Berlin.[15]

The tradition of public service inherited from his father and foster father were not lost on young August von Willich. In 1848, he described the debt he owed to posterity. "Our fathers tell us of the enthusiasm which the whole nation burnt through," Willich remembered. "Our fathers, bleeding from their wounds, exhausted from fighting, tired of old age, have put their achievements into our hands. Only a few of us still shine with the spirit

of that time on the orbits on which we can prove ourselves as their sons."
Willich was determined to honor his forbears' legacy through his own efforts
on behalf of what he called "a German national spirit."[16]

Emulating their dead father, Julius and August von Willich prepared for
careers in military service. It was a privilege to serve the Fatherland and continue the family legacy, and their title alone was enough to secure them a place
among prospective cadets. The brothers, however, would end up taking their
education and military training down divergent paths, and they were never
to fully reconcile as grown men. Julius, raised in a traditional military family, became a loyal career soldier for the Prussian government. August, the
product of a liberal upbringing, eventually rebelled against country and king.

• • • • •

August von Willich entered a newly reformed military system destined to
become the envy of the world. His schooling concluded under the direction
of one of the preeminent military strategists of all time. Carl von Clausewitz
served as aide-de-camp to Prince August during the Jena Campaign, and he
was one of more than twenty-five thousand Prussian soldiers captured in
October 1806. After spending nearly two years in a French prison, Clausewitz
joined his mentor and fellow reformers Hermann von Boyen and Karl von
Grolman in their efforts to restructure the Prussian Army. Clausewitz was
a graduate of the old military academy at Berlin, so he was aware of both its
successes and its shortcomings. He also served as director of the academy
from 1818 to 1830. During his leadership, the school regained a reputation
for excellence that would have made Frederick the Great proud.[17]

August began his military education in 1823 at the age of twelve, entering the cadet school at Potsdam. One hundred fifty students boarded at the
school, nine to a room, assisted by resident tutors. The boys had clean, comfortable beds, ample food, and laundry service. Their uniforms mimicked
those of the Landwehr, the national citizen militia: blue tails, red cuffs and
collars, a gray overcoat, and a tall cap or shako adorned with the badge of the
Prussian king. Cadets studied Latin, French, arithmetic, history, geography,
and drawing. Religious education was offered twice a week, and students
could spend the noon hour learning music and dance at their own expense.[18]

Cadets immersed themselves in an insular military culture that emphasized a convivial esprit de corps combined with rigid discipline, based on
the Spartan model of the ideal youth. Willich and his fellow students went to
great lengths to prove themselves "Spartan-like." A classmate recalled ritual

self-torture such as "bearing blows, sticking needles in [the] flesh or making deep cuts" as customary. He also described more elaborate demonstrations: "the burning of elastic bands into our hands, melting a snowball over the palm of the hand, or letting a rooster crawl over your face without turning a hair." When a cadet who had dislocated his arm in a wrestling match let out a whimper, his doctor sneered, "Pshaw! A soldier should be able to dance on needles!"[19] School authorities encouraged Spartan ethics to build fraternal relations and harden the boys for a long military career. The combination of strict discipline, ascetic lifestyle, and strong brotherly bonds would become hallmarks of Willich's leadership for the balance of his military career.

Following three years at cadet school, fifteen-year-old August entered the Allgemeine Kriegsschule, or German Military Academy. The school, founded by Frederick the Great, boasted an impressive campus on Neue Wilhelm-strasse. Unlike private military schools, the academy was specifically designed to prepare cadets for the officer examination. A select group of only fifty-five cadets were admitted to the program each year. After watching his brother Julius complete the three-year course and obtain his commission, August set his mind to the same task.

Officer candidates lived five to a room, with a common area available for studying. The library boasted nearly ten thousand volumes, support from officers and tutors was readily available, and discipline was exacting. Cadets studied for nine months a year and completed typical university-style course-work with an emphasis on military science. The remaining three months were dedicated to practical service-related exercises. Willich rose at half past five each morning, ate breakfast, then took an hour to prepare for the day's lessons. Following a lunch break at noon, lessons resumed from two o'clock until four or five in the afternoon. After supper, study with tutors resumed from six to eight in the evening, followed by an hour and a half of free study time. Wednesdays and Saturdays were half holidays, and cadets had all of Sunday free following church services.[20]

Coursework and exams were rigorous. Year-one cadets studied elementary tactics, fortifications, military history, French, and mathematics. In the second year, students learned specifics of fortification and tactics of past campaigns, as well as geography, French, history, logic, physics, and advanced mathematics. In their final year, Willich and his classmates pored over subjects as diverse as general strategy, sieges, chemistry, Latin, trigonometry, French and German military history, and mapmaking. Studies culminated in a general exam before the Supreme Board in Berlin, and students who passed it were awarded a special sword knot indicating their status as ensign officer candidates. They then did six months' service in the field before subjecting themselves to the officer's examination. Like the general exam, this test lasted many hours and contained both written and verbal components.[21]

Eighteen-year-old August von Willich passed his exams and earned his commission as second lieutenant in 1828. For six years, August had followed the example of his father and brother, fulfilling his duty as a loyal son and subject. But time in a new environment amid the emergence of liberal rumblings in the German provinces would soon change Lieutenant von Willich in ways no one expected.[22]

Chapter Two

● ●

POET PROPHECIES

SEVENTEEN-YEAR-OLD 2nd Lieut. August von Willich made his professional debut during a time when war-weary Europeans seemed content to slumber under the rule and protection of traditional monarchial regimes. The Bourbon dynasty ruled France again. Friedrich von Sallet, Willich's classmate at Potsdam, decried the demise of the French Republic in a poem describing a veteran of the French Revolution: "At the Bastille storm, how he was power and fire! / Now he is lying on his bed, his hair white, / the limbs cold and damp, a long-forgotten old man." Dreams of liberty, equality, and fraternity had all but vanished in the quarter century since Napoleon had declared himself emperor, but dormant forces for social, economic, and political reform lingered. The people of the German Confederation's thirty-four states grew increasingly restive during the second quarter of the nineteenth century, a period that became known as the Vormärz or "pre-March."[1]

Sallet and Willich received commissions as officers in the Rhineland region. Sallet was sent to the large fortress at Mainz, which had joined more than a hundred other towns and villages declaring the region a separate republic for a brief time in 1792. The area was a part of France for nearly twenty years until Napoleon Bonaparte was defeated and large portions of the Rhineland returned to Prussia. There and in the Grand Duchy of Baden to the southeast, a complex brew of socioeconomic ingredients combined with intellectual yeast from Romantic poets, philosophers, and politicians to ferment a potent elixir of progressive ideas that ultimately produced revolution.

Economic change in the Rhineland progressed rapidly during the nineteenth century. Mechanization and commercialization in industries

GERMAN POET AND WRITER FRIEDRICH VON
SALLET (1812–1843). ENGRAVING BY UNKNOWN
ARTIST, C. 1859. AUTHOR COLLECTION.

traditionally controlled by artisans and master craftsmen resulted in lower wages, lower prices for finished goods, and reduced quality. Manufacturers of wool, for example, encouraged the exploitation of common pasturage rights, sponsoring large herds of animals who stripped the land bare and created hardship for peasants and small farmers. Large vineyards squeezed small vintners in a battle to maintain market share amid falling prices. Rhinelanders vocally opposed indirect taxes the Prussian monarchy imposed during the 1830s.[2]

Social division played a critical role in kindling revolution in Europe but these same divisions ultimately hastened its failure. Aristocrats occupied the highest rung on the social ladder, as they had for more than a thousand years. Dynastic rulers, landed nobility, and influential clerics controlled the vast majority of land and resources. Their power and position, however, was eroding. Upper-middle-class bourgeoisie often led reform efforts. Yeomen farmers, artisans, and laboring peasants filled out the bottom ranks of society. The bourgeoisie successfully reengineered English rule in the seventeenth century to create a constitutional monarchy. Affluent middle-class leaders helped depose the monarchy in subsequent revolutions in America and France in the eighteenth century. The French model of social equality had failed, but the rise of capitalism as the dominant form of economic exchange in the West gave hope to bourgeois intellectuals that another enlightened revolution would come soon.[3]

When Sallet and Willich arrived in the Rhineland, they found a society that was quite different from Berlin. The power of the nobility, already on the wane due to the abolition of feudal practices, was further diminished in their new environment. In the Rhineland, the nobles were few in number and limited in influence. The predominantly Catholic bourgeoisie held most power. They neither needed nor desired Prussian help, military or otherwise, in meeting the challenges of a changing social and economic order.

Economic upheaval driven by changes in the market economy created further division. As bourgeois capitalists amassed huge fortunes and ascended from the middle to upper ranks of society, small business owners, or "petite bourgeoisie," came into increasing conflict with their wealthier peers. Doctors, lawyers, and teachers also occupied the middling economic stratum. Their influence was much greater than their numbers might suggest. These men acted as moral spokespersons for a populace less inclined to hew solely to the directives of a church hierarchy many viewed as corrupt and wedded to the aristocracy. True believers were increasingly divided. Interfaith conflict between Protestants and Catholics bubbled near the surface, frequently emerging during policy interventions by a prince of state.

The greatest change in social relations was happening at the bottom of the class hierarchy. Perpetually struggling peasant farmers were joined by increasing numbers of laborers needed to feed the burgeoning capitalist machine. Activities that formerly took place in the home, with families controlling the means and deriving the benefits of their own labor, were moving to distant city factories. Workers from the countryside often toiled and lived in crowded, unsanitary urban conditions. Those who remained at home had fewer options and were often one or two bad harvests away from starvation. As ruling elites commiserated over commodity shortages and debated ways to offset falling prices by increasing production, they had one ear turned to the working class. Would they rise if conditions worsened? They would not wait long for an answer.[4]

A four-year cycle of poor harvests began in 1828. Food became scarce and expensive, and Europe's workers grumbled. That summer, southern provinces of the Netherlands seceded and formed the new Kingdom of Belgium, followed weeks later by the fall of the Bourbon dynasty in France. On September 6 the Duke of Brunswick fled his throne in the northern part of the German Confederation. A new monarch was installed in each case. In August, mobs ran through the streets of Cologne calling for an end to excise taxes and cheering Napoleon. This was hardly cause for panic, but Rhenish bourgeois leaders sensed an opportunity to press for liberal reform. Monarchs in southwestern Germany reacted swiftly and little was accomplished. By the spring of 1832, however, bread and forest riots in Bavaria were gaining momentum. When democratic leaders organized a National Festival of the Germans in Hambach on May 27, 1832, over thirty thousand people attended. Some carried flags bearing the German national colors of black, red, and gold. Others wore red Phrygian caps copied from the French Revolution. Orators spoke and people cheered, but festival leaders had no plans for next steps. Bavaria's King Ludwig sent 8,500 troops to the province, censored its newspapers, and arrested the revolutionists. Despite its failure, the Hambach Festival proved that large numbers of people could be mobilized quickly to support liberal and national goals. Revolution appeared attainable.[5]

Willich came to believe that the laudable military reform goals of Scharnhorst, Clausewitz, and others had been subverted by reversion to tradition. The resurrection of the old system of Junker privilege alienated the people from the army. Officers perpetrated acts of violence against citizens they were supposed to protect. Soldiers suppressed their humanity and became an unthinking weapon of the state. "Where human law is contrary to the law of the state," Willich insisted, "the state is wrong; where military law is in conflict with state law, the military is wrong. . . . Humanity and human rights constitute the foundation of the state as well as the rank."[6] Sallet agreed. In 1832, the poet-soldier was imprisoned in the fortress at Jülich for publishing satirical essays and poems criticizing the military.[7] Willich himself was punished that same year, accused of harboring "extravagant ideas."[8]

Events in the early 1830s gave pause to monarchs throughout the German Confederation. They responded with sweeping measures designed to intimidate opposition, limit free speech and free press, ignore parliaments, and clamp down on free association. They created secret political police forces. Germany's monarchs co-opted the liberal nationalism of the Hambach Festival, inventing fears of war with France to promote patriotism for the existing order. These tactics worked for a while, though many Rheinlanders never bought into royal propaganda. Democratic and republican movements went underground for a time. This gave Willich and his officer friends time to read, discuss, and debate the future of the army and society. In a period of intense reflection, these men attempted to reconcile loyalty to their country with their code of morals. They turned to the great philosophers and poets for guidance and inspiration in this time of intellectual turmoil.[9]

Significant molders of Willich's social consciousness were followers of influential German Romantic intellectual Georg Wilhelm Friedrich Hegel. Hegel was a giant of modern philosophy, an idealist who believed in dualities he called "dialectics" that were inherent in every sphere of spiritual life. Dualities are self-conscious pairs of seeming opposites, like master and slave or being and nothing. Hegel argued that human relations constantly evolved toward perfection. He also contended that political states closer to achieving full realization, like Prussia, would end up eliminating other states of lesser consciousness. According to Hegel, the state ultimately subsumes and fulfills the needs of family and civil society. An individual achieves an ethical life only in the fully realized state.

Hegel believed that the concepts of freedom and reason had reached fulfillment in the Prussian state. In his view, Prussia was the culmination of an inexorable march toward an ideal existence. His followers split on this claim along political lines. Conservatives cherished the idea that their state had achieved perfection, and liberal thinkers saw contradictions in Hegel's work and much room for improvement in Prussian civic relations. Leftists retained Hegel's insights on dualism, stressing that man's ultimate destiny was to banish encumbrances to freedom and reason. In practice, this meant an end to absolute monarchy and a turn toward democracy. Liberals influenced by the philosopher became known as "Left" or "Young" Hegelians.[10]

The flash point for the politicization of the Young Hegelians came when Friedrich William IV assumed the throne of Prussia in 1840 and began limiting political freedom. Willich was already leaning in a liberal direction by 1837, when a major accused him of being more of a republican than a loyal Prussian subject.[11] This was not true, at least not yet; Willich was still wrestling with his conscience. Not so with his poet friend, for Sallet resigned from the army in 1838 to focus on his writing. Both men adopted a view of religion and society that mirrored the radical Young Hegelian philosopher Ludwig Feuerbach.

Feuerbach was the son of a Bavarian jurist whose other sons attained distinction in academic and scientific circles. A student of Hegel, Feuerbach had once challenged his master on assertions about God and Creation. Hegel had ignored him. To Feuerbach, God was simply a projection of human nature, not a divine being or creator. The philosopher believed that religion isolated a person from his true essence. Religious alienation inhibited the natural state of collective life through egoism and individualism in pursuit of a false doctrine of salvation outside one's own self. Schleiermacher had encouraged Willich to question authority. Feuerbach freed him to abandon traditional conceptions of God and the superfluous superstructure of organized religion, and to substitute an anthropological explanation. Willich ultimately became an atheist and a revolutionist.[12]

Willich believed in a universal human consciousness. He saw the universe as a dynamic and self-existing whole in which humans evolve to benefit their fellow beings while sustaining their individual selves. These conflicting drives represent a personal struggle to reconcile death and immortality, self-interest and charity. The perfection of humanity would not come from Christianity or politics, in Willich's opinion. It would be achieved through labor. Existing systems should be reorganized so that people could follow their natural inclination to work in a community for the common good. Only then could individuals abandon selfish inclinations and become fully realized as "the reconciled man, the man of the community."[13] Willich had little idea what that concept might look like in the real world. For the time being, he continued his quest for understanding within the confines of his military career.

Thirty-one-year-old August von Willich returned to Berlin, passed the artillery master's exam in 1838, and was commissioned first lieutenant. He then moved back to the Seventh Royal Artillery at the fortress of Wesel in the northwestern province of Westphalia. There, he was responsible for eighty soldiers, forty-five horses, and two artillery pieces. Some Wesel citizens were sympathetic to liberal ideas. For example, the young officer's friend and landlord Friedrich Veenfliet would later publish a radical leaflet and be forced to immigrate to the United States. Willich was godfather Veenfliet's daughter Wilhelmine. Gymnasium (secondary school) director Ludwig Bischoff was eventually compelled to leave for political reasons as well.[14]

In March 1844 Willich earned promotion to company commander. He subsequently started a reading circle that included fellow officers Fritz Anneke and Joseph Weydemeyer. Members read and discussed many forbidden books, including those of the Hegelian philosophers, and they often debated long into the night about the monarchy and the military's place in the kingdom. Under Willich's influence as the oldest company commander, the Seventh became infamous as a hothouse of open inquiry during the Vormärz period.[15]

Another Young Hegelian who profoundly influenced Willich's thinking was the Jewish philosopher Moses Hess. Hess attended Bonn University but never graduated. After years of moving in Young Hegelian circles in the Rhineland, he anonymously published the *Holy History of Mankind* in 1837. Applying Feuerbach's concept of religious alienation to emerging social and economic realities of capitalism, Hess compared the subordination of man's essence to divinity and false religion to the relationship between workers and the value they produce. Workers must sell their labor but relinquish its fruits, thereby alienating themselves from their essence and becoming slaves to the aristocracy of money. To emancipate laborers from the yoke of forced toil, capitalism must be eliminated and a new communist economy established in its place. In Hess's ideal society, people could realize their true nature in a collective life based on love for their fellow humans. The result was a variant of French utopianism that became known as "True" Socialism. Hess was its architect.[16]

By 1842, Friedrich William IV's reactionary program had crushed most liberal reform efforts. Frustrated Young Hegelians split into two factions. One group, led by Bruno Bauer and Max Stirner, set their course toward individualism and anarchy. Others, including Feuerbach, Hess, Karl Marx, and Friedrich Engels, moved away from liberal bourgeoisie concerns and threw their weight behind the working class. On January 1, 1842, a group of prominent Rhenish businessmen established a newspaper in Cologne called the *Rheinische Zeitung*. Hess was its first editor and Marx served as a frequent contributor. Later that year, Hess introduced his young protégé Friedrich Engels to Marx, and the two became lifelong friends and collaborators.

Marx joined the editorial board of the *Rheinische Zeitung* on October 15, 1842, and published an influential article on timber theft. In January 1843 the paper ran a series of essays criticizing the Prussian government for ignoring peasant grievances. Rheinlanders had enjoyed liberal French rule in the days before the region was returned to Prussia, and many viewed the Prussian state as an alien enemy. Subscriptions to the periodical exceeded three thousand copies, making it one of the most popular German-language newspapers of its day. Fearing burgeoning democratic sentiment, the king ordered the newspaper suppressed on January 21, 1843. On March 17, Marx resigned rather than tone down his rhetoric. He and Hess spent the next five years shuttling to Paris, Brussels, and elsewhere, anticipating the day when they would return to the Rhineland to fight for worker freedom and democratic rule.[17]

In the meantime, Willich and officer friends in Westphalia became radicals. They realized that the elite military class in Prussia was alienated from both the state and the people. To serve the state, an officer was expected to be "a soldier and nothing but a soldier." Officers were also kept separate from the people to build esprit de corps, according to Willich, so that "they would be ready at any moment to give their lives in a struggle against strangers." This meant not only battling foreign invaders, but also fighting against their fellow citizens.[18] A tragic example was the 1844 weavers' revolt in Silesia, an important Prussian province and a center of textile manufacturing. Market changes brought on by industrialization created overseas competition for the Silesian weavers, lowering prices and depressing earnings below sustenance levels. Protests to the Prussian government were largely ignored. In June, mobs of angry weavers went on a rampage, attacking homes and businesses and demanding money from local merchants. The army mobilized and fired into the crowds. Eleven weavers died in the melee. German radical Heinrich Heine, who had moved to Paris to escape German censorship, composed a poem dedicated to the Silesian weavers. Marx published the work in his Parisian newspaper *Vorwärts!*, distributing fifty thousand copies throughout the Rhineland.[19] Battle lines between the Prussian Army and its citizens were drawn. Officers like Willich were trapped in the middle, forced to choose between duty and humanity.

Willich and his peers tried to push the army toward reform from within. They treated subordinates with dignity and respect while forging strong connections with citizens in their neighborhood. Above all, they used self-education to foster an inner spirit of compassion to guide them in their actions. That strategy was destined to fail within the rigid confines of the Prussian military system.

Sallet died in 1843 at the age of thirty. Willich eulogized his childhood classmate as a man who overcame military indoctrination "with warlike heroism," a man who, "without fear and reproof, inspired truth and freedom in the breasts of his fellow-citizens."[20] It was high time for others in Sallet's circle to step up and be counted—to follow their conscience despite danger to their careers and their persons. Weydemeyer was the first to leave, resigning from the army to edit a radical newspaper in Trier. Willich's closest friend and confidante, Fritz Anneke, was the next officer to come to a crisis of conscience. Anneke's conflict with his superiors would ultimately force Willich to make the most difficult decision of his life.

Chapter Three

● ●

INQUISITION

LIEUT. GEN. WILHELM von Tietzen und Hennig, who later commanded the Seventh Corps of the Prussian Army, spoke to officers and volunteers of the Landwehr at military maneuvers during the summer of 1846 in Münster:

> Recent incidents compel me to have a serious word with you. Unfortunately, there are people in our midst who are making it their business to seduce young people and sprinkle poison in their hearts. . . . Do you know what it means to be a socialist and a communist? I will tell you. It means to plot behind His Majesty's back. Communism wants to take the property of the quiet, prosperous citizen and distribute it equally. He will use all means to accomplish this: rape, arson, robbery, murder. Such is the communist pest. It is preached by clever, witty people and is therefore dangerous for young, inexperienced minds.[1]

What compelled a high-ranking officer like Tietzen to express such grave concerns? After all, Prussian censors were adept at stifling dissent. They had moved beyond banning religious polemics, adding liberal and radical authors to the forbidden books list. For many at the Münster review, the label "communist" was new and carried uncertain meaning. Prussian military leaders, however, saw discontent brewing among peasants and workers. Divisions within the army itself were even more troubling. The military establishment demanded strict discipline and unquestioned loyalty to the crown. Nowhere in the army was dissension more pervasive than in the Seventh Artillery Brigade.

Although seven years younger than Willich, Fritz Anneke earned promotion to company command before his outspoken peer. Assigned to Wesel

FRITZ ANNEKE (1818—1872). DAGUERREOTYPE, C. 1855.
WISCONSIN HISTORICAL SOCIETY.

in the Seventh Artillery in 1841, Anneke won his men's love and respect due to his unblemished character and fairness. He and Willich subsequently became close friends. When Joseph Weydemeyer resigned in 1844, the two lost a comrade and an ally in their efforts to reform the service. Willich's circle was dealt another blow when Anneke was transferred from Wesel to Minden in September. Anneke neither wanted nor appreciated the new assignment. His transfer was designed to break up what Prussian military officials feared was a coterie of dangerous influences. Their suspicions had merit.[2]

Anneke stoically accepted the move and started another reading club in October 1844, ordering books on politics, military affairs, and history, along with a few fiction titles. Some club members suggested that they also read forbidden books. Anneke, not suspecting the elaborate trap, fell right into it.[3] His peers began reporting his activities to senior officers, and the group disbanded after nine months in operation. Anneke tried to maintain a low profile, but he had made enemies in high places that doomed his career. He was suspended from the service.[4]

Investigators began intimidating Anneke's closest friends, warning them to avoid contact with their comrade or be subject to discipline themselves. Former roommate Lieutenant von Kalinowski pushed back. "Lieutenant Anneke is my best friend," he admitted. "I hold the same views." Kalinowski was then urged to resign. Some officers openly accused Anneke of disloyalty, even challenging him to a duel on one occasion. Rather than accept, he referred the dispute to the honor court of the Seventh Artillery Brigade.[5]

Brigade commander Colonel von Schlemmer had trouble stifling rage when Anneke appeared in honor court at Münster in full beard—a silent and foolish protest. Honor court was held in the five garrison towns of the region. Anneke had friends, including Willich, in the Ehrenrath, a group of honorary judges selected annually. Once judges collected evidence and heard Anneke's defense, thirty voted for acquittal, eighteen recommended warning, and another eighteen counseled dismissal. That should have ended it. However, Schlemmer appealed to the Court of Justice, claiming that since Anneke's case had not been settled by two-thirds' majority verdict, it should be remanded to staff-officer court in the Thirteenth Division. The king agreed, expressing his dissatisfaction with investigative procedures in the action. In July 1846 he issued a cabinet order directing a retrial; the edict was read by Prince Adalbert, general inspectorate of the Prussian artillery, at a review.

Colonel von Schlemmer assembled the officer corps of the brigade a few days after the cabinet order was read. He emphasized that officers engaged in political discussions in public places were expected to make their commander aware of such conversations. Anyone who did not share His Majesty's political sympathies could no longer be an officer. As Schlemmer moved to leave the circle, Willich stepped forward and asked the council to explain why a fellow soldier's insult against Anneke was not also worthy of consideration. The colonel responded that "this was not the place to do so." Willich pressed him, insisting that the honor of the entire officer corps was at stake. Schlemmer left the circle momentarily to confer with staff, then returned and assured his men that he would do his duty to represent the honor of the officer corps in every circumstance. Willich had embarrassed the colonel in front of other officers. Schlemmer was not one to forgive such slights.[6]

Anneke was jailed and dismissed from service a month later. The proceedings of the staff honor court were kept secret, and the case was closed. Anneke traveled to Wesel upon release and met with Willich for a few days to discuss the future. Willich implored him to accept a monthly subscription of twenty-five thalers raised by friends until he could establish himself in another profession. The men visited with officers and their families, enjoying the fellowship of coffee, wine, and music. After Willich retired, Anneke raised a glass with old comrades in the tavern. When he returned to Münster, the former officer accepted the subscription support for the time being. Even this innocent send-off was cause for concern among Prussian authorities.[7]

Münster military officials insisted that officers swear an oath stating they did not share Anneke's sentiments. Willich refused. The oath was never formally administered, and the issue was forgotten. Some officers distanced themselves from Anneke, and a few days later, Colonel von Schlemmer circulated a letter stating, "Under the present circumstances, it would be very desirable to know which officers contributed to the salary of Lieutenant Anneke." He used the word "salary" to imply that the king's decision to end Anneke's financial compensation had been subverted. Each officer of Wesel corps gave the same one-word reply: "No." Other officers admitted that they only contributed to Anneke's temporary support. They were stonewalling. Schlemmer followed up with four questions from the general inspectorate: Did you support Lieutenant Anneke? Did you do this voluntarily or on request? Who asked you to do it? Who took the money to Anneke? Officers refused to answer the questions, claiming that such inquiries constituted an invasion of privacy. All citizens had the right to dispose of their own resources in any way they deemed fit, they claimed. Willich's reply was more pointed.[8]

"I do not stand with Lieutenant Anneke or anyone else in any connection through which the service is compromised," Willich wrote. He continued, "In the innermost circle of my sensations, thoughts, and relations with others, you must not intend to enter, as this is a sphere in which only the benevolent friend and brother is voluntarily tolerated. This is why your superiors will surely agree with me if I only explain in general that I am neither in any relationship with Lieutenant Anneke, nor anyone else, in whom threats, honor, or conscience are threatened." The colonel replied that if the Wesel garrison had admitted its support for Anneke, as other garrisons had, there would have been no need to resort to special questions. Obfuscation ended, and Wesel officers came clean. Willich admitted that he had taken part in the Anneke subscription and that Anneke himself had stopped it due to unfavorable newspaper reports. In addition, Willich said that Anneke was his friend and that he had come to visit him in Wesel immediately after his dismissal. Military leadership issued a response to these revelations a few days later. It was an arrest order.[9]

Officers from the Seventh Artillery began disappearing, and Willich was arrested and held for three days. When everyone had returned from their banishments, their spirits were light. Surely the controversy would blow over, they reasoned. What more could officials do? Willich and his colleagues renewed their commitment to the Prussian Army, believing they could still shift its focus to a more humane form of civil service. This was a naïve vision.[10]

Willich should have known that he was a marked man before Anneke was released from service. Colonel von Schlemmer was annoyed because Willich had complained about a junior staffer's insult against Anneke. The colonel thus chose the general review to find fault with Willich, who stood on the left wing of a long line of troops being reviewed by Prince Adalbert. Stifling heat caused the soldiers to scatter; some of them were sitting and smoking cigars. Willich put a cigar in his own mouth and paced back and forth in front of the broken company. Then adjutants appeared on the scene and chastised the smokers. Schlemmer saw this behavior as a sign of disrespect akin to Anneke's beard. When the review ended, the prince gave orders not to march, so Willich instructed the men to walk "without a step." Schlemmer appeared on the scene, criticizing the crooked knees of the marchers. Willich ignored him and repeated the command. The irritated brigade commander remarked that he would remember such insolence.[11]

Willich had just finished morning training exercises when he was ordered to report to the interim division commander. Awaiting him was a transfer to the Second Artillery Brigade in Kolberg on the Baltic Sea in East Pomerania. He would be placed under the special supervision of a junior officer, and he was instructed to leave within four days. When Willich returned to the barracks, he found that six other officers had been transferred to six different locations. It was bitter blow to a man whose only family was the Seventh Artillery. Reassignment to one of Prussia's remote outposts and diminishment of his role made Willich sad and insecure. Warm embraces and a few tears marked his departure.[12]

Yet he resisted the impulse to resign, which was what Colonel von Schlemmer expected him to do. Willich had another idea and traveled to Berlin to seek an audience with the king. Once he arrived in the capital, however, a man with court connections convinced him that a live audience was impossible. Orders were already in place to intercept Willich when he arrived at the palace; that sounded ominous. Suffering from high fever and overcome with nervous exhaustion, Willich then checked himself into the Second Guard Regiment hospital. His condition worsened, and eye infections disabled him for several weeks. Frayed nerves gave way to somber reflection. Willich used his month in hospital to weigh options and make plans for the rest of his life. When he was finally well enough to travel, he knew what he had to do.[13]

• • • • •

The former orphan, now a thirty-six-year-old man, lacked guidance at the most critical moment of his life. Willich's father was a faint childhood memory, a mute icon to be revered but never consulted. His mother had a new life and family, and he wanted nothing to do with her. Schleiermacher had been

EDUARD SACK (1794–1866), PRIVY GOVERNMENT
COUNCILOR IN DÜSSELDORF AND WIFE SOPHIE,
C. 1865. COURTESY OF BRIGITTE VON DER OSTEN SACKEN.

dead for sixteen years. Older brother Julius was steadfast in his loyalty to the king and would not understand. Fortunately, Willich had acquired a mentor during his years in Westphalia who became, in his own words, a "fatherly friend." With personal and professional crises peaking, Willich turned to an older man he loved and respected, Düsseldorf town councilor Eduard Sack.

Eduard Wilhelm Hieronymus Maximilian Sack's father had served in the Prussian Army. At the tender age of twenty-one, Eduard Sack himself became a military hero when he was wounded three times at the Battle of Ligny on June 16, 1815. This was Napoleon's last military victory, occurring three days before the decisive battle of Waterloo. Sack achieved lasting fame commanding the First and Second Battalions of the Twenty-Second Regiment. In this role, he stopped the advance of the French cavalry, covering the Fifth Brigade's retreat. After the war, Sack enrolled in the University of Göttingen and studied law. In 1826, he was appointed counsel and adviser to the Directorate of Cologne. He then advocated successfully for the completion of the Cologne Cathedral and co-founded an association to improve the region's prison system. Ultimately, Sack dedicated more than fifty years of his life to public service in Düsseldorf. To address mounting social problems in Prussia, he developed an original scheme called "the Brotherhood."[14]

In Sack's Brotherhood concept, Willich found answers he had been seeking since he began reading radical literature. While Willich leaned toward communist ideology but had no viable plan for its implementation, Sack's blueprint went beyond early theories of communism and devised a way to transform rhetoric into reality. The Brotherhood's model society was grounded in the ecclesiastical community. Three classes of working citizens existed, according to Sack. The first class consisted of independent businessmen and landowners who paid the bulk of state taxes. Members of the second class, or proletariat, were able to work but lacked resources. The third class was unemployed. Communities would form small cooperatives made up of twelve families from each class. First- and second-class households would contribute a weekly sum of money according to their income, and they would also choose a foreman and a secretary to administer these funds. First-class heads of households would be assigned a comrade from the second class to mentor. Finally, the unemployed would be supported by the other classes until they became contributors and eventually helped form new circles. The Brotherhood was self-sustaining; all people would become truly free through interdependence.[15]

Willich finally had a concrete vision that comported with his commitment to improving the human condition. He would spend nearly a year in deep thought and lively conversation while refining this concept and advocating for its ultimate fulfillment. In the meantime, he appealed to Minister of War Hermann von Boyen to review his case, cancel his transfer, and return him to his former rank and responsibilities. Three days later, Boyen replied that Willich was being punished for insubordination and that regulations must be upheld. When Willich requested a private meeting, Boyen did not reply. Then the officer sent a third letter, but Boyen still did not budge. On March 11 Willich decided to resign from the army, collect his pension, and begin learning a trade.[16]

Willich's resignation letter cited the "moral impossibility" of remaining in the service. He felt he had lost the opportunity to gain meaningful civilian employment after nearly nineteen years in the military. Despite his hernia, he ignored the regimental physician's orders to limit his activity. Finally, he requested travel money to Düsseldorf, where he planned to begin civilian life. Hoping to have an answer to his resignation petition by the middle of April, Willich left for his new post at Kolberg to begin what he anticipated would be a short stay.[17]

Willich journeyed to Stettin to meet his new commander, then continued to Kolberg, where he received a reply to his resignation letter just a few days later. The petition was rejected on the grounds that Willich needed a formal certificate certifying his invalid status. He replied that he was no invalid, but he attached the medical certificate and requested his release as soon as possible. "I am no longer young, and every month, every day, is important to use toward gaining a bourgeoisie profession," Willich pleaded. The prompt reply stated that he needed to submit for examination by a physician to determine if he was partially disabled by his injury. At this point, Willich felt offended. His request to leave the army was not based on his medical status but on moral grounds, he retorted. Furthermore, he was entitled to a pension for his long service. Willich appealed to Prince Adalbert to be allowed to lay his case before the king. His request was granted.[18]

Willich labored for weeks crafting a letter to King Friedrich William IV. He began by summarizing the merits of his case, claiming that his superiors had made factual misrepresentations about his service record, then ignored his request for an audience. Appeal to the king was his last resort. Willich told the ruler that he had examined his conscience and had decided to leave His Majesty's service. The first part of the letter was a boilerplate appeal to the mercy of the king. What came next, however, surprised and enraged the powerful monarch. Willich wrote that he had sought truth and justice since he was young. The rebirth of the Prussian spirit following defeat by Napoleon and the army reforms that ensued had inspired the officer. He yearned for a military profession he believed was noble and just. Willich reminded the king that, though acquitted by a jury of his peers in a court of honor, Anneke had still been driven from the service. Punished for remaining friends with Anneke, Willich could no longer serve in an army that had lost its sense of humanity and respect for human dignity. As for the pension, he would no longer accept it consistent with his honor. Willich begged His Majesty not to delay in releasing him, as he felt "completely destroyed." Six weeks passed before a corps auditor from brigade headquarters in Stettin arrived in Kolberg on July 24, 1847. The king wanted answers.[19]

The investigator summoned Willich and demanded replies to three inquiries. First, what did Willich mean when he suggested that military authorities stood between His Majesty and the people? Second, why did Willich pursue his resignation and pension in a legal manner, then decide it was inconsistent with his sense of justice? Finally, why did Willich appeal to His Majesty in such an improper way? Willich insisted that he did not mean to imply that the king was alienated from his subjects; rather, he meant to say that senior military officials for Friedrich William IV had acted as agents of the government between the king and his people. The only way to overrule these officials in a case of injustice was to appeal to His Majesty. Willich argued that the administration of his case was unjust because it had not been adjudicated. He was being reprimanded despite an absence of proven criminal offenses. To the third question, Willich answered that he appealed directly to the king because he had lost confidence in the fairness of his superiors. Two of his letters remained unanswered, and he denied feelings of impertinence toward the king. Willich stated his innermost feelings and the facts of the case simply and honestly. The investigator then departed, leaving him to wonder what would happen next.[20]

The months that Willich spent in limbo at his new post in Kolberg allowed him ample time to consider his future. He took long walks on the seashore, rejuvenating his soul and connecting with nature. He rowed in the Baltic Sea during a storm, reveling in waves breaking over the sides of the boat and the wind taking his cap away. He spoke with peasants who participated in the Pomeranian Bread Riots, incredulous that the Prussian United Diet had refused to aid them. Willich's letters to Sack and Anneke during this period sing with renewed energy and purpose. He spoke often of the Brotherhood, predicting that humanity was "close to a rebirth." Despite his perilous situation, he was full of optimism.[21]

The king replied to Willich's letter with restraint. His Majesty noted several "unsuitable statements," suggesting that the soldier was "still caught up in the erroneous conception that his opinions carried weight when juxtaposed against the laws of the state." Willich decided he would no longer fight. Instead, he submitted a brief statement explaining that he reserved the right of defense in the future should the government bring him to trial. Since Willich had renounced his protests, the king commanded his release. Willich received his dismissal in the middle of November, and officer friends from the Seventh Artillery in Wesel returned from their respective banishments immediately afterward. The inquisition was over, but not the potential threat to the Prussian state. Dissent simply went underground.[22]

Chapter Four

• •

REBELLION

A MIDDLE-AGED MAN discards a twenty-year career, renounces his social status, and abandons his military family for what? Honor? Principle? Utopian dreams? Instead of feeling anxious and uncertain, August Willich was exhilarated. His dismissal was half an hour old when he dashed off a letter to Eduard Sack. It was a personal declaration of independence.

During his stay at Kolberg, Willich had collected his thoughts and planned his future. He shared Sack's Brotherhood idea with influential lay and clergy leaders in Pomerania, encountering real enthusiasm for socialism but no bias for action. Willich eventually came to view religious leaders as the problem in Sack's ideation. "What is the use of water from a well, cleansed and purified, and then reinjected," he asked his mentor, "if the well has a sulfurous side-source?" Willich came to believe that God existed in man as part of his spiritual self-awareness. "My strength is to feel more and more penetrated by this spirit," he explained, "to be content with it, to be able to give up everything without pain." He asked Sack for ten thalers in travel money to fund his move back to the Rhineland and for help in securing a carpenter's apprenticeship. "I am filled with joy as I look at myself," Willich exclaimed to his friend, "as I have become a vagrant to others, but a free man to myself."[1]

Fritz Anneke did not trust Eduard Sack, suspecting that his true loyalties lay not with Willich but with "the priest or the government." Anneke warned that Sack was trying to keep Willich out of the Rhineland "at the behest of higher authorities." Willich made the eight-hundred-kilometer journey to meet with his mentor a final time, hoping that Sack would avoid compromise with the Prussian government. In the end, Willich became a rebel and Sack sided with the king.[2]

In January 1848 Willich continued to Wesel, where he enjoyed the fellowship of old army friends. He spoke to them from the heart: "And now, my former comrades, I bid you farewell. Fate and my outlook on life lead me to the working class, to the handicrafts. Whomever still accepts my handshake, tells me that he acknowledges my conscience and actions as true. Farewell, my former subordinates, as you accepted my hand as your superior, do not refuse me now as one of your own." Willich subsequently departed for the city of Cologne, the bustling metropolis of the Rhineland and the nerve center of the republican movement in the region.[3]

Cologne's one hundred thousand residents lived in the most industrialized region of Germany—an ideal place to sow the seeds of worker revolution. The Communist League met twice weekly, singing songs, debating social and political topics, and manufacturing propaganda. Their leaders were Fritz Anneke and Andreas Gottschalk, the son of a Jewish butcher. Dr. Gottschalk was a local folk hero who dispensed free medical care to the city's poor. Shortly after Willich's arrival local communists feted him at several banquets. In addition, Anneke and Gottschalk convinced Willich to take a leadership role in the local chapter of the Communist League.[4]

Willich donned blue blouse and rough trousers and slung a carpenter's axe over his shoulder. He walked to work, parading his humble status before local army officers whenever he had the opportunity. In addition, he issued a pamphlet recounting his experiences in the army and his reasons for leaving, and published his political philosophy, describing the ideal future social order. Willich's secularization of Sack's Brotherhood concept was innovative, but social reform was hardly a novel idea. By the 1840s there were nearly six hundred mutual benefit societies in the Düsseldorf District of Rhine Province alone. Most were politically conservative. Willich's radical philosophy, on the other hand, advocated upending the existing social and political system.[5]

The moment had finally arrived, Willich reasoned, when man would realize his ultimate fulfillment and humanity in a cooperative community. Hegelian theory convinced Willich that the forces of nature drove humans inexorably toward unity. Once they achieved consciousness, people could build a better world by eliminating religion and selfishness. "Longing and self-seeking have attained their highest degree," Willich predicted, "[and will] collapse in a witnessing life-spark" with the rebirth of the reconciled human being. In Willich's ideal future, people would be healthy and good, and criminal and

IN THE PRUSSIAN ARMY BY AUGUST VON WILLICH,
1848. PRUSSIAN GOVERNMENT CENSORS BOUGHT
MOST OF THE PAMPHLETS TO LIMIT CIRCULATION.
AUTHOR COLLECTION.

other bad behavior would disappear. His plans to construct this new community were ambitious.[6]

In the initial stages of the new society, Willich declared, "nothing can be disturbed, neither the well-being of an individual nor a business." Once local infrastructure was converted into a single municipality incorporating urban and rural areas, artisans and craftsmen would elect a board of directors. Enlightened bourgeoisie would grasp the benefits of the new system, thereby embracing a more humane and just social order. Private business would be taken over by the municipality through simple consent. Furthermore, the resources of what Willich called the "many rotten and dead forces of the church" would be reallocated to various workshops. Willich had become a "true socialist" in the mode of Moses Hess and German tailor turned utopian philosopher Wilhelm Weitling. The former officer's dream of an ideal society was politically naïve, for he underestimated the conservative nature and religious allegiances of the very working class he was trying to help. As a committed revolutionist, however, Willich displayed perfect timing.[7]

* * * * *

Conservatives, liberals, and radicals throughout Europe greeted 1848 with a sense of dread and nervous anticipation. Alexis de Tocqueville spoke for many educated and informed elites in the French Chamber of Deputies when he warned that all of Europe was "sleeping on a volcano." "Can you not feel," he asked his fellow countrymen, "the wind of revolution in the air?" Brief civil war in Switzerland ended in 1847 with liberal and radical cantons defeating the secession efforts of conservative Catholic cantons in open warfare. The fact that Catholic Austria refused to intervene signaled unease in that regime, which was led by powerful Prince Clemens Wenzel von Metternich. The Austrians had troubles of their own in their Italian provinces. Those difficulties came to a head in January 1848, when young nobles in Milan boycotted Viennese tobacco, spawning a riot in which six civilians were killed and fifty wounded by Austrian troops. One week later, Sicilians rebelled against Bourbon rule. Full-scale revolution broke out, unleashing pent-up dreams of a united Italy and creating crises across the peninsula. Dukes of Papal States and Pope Pius IX scrambled to stem pockets of resistance that were popping up everywhere. Was de Tocqueville's volcano about to erupt? France provided the answer.[8]

Unemployed workers, men, women, and children gathered on the Place de la Madeline in Paris to march on a gray, windy late February morning. French National Guard troops confronted the protesters. All watched as a column of more than seven hundred students crossed the Seine and arrived on the scene singing "La Marseillaise." A surge toward the Chamber of Deputies devolved into street fighting, and Paris was consumed with rioting in just hours. Barricades arose overnight. Despite having more than one hundred thousand troops at their disposal, local officials fearing a popular backlash hesitated to use force. This gave rebels time to mobilize. When King Louis Phillipe abdicated two days later, revolutionaries entered the palace and took turns sitting on the throne. Someone scrawled a note on the big chair: "The

People of Paris to All Europe: Liberty, Equality, Fraternity, 24 February 1848."
Rebels then took the throne to the Place de la Bastille and burned it. Out of
its ashes rose the Second French Republic.[9]

News of the Paris uprising created a sensation across Europe and throughout the civilized world. By the end of the year, revolutions in Italy, Hungary,
Prague, Slovakia, and Vienna would topple princes and result in a dire struggle between advocates for democratic change and the forces of conservative
reaction. Excitement ran particularly high in the German Confederation.
Eighteen-year-old student Carl Schurz was working on a manuscript for history class in his attic chamber at Bonn University when a friend rushed in to
share the news. He and his fellow students poured into the streets, where they
encountered friends and strangers feeling, "confused, astonished, and expect-
ant." Was this the moment when Germans would finally create a united and
powerful empire with freedom of speech and press, free elections, and other
civil rights? Democracy, whether in the form of constitutional monarchy or
a full-fledged republic, was the fervent hope of many educated Germans,
though they dared not express it too strongly. Now they sensed opportunity.
Some students like Schurz could think of nothing else.[10]

In Cologne, communists wasted no time seizing the initiative in the wake
of Parisian events. Willich, Anneke, and Gottschalk organized a massive demonstration outside the town hall on March 3, 1848. Inside, liberal politicians
debated the wording of a reform petition to the king. The crowd outside grew
to nearly five thousand by afternoon. Then the three leaders rose together
and read "the demands of the people." The revolutionaries insisted that town
fathers disband the standing army, replace it with a citizen militia, and establish laws enacting universal manhood suffrage, protection of labor, and
free education. In addition, the rebels issued a vaguely worded admonition
for "legislation and administration by the people." When a delegation led by
Gottschalk and Willich interrupted a council meeting to read the demands,
they were rebuffed. The crowd then took matters into its own hands, surging
into chambers and forcing city councilors to flee. One municipal leader broke
his leg when he jumped from a second-story window to escape the throng.
Troops arrived, dispersed the crowd, and arrested the ringleaders. Willich
and his two coconspirators were arrested, charged with inciting a riot, and
carted off to prison for several weeks. Their protest inspired similar scenes
in towns throughout the Rhineland. While Willich and his friends stewed in
jail, the contagion of revolution raced across the German Confederation.[11]

Berlin exploded with civil unrest on March 18. Streets were blocked with
barricades, and thirteen hours of open warfare between Prussian troops
and Berlin citizens ensued. When the military withdrew, it left hundreds

dead and many more wounded. King Friedrich William IV assured dem-
onstrators that he would reorganize his government, arm the citizenry, and
implement further reforms. Three days later, the king appeared with his
minsters and generals at a funeral for civilians killed in the uprising. They
wore the revolutionary colors of black, red, and gold as 254 coffins lay in the
Gendarmenmarkt. Forty thousand marched to the burial at Friedrichshain.
Throughout the federation, public pressure to release jailed radicals mounted.
Willich, Anneke, and Gottschalk were released from prison on March 21. In
the meantime, the situation in the most liberal German duchy was dynamic
and dangerous.[12]

The Grand Duchy of Baden had a long legacy of liberalism beginning
with the constitution of 1811. That compact lasted fourteen years until the
aristocracy snuffed it out. When Leopold became grand duke in 1830, he
reinstituted liberal reforms in politics, law, education, and civic life. Despite
these concessions, when news of the Paris insurrections reached Baden,
peasants revolted spontaneously and burned the mansions of several wealthy
aristocrats.[13]

Politicians Friedrich Hecker and Gustav Struve had worked together for
years to push Baden toward democracy. Hecker was a charismatic and popular champion of the people and civil rights. An attorney by trade, he became
impatient with the slow pace of reform in his native Baden. The more time he
spent in politics, the further left he moved. By 1848 he was a known socialist
and republican. Struve was just as committed to radical reform, but he lacked
his ally's personal magnetism. Critics mocked Struve for his vegetarianism
and his obsession with phrenology, the study of skull shapes. The former
surgeon, lawyer, and journalist renounced his nobility in 1847 and committed himself to a lifetime of reform.

Hecker and Struve's chief propagandist was Joseph Fickler, whose influential newspaper *Seeblatter* first appeared in 1836. One secret police agent
considered him the most important and dangerous revolutionary figure in
Prussia. Fickler and Willich became acquainted during the winter of 1847–48,
when Fickler spent three months hiding in the Rhineland countryside. The
editor argued that violent revolution was the only path to justice for oppressed
classes. He began actively plotting violent rebellion in 1847, urging Hecker
to adopt that same course.[14]

In September 1847 Hecker presented the Offenburg Assembly with thirteen "demands of the people," including familiar themes of freedom of press,
speech, assembly, religion, and representation. He demanded abolition of
privilege, institution of a progressive income tax, and rectification of the

imbalance between labor and capital. It was a bold document. On February 27, 1848, Hecker and Struve presented their demands to the Mannheim People's Assembly, which forwarded them to the Second Chamber of the Baden Landstände, then on to the capital at Karlsruhe. On March 1, twenty thousand people gathered in front of the parliament building, where Hecker demanded the renunciation of noble privilege and the liberation of peasants from feudal encumbrances.

Events in Vienna on March 13 further emboldened the Baden radicals. Austrian troops mowed down Viennese students demonstrating for a constitution and an elected assembly. Chancellor Metternich resigned and slipped into exile, and King Ferdinand promised his subjects a constitution. On March 19, Hecker and Struve told more than twenty thousand people gathered at the Great People's Assembly in Offenburg that the Baden government was stalling, suggesting the representatives would renege on the thirteen demands agreed to back in September. Peasants revolted throughout North Baden, then the violence spread to neighboring duchies. Rulers in Württemberg, Nassau, Hessen-Darmstadt, and elsewhere acceded to similar demands. Meanwhile, Fickler scurried from one mass meeting to another, whipping up enthusiasm for revolution.[15]

At the end of the month a preliminary parliament formed by progressive leaders of the German states met in Frankfurt to prepare for an election of a constituent national assembly. Frustrated by the group's inaction, Hecker and Struve walked out two days later. Their departure prodded the pre-parliament to act; members called for a German National Assembly and universal manhood suffrage. However, radicals in Baden did not wait for the assembly to convene. Instead, they crossed the line into open rebellion. A hysterical Fickler called for revolution in the April 2 issue of *Seeblatter*. "Strike down the thrones of the traitors of the people," he wailed. "Take the scepters from their bloody hands, abolish and destroy their satanic power." Hecker and Struve prepared for war.[16]

Willich hurried to Konstanz in southeast Baden. Former Baden infantry lieutenant Franz Sigel joined the rebels. As leaders gathered, Hecker entered the room and greeted Willich with a question: "You are my commander in chief, aren't you?" The Prussian replied simply, "Yes." Clearly, the appointment had been prearranged. Sigel was disappointed at not getting the job and never overcame his bitterness. Hecker subsequently directed him to raise an independent corps at his former post in Mannheim. Exiled poet Georg Herwegh promised that five thousand Germans, Poles, and other workers from Paris would join the fight, and that he would move them to the banks of the Rhine when the time was ripe. Johann Phillip Becker prepared a force of thousands of native Germans from Switzerland for a similar mission. Hecker was jubilant—the Baden folk hero expected to lead an army of between thirty and forty thousand men that would grow exponentially as he traveled north and encountered the adulation of long-oppressed German peasants and workers. However, his imagination clouded his judgment.[17]

The Baden Landtag was nervous. The assembly was split between moderates who wanted to implement progressive reforms gradually and radicals who were fully committed to overthrowing the regime. Fearing that Herwegh and other revolutionary exiles would lead an invasion from France, the Baden government asked for protection from the German Confederation on April 4. Radicals saw this as the final indignity. On April 7, Hecker stormed out of the Landtag in protest. After the session ended, a closed meeting convened to hear evidence of Hecker's and Fickler's conspiracy to commit high treason. That same day, Fickler and Willich attended a mass meeting in Mannheim and urged the populace to rise in rebellion. Moderate politicians intercepted the men at a railway station on April 8 and had Fickler arrested before he could depart on the train for Konstanz. Willich managed to elude police agents. Shaken by Fickler's arrest, Hecker made his way to Konstanz in secret, traveling through Bavaria, France, and Switzerland. He arrived on April 11, and friends urged him to reconsider armed insurrection. Yet Fickler assured Hecker that tens of thousands would flock to the rebellion from Fickler's hometown of Konstanz alone.[18]

Willich watched with a mixture of excitement and trepidation as Hecker and Struve announced the mobilization of a citizen army before throngs of cheering supporters in Konstanz on April 12. Hecker had no understanding of international diplomacy and even less knowledge of military matters. No advance planning was done for logistics, and supplies and arms were scarce. Only fifty volunteers accompanied the rebels as they marched north on April 13. According to Hecker himself, many of these men had been shamed into volunteering by women and girls who told them it would be cowardly to stay home while others fought for their freedom. Nevertheless, Hecker's mood was ebullient.

"Indubitably, a mass rising is taking place," Hecker wrote shortly after the march commenced. "The blue sky smiled down from the torn rain clouds beside the bright magnificent lake. In the distance were the free Alps, and before us lay . . . a world of ancient sagas. . . . Martial songs sounded and white gulls swirled over our heads." The tiny force arrived at Stockach, less than forty kilometers north of Konstanz, expecting to join three thousand reinforcements there. Fewer than two hundred men showed up. Hecker accepted two ancient long cannons called *feldschlangen* that he admitted had probably last been used in the Thirty Years' War. He then raided the local armory, taking four thousand cartridges. Hecker had no communication with Struve and Sigel, who were presumably raising and organizing armies. The three planned to unite forces and march to Karlsruhe, where they would proclaim a republic. Hecker and Willich trudged on toward Donaueschingen, thirty kilometers west, intending to join Struve's troops recruited from the southern Schwarzwald. That never happened.[19]

Two thousand federation-sponsored soldiers from Württemberg in the east arrived in Donaueschingen ahead of them, foiling plans to seize the fortress. Struve and his men retreated sixteen kilometers south to Bonndorf, where Hecker met them on April 16. Plans to capture Freiburg to the west and Offenburg to the north were scrapped. In the meantime, Hecker sent mixed signals to Herwegh, who was at the French border with a large force ready to roll east. Hecker still believed that the Baden army would defect to his side, and he did not want to employ a foreign legion that the Baden people could perceive as a threat. Instead he sent Herwegh's wife, Emma, to Becker in Switzerland with vague instructions to bring his legion north at a time and place of his own choosing. The entire enterprise was collapsing from within, as Willich later wrote, from "mutual deceit, jealousy, political and military ignorance." However, the biggest obstacle was not poor leadership and planning. The fatal flaw in the revolution, according to Willich, was the "indifference of the rest of Germany," which doomed any small success the rebels might enjoy in Baden.[20]

Sensing that things were not going well for Hecker, the German Confederation sent delegates to Bernau for talks with the rebel leader. Emissaries found a disheveled band of misfit insurrectionists wearing borrowed clothing and mismatched shoes, singing and drinking while their wet garments dried by the fireside. Willich had adopted the romantic Hecker visage, replete with wide-brim slouch hat, saber, musket, and flowing red beard. When government delegates offered amnesty should he surrender and disband his army, Hecker replied that he would offer amnesty to German princes if they chose to abdicate. The peace commissioners left, appealing to the people of Baden not to throw away the promise of the upcoming national assembly by participating in this illegal and ill-advised rebellion. Most Badeners agreed with them.

Meanwhile, Hecker's generals were operating solo. Struve headed south from Saint Blasien on April 17 to join a volunteer force near the Swiss border.

Hecker, Willich, and nine hundred men recruited on the march continued southwest through mountain passes in snow and freezing rain. They had no rations. In the meantime, Sigel had made progress. He left Hecker and returned to Konstanz on April 14, managing to enroll another hundred recruits. As he marched west, Sigel added scores of volunteers impressed by his enthusiasm and military bearing. Unlike Hecker's army, Sigel's column had a supply train of twenty wagons and a martial appearance. His three thousand troops reached Tiengen, just a stone's throw from the Swiss border, on April 18. At this point, he set his sights on Todtnau as a base of operations. While Sigel intended to move north and capture Freiburg, he unfortunately had little idea of the obstacles arrayed against him.[21]

Two successive commanders of the Baden army had resigned by that time, so government officials appointed Friedrich von Gagern, a splendid soldier and the brother of Germany's leading liberal politician, the commander in charge of stifling the rebellion. On April 16, the Bundestag combined troops from the duchies of Hesse and Nassau with the Baden army to form a force of more than thirty thousand men to stop the rebels in their tracks. Fresh, well-equipped troops departed the railway terminus at Schliengen and moved south, compelling Hecker to retreat farther to the southwest. Exhausted insurgents were in danger of being pushed all the way to the Rhine and out of Baden. Hecker ordered Struve's troops into the Black Forest, while Willich led his column toward Kandern. Willich planned to delay the enemy long enough for local sympathetic militias in the south to mobilize. He wanted to draw Gagern's army to Lörrach, thus allowing Sigel in the east and Struve in the west to outflank government troops.

Willich reached Kandern the evening of April 19 and found Emma Herwegh waiting for him. "We are in a mousetrap," Hecker told her. Emma said that her husband's legion in France was growing restless and short on supplies. Would Hecker finally order Herwegh to cross the border? Hecker equivocated. "Well, tell Herwegh that I cannot call him," he replied, "but if he wants to come quickly, and in large numbers, I would like it." At daybreak Hecker was confronted by more than two thousand well-armed soldiers of Gagern's advance guard. Only half of Hecker's 1,200 men had muskets and the remaining rebels carried sharpened scythes. Despite Willich's protest, Hecker insisted they give battle at Kandern rather than continuing south to Lörrach. It was to be Hecker's final blunder.[22]

Kandern sat at the southeast entrance to the Southern Black Forest, a rugged land of high mountains and picturesque valleys. The road southeast from Kandern to Steinen through the Kandern Valley was lined with trees on both sides. Hecker instructed Willich to halt his troops on this road a few kilometers east of town. Willich arrayed his forces facing back toward Kandern and Dog Stable Bridge, which spanned a small creek. His right wing took position along the wooded heights next to the bridge and the creek. In the center, behind a small hill on a meadow next to the road and the bridge, Willich deployed his only trained company, the fifty-three men of the Konstanz Worker's Militia. Hecker took the remaining companies to the hills left of the meadows, an area isolated from the rest of the army. Willich stood in the center next to Company Konstanz and watched as the enemy drew near. When a single horseman galloped over the bridge in his direction, Willich hailed the rider and asked him his purpose. The aide replied that Gagern wanted a parley with Hecker.[23]

The two leaders met on the bridge. Gagern wore a brown civilian overcoat and green cap with a saber in his belt, symbolic of his desire to be seen as the "citizen general." He called Hecker a brave man but a fanatic, proposing that he surrender at once. Hecker refused. "If devotion to the freedom of a great people is fanaticism," the rebel leader replied, "you are free to use that term, but there is fanaticism on the other side, the one you serve." Hecker turned and walked back to confer with Willich.[24]

In the meantime, volunteers on the rebel right wing became anxious and disorderly, so Willich rushed to steady them. When he returned to the center, he found that the Konstanz's men had departed to join Hecker on the left wing. Willich knew it would be disaster to wage battle with his center abandoned and outnumbered two to one, so he ordered a slow retreat up the steepest section of the Scheideck Road. Gagern pursued methodically, and neither side appeared willing to fire first. Hecker and Willich argued vehemently on the march. Willich felt Hecker never completely trusted him because he was a Prussian. When it became clear that his comrade would not be convinced to withdraw, Willich relented, forming his troops into line of battle near the top of a long, narrow 543-meter grade known as the Scheideck Pass. He placed the two ancient cannons on opposite sides of the road, thinking they might intimidate the enemy, who would hardly imagine that they were not loaded. Alongside the cannons he placed two companies of riflemen on the right and Hecker's own men on the left. Willich positioned the scythe bearers as far in the rear as the terrain allowed.

Gagern's troops marched up the steep hill without skirmishers, maintaining a closed-rank formation half a platoon wide. Then they walked boldly into the enemy skirmish line between the two flanks of the rebel army. Willich met the soldiers himself, walking within thirty paces of their line and about the same distance in front of his own line. When he commanded them to "Stop!" Gagern's men replied that they only took orders from their own commander. They halted nonetheless, and Willich's men then employed a risky tactic.[25]

Rebels shouted to government soldiers, "Come over, brothers! Join us! Come to freedom!" Taunts and laughter continued from both sides. "We do not want to shed the blood of citizens," Willich's men continued, adding, "We are all Germans." Some rebels advanced, offering a handshake instead of a bullet. Gagern's troops wavered; some appeared eager to fraternize with the insurgents. "Let the general come forward," Willich's troops pleaded. Gagern rode to the front, conspicuous in his civilian garb. A rebel shouted, "Don't shoot your German brothers!" Gagern replied, "Lay down your weapons and go home!" The federal line appeared on the verge of breaking, and Willich's force let out a cheer as Hessian volunteers encircled the wobbly government front line.[26]

Sensing the moment was critical, Gagern shouted, "What? Brothers? Scoundrels and vagabonds, that's what you are!" He drew his saber and screamed, "Fire! Fire! Fire!" A scytheman dropped as bullets clanged off farming implements in the rebel rear. Company Konstanz responded. Gagern grasped his breast, toppled from his horse, and fell dead. The battle that followed lasted all of fifteen minutes, including a brief pause to allow Gagern's body to be exchanged for a rebel battle flag. The scythemen were the first to run, followed by most of the rebel contingent. The fleeing troops scattered into the forest. Hecker and Willich managed to escape while government troops pressed forward, killing ten insurgents. That same day, royalists encountered and defeated volunteers led by Struve, sending many scurrying across the Swiss border.[27]

Sigel had not heard from Hecker for days when word reached him of the battle near Kandern. He was astounded; he had presumed that Hecker was already in Freiburg. Sigel responded to multiple appeals from Hecker's fleeing troops but could not reach them. Thus, he spent ten hours marching in the rain for nothing. By the time he heard that Hecker and Struve had crossed the Rhine, Sigel had lost two precious days in his planned assault on Freiburg. Government troops from Baden and Hesse formed a barrier south of Freiburg, while Württemberg troops moved west to cut him off. At the same time, Bavarian troops closed off his retreat to the east. Sigel pressed forward through the mountains in a last-ditch effort to salvage the insurrection, but he had no chance for success and was also forced to flee.[28]

Herwegh's 650 men finally crossed the Rhine on April 23 only to learn of the Kandern defeat. Willich tried to join them. The soldiers planned to meet

DEATH OF GENERAL FRIEDRICH VON GAGERN IN BATTLE AT KANDERN.
LITHOGRAPH BY UNKNOWN ARTIST, C. 1849. HECKER IS PORTRAYED POINTING
IN THE UPPER RIGHT, WHILE WILLICH, THIRD FROM THE LOWER RIGHT,
COMMANDS REBEL SOLDIERS. ALAMY STOCK PHOTO.

Sigel near Todtnau and were unaware that he had already fled. With Sigel's
three thousand men gone, there was nothing left to do but conduct an orderly retreat south into Switzerland. Unfortunately, Herwegh was ambushed
at Dossenbach by Württemberg forces, losing eight men in the process but
killing forty of the enemy. Dozens of rebels were hunted down and hanged
in the woods, or drowned in the Rhine while attempting to swim to Switzerland. The Herweghs ultimately escaped. The rebellion was over. Liberal
leader and poet Robert Blum wrote to his wife about the uprising the week
after its end. "Hecker and Struve have betrayed the country in the eyes of
the law," he complained, "that is trivial. But they have betrayed the people
by their insane insurrection and checked us on the way to victory. That is a
serious crime."[29]

Willich traveled west on news that 250 rebels were trapped in the southwest corner of Baden. Willich led remnants of the disheveled army to a tentative position on the small island of Schusterinsel on the Rhine on April 25. Their refuge was a tiny speck of Baden territory bordering both France and Switzerland. Once the outworks of the massive French fortress of Huningue, the former bastion was by then just a pile of rubble. Willich and his band stayed only long enough to consider next steps, and they were faced with few options. Staying in Germany meant annihilation. Switzerland was in no position to challenge the German states by housing a large force of armed, violent revolutionaries. Powerful France, recently reborn as a republic, was the revolutionaries' only viable place of refuge.[30]

Chapter Five

● ● ● ● ● ● ● ● ● ● ● ● ● ● ● ● ● ● ●

REFUGEE

THIRTY-SIX THOUSAND residents of the ancient city of Besançon, regional capital of the department of Doubs in northeast France, enjoyed a beautiful spring day on May 24, 1848. Nearly two thousand patrons waited in hushed anticipation in the city center for what would certainly be one of the most unusual concerts of the season. The venue was a marvel of late eighteenth-century engineering. Noted architect and city planner Claude Nicolas Ledoux had created the blue and ochre limestone theatre in 1784. Simple Ionic columns at the building's entrance lent gravitas to an exhilarating public space inside. Ledoux's revolutionary design eliminated interior divisions and located the orchestra in a pit below the stage, giving spectators unobstructed views of performers from all angles. Never in the five decades since its construction had the theatre witnessed an event such as the one that took place that evening.[1]

The curtain drew back, revealing forty young men dressed in simple blue blouses and rough trousers held together by rude leather belts. A writer for local newspaper *Franc-Comtois* stated that the workers sang twelve choruses "with an accuracy, a musical ensemble, a musical intelligence, that was a taste above our praises." The singers performed three choruses of Conrad Kreutzer's part-songs for male voices, including the popular "Evening Chant." A quartet of Friedrich Heinrich Himmel works followed, then Ludwig Spohr's "Song of the Flag" and "The Homeland." This last piece was rendered with feeling and gusto, and the audience responded with thunderous applause and bravos. As he watched men "singing with recollection the hymns of the absent homeland," the editor said he was witness to "a touching spectacle."

The singers' garb was not the only thing that made them extraordinary. The group had never performed together in public; in fact, many had first become acquainted with one another just weeks before the event. "We cannot overly admire this exceptional organization," an observer gushed, "who without preparation, study, or practice, performs the most difficult choral music, and for which the song seems to be their mother tongue." The conductor of the group, August Willich, had little formal musical training. He had responsibility for nearly three hundred political refugees, and his impromptu benefit performance promised to boost their morale and solicit financial support for their basic needs. Citizens of Besançon responded enthusiastically.[2]

• • • • •

French subsecretary of state for the interior Nicolas Henri Carteret answered Willich's plea for asylum by designating the department of Doubs to receive German rebels at Besançon. The French were ill prepared to deal with a refugee crisis; by the first week of May, 463 displaced revolutionaries had arrived with no place to live or work. Yet the local community responded with charity. Commissioners gave the men man five francs each to tide them over until a subsidy could be approved. Provisional mayor Thomas Deprez appealed to Monseigneur Mathieu, Catholic bishop of Besançon, who immediately agreed to house the refugees at the ancient convent of the Cordeliers, a commodious three-story edifice on the Rue du Lycée. On May 9, republican commissioner François Gindriez ordered French soldiers to deliver five hundred pallets, five hundred blankets, and five thousand kilograms of sleeping straw for the exiled revolutionaries' use. Willich and his men were also given bread, utensils, firewood, and cookware for making soup. Despite this generous response, local authorities knew they could not house so many refugees indefinitely. They made plans to send the French citizens among the refugees back to their homes, and to disperse some Germans to other locations in the department of Doubs. This plan did not sit well with Willich and his men.[3]

Refugees protested the breakup of their column and urged commissioners to allow them to return to Germany with their confiscated weapons. The rebels planned to retake the abandoned fortress at Huningue for starters. If that proved impossible, they asked for a subsidy from the French government to sustain them. Willich organized the column into ten companies, including two detachments from Habsheim in the Alsace region. In addition, he established rules of strict discipline, such as a 10:00 p.m. curfew enforced by in-house police. The men drilled in the streets every day, expecting to be called back to action at any moment.[4]

That same day, the *Franc-Comtois* ran an editorial praising the refugees' efforts as a "holy cause, sister to [France's own]" in the name of liberty. "They deserve our generous hospitality," the paper said of the exiles, then it offered a promise: "Our fellow-citizens would not hesitate to come to the assistance of a misfortune which obliges us all." The day after entering their protest and reading the article, several members of the column decided to test the goodwill of their hosts. They assembled a small musical ensemble in the courtyard of the elegant sixteenth-century Granvelle palace, sang songs, and passed the hat. They returned to the convent with sixty francs. Willich began to think big.[5]

In the meantime, Mayor Deprez and Commissioner Gindriez lobbied the French government for the subsidy. "After the deduction of 110 Germans on the neighboring departments," Gindriez enumerated, "there are still 380 of these refugees in Besançon, all in most complete deprivation. Every day a considerable number of them, who suffer misery and agglomeration in the same dwelling, become ill and are admitted to the hospices of the city." Willich sent a pleading letter to Fritz Anneke in Cologne, proposing that the new workers association founded by Gottschalk and the democratic association chaired by Karl Marx start subscriptions for the refugees at Besançon. When Anneke read Willich's letter aloud to the democrats and asked for unanimous consent, Marx and others balked. Marx's clique did not want to be seen as sharing the extreme ideology of the insurgents. Gottschalk and Anneke resigned from the democratic group and launched a subscription drive that proved successful. The rift was a preview of similar divisions that would later split the Communist League.[6]

After the concert at Ledoux's theatre, support from the community strengthened. Women formed a relief organization to help refugees with basic needs like sewing and laundering. However, brewing tensions threatened support for the German visitors. City librarian Charles Weiss, a beneficiary of the old monarchial regime, confided to his journal, "Public good sense is not and cannot be favorable to youngsters who enter the country in order to impose their liberty. They are, however, less guilty than the government, as stupid as it is anarchist, who has thrown them on the Rhine and disavowed them." Such skepticism regarding the French Second Republic was well founded.[7]

The new French regime had a split personality. While Alphonse de Lamartine, the poet who proclaimed the republic, was running a conservative provisional government as foreign minister, social democrats demanded reform of the entire society in an effort to elevate the worker to true equality. Socialists led by Louis Blanc set up a shadow government and successfully implemented a short-lived right-to-work scheme to aid the unemployed. This plan ultimately failed due to financial pressures and opposition from the provisional government. German officials worried that France was allowing dissidents to assemble on the border between their countries for another attempt at revolution. A confused mixture of genuine sympathy and geopolitical concerns colored French officials' attitude toward the refugees. Uncertainty within their own regime caused some in France to worry that Germans might start a border war. Despite their concerns, French representatives approved a subsidy of fifty centimes per refugee "in cases of essential need" retroactive to May 15. By the end of May, Willich and his men were demoralized and restless. They had no particular purpose or plan in sight.[8]

Meanwhile, in the German Fatherland, government officials and politicians of all stripes were setting a new course for the confederation in light of recent upheavals. The Frankfurt National Assembly, Germany's first freely elected parliament, opened on May 18 with the long-term goal of a drafting a national constitution for a unified country. Liberal politician Heinrich von Gagern, whose brother had fallen in the late rebellion, chaired the nascent body, which regional and political divisions plagued from day one. Despite a lack of common ground, the table was set for deliberation on the future makeup of a presumptive German nation-state.[9]

In early June, German refugee democrats established a central committee under the leadership of Johann Phillip Becker in Switzerland. Besides Willich and Becker, the group included Gustav Struve and Alexandre Martin, a French Blanquist member of the French provisional government. Martin earned the nickname "Albert the Worker" by being the first member of the industrial working class to hold office in his nation's administration. He manned barricades in the 1848 revolution, and he collected six hundred francs for Willich's column. As politicians jockeyed for position in France and in other teetering regimes, Willich and his allies pledged themselves to a radical international agenda.[10]

The French government forced Willich to break up his column on June 3. Four companies composed of 142 men stayed in Besançon, while four other companies dispersed to Ornans, Beaume le Dame, Pontlarier, and Saint Hippolyte. French officials insisted that all refugees seek work so that they could be taken off the dole. Willich's exiled soldiers remained proud. On June 13, refugees from Saint Hippolyte wrote Willich and claimed that their enclave no longer wished to exist on the alms of France. Rather, the exiles were willing to "risk all" to escape their humiliating life. "We are all ready to take on the battle of life and death for the cause of the German nation beyond the Rhine," they vowed, "and if all the blood of the German nation should be digested, later generations will stammer words of gratitude on our bodies." No one knew when the next opportunity for revolution might arise in the German states. In the meantime, Willich and Becker were devising a different plan to escape the doldrums and take up arms for the cause of pan-European liberation.[11]

Across Europe, the pace of change accelerated during the summer of 1848. Sparks of discontent among the peoples of various regions coalesced into yearnings for reform in two main arenas: social justice and political freedom. How Europeans dealt with increased economic inequities in an emerging industrial society was a thorny moral issue. The subtext of this discussion revolved around the need to reconcile social justice with individual liberty. Potential remedies to the social question itself, ranging from moderate change within existing systems to a wholesale restructuring of society based on communal norms, fractured assemblies of reform advocates and created little revolutionary consensus.

On the political front, similar divisions frustrated leaders of all parties. The chaotic situation in the French Second Republic made German revolutionists doubt the best way to create new government structures. Should the new administration be a constitutional monarchy like Britain or a full-fledged republic? If Germany became a republic, should its goal be the attainment of true democracy or merely liberal reform? And what of the equally important role of nationalism in replacing the existing hodgepodge of small European states and principalities? Should feelings of brotherhood among peoples be based on ethnic origins, or should they make a radical progression from civic nationalism on the French model to a European citizen nationalism transcending artificial borders?

One man with whom Willich shared a vision of pan-European social justice was Italian radical Giuseppe Mazzini, who was just five years his senior. Like the Prussian, Mazzini was born into favorable circumstances. In his midtwenties the Genoa attorney was a member of the Carbonari, a secret society bent on expelling Austrians from the Italian Peninsula and creating a united Italian democratic republic. His vision and his motivation, however, went far beyond Italian nationalism. Mazzini believed that an impending revolution would liberate all oppressed Europeans, and he maintained that it was the destiny of Italian patriots like himself to lead this effort. He first founded the "Young Italy" organization while in exile in 1831. By 1834, this association had morphed into "Young Europe." Mazzini and his fellow radicals believed they could use moral suasion to convince Europeans to settle political and ethnic differences peacefully and work for the betterment of all peoples. That same year, he and one of his disciples, the fiery revolutionist Giuseppe Garibaldi, were sentenced to death in absentia by Piedmontese authorities. By 1847, Mazzini's radical escapades had landed him in exile in France, England, and Switzerland. Monarchs across Europe lost sleep as they monitored Mazzini and his activists, who stood ready to act as soon as the opportunity presented itself.[12]

Mazzini's moment came on April 7, 1848. He arrived in Milan from Paris a few days after the Milanese had revolted against the Austrians. Venice then followed suit and established a revolutionary government. With much of the Kingdom of the Two Sicilies having thrown off the yoke of Bourbon monarchy and constitutions forced on the rulers of Tuscany and Sardinia, Mazzini's dream of a unified Italian republic appeared close at hand. His followers gathered in droves in Turin and Genoa to fight against the Austrians. But Mazzini's leadership was short-lived. King Charles Albert of Sardinia sensed an opportunity to enhance his own prestige by simultaneously taking on the Austrians and blunting the efforts of republicans like Mazzini. The Genoa rebel was compelled to offer tepid support to the king in order to the wrest the peninsula from Austrian influence. The republic and democracy would have to wait. When the king later pressed him to accept the monarchy in exchange for a democratic constitution in the north, Mazzini refused. His dream of a unified Italy was unraveling as individual states looked after their own interests. Pope Pius withdrew his support of the revolution against Catholic Austria, and despite early successes, revolution in Italy stalled.[13]

Willich was anxious to go to Mazzini's aid and fight for freedom in Italy. On June 22, he sent a letter to Becker outlining conditions for his involvement. He wanted to lead an all-German corps that was answerable to the Italian supreme command. However, if revolution broke out in Germany, Willich's column would leave Italy immediately to join it. Food and arms for this proposed force would come from the refugees' central committee.[14] Unbeknownst to Willich, Becker had received word from neutral France that refugee troops would be blown out of the water if they tried to sail from Marseilles. Learning of the threat, Willich drafted a revised plan for Becker that emphasized the importance of their mission and suggesting that his own column enter Italy through Swiss territory. "The struggle which is now being conducted is not a national one," Willich argued, "but a universal one;

it is concerned with the liberation of mankind. We are all struggling for the same thing. Every victory or loss at a point in Europe has a direct effect on everyone." He asked Becker whether the Swiss authorities would allow them safe passage to Italy. The answer was a resounding "no."[15]

At precisely the time that Willich was trying to get to Italy, French radicals were pushing the renewed republic to honor commitments to their worker constituency. A newly elected moderate French provisional government decided to close the national workshops that had been providing work for indigent citizens. Frustration boiled over. Alexandre Martin, Auguste Blanqui, Armand Barbès, and others incited a riot in Paris on June 23 that lasted three days. When French National Guards finally put down the insurrection, over ten thousand people lay dead or injured, and another four thousand were deported to Algeria. The "June Days," as the events came to be called, sounded the death knell of radicals' hopes for a democratic social republic and marked a victory for conservatives and moderates.[16]

Ironically, Willich received news of the uprising while in Dole attending a celebration of the fifty-fifth anniversary of the signing of France's first republican constitution. While at the meeting, Willich presented an overview of the situation in Germany and made an urgent request to abandon national feuds and support oppressed people everywhere. Local officials convinced him to join their Masonic lodge. Six thousand seated guests rose as Willich delivered a toast "to the unity of all peoples, to the universal republic." He was speaking strictly from the heart.[17]

Two weeks later, Willich admitted that fallout from the events in Paris was little understood. However, one thing was clear—earlier predictions that a better world could only emerge from working-class agitation had become his life commitment. "The complete radicalism of the deed," Willich stressed, "leads to large and small gains. If you act, act only under the most radical laws of war." The downtrodden had inherited "weakness, cowardice and subjugation" from their perpetual state of misery, he maintained, further stating, "Only the certainty of death can paralyze manifestations of those qualities." Violence, not mere moral reasoning, was the path to ultimate justice. Willich's epiphany had immense consequences for his future as a radical reformer.

Morale in Willich's column reached low ebb. Only a hundred German refugees remained in Besançon; the rest had gone to other departments in search of work. Moreover, Willich himself showed signs of disillusionment. Infighting among radical leaders had poisoned the entire enterprise and further fractured what had never been a unified cause. "Had I had any idea of the spirit of the Baden Republicans," Willich confided to Fritz Anneke,

"I would not have gone there." Only in defeat could Willich see "the masses of small passions" that overtook larger aims of the rebellion. He expected his column would gradually diminish before being absorbed into Becker's worker's organization in Biel, Switzerland. In the meantime, Willich waited for another chance at revolution.[18]

· · · · ·

July 1848 found Willich attempting to enjoy the beauty of his surroundings and his newfound celebrity among the French people. If one had to flee into exile, Besançon was certainly a delightful place to take refuge. Situated on the western slope of the Jura Mountains at a hairpin turn in the River Doubs, the city had been a place of strategic importance since Roman times, when Julius Caesar called it Vesontio. Charlemagne made Besançon a key stronghold of his empire, but it was the acclaimed French military architect Vauban who built massive fortifications on a steep rock overlooking the verdant countryside. Set amid vine-covered hills and poplar and beech forests, and boasting an endless supply of some of the finest water in all of France, nineteenth-century Besançon was the political and cultural center of the region. The city boasted a free academy of arts, sciences, and belles lettres, free art and music schools, and a technical school for the training of watchmakers, all open to students of both sexes.[19]

Willich took long walks in the hills surrounding the fortress with his chief lieutenant August Gebert, or with his girlfriend, described by one visitor as "a lavish Jewess."[20] When he was not drilling his volunteers daily, the rabble commander could be found strolling over the stone bridge that linked the two sections of the city. Willich walked down the ancient Boulevard Chamars, which ran southeast to the Black Gate, a triumphal arch raised in honor of Crispus Caesar, son of Constantine. He had access to the same great library where native sons Victor Hugo, Charles Fourier, and Pierre-Joseph Proudhon had once perused its fifty thousand volumes.

For the first time since his childhood in Berlin, Willich basked in the presence of elite social circles, appearing equally comfortable there as in the company of workers in their makeshift barracks. On July 23, Willich and his column participated in a ceremony on the Chamars honoring 1,500 volunteer national guardsmen sent to Paris during the June Days uprising. The mayor of Besançon welcomed the honorees, whom he called "these refugees, our guests for several days, who represent German liberty." Willich replied at length: "French Citizens, you provide a great and beautiful example to people and princes. The former will rise up as the latter will tremble. In the great struggle that shook the whole body of society, you chose the most perilous place. You have not been surpassed in history. No mother nation has suffered as much as you have in this noble struggle, nor sacrificed as much. Most civilized peoples walk in your footsteps and all applaud every step you take. All will unite with you for freedom, truth and humanity when the fighting is over. Then all plagues will be cured. All peoples will see each other as members of the same body, and the cry that comes now from a German heart will be realized: To the fraternity of nations: Honor, glory and prosperity to the French Republic!"[21] Willich was not celebrating the reactionary France of the June Days in his speech, but rather the France of the February 1848 Revolution.

As her husband had no purpose before him, Mathilde, Fritz Anneke's wife, wrote to ask Willich whether he saw himself going to America. Some failed revolutionists like Hecker had already done so. Willich replied by saying he would stay with his column. Rather than live elsewhere, he vowed to "die as a democrat" while attempting to "convert Germany to a dwelling for humanity." Many of his comrades felt the same way. Willich admitted he found strange pleasure in "being the object of noble sympathy in apparent miseries."[22] With this in mind, on July 28 he and his 160 men appealed to the German Parliament in Frankfurt for amnesty. Willich asked legislators to safeguard the exiled revolutionaries from persecution by a new French regime that they themselves might not be willing to tolerate much longer. "Let us again participate in the great work of the German people," he pleaded, "to create a higher, more just principle of unity of the people than is present."[23] Parliament denied his request. Willich and his band settled in to an unknown future as the summer dragged on.

The Central Committee of Republican Refugees planned for the next opportunity to mobilize and act. Frustration and petty jealousies within this circle made some question Becker's leadership. Gustav Struve had been harried from place to place by Swiss secret police and was running short on funds. He was anxious for action, perhaps a little too anxious. When riots broke out in Frankfurt, Cologne, and Baden following the Frankfurt Parliament's ratification of a peace treaty with Denmark, Struve thought his moment had arrived. Without consulting Becker, Willich, or other key leaders, he gathered a small group of acolytes, crossed the Swiss border into Baden unarmed, and entered the town of Lörrach late in the afternoon of September 21. From the balcony of town hall, Struve proclaimed a German republic with himself as provisional head of state. Surprised republican leaders had little choice but to join in the poorly planned and self-serving fiasco. Months later, when one of the central committee members had had time to reflect, he held nothing back: "We had a much wider sweeping plan that Struve completely ruined with his ill-calculated coup."[24]

Willich was visiting Becker in Switzerland when Struve's request for military assistance arrived. Becker advised his German workers association not to participate, but after hearing inflated reports of Struve's initial success, he ordered the group to mobilize on September 24. That same day, Willich ordered his column in Besançon to cross the border while he rushed to Baden. One of Willich's lieutenants assembled the troops on Saint Pierre Place and read a letter wherein Willich both thanked the mayor for his support of the refugees and addressed the men with a short speech. Those gathered were told that a republic had been declared in Germany and that they would find scores of workers there ready to rally to their cause. Willich's address finished with the cry "Long live the universal republic!" The column then marched out of the city. The new conservative French government neither supported nor hindered Willich's movements. The *Union Franc-Comtois* wished him and his men success. "Whatever may be the chances of the struggle," the paper's editor predicted, "its outcome is certain. Between the democratic principle and the monarchial principle, God has already declared whom the victor shall be." With men such as these, the paper continued, "Germany elevates all parts by the revolution . . . to realize the prophecies of its popular poets." By the time Willich's column left Besançon, Struve's ill-conceived coup had already been crushed at Stauffen and its leader made prisoner.[25]

Willich learned of the defeat and dispatched a messenger ordering his troops to abandon the mission. The message arrived too late; his men had already crossed the Rhine and were advancing toward southern Baden. At Müllheim, Willich gave a fiery speech to a large crowd of soldiers and republican sympathizers, urging them to press on. Not long after the cheering corps marched off, the men encountered some Baden dragoons and started to panic. Willich demanded that those who wanted to hide behind their wives' apron sleeves go home immediately. Most departed, leaving him with a hundred men. Willich was subsequently joined by Becker, who had also arrived too late to do anything but cover the retreat of Struve's remnant forces. On September 27, Willich made his way to his familiar refuge in the Schuster-insel near Weil am Rhein. Along with seven hundred rebels, including the recently arrived Besançon column, he took position on the left bank of the

Rhine near a bridge of boats that held their weapons. Lieutenant Colonel von Stoecklern of the Baden military demanded that the insurgents withdraw. However, they refused to leave.[26]

Willich assembled the remains of the rebel army in an old riding arena on October 1 and announced the establishment of the German Republican Military Association, a mutual-aid society for radical refugees in France and Switzerland. Becker was given political leadership of the group, and Willich was appointed its military commander. A joint statement from the two leaders called Struve's rash action "the still-born idea of an improvised revolution." The new association would protect the German expatriates from "taking part in ridiculous putsches and premature insurrections." French authorities offered to receive the column back, so the revolutionaries crossed the river at Huningue, where they remained for a few days. Before crossing into French territory, Willich gathered his column under a large apple tree; there, the men swore an oath to die singing the next time they entered their homeland, rather than forsaking German soil again.[27]

Baden troops massed on the border, fearing invasion. Anxious to avoid war, the French cooled tensions by assuring Baden officials that the insurgents would be quickly dispersed. Among the hundreds of rebel soldiers sheltered in Huningue, 150 were Swiss citizens, mostly from Becker's corps. They returned to their homes, and the French marched the Germans back to Besançon, where they began arriving on October 5. That same day, a *Franc-Comtois* editorial, probably written by Willich himself, tried to explain the failed revolution to the public. "Willich's column had nothing to do with the errors committed by Struve," the article read. "It is very possible that a combined movement between the different leaders could have succeeded. This is what cannot fail to happen, for it is not the Revolution that must perish in Germany." Readers were urged to continue their support for the refugees. "In the present state of Europe," the paper noted, "France is a land of asylum, until it is a land of deliverance."[28]

Willich and his men settled into an uneasy purgatory at their Besançon barracks while the forces of reaction throughout Europe regained the upper hand. On October 16, Berlin militia fired on demonstrating workers. November found both Vienna and Berlin under the control of royalist forces. In December, Prussian king Friedrich William IV agreed to pacify dissidents by adopting a constitution. That same month, Louis-Napoleon was elected president of France and Franz Joseph declared emperor of Austria.[29] The future for European republicans looked bleak.

Willich's corps spent the gloomy winter of 1848–49 drilling, learning

French, and singing patriotic songs in the cavernous, dimly lit hall. It was a tragic scene. Eleven members of the column died in hospital during the first three months of 1849, and nine of the dead were in their early twenties.[30] Saxon army deserter Phillip Wagner, whom Willich rejected for membership in the unit, later recalled the exiled revolutionary leader as "a true Cherusker, like a Christ among his children." Clinging stubbornly to an elusive vision of a brotherhood of man, Willich was "the Christ of Besançon as a living Don Quixote."[31]

Chapter Six

● ● ● ● ● ● ● ● ● ● ● ● ● ● ● ● ● ● ● ●

REHEARSAL FOR REVOLUTION

REACTION CLOSED IN on Willich and his column at the beginning of 1849. The Grand Duchy of Baden offered amnesty to its nationals if they swore an oath not to conspire against the monarchy, but it offered no pardon for revolutionary leaders. Newly elected French president Louis-Napoleon's conservative government threatened to end subsidies for the Besançon refugees. By the end of February, 40 of the 150 German exiles under Willich's leadership at the close of 1848 had left for jobs in the French interior. J. P. Becker, political leader of German émigré republicans, joined Willich in forming the military-focused Wehrbund. Marx and Engels were active in less radical worker associations. They opposed Willich and Becker as dangerous adventurers whose dream of a spontaneous rising of the German proletariat was destined to fail.[1]

While the Frankfurt Parliament debated the future of Germany, Becker and Willich began building a European network of worker organizations that would support one other in the quest for basic rights and republican government. They focused their energies on Italy, where Rome revolutionaries had seized power and forced the pope to flee. Becker and Willich negotiated a secret alliance with the nascent Roman Republic and communicated frequently with Mazzini and Garibaldi. Concerned that he would be unable to return to Germany to participate in an anticipated rebellion there, Willich declined Mazzini's offer to command a revolutionary army in Sicily.[2]

Willich's missionary zeal and desperation for immediate action worried Becker, who began to distance himself from his radical ally. Nevertheless, Becker supported Willich's efforts to form a German-Swiss legion to aid

Mazzini in an expected conflict with Catholic Austria. In late March, Willich slipped out of Besançon on a covert mission to recruit soldiers for his battalion. French police agents followed him.[3]

Italian republicans had expressed the hope that their French brethren would intervene and save them from extermination by the Austrians. But Louis-Napoleon was plotting to crush the Roman Republic himself, restore the pope to power, and consolidate his political position with French Catholics. As Willich made his way to Lyon, the French National Assembly voted to send six thousand soldiers to occupy the Port of Rome. French police arrested Willich, placed him in chains, and forced him to walk to the border, where they intended to turn him over to Prussian authorities and a certain trial for treason. Willich had made many friends in the region during his eleven months of exile. French newspapers hailed him as a republican folk hero and protested against such horrendous treatment of a political refugee. The country's officials responded by escorting their prisoner to the Swiss border at Geneva and setting him free. When Willich arrived at Geneva on April 10, Moses Hess and Becker were waiting for him; they had been busy assembling a German worker's association composed of democrats and communists. Excitement grew as radicals waited for their moment. It came unexpectedly.[4]

• • • • •

Deliberations in the German Confederation's first freely elected parliament during the final seven months of 1848 had not gone well. The Frankfurt Parliament's mission was daunting: draft a constitution that would serve as the legal framework for a unified German nation-state. As the sessions dragged on, advocates for absolute rule by hereditary monarchs gained strength while the legislature floundered. Radical democrats like Gustav Struve broke with liberals once and for all. An October rising in Vienna was put down violently. That same month, Prussian troops occupied Berlin.[5]

Berlin and Vienna paid no heed to the parliament, as internal squabbling had further weakened it. An emboldened King Friedrich rejected Prussia's draft constitution and disbanded its national assembly. In a last gasp of audacity, the Frankfurt Parliament issued a declaration of basic rights on December 27, 1848. Members of parliament further proclaimed that these rights, which included freedom of assembly, press, trade, and education and the abolition of class-based privileges and capital punishment, were inviolable and immediately in force.

Willich was escorted to the French border with an iron collar around his neck while the denuded Frankfurt Parliament passed a constitution on March 28, 1849. This development was hardly cause for celebration among democrats and radical republicans. The constitution proposed a federal state with a bicameral legislature and the Prussian king as hereditary emperor. The crown was offered to King Friedrich the next day. Twenty-eight German states approved the federal constitution immediately, but Hanover, Saxony, and Bavaria balked. The success of the entire enterprise now relied on a favorable reply from Prussia.[6]

King Friedrich was not anxious to accept the title of Emperor of the German People. Such titles were traditionally bestowed by God, not as a gift of "a sausage sandwich" from a "master butcher and baker," as the monarch told some of his confidantes. Other intimates recalled him describing the offer as "a pig's crown" and "a crown from the gutter." The king was concerned that a unified Germany with Prussia at its core would threaten Russia and destabilize Europe. Many of Friedrich's subjects, however, urged the new Prussian parliament to accept the constitution, which both chambers did on April 24. Friedrich wasted no time in responding. He dissolved parliament, rejected the crown, and promised military support for German states who followed his lead. Germans across the confederation were outraged.[7]

While the Frankfurt Parliament disintegrated under Prussian pressure, radicals like Willich sensed opportunity. They held their noses and harnessed public anger, supporting a campaign for a constitution they did not believe in. Revolutionaries reasoned that further reforms would move in a democratic direction once Germany was unified. Ultimately, then, their dream of a red republic could be realized. It was a farfetched hope, but at this stage of the revolution, it was all they had.

Willich and his radical allies had been planning for an opportunity like this for a year. This rebellion would be neither a spontaneous uprising like the one in March 1848, nor a reckless action like Struve's September putsch. Now that the flame of public indignation had been reignited, leaders focused on regions in southwest Germany most likely to support them: the Bavarian Palatinate and Baden. On May 1, twelve thousand people assembled at Kaiserslautern in the Palatinate for a meeting of various democratic people's associations. Bavarian king Maximilian had defied popular approval of the Frankfurt Constitution by adjourning parliament and convincing his supreme court to nullify the recently approved Fundamental Rights for Bavarians. Angry democrats declared the king's actions a violation of law. They demanded that the territories of Swabia, Franconia, and the Palatinate adopt the Frankfurt

Constitution, separate from the Kingdom of Bavaria, and abolish the monarchy. Any use of force to prevent these actions would be considered treason against the prospective German nation. The assembly appointed a ten-man committee to defend the constitution, establish a people's militia, and form a provisional government.

Meanwhile, riots broke out in the city of Dresden in Saxony on May 3. Friedrich August's entire cabinet resigned when the king refused to publish the Frankfurt Constitution. The sovereign and his ministers fled the city, but instead of pressing their advantage, moderate democrats established a brief truce, allowing counterrevolutionary elements to organize. By the time the cease-fire had expired, five thousand men from the Saxon army had entered Dresden. The Prussian Army also arrived in support with artillery and Dreyse needle guns, the latter of which were new breech-loading rifles capable of firing as many as ten to twelve rounds per minute. Vicious combat ensued in the barricaded streets of Dresden, where composer Richard Wagner and anarchist Mikhail Bakunin were among the rebel fighters. Prussian soldiers gave little quarter and encouraged their Saxon allies to do the same—King Friedrich of Prussia was living up to his promise. These events presaged gloom for the revolution.[8]

The rebellion gained steam quickly in southwest Germany, fueled by the shocking news on May 9 that hundreds of soldiers from the Baden army in the federal fortress at Rastatt had mutinied. Government soldiers in Freiburg followed suit two days later. Across the Rhine, thousands of Royal Bavarian Army soldiers defected to the revolutionaries, and Grand Duke Leopold fled his residence at Karlsruhe the night of May 13. Five days later, a military alliance was completed between the provisional government in the Palatinate and Baden rebel leaders. Riot and rebellion threatened to become outright war. No one knew just how many government soldiers could be converted to the cause and how quickly public enthusiasm, money, arms, and volunteers could be marshaled to defend the imperial constitution. There was only one certainty—the Prussians were coming.[9]

• • • • •

Willich departed Geneva for the Rhineland on May 16. That same day, secret police arrived at Karl Marx's home and ordered him to leave Germany. Three days later he published the last issue of the *Neue Rheinische Zeitung*, printed entirely in red ink. Marx and his followers opposed the Frankfurt Constitution, but events were outrunning ideology. Radicals to the left of Marx like Willich, Struve, and Becker remained committed to armed insurrection. Legions of volunteers began moving toward the provisional capital at Kaiserslautern, where the revolutionary army of the Palatinate was assembling.[10]

Before key rebel military commanders could gather, Ludwig Blenker, a popular colonel in the Worms militia, amassed a corps of insurgents, took Ludwigshafen, and occupied Worms. He then set out to capture the federal stronghold at Landau with a motley assemblage of three hundred Bavarian Army deserters, fifteen hundred local militiamen, and various peasants carrying pitchforks and scythes. Blenker expected the castle garrison to come over to the rebels en masse, as they had done at Rastatt in Baden. On May 19, he marched to the castle gate shouting, "Brothers, don't shoot!" and was wounded instantly. Blenker's troops then wheeled and departed.[11] Austrian Ferdinand Fenner von Fenneberg, the military leader of the Palatine revolution, resigned the following day. The provisional government appointed a military commission led by Fritz Anneke to reorganize the burgeoning rebel army.[12]

The commission settled on former Polish general Franz Sznaide as their leader. It was a poor selection; Sznaide was incompetent and listless, a man with few ideas and no charisma. Moreover, his recruiting efforts were pathetic. It was hardly surprising that volunteers had to be "dragged in by the hair to report" for what was supposed to be compulsory military service, since the provisional government had no money, no provisions, no ammunition, and barely eight thousand muskets. France, Belgium, and Switzerland closed their borders to arms shipments. Though thousands of government soldiers deserted to the cause and a like number of workers and peasants were caught up in the initial excitement, commitment to revolution remained shallow. Only hard-core rebels were willing to risk all for the cause, and Sznaide was not one of them. He confided to one of his corps commanders, "The only thing left for me to do is to get killed." Willich, on the other hand, was fully invested.[13]

Willich joined Marx and Engels in Speyer, and they arrived in Kaiserslautern on May 20. The rebel force numbered approximately 5,500 soldiers and more than 1,500 scythemen. With Engels as his adjutant, Willich assumed command of 2,000 Palatine volunteers, including 90 men who had trained with him at Besançon. These soldiers made up the heart of the force. Alexander Schimmelpfennig and his battalion of Palatinate militia were also at Willich's disposal, along with about 1,100 workers recruited from various towns.[14] While other volunteer forces spent early June needlessly marching and countermarching against an enemy who failed to appear, Willich left to lay siege to the fortresses at Landau and Germersheim.

Before departing, Willich read his men the articles of war. The *freikorps* was open to everyone. War crimes such as murder, arson, and robbery were punishable by death, and conduct unworthy of a soldier would result in expulsion from the corps. Commanding officers could summarily shoot combatants who disobeyed orders while engaged with the enemy. Desertion for more than twenty-four hours, leaving a comrade under fire, or abandoning a guard post without leave could also result in a death sentence upon conviction in a court of war. Punishments for lesser offenses remained solely at the discretion of the corps commander or, in the case of minor infractions, the company leader. All corps members were required to swear an oath: "I pledge my word as a man to campaign for the constitution and the legitimate provisional government, and I shall be without honor should I leave my corps without permission of the government before the end of the battle."[15]

Willich and his men might have sworn to defend the Frankfurt Constitution and the Palatine Provisional Government, but many were committed to larger goals. They carried the black, red, and gold banner of the Palatinate

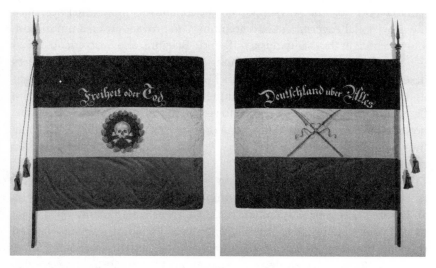

REUTLINGEN FREISCHAR BANNER, MAY 1849 (OBVERSE AND REVERSE).
MADE BY THE REUTLINGEN VIRGINS FOR THE VOLUNTEERS. MOTTO:
'FREEDOM OR DEATH.' HEIMAT MUSEUM, REUTLINGEN, GERMANY.

Army alongside red pennants. They intended to use the uprising to ignite an international socialist revolution. Radicals like Willich hijacked the campaign for a German national constitution, making it less likely that moderates and liberals among the middling classes would join the rebellion. Most Germans did not support drastic social reengineering.[16]

Capturing a large fortress was out of the question for such a small force with only negligible artillery, but keeping loyal Bavarian soldiers bottled up inside their stronghold was the next best thing. The fortress at Landau held only a third of its typical complement of 4,500 soldiers. The balance had left in May, refusing to fight against fellow Rhinelanders. Inside the fortress was a huge store of guns, ammunition, and artillery that the rebels desperately needed. Willich had studied siege tactics extensively in Berlin and knew how to put pressure on the fortress. He cut off its fresh water supply, and his forces worked with the local militia to blockade all roads between Landau and the smaller fortress at Germersheim, thereby interrupting communication and movement.

Willich issued an ultimatum to Landau's commander, sixty-three-year-old Maj. Gen. Christian Wilhelm Freiherr von Jeetze, on June 9: "The Nussdorf-strasse well has been dug up at my command by local citizens and will remain inoperable as the fortress must be ours." Willich explained that the rebels' cause was righteous and that surrendering government soldiers would be treated honorably as long as they acted in that same spirit. If the garrison took up arms against the townspeople, however, they would be treated as enemy combatants. "Remember that the time in near," Willich warned, "when the people will sit in judgment. Much will be forgiven, but not inhumanity. . . . Consider this your last chance." Jeetze did not reply. He instead sent the mayor of Nussdorf a note, saying that he would deal fairly with the local populace as long as they did not participate in armed rebellion. In reality, the fortress was close to capitulation. Two days later, however, the advance guard of the of the First Division of the First Prussian Army Corps crossed the Palatine border without opposition and marched south. Their advance forced Willich to abandon the siege and prepare for an onslaught of Prussian bayonets.[17]

Willich and other rebel corps commanders operated independently, as Sznaide had issued no orders for weeks. More than twenty-eight thousand Prussian troops of the First Corps under the command of General Moritz von Hirschfeld, along with a few thousand Bavarian Chevaliers, bore down on the rebels. Willich moved reinforcements to Bellheim on June 13, placing a small force composed of raw volunteers and scythemen in the rear. These supporting troops ran from the first shots fired by Bavarian royalists, but reserves conducted a brazen counterattack. The battle raged for two hours until additional men from Willich's corps arrived to help drive the Bavarians out of the village. The rebels were outnumbered by more than ten to one. Between twenty and thirty members of Willich's corps perished in the battle, and one French rebel volunteer was shot in the upper arm before he could fire a ball. Nevertheless, the Frenchman requisitioned one of the scythemen to load his musket for him and discharged all sixteen of his cartridges.[18]

Prussians appeared at 5:00 a.m. on June 14 near Kirchheimbolanden, where Rhenish-Hesse rebel volunteers were surrounded on three sides and routed. Fifty revolutionaries were killed and another thirty captured, including Mathilde Hitzfeld. She was so frustrated by her timid townsmen that she ripped a pistol from one of their belts and advanced against the invaders. She also saw service on the barricades.[19] Accompanied by his wife, Mathilde, Fritz Anneke set off with his artillery to join Willich. At Edesheim, north of Landau, Anneke's party met a young woman carrying a scythe. Earlier, the maiden had stridden boldly up to her father, the blacksmith of the village. "What do you want?" he asked her with some irritation. "It is not mowing time." His daughter replied that, indeed, it was not time to mow but to fight. "Beat the sickle straight!" she implored him. "What do you plan to do with it?" the blacksmith asked. "Beat it straight!" she repeated earnestly. The maiden then stood over her father as he worked with hammer and anvil. When the job was done, she took the weapon and walked away. The blacksmith then asked his apprentice, "What does she want with that?" The young man replied, "Our brother Willich calls us, master. We must leave and go into battle." Then he walked away and did not return. The following evening, a rebel soldier woke the Annekes with news: "Colonel, the Prussians are here!"[20]

Anneke, Adjt. Carl Schurz, and their troops departed at 3:00 a.m. on June 16 and headed west. They arrived in the village of Frankweiler, where they met other corps of the revolutionary army, some of whom adorned their hats and blouses with green oak clusters. Provisional government leaders conducted business in the tavern. Willich's and Anneke's former comrades in the Prussian Seventh Artillery were among Hirschfeld's enemy corps, and Mathilde Anneke composed a few lines chastising them: "Your mothers will never bless you, your wives will curse you, your brides will kill you one day." Before long, the Annekes encountered the Willich *freikorps*. They were taken aback by Willich's changed appearance. "His face was paler, his head and beard longer," Mathilde wrote. She also observed, "His whole appearance was almost spiritual." The old friends hugged and kissed, but it was a short reunion. Willich climbed on his white horse and rode away with his corps, red flags flying, straining to appear triumphal in the face of imminent defeat.[21]

Prussians advanced in two huge columns as far as the outskirts of Landau and Germersheim. The rebels had lost the northern half of the Palatinate. Now loyalist armies would link up and move swiftly over the clear, flat plain of the Rhine Valley to secure the remainder of the province. Nothing could stop them. While the main body of the rebel army prepared to abandon the Palatinate and cross into Baden, Willich assumed the daunting duty of covering the retreat with his corps. He joined Schimmelpfennig's militia in the mountains near Rinnthal, convinced that the Prussians would pursue. He was right. One June 17, the Second Division of the First Prussian Army Corps came after the insurgents.

Willich had a sound defensive plan, but it failed through poor execution. He would slow the advance on Landau by controlling a key road at a narrow point in the Queich River valley between Wilgartswiesen, where the Prussians were assembled, and the town of Rinnthal to the east. Willich ordered Schimmelpfennig to man the heights on either side of the road so the Prussians would walk into a shooting gallery in the defile fronting the town. Schimmelpfennig instead barricaded the road, ignoring those orders and his pickets' reports. Prussian Jägers easily stormed the heights and turned the tables on the rebels. By the time Willich's troops arrived in Rinnthal, Schimmelpfennig's militiamen were already under fire in a trap of their own making. Engels led a daring mission to dislodge some of the Prussian sharpshooters, but he was forced to call it off because an attempt to cross an open area measuring two hundred fifty paces would be suicide. The rebels were outflanked.[22]

Once Schimmelpfennig himself was wounded, his troops broke and ran. With the road back to Rinnthal blocked by barricades, Willich and Engels led a retreat through wet meadows and swamps to the village. The rebels lost most of their men on that pullback. Dense columns of men crowded together allowed the Prussians to find their mark with many volleys, killing about twenty enemy soldiers. Forty more were wounded or captured. In contrast, no Prussians were killed and only nine were wounded. Fortunately for the rebels, they were not pursued on their grueling sixteen-hour retreat. Willich displayed such personal bravery in the fight that some soldiers believed he sought his own death.[23]

By the time reinforcements arrived in Albersweiler, some volunteers had seen enough. "They want to lead us to the slaughter!" a grizzled, drunk rebel cried. When his comrades voiced support for the coward, Willich dismissed

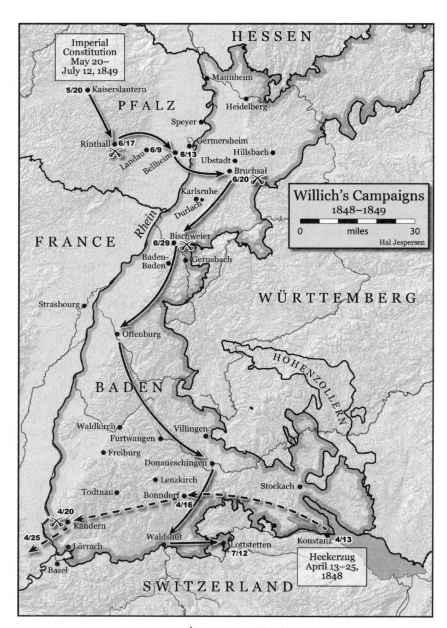

HESSEN

Mannheim

5/20 • Kaiserslautern

PFALZ

Heidelberg

Speyer •

Germersheim

Rinthall • 6/17
Landau • 6/9
Bellheim
6/13

Hillsbach •
Ubstadt
Bruchsal
6/20

Karlsruhe

FRANCE

Durlach

Rhein

Bischweier
6/29

Baden-
Baden

Gernsbach

WÜRTTEMBERG

Strabourg •

Offenburg •

HOHENZOLLERN

BADEN

Waldkirch •

Villingen •

Furtwangen •

• Freiburg

Donaueschingen •

• Lenzkirch

Stockach •

Todtnau •

Bonndorf
4/16

4/20
Kandern

4/25

Lörrach •

Waldshut •

Lottstetten
7/12

Konstanz 4/13

Basel •

SWITZERLAND

Willich's Campaigns
1848–1849

0   miles   30

Hal Jespersen

Heckerzug
April 13–25,
1848

WILLICH'S CAMPAIGNS, 1848–49

the entire company, saying he was sick of their complaints. Willich then learned that the enemy had entered Landau, and he rushed to the bridge at Knielingen. On June 18, most of the Palatinate rebel army crossed into Baden. Willich's column followed later that day. While hopes for the liberation of the Rhenish Palatinate evaporated, even worse news arrived from France.[24] The June 13 Paris insurrection had been crushed. There would be no pan-European revolution in 1849. As the entire enterprise was collapsing before Willich's eyes, there was little to do but regroup and make a last stand in the provisional republic of Baden.

• • • • •

The revolution had a promising start in Baden. Widespread defection of the duke's troops and possession of the stronghold at Rastatt gave revolutionists hope. J. P. Becker commanded the Baden Volkswehr militia, which faced enormous odds. Combined Baden and Palatinate rebel forces numbered more than twenty thousand, but arrayed against them was an enemy force of more than fifty-three thousand federation troops led personally by Prussian crown prince and future emperor Wilhelm. The loyal army was also armed to the teeth and amply supplied. In contrast, the Baden provisional government had limited resources. Its military leader was former Polish general Ludwik Mieroslawski, who had been a key figure in the Poznan uprising of 1846 against Prussia. Mieroslawski avoided execution via a general amnesty proffered to revolutionaries by the Prussian king after the 1848 revolutions. Republican forces subsequently won a series of four quick victories on the line of the River Neckar from Mannheim to Hirschorn, north of Heidelberg.[25]

Wearing their blue worker's blouses, members of the ragtag Willich corps greeted Baden regulars sporting beautiful, shining uniforms. Anneke and the balance of the defeated Palatine Army were already across the bridge. Upon meeting them, a Baden soldier named Hofer removed his helmet, replete with the emblem of the exiled Duke Leopold. "If you have any doubt that I have loyalty to that cursed name," the soldier announced, "I will give you proof against it." He placed his helmet on a stone, drew his saber, and hacked off the letter _L_. Finally, he handed the keepsake to Mathilde Anneke. Fritz Anneke then gave the order to his artillerymen to destroy the Knielingen Bridge. Two days later, Prussians crossed the Rhine near Germersheim.[26]

Willich rode to Daxlanden and billeted his troops, who slept on the bare ground with little to eat or drink. Rebel officers drank wine from large goblets to disguise their melancholy, and the Annekes encountered Willich at a table in the tavern. "Mathilde!" he exclaimed with typical dramatic pathos, "I feel as if I would like to lie in my grave today!" She protested, but Engels whispered to her about the Rinnthal battle where one of Willich's dearest friends had died in his arms. After laying the fallen man down, Willich had mounted his horse and charged forward, only to have the beast shot from under him. When he tried to advance on foot, Engels had shouted, "Willich, if you go forward, *we* will shoot you."[27]

Trailing behind Willich on an evening march, Anneke left for Heidelberg to assume command of the Baden artillery. Locals with torchlights guided the troops along the route. At Blankenloch, an hour and a half northeast of Karlsruhe, Willich stopped to feed his men and hold a council of war with other rebel leaders. Here they learned that Hirschfeld's Prussians had advanced in two columns. Willich lobbied for an immediate attack, but other leaders felt that their inexperienced men could not make a night assault. They decided to continue northeast to Karlsdorf, where Willich would attack before daybreak, attempt to break through the Prussian line, then link up with allied forces at Bruchsal. This risky plan would pit Willich's column of about seven hundred men against a force of four thousand Prussians. After a brief rest, Willich and his rebels set out at midnight.[28]

Fritz and Mathilde Anneke remained in Blankenloch while Willich marched on Karlsdorf. Mathilde was asleep in her chair when her husband woke her. "To the horses!" he shouted, waving his arm. When asked the reason for such urgency, Fritz responded in a grave whisper. Their dear friend was dead. The general staff told Fritz that Willich's corps had been decimated in the night battle; informants claimed the men had been mowed down with case shot and fiery cannon balls. As the Annekes rode toward the battlefield in the rising morning fog, Mathilde's teeth chattered. "We ride quietly, we ride silently, we are going to our ruin," she thought.[29]

The Annekes encountered stragglers who claimed that the valley was "black with Prussians." They had only traveled a short distance when they encountered Willich himself, astride another white horse and looking quite robust for a dead man. The false rumors had been spread by a few cowardly Baden dragoons and local reactionaries.[30] General Sznaide met Willich and Engels outside of Blankenloch. "Where are you going?" the old general asked. "The enemy is that way!" Willich ignored him and led his troops back to town for some much-needed rest and nourishment. Two hours later Sznaide and the rest of the army returned, having failed to engage the enemy. They had no idea that at that very moment, another battle was beginning twenty-eight kilometers to the north that would seal the fate of the Baden revolution.[31]

Leading the combined revolutionary armies, Mieroslawski opted to move the corps under his immediate command south from the River Neckar and attack Hirschfeld's First Prussian Corps. It was a desperate gamble. The rebels had initial success at Wiesental and Waghäusel, pushing the enemy back to Phillipsburg. Prussians suffered 21 dead, more than 100 wounded, and 130 missing before reinforcements turned the tide. Then Peuker's corps crossed the Neckar River, threatening the rebel right flank. On June 22 Mieroslawski's center collapsed, and he made a dash south toward Rastatt that saved the revolutionary army from certain annihilation.[32]

In the meantime, Willich moved to protect the right flank of Sznaide's army. It took him five hours to reach Weingarten, where panicked locals were reporting sightings of Prussians at every turn. The reports were false. Just as Willich and his men were entering the town of Bruchsal, the Prussians had moved back to Waghäusel. Anneke's six hundred troops were in an advance position to the north at Ubstadt. On the morning of June 23, Willich received a note from Anneke with the news that a council of war had been held and the decision made to withdraw. Willich could not believe it. He jumped on his horse and galloped to Ubstadt.[33]

Willich convinced Anneke and his officers to give battle outside of Ubstadt. Willich formed his men on the right flank as Anneke's force cried, "Long live Willich!" He shouted back, "And I will die with you!" Anneke surveyed their position and deployed his twelve cannons between Ubstadt and Stettfeld to the north. While the troops were assembling, Willich and Anneke received a dispatch from headquarters stating that the main body of the army was in retreat.[34] Willich again maneuvered to protect Sznaide's right flank, marching northeast by way of Odenheim to Waldangelloch. If the Baden army was defeated, Willich would be cut off from the rest of the rebels and compelled to flee into the mountains. The soldiers soon encountered Sznaide's forces retreating to Bruchsal. The situation was beginning to look like Willich's worst nightmare.

Fortunately for Willich and the rest of the revolutionary army, the Prussians had taken quite a beating from Anneke's cannons and had pulled back after a battle at Ubstadt. Of greater concern, however, were the ten thousand Bavarian troops billeted just an hour and a half to their northeast at Sinsheim. On his retreat just two days earlier, and after skirmishing with Bavarians on the way, Mieroslawski and his troops had spent the night there. Willich, who passed the night with his men at Hillsbach, left early in the morning of June 24 to catch up with Becker, who had formed the rear guard of the retreating main body of the army. The next morning, they marched south toward Rastatt.

Prussian soldiers and their allies pushed the rebels into the southern extremities of Baden with methodical precision, accepting battle when they had the opportunity and dealing savagely with armed insurrectionists along the way. In Ubstadt, several snipers in the church steeple were executed. Fifteen captured rebels were shot down in the churchyard. The Prussians knew that, despite strong yearnings for self-rule, the average Baden citizen most yearned for peace and prosperity. There were many more desertions along the retreat route than there were inspired workers joining the revolution.[35]

Discouraged by defeat and looking for a scapegoat, Baden troops took their anger out on Sznaide as the rebel army made its way south toward Durlach. The revolutionaries had just left Weingarten when about fifty members of the rear guard surrounded the general, pointed their guns at him, and ordered him to dismount. "Come down, betrayer of the people!" one soldier shouted. Four shots rang out, none of them taking effect. Soldiers then tore Sznaide from his horse, and one of the sappers struck him on the head with the blunt end of an axe. The attackers then took the bleeding general's sword, ripped off his scarf and orders, and beat him with the butts of their guns. Apparently mistaking the Polish general's surname for "Schneider," one attacker cried out, "All Prussians are traitors!" As they began to stomp on Sznaide, other soldiers pushed the mutineers aside and spirited the shaken old man away. The humiliated general resigned the next day.[36] Franz Sigel, Mieroslawski's personal favorite, offered Sznaide's command to Willich, who declined. That dubious honor was bestowed on Becker.

By the time the revolutionary army reached the environs of Rastatt, most saw further resistance as futile. Many made their way to safety in Switzerland. The Prussian government incited more defections by declaring amnesty for all Palatinate troops at Rastatt who returned home before July 5. Willich relinquished command of his *freikorps* in a reorganization of the army and was named chief of staff of the First Division of the combined army. Becker was the last to arrive at about eight o'clock in the evening, bringing fifty wagons of supplies and ammunition Mieroslawski had abandoned in his hasty retreat. Various rebel corps mustered at Rastatt around midnight. Mieroslawski positioned his fifteen thousand remaining men in a line north of the Murg River. Becker acted as rear guard to protect people and supplies fleeing south from Karlsruhe. He and his troops spent the night building barricades, tearing up railway tracks, and sleeping on the ground under continuous rain. They awoke on June 25 to the footfalls of two Prussian divisions. Meanwhile back at Rastatt, Mieroslawski prepared to face a consolidated federal force more than four times larger than his own.[37]

Willich was having breakfast with division staff three days later when the Prussians attacked at Michelbach. The fighting was over by the time Willich reached the scene of battle, and both sides had suffered only trifling losses. The next day, June 29, the Prussians made an assault at Bischweier, on the right bank of the Murg, near Willich's left wing. Willich faced a decision. He could move toward the firing, or he could hold his position at Gernsbach, as the largest Prussian attack was expected in that sector. Willich's instincts told him to wait for the larger assault, but others reasoned that nearby troops would cry "treason" and run if other units did not come to their aid. So Willich marched on Bischweier.

A half hour out of camp they met the enemy, and a desperate firefight ensued. Soldiers from the Prussian Neckar Corps approached the rebels crying, "Don't shoot, we are brothers," then opened fire on the insurgents at eighty paces. Willich's men advanced with red banners fluttering, shouting in French *En avant! En avant!*, or Forward! Forward! Willich's forces pushed the Prussians back to Bischweier in close combat with muskets and bayonets. Enemy reinforcements then arrived on the scene and forced the rebels to withdraw. Willich's corps suffered thirty casualties, and the Prussians lost fifty-nine dead and wounded. Willich reassembled the troops near the Murg Bridge, looked south, and saw smoke rising from the vicinity of Gernsbach.[38]

The Prussians attacked along the entire rebel front that day, but Gernsbach took the brunt of it. Prussian troops under Peuker crossed neutral Württemberg, convincing defensive troops massed along the border to accompany them against the Badeners. After a courageous stand by Baden regulars at the bridge, the Prussians crossed the Murg and advanced northwest to Gaganeau. In so doing, they turned the rebel right flank and spread panic across their lines. Willich scouted an advantageous high ground where he intended to place artillery and slow the enemy advance, but the guns had already been taken away. Willich had no choice but to gather his remaining men and retreat.[39]

Franz Sigel assigned Becker the impossible task of covering the army's retreat to Oos while also preventing the capture of the supplies and men at Rastatt. Becker's actions were enough to ensure that the two leaders and their reserve artillery could withdraw in safety. Six thousand rebels were left behind in the fortress and cut off from communication with the outside world. The Second Prussian Corps laid siege to the fortress while the rest of the Prussian Army pursued the remnants of the rebel army.[40]

The Baden government fled to Freiburg via Offenburg. They might have called up conscripts from Upper Baden to mass at Freiburg and

Donaueschingen, but most had lost the will to continue the struggle. On July 1, Mieroslawski resigned, leaving four thousand rebels in the field commanded by Sigel. Meanwhile, Willich led his men through the Kappel Valley into the mountains to defend the border with Württemberg. He and his troops marched through the Black Forest for three days without sighting the enemy. A messenger arrived on July 3 stating that the government in Freiburg was considering abandoning the town. Willich ordered his men to march there as fast as possible, hoping to convince Sigel not to leave without a fight. They were too late. When he arrived at Waldkirch that evening, Willich learned that Freiburg had been evacuated and remnants of the government moved to Donaueschingen.[41]

To defend the rapidly shrinking Baden republic, Sigel established one final line extending 130 kilometers northeast along a ridge of mountains near the Black Forest. Willich positioned himself to protect Sigel's likely retreat into Swiss territory.[42] The brash young leader was a mere four hours from the border. Becker requested that Willich attack the Prussians from Vohrenbach, but Willich refused. He had only 450 men left, barely enough to occupy three

WILLICH IN THE BLACK FOREST. WATERCOLOR BY OTTO VON ERXLEBEN, 1849.
WILLICH APPEARS ON HORSEBACK SURROUNDED BY REBEL VOLUNTEERS.
ALAMY STOCK PHOTO.

square miles of territory he had been assigned to hold. Instead, he went to meet with Sigel.

Willich arrived at Sigel's headquarters at ten in the evening and received disheartening news. At the constituent assembly in Freiburg, Gustav Struve claimed that all was lost and insisted the revolutionaries move to Switzerland at once. Thus, Sigel ordered a general retreat. While Sigel looked for a place to cross the Swiss border, Willich and Becker took up favorable positions near Wutöschingen. Rebel leaders convened at Riedern on July 10 to hold a final council of war. Willich alone argued for continued defense. Meanwhile, Swiss emissaries told Sigel that their government would not offer the rebels asylum if they continued to fight. Early the next day, Sigel and Becker crossed the border with their troops. Willich and his men covered their retreat and were the last rebels to cross into Swiss territory near Lottstetten on July 12. Revolutionists under siege at Rastatt were not so lucky.[43]

Twenty thousand patient Prussian soldiers stood by for three weeks as rebels inside fortress Rastatt awaited deliverance. Prussian leaders eventually allowed their captives to send emissaries to the far corners of Baden to confirm what the insurgents themselves refused to believe—the Baden provisional government no longer existed. The castle garrison surrendered on July 23. Defenders were imprisoned in horrible conditions while they awaited trial, many of them dying from typhoid fever contracted in the stinking casemates. Nineteen survivors were shot by firing squad, and the Prussians dumped them in a mass grave. Eight other rebels were shot in Mannheim and Freiburg. More than seven hundred individuals were sentenced to ten-year prison terms. Carl Schurz escaped through a sewer drain, but Willich and fifty other ringleaders were sentenced to death in absentia, ensuring most would never return to their homeland.[44]

Willich did not know that his crusade to win liberty for the German people in his native country was nearing its end. He crossed the border into Swiss territory fully expecting to return when the next window of opportunity opened. Willich could hardly imagine that a mere dozen years in the future, he would take up arms again thousands of miles away in the largest and most radical revolution of the nineteenth century. The lessons and memories of 1848 and 1849 would be reshaped into rhetorical weapons inspiring thousands to risk their lives in a war for the very survival of free government, while he himself fought for even more ambitious goals of social justice and universal human rights.[45]

Chapter Seven

• •

DUELING KARL MARX

DEFEATED BUT NOT DISHEARTENED, Willich and his corps were again refugees. The Prussian royal family had seen this drama play out previously; they were not about to allow revolutionaries to reestablish base camp in nearby France and launch yet another campaign. The loyal German press circulated rumors that a dozen men in Willich's corps were using false names and forged documents to spread propaganda in the border cantons of Switzerland. Journalists suggested that rebel agents stood poised to cross the border into the German states and stir up trouble. When these stories were picked up and printed by liberal periodicals like Hermann Becker's *Westdeutsche Zeitung*, Willich was incensed. "Is it not enough that there are victims who gave their lives, killed by princely lead, crying for freedom?" he pleaded. "Not enough captives in prison cells condemned to death? The day will come," Willich predicted, "when the people itself will dispense justice."

Bowing to pressure from their powerful neighbor, the Swiss general council ordered Willich and other revolutionary leaders to leave the country. "The Swiss would not suffer that fellow humans will perish in misery," Willich complained. He concluded, "Therefore these refugees must vanish." France also vowed to close its borders to German republicans. According to Willich, the French remedy for such exiles was to "transport them quickly through her territory like a contained agent of sickness and throw them at the English coast." The one safe haven left for political refugees was indeed England, the most liberal monarchy in Europe. By October 1849, Willich and other rebel leaders had settled in London to lick their wounds, organize, and attempt to keep the revolution alive.[1]

Midcentury London was a sprawling international city of 2.5 dents, more than twice the size of Paris. It was also a hothouse ı democratic ideas, second only to the French capital in its reputatı cutting-edge political exchange. Café and tavern culture thrived among mı dling and lower classes while the upper crust preferred the more formal atmosphere of intellectual salons. Refugees from failed revolutions throughout Europe found in these meeting places not only comradery and moral support, but also political associations formed by their democratic and socialist predecessors. One important radical group was the League of the Just.

The league was a secret society inspired by democratic conspiracies in Paris during the late 1830s. Dominated by artisans, it aimed to liberate Europeans from "the yoke of disgraceful oppression" and promote "cooperation to free mankind." The League of the Just preached strict adherence to the principles espoused by the French Revolution's Declaration of Rights. One of its leaders, tailor Wilhelm Weitling, became a pioneer of German socialism. Weitling believed that money and private property caused most societal ills. Communal property, however, was a Christian ethic. Only worker revolution from the ground up could achieve perfect equality. Weitling's French counterparts had a different strategy. The French League of the Just, led by Auguste Blanqui, envisioned a secular revolution by a secret clique of conspirators. Blanqui's chapter was suppressed following a failed uprising in 1839. Karl Schapper, a German disciple of Weitling who had been linked to the French conspiracies, established a London branch of the organization in 1841. All three men played important roles in the emergence of August Willich as a leader among the émigré community in London in the early 1850s.[2]

A local worker's organization also existed in London. It operated alongside the League of the Just and the Communist League. On February 7, 1840, Schapper and six others founded the German Worker's Educational Association, which became known as the Communistischer Arbeiter-Bildungsverein, or CABV. The CABV served to instruct ethnic German workers on a wide range of cultural subjects, from music and fine arts to history and science. Members attended lectures, participated in political discussions, and took field trips. Supplied with books, maps, and musical instruments by wealthy donors, the CABV helped exiles feel at home. They even promoted a health insurance scheme. On the surface, the CABV was apolitical, but in practice the organization recruited German refugees for radical groups. The three principal radical societies suffered from the same malaise that helped doom the revolutions themselves: clear differences in political ideology and violent disagreement over how the next phase of European revolution should proceed. Willich and his allies worked tirelessly for several years to reconcile these competing visions and unify the movement.[3]

By the time Willich arrived in London he had become an international figure. Newspapers on three continents chronicled his military exploits in southern Germany.[4] True to his sympathies with the dispossessed, the ascetic rebel leader elected to live with his citizen-soldiers in a barracks-style ghetto in London's East End. They made brooms to eke out a living, and Willich also taught lessons in German and mathematics. Those efforts failed, and the column was then forced to live off the goodwill of wealthier sponsors and emigrants from the homeland. The men's favorite haunt was the German Stores Hotel tavern at Twenty-Seven Long Acre near Leicester Square. It was owned by Willich's close friend August Schärtner, who had led a Turner company in the Baden rebellion and was a member of the Central Authority of the Communist League. A lodger described the place as "a robber's den" in one of London's dirtiest streets. Waiters in a large, dark room on the ground floor served ale and porter. The tavern also featured a huge round table piled high with old issues of democratic newspapers from around the world. Most evenings, traveler Theodor Fontane wrote with irony, "future presidents of the united and indivisible German republic settle down to expound their views on government."[5]

Only 5 percent of an estimated twenty-five thousand German-speaking residents of London were political refugees.[6] The rest were simply emigrants fleeing the uncertainty of life in central Europe and yearning for better economic opportunity in the bustling metropolis. Political émigrés from Germany in Willich's neighborhood were predominantly journeyman artisans and tailors in this motley collection of struggling idealists. Willich was their clear champion, their Volk hero.

Karl Marx and Friedrich Engels had arrived in the city a few months earlier and welcomed their comrade into the London chapter of the Communist League. Willich later became a member of the organization's central committee, and his radical views nudged the group further left. In March 1850, the central committee called for renewed rebellion in Germany. The next month, the World Society of Revolutionary Communists formed via an alliance with French radical Auguste Blanqui and English Chartists, a group dedicated to promoting socialism in Great Britain. However, Marx's partnership with Willich was destined to be brief, as he and Engels developed a strong distaste for the old Prussian. Willich's inflated ego, according to Marx, stunted his other talents. Engels described his former commander as "brave and cool in battle but a boring ideologue and true socialist dreamer."[7]

KARL MARX IN EXILE, LONDON, C. 1861.
PRIVATE COLLECTION.

Marx had good reason to see Willich as a threat. The former lieutenant had a habit of visiting Jenny Marx while her husband was away. Strolling into her bedroom "like a Don Quixote, dressed in a gray woolen doublet with a red sash in place of a belt," Willich would "roar with laughter in real Prussian style" and engage Mrs. Marx in long theoretical discussions on the merits of socialism. "He would come to visit me," Jenny claimed, "because he wanted to pursue the worm that lies in every marriage and coax it out." To Jenny and her husband, a man so popular and powerful who appeared to think more with his heart than with his head was a dangerous rival indeed.[8]

While Willich and other radicals pressed for immediate violent revolution in Europe, economic conditions on the Continent improved. Some leaders of the Communist League questioned the wisdom of the Blanquist approach. Marx and Engels believed that the window for action against the European princes had closed. Marx now maintained that certain economic preconditions were needed before attempting wholesale political and social change.

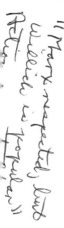

:rm revolution should progress in an evolutionary manner through
ive phases of economic development, he argued. Marx wrote col-
in Cologne that "Willich with his trash . . . had vehemently opposed
ıd said that "socialism would have to be introduced in the next revo-
even if only through the force of the guillotine." A pitched battle for
;hip of the London Communist League got underway.[9]

lich's circle of friends included the most radical revolutionaries in
e. Some were so zealous they would consider any measure justified
vanced their cause. One such unsavory character, French Blanquist
ınuel Barthelémy, had already tried to murder a police agent by the time
nned the barricades in Paris. Escaping prison, he arrived in London
1849 and became one of the leaders of the French émigré contingent.

et his end six years later when he was hanged for the murder of two
Englishmen. Carl Schurz retained vivid memories of Barthelémy's dusky, pale
face, black mustache and goatee, and dark eyes glowing with fire. Barthelémy
spoke slowly and carefully with a disturbing coolness. The French murderer
believed that all views contrary to his should be exterminated.

Barthelémy was also a fencing master, and he gave lessons to Karl Marx
soon after the German philosopher's arrival in London. Eventually, he grew
tired of Marx's sour temperament and made Willich his star pupil.[10] As Marx
and Willich's disagreement over the future of the Communist League grew,
the French assassin and the Prussian ex-lieutenant found that their political
views were compatible. Willich was keeping dangerous company.

Marx grew irritated as Willich's renown soared among German political
refugees. A contemporary remarked that "Marx was respected, but Willich
was popular." Barracks artisans identified with their bachelor military hero
who drank with them in the taverns, made brooms with them, and shared
their Spartan lifestyle. For his part, Marx spent much of his time studying
and writing in the British Museum and enjoying the relative comforts of an
apartment, wife, and housekeeper. Willich's carefully crafted image as savior
of the working class also grated on Engels. "He was entirely the prophet,"
Engels jeered, "convinced of his personal mission as the predestined liberator
of the German proletariat." Engels further claimed that Willich desired to
establish a military dictatorship, calling his former corps commander's philosophy "a kind of communist Islam." In truth, Willich was so anxious to for
revolution that he considered most any approach worthy of consideration.[11]

Willich was not content to sit back and discuss philosophy while workers
were denied their natural rights to liberty and prosperity. He valued action
over talk and refused to embrace calls for measured prolonged revolution. In

August 1850, Willich proved he had workers on his side when thirty members of the CABV undertook a secret journey to Hamburg, attempting to join the Schleswig-Holstein army in its revolt against Danish rule. They were sent back upon arrival. As Willich's long shadow began to obscure their leadership in the summer of 1850, Marx and Engels tried to undermine his reputation to anyone who would listen.[12]

Willich and close ally Karl Schapper, who was released from prison in June 1850, responded to Marxist attacks on their characters by framing the dispute as a power struggle between elite pseudointellectuals and men of action. Marx considered the workers "zeros," according to Willich. "As soon as they started to refuse blind obedience [to Marx], they were rogues, asses, rotters, rabble," he explained. Schapper attempted to mediate the conflict, but for Marx and Willich, the dispute had gone far beyond ideology. It was personal.[13]

In the late summer of 1850, the animus between the Marx and Willich factions accelerated out of control. At an August meeting of the CABV, an argument broke out that nearly led to blows. Afterward, Willich resigned from the refugee committee in a huff. The next meeting of the worker's society also turned ugly, with Marx and Engels storming out after the Willich party shouted them down. "We'll make you remember this yet!" Marx cried out amid jeers and laughter. The final straw came on September 1 at a meeting of the Central Committee of the Communist League. This particular conclave ended up splitting the organization and diminishing Marx's influence among the London exiles.[14]

The meeting was barely underway when Marx began hurling insults at Willich, calling him "an uneducated, four times cuckolded jackass." Willich lost his composure, calling Marx a liar. Marx responded with silent insolence. Conrad Schramm, a young Marx acolyte, then intervened and challenged Willich to a duel on his idol's behalf. Willich accepted, but since dueling had been outlawed in England, the combatants had to cross the channel to Ostend on the Belgian seacoast to hold the frightful event. Willich chose Barthelémy as his second.[15]

The mismatched duel promised a horrifying result. Willich chose pistols. While Young Schramm had never held a gun in his life, it was said that the former lieutenant never missed the ace of hearts at twenty paces. Willich and Barthelémy had a busy day planned, as the Frenchman had arranged for his own duel with a rival countryman. Fortunately, that opponent never appeared. Willich had already marked out the dueling ground when Schramm arrived with his second. Willich chose his place in the shade, leaving his rival in the sun. Schramm stepped forward one-half pace and pulled the trigger, missing his target. Willich took careful aim and fired.

The next evening a somber Barthelémy knocked on Marx's door and entered. The philosopher was not home, but Jenny Marx could not restrain her curiosity. "What news?" she asked anxiously. "Schramm a une balle dans la tête" (Schramm has a bullet in the head), Barthelémy announced. He bowed abruptly and exited, and Madame Marx nearly fainted. The following day brought another knock at Marx's door. To Jenny's amazement, a bloodied and bandaged Schramm gleefully burst into the house, explaining how Willich's shot had only grazed his head and rendered him temporarily unconscious. He woke up on the beach with his second and a doctor by his side. Willich had already left. The duel ended happily for everyone, especially Willich, who proceeded to assert his dominance over the Communist League, consigning Marx and his supporters to the periphery of London émigré politics.[16]

While Willich and Schapper pressed their radical program, Marx and Engels moved their focus from London to Cologne and preemptively abolished the London chapter of the Communist League. In reality, the league was still in operation and about to reach its zenith under Willich's leadership. On November 16, 1850, Willich and Schapper joined with the Blanquists in issuing a pamphlet titled *Aux democrats des tous les nations* calling for international unity and a revolutionary agenda. Willich and his former lieutenant in the 1849 revolution, Alexander Schimmelpfennig, actively solicited Prussian Army officers to resign and join the anticipated rebellion. Few listened.

The alliance with Schimmelpfennig, Franz Sigel, and others marked a resumption of London-based revolutionaries' focus on violent overthrow of European monarchs. Former army officers planned to assemble caches of guns and ammunition, drill and train prospective citizen-soldiers, and stand ready for mobilization when the time was right. On December 6, 1850, Willich wrote Cologne editor Hermann Becker detailing his latest scheme for revolution. The letter was a call to arms.[17]

Willich's revolution would begin with a press release directing home guards in southern Germany states to retain their weapons and defend their homeland against a phantom Prussian-backed invasion by Austrian and Russian troops. A revolutionary council of citizen armies would ensure that local government authorities fed and financed the home guards; those who didn't comply would be court-martialed and shot. In addition, anyone attempting to oppose local councils by judicial or other means would be executed. Willich urged Becker to wait for a flash-point event in Vienna, Italy, or France that would set their plans in motion. Three weeks later, Becker received another note from Willich with further instructions.[18]

Willich believed that his planned uprising would succeed. "Just as the total effect of a bullet is determined by speed and mass, and one of these can largely compensate for the other," he reasoned, "in revolution there exists a similar relationship between energy and means." The revolutionaries could compensate for their lack of manpower and resources by adopting a military dictatorship with unanimity of purpose and zero tolerance for dissent. Exports of money and emigration from the country would be punished as high treason. Only one newspaper would be authorized as a propaganda organ for the rebellion. The revolution would thus be "electrified" down to the last cottager.[19]

Becker did not share Willich's fantasy. "The other day we laughed till the tears came," Becker wrote to Marx. "His idiocy will spell disaster for the people." Of Willich's offer to assume leadership after Becker completed the work in Cologne, Becker tittered, "Very kind of him!"[20] Jenny Marx was not humored by Willich's adventurism. "If Willich is not ripe for the lunatic asylum," she wrote to Engels, "I don't know who is."[21] By February 1851, Willich still lacked funding for his secret enterprise. "In any case, we shall not let a business, just begun, go bankrupt," he assured Becker.[22]

Willich, Schapper, and Blanquist leaders reached out to English Chartists, Poles, Italians, and Hungarians in an attempt to unify the movement. French socialists sponsored the "Banquet of the Equals" on February 24, 1851, drawing over a thousand attendees to Highbury Barn. Noticing this celebration of the third anniversary of the Paris uprising, Marx and Engels and planned to disrupt the meeting and discredit their chief rivals. Their scheme worked even better than expected. Marx, who had a talent for spewing scathing denunciations while letting others face the music, sent protégé Conrad Schramm and an accomplice to the meeting to stir up trouble. They began by harassing English attendees, then waited for a response from Willich's acolytes. Just as the band was about to strike up "La Marseillaise," a dozen members of Willich's delegation, including Barthelémy, surrounded Schramm and his friend and attempted to snatch their hats. Fists flew while the meeting chair did nothing to stop the fracas. Throughout Germany, Marx gleefully spread a fable of a hundred men against two, characterizing Willich supporters as "cowardly, calumnious, infamous assassins." Many who knew of Barthelémy's reputation and disapproved of Willich's penchant for violence believed the rumors. If that was not enough, event host Louis Blanc and Barthelémy committed a gaffe that Marx and Engels were happy to exploit.[23]

Toasts for the meeting were mailed in from all over Europe. When Barthelémy previewed the message sent by Auguste Blanqui, then in prison in France, he decided not to have it announced at the banquet. Blanqui's letter called Louis Blanc and his followers "traitors" masquerading as champions of the people. When a copy of Blanqui's letter appeared later in a French newspaper, both his disparagement of Blanc and Barthelémy's attempt to suppress it were made public. Marx and Engels pounced on the opportunity to embarrass their political opponents by translating the letter into German, then printing and distributing thirty thousand copies. A celebration of émigré unity ended up feeding Marx's insatiable appetite for character assassination. Willich and Schapper reeled from the fallout.[24]

Blanqui was the undisputed martyr of the radical wing of the revolution. To have him at odds with Blanc and other Willich allies impugned the Prussian's credentials as the true leader of the worker's party. The scandal lessened enthusiasm for the Willich-Schapper Communist League and bolstered support for the less radical Marx contingent. As prospects for imminent military uprising dimmed, Willich reached out to diverse groups of potential allies as a way to keep hopes for revolution alive. Partnership with a liberal democratic group led by Baden Uprising officer Gottfried Kinkel was an unexpected and ultimately unsuccessful effort to maintain leadership of German exiles in London.[25]

Kinkel was an unlikely partner. From a gentry family, the professor of art history wrote sentimental poetry. But Kinkel was also a doer. He suffered wounding and imprisonment in the 1848–49 risings, and after that rebellion ran its course, he remained in prison and became a popular promoter of German unity. Kinkel's wife, Johanna, conceived and executed a propaganda campaign that made her husband a symbol of the democratic movement. She printed his poetry and other writings, making him a household name in Europe. On November 6, 1850, Carl Schurz, one of Kinkel's young students, helped him escape from prison and accompanied him to London. Kinkel then became the leader of the city's German social democratic circle. As he lived in posh circumstances in the wealthy suburb of Saint John's Wood, the professor and activist irritate who cobbled farthings together in an effort to survive.

Guilt gnawed at Kinkel led him to acknowledge the debt he owed to radicals who had saved his life. "I belong to my fatherland and to the coming republic," he wrote to a group of his critics in Saint Louis in March 1851. To prove his loyalty, Kinkel and his friends decided to embark on a scheme in the spring that consumed London's German émigré community for the next two years. It would ultimately prove a swan song for efforts to reignite revolution.[26]

The German National Loan Project, as it came to be called, was an ill-conceived and poorly managed enterprise from its beginning. The idea was to raise a large sum of money to fund German revolution at some undetermined time in the near future. Subscribers to the campaign would presumably recoup their investment with interest after a united Germany was established. Organizers ignored persistent division among various political factions, concentrating instead on efforts to achieve their ultimate goal. To demonstrate unity, figures like Schurz established a tripartite committee to oversee the loan. Willich represented workers and communists, Kinkel the social democrats, and Silesian count Oscar Reichenbach the moderate parliamentarians. While the initial response to solicitations in Europe was encouraging, the primary fundraising targets were successful German-speaking immigrants in America.[27]

Kinkel had become a folk hero of the revolution. As Willich and friends convinced him to act as the loan's pitchman in the model republic across the Atlantic, Kinkel left for New York in September 1851. He raised more than $15,000 at one meeting in Cincinnati. The appeal was off to a promising start, but success was short-lived. A rival group headed by former Baden rebel Amand Goegg sailed for America that same year, soliciting the same prospective donors. Meanwhile, acclaimed Hungarian revolutionary Lajos Kossuth also toured the United States while drumming up financial support. Americans grew weary of such appeals. In addition, Marx and Engels saw the teetering loan project as another opportunity to criticize their radical rivals. They suggested that loan guarantors, and Willich in particular, were using contributions for personal benefit; after all, donors had received no detailed accounting. Just when it looked as if rival German loan committees might join forces and salvage the effort, an event took place in France that demolished hopes for imminent revolution in Europe.[28]

• • • • •

The collapse of the French Second Republic on December 2, 1851, shocked European radicals. Louis-Napoleon Bonaparte, frustrated by the French Assembly's opposition to reform proposals, staged a successful coup coinciding with the anniversary of his uncle Napoleon Bonaparte's coronation in 1804. He dissolved the assembly, restored the vote to all male citizens, and drafted a new constitution. Less than a year later, Louis-Napoleon was crowned emperor and the Second French Republic became yet another failed experiment. Dreams of returning to their homeland ended for many German exiles after Bonaparte's coup.

Willich made a desperate appeal to continue the struggle despite the depressing news. "What has been lost? Nothing!" Willich declared shortly afterward. "The people with their social demands now find the field all cleared of sham and mockery," the communist leader suggested halfheartedly.[29] Even-tempered fellow exile Carl Schurz called further agitation "a reckless and wicked game." Finding refugee life empty and depressing, Schurz sailed for America, where the ideals he had fought for were still "struggling for their full realization." Before he left London, Schurz ran into Louis Blanc in a park just days after the coup. "C'est finis, n'est pas?" Blanc muttered. "C'est finis."[30]

Willich also knew the game was up. Unable to find permanent employment in England, disillusioned refugees eagerly accepted the British government's offer to bankroll their immigration to America. Exhausted comrades had to yield, in Willich's words, "to the law of self-preservation." With prospects of imminent political revolution dimmed, Willich turned attention to the social causes that had always informed his radicalism.

Despite his split with Marx, Willich agreed with his chief rival's insistence that workers needed to control the means of wealth production. At meetings of both the Communist League and the CABV, he led discussions aimed at developing a coherent picture of a future communist society. "No revolutionary form of state is tenable," Willich insisted, "unless it is founded on an equally revolutionary organization of economic conditions." Simply declaring a republic was not enough. Willich and William Weitling, who had immigrated to New York, shared similar visions. A communist society organized by branches of industry would replace traditional political institutions.[31]

The Communist League and the CAVB had robust philosophical discussions, sometimes on the hot topic of religion. Willich renounced organized religion and especially the Catholic Church. They were simply powerful accomplices of oppressive monarchs. In Willich's model society, there was no need for religious organizations. He suggested that church and religion could remain for a time in a transitional period as a moral doctrine since personal belief was irrelevant for communism. Willich had enough enemies without alienating believers.[32]

Willich fought a losing battle throughout 1852, struggling to keep a shrinking cadre of radical revolutionaries active and engaged. When a group of workers talked of petitioning the British government for support in emigrating from the country, he threw them out of the CABV. In April 1852, some workers arrived in New York angry with Willich, while others started a military association in the United States on Willich's behalf to maintain readiness for the coming revolution. A trial of revolutionaries in Cologne damaged Willich's and Schapper's reputations by revealing dubious associations with spies and other intrigues. Their leadership withered, and alliances unraveled. In a comedy of bad timing, personal scandals sent both men's reputations into a tailspin.[33]

Schapper was under increasing suspicion as a spy due to his burgeoning waistline and a lack of transparency in managing refugee committee funds. The real stain on his character, however, came from his affair with the wife of fellow communist Friedrich Lessner. Willich elected to distance himself from Schapper on moral grounds. "Whoever is unreliable in his private life," Willich preached, "is also unreliable politically." Despite several occasions on which he had had a late night in the taverns and been seen hopping the barracks wall after curfew, Willich worked hard to present himself as a paragon of virtue. His self-righteous act was wearing thin with friends and enemies, and it backfired on him one evening in May 1852.[34]

Baroness von Bruiningk's salon in Saint John's Wood became a social nexus for liberal German refugee leaders soon after her arrival in London in the autumn of 1851. Born Princess Lieven in the Russian province of Estonia in 1818, Bruiningk became enchanted with democratic notions. She and her dutiful husband, who did not share her radical politics, were compelled to leave their home for brief stints in Germany and Switzerland before settling in London. The baroness furnished part of the bribe money Carl Schurz used to free Kinkel from prison, and she had helped innumerable other political exiles. She was so committed to alleviating refugees' suffering that she wore the same threadbare and patched evening gown night after night so she could use her sizable allowance for charitable purposes.

Schurz, Kinkel, Willich, and Blanc were part of a circle who assembled frequently in Bruiningk's drawing room. Schurz remembered that the baroness "was not a woman of great mental gifts" and was "frequently accused of an inordinate desire to please."[35] In truth, she was a flirt. Willich was a frequent and favorite visitor, dining at her home at least once a week. According to Marx, it was a source of amusement for the baroness "to tease the old he-goat, who play[ed] the ascetic." One evening, after a few too many glasses of wine, Willich made unwanted sexual advances on Bruiningk and was shown the door. News of what Marx called a "brutally brutish assault" circulated throughout the refugee community. Willich was humiliated, and Marx and Engels were beside themselves with glee.[36]

Willich's chief rivals swept in for the coup de grace, eager to report on what they hoped would be his final act in the public sphere. Marx wrote Engels on May 22 with the happy news. "So fate has caught up with that pure and noble man after all!" Engels replied.[37] Marx also dashed off a letter to his New York press agent, Joseph Weydemeyer, relating the story.[38] Engels followed up two weeks later, adding juicy gossip to further prejudice recent emigrants from Germany against his former commander. "The morally pure stoic," Engels suggested, "who as a rule felt a far greater sympathy for fair-haired young tailor's apprentices than for pretty young women, may thank his stars" that he did not land in jail "as a result of this involuntary, instinctive outbreak of his physical ego so long kept enchained." Engels further indicated that Willich might turn up in New York before long. "In America, Willich would be in his element," Engels predicted, among his old crew of "rowdies and loafers." New Yorkers would soon "grow sick of him and beat him black and blue." In London, Engels continued, "[Willich's] relationship with the swine finally degenerated into the low vulgarity of a mob of rogues bickering over plunder." Willich's reputation was compromised, but he was not done fighting. The wounded warrior was still a dangerous opponent.[39]

The Bruiningk affair accelerated the war of words between Marx and Willich to a level of character assassination that bordered on the absurd. Initially, Willich denied news of the infamous incident. Later, he concocted a tale that no one believed, characterizing the baroness as a Russian spy who had tried to entrap refugees. When Willich stood in her way, the story went, the baron circulated a rumor of Willich's carnal advance to discredit him. Schimmelpfennig admitted that Willich had invented the spy story but claimed that the old Prussian was trying to magnetize the baroness. Kinkel and Count Reichenbach began to distance themselves from Willich. In contentious meetings of the Communist League during the summer of 1852, friends debated questions of Baroness von Bruiningk's loyalty to their cause while Willich sat silently.[40]

Marx and Engels were not content to watch Willich self-destruct. They finished a satirical exposé of leading political opponents titled "The Great Men of the Exile," intending to issue it in pamphlet form. This jewel of defamation illustrated the depth of the animus between Marx and Willich. Besides describing the Bruiningk assault, Marx and Engels repeated the accusation that Willich was a closet homosexual. "Feminine charms should leave him cold," they wrote, adding, "as Cromwell did with his non-commissioned officers, [Willich] takes a tailor's apprentice into his bed from time to time." The pair went on to describe the Prussian as a fool, "Don Quixote and Sancho

Panza rolled into one," and a caricature of "intrigues, sordid prevarication, the occasional lie." "His real future," Marx and Engels claimed, "lies in the prairies of the Rio Grande del Norte." It was a prescient prediction.[41]

Willich caught wind of the manuscript and worried that such scandalous accusations would reach a wider audience. He need not have been concerned, as a comedy of errors prevented its publication. First slated to appear in Weydemeyer's weekly *Die Revolution*, that paper went belly-up before the piece could be printed. In early July 1852, Marx gave the manuscript to a Hungarian refugee who promised to publish it in Germany. That never happened. The Hungarian was actually a spy for the Prussian police, who purchased the work. Fortunately for Willich, the article sat in an archive until long after Marx's death.[42]

Meanwhile, Count Reichenbach insisted that money raised by the German National Loan project be repaid. Kinkel and Willich overruled him, convincing colleagues to deposit the funds for future use under their assurance. In August 1852, London communists sponsored an international congress and Willich prepared a paper titled "A Proclamation to Germany." He argued for violent action against the aristocracy: "I preach hatred because I want love, I preach barbarism because I want it to destroy our enemies, to introduce our rule and our happiness. I preach war against the world because I want peace." Cologne tailor Julius Grozinski summed up the appeal of Willich and his allies as true representatives of the working people. "Don't let yourselves be carried away by this infamous literary clique around Marx," Grozinski cautioned, "who can achieve everything with their evil pens, in order to push aside those aiming for the true welfare of the workers." Marx and company could stir up trouble "by impugning men of action," Grozinski stressed, but "these literary loudmouths" could not lead a people's revolution.[43]

Barthelémy wrote Willich from Paris in September, saying that he was "reduced to impotence and this [made him] despair." His plan to rescue Blanqui from prison had failed, ensuring that leadership needed to oppose Louis-Napoleon's rule would not materialize. "It is impossible for me to resign myself to leaving Bonaparte enjoying his triumph peacefully," the French radical moaned.[44] Barthelémy returned to London later that month ready to vent his anger and frustration. He found a soft target in fellow French émigré Frederic Cournet.

Cournet was a former French naval officer lauded by Victor Hugo in his epic novel *Les Misérables* for constructing a monstrous barricade in Faubourg, Saint Antoine, three stories high and seven hundred feet long. Barthelémy constructed an equally impressive barricade at Faubourg de

Temple. Resistance to Louis-Napoleon's coup was planned at Cournet's house, where he read Hugo's proclamation of rebellion to the crowd.[45] Cournet and Barthelémy fell out over Cournet's embrace of Alexandre Ledru-Rollin as leader of the opposition, rather than Louis Blanc. Barthelémy sprung a trap by insulting Cournet's former Italian girlfriend, prompting a barrage of personal insults from the former naval officer. Willich knew both men and stepped in to mediate. He suggested Cournet write down the facts of the dispute. A friend of Cournet's proposed that the men apologize to each other, but Cournet refused. He issued a challenge to his rival, precisely what Barthelémy had hoped for. A duel was set for dawn at Priest's Hill in the Surrey countryside.

The two men and their seconds met on a cold, gray morning in October 1852. Custom dictated that the man challenged had choice of weapons, and Barthelémy chose pistols. Cournet was a deadly swordsman but a notoriously poor shot. The men paced and turned. Cournet fired, missing badly. Barthelémy tried to fire, but his pistol failed to discharge. In strict observance of the Irish code duello, a set of rules governing duels between gentlemen, Cournet stood straight and still while his opponent reloaded and pulled the trigger. Another misfire. The chivalrous Cournet then did something hard to fathom. He had his second reload his own pistol and hand it to Barthelémy, who certainly did not share his rival's sense of fair play. He shot Cournet in the chest, killing him instantly, then fled the scene. It was the last fatal duel on English soil.[46]

Willich learned of the tragedy and ran to Louis Blanc for advice. Willich then sent Russian exile Alexander Herzen to consult with Giuseppe Mazzini, but there was little to be done. Police apprehended Barthelémy and brought him to trial for capital murder. The cunning criminal pleaded self-defense on the grounds that Cournet had shot first and tried to kill him. Incredibly, the jury bought this explanation and acquitted him.[47] The affair tarnished Willich's reputation further.

Word reached London that Willich's American allies had convened a mass meeting and decided to offer him a leadership position in a new workers' organization based in New York. Meanwhile, expelled members of the Communist League accused Willich of "unmistakable insanity." His London leadership was crumbling. Marx reported that his chief rival was "gone to the dogs," forced into "tumbling his old philistine of a landlady" to pay room and board. A cartoon by Karl Heinrich Schmolze, who had fought beside Willich in Baden, depicted Kinkel as Old King Lear and Willich as The Fool. Trials of jailed rebel leaders in Cologne revealed a complex and confusing web of intrigue that embarrassed both Marx and Willich. Marx claimed that Willich was "a spy and a rogue unmasked." Rhetoric from all sides reflected just how bleak the refugee situation had become.[48]

Willich watched his dream of imminent revolution evaporate in November 1852. The final blow was struck in the Cologne trials. Willich admitted that he had forged documents while exchanging money and secrets with police agents. In fact, Willich had been duped by these spies, tricked into believing that one of them was a double agent acting in the best interests of the refugees. It was a poor, if sincere excuse. No matter who was telling the truth, Willich was "done for here," according to Marx. The Prussian sailed for America in mid-January.

Willich ran from his troubles, pursued by Marx's pen. Marx had just completed his *Revelations Concerning the Communist Trial in Cologne*. He informed associates in Washington, DC, "At least those parts of the pamphlet which relate to [Willich] should appear in the press."[49] Willich began a new life in New York, but his old nemesis made sure that the German American community heard Marx's side of the story. The battle of words between Willich and Marx continued for a time across the Atlantic, where both men saw opportunities to promote their vision of socialism in the context of the world's largest democratic republic.

Chapter Eight

• • • • • • • • • • • • • • • • • • •

DIASPORA

A LARGE CROWD of German immigrants assembled at the Port of New York as William B. Smith, master of the *Ocean Queen*, guided his passenger ship to the dock on Saturday, February 19, 1853. A tall man with a long red beard stepped off the gangplank, and the crowd erupted in cheers. August Willich's triumphal entrance into New York Harbor stood in stark contrast to his solemn exit from London six weeks previous. Like Carl Schurz, Franz Sigel, and Friedrich Hecker before him, Willich was welcomed as a Volk hero who would keep the faint hopes of homeland revolution alive among many thousands of Forty-Eighters who settled in America as a refuge of last resort.[1]

Willich was energized by the outpouring of warmth from the third-largest German-speaking metropolis in the world. Many lived in an ethnic enclave on Manhattan's Lower East Side known as Klein Deutschland, or "Little Germany." Willich arrived near the peak of a huge wave of immigration that doubled the German population of New York to more than 257,000 residents over the course of the 1850s, or a quarter of the residents of America's largest urban center. Two-thirds of these newcomers came from the same south-western states of the German Confederation where Willich and his fellow revolutionaries had fought for social justice and popular rule. They were predominantly artisans and skilled craftsmen. Despite fleeing economic and social disruption, New York's German community was anything but a social and political monolith, as Stanley Nadel reveals. The challenge for Willich and other leaders was to take a complex brew of allegiances and mold them into some sort of "organic solidarity and tentative unity," thus forming the basis for a nascent sense of German American ethnic identity.[2]

Radicals planned to use Willich's arrival as a springboard to unite various émigré factions behind a scheme to topple the monarchs of Europe, beginning with the princes of the German states. These plans had been in place for more than a year. Hanau Turners who had fought side by side with Willich's Besançon column formed a Socialist Turner society in New York, which boasted over five hundred members. The group published Franz Sigel's *Drill Regulations* manual in 1852. In March of that year, Sigel and Hungarian revolutionist Alexander Asboth purchased fifty thousand percussion caps from a New York arms dealer and kept them ready to be shipped overseas the moment the next phase of European revolution began.[3]

At London's international communist conference in August, Willich, Kinkel, and Amand Goegg had drafted a contract of union between the German National Loan and the American Revolutionary League for Europe. The newly unified group had four major objectives: overthrow monarchs across Europe, implement universal male suffrage, replace standing armies with citizen militias, and destroy all who oppressed the people. Key members of the Central European Democratic Committee like Italian revolutionist Giuseppe Mazzini supported these aims. When the league held its first US conference in Wheeling, Virginia, in September 1852, however, American delegates used the failure of 1848 to reinforce notions of the United States as an exceptional nation. European revolutionists, they maintained, should follow the example of 1776 and create a peaceful republican nation free of the violence and despotism that plagued its transatlantic neighbors. These arguments took the league's ideals into the realm of fantasy.[4]

The American Revolutionary League for Europe issued a manifesto that called for the United States to fulfill its destiny as the leader of a new and free world. To achieve this, nation-states of Europe would dissolve and adopt what they described as "the universality of the American character." In practice, this meant the creation of a single worldwide republic on the American model—the Western world would be governed by "one universal federal state" with open borders and a shared economy. The plan drew little support.[5] By the time Willich arrived in America the following year, the idea of a global republic was under attack from rival socialists like Karl Marx and Joseph Weydemeyer, who viewed these schemes as the immature dreams of second-rate thinkers.

One dreamer aligned against Marx and sponsoring Willich was German American communist Wilhelm Weitling. Weitling had supported Willich and Kinkel's German National Loan project alongside his own cooperative Trade Exchange Bank, which never gained traction. His worker's league was at its zenith when Willich came on the scene, but that success proved fleeting.[6]

Radicals feted Willich at the Shakespeare Hotel on March 2, 1853. The celebration was organized by Weitling and attended by more than three hundred committed German revolutionists. "I have found a great number of comrades-in-arms," Willich wrote Alexander Herzen shortly after the event, "who are all ready to return to Europe" and "throw themselves into Germany despite their wives and infants." Many German immigrant workers in America had a few hundred dollars in the bank and were willing to risk it in joint ventures for revolution. "They need only a confident leader for that," Willich assured him.[7]

Banquet tables were festooned with red flags and Weitling's triangle symbol. Willich gave an impassioned address arguing that bread was even more essential than liberty. He predicted that rebellion would erupt again in Europe due to the oppression of the working class. In his keynote speech Weitling claimed, "Communism alone is the alpha and omega for the redemption of a suffering humanity." He likened the philosophy's credo to "a gospel for the poor and the oppressed, for whom a prophet, deserted by his people, had been crucified on Golgotha." Weitling then turned to Willich, who was attired in his emblematic red scarf, and presented him with a sword from the workers of New York. Weitling reminded the audience of Christ's coming not to bring peace but armed with a sword, and he urged Willich to use this weapon "in the holy battle for the finest treasures of mankind." Some attendees had heard quite enough of Weitling's Messianic references.[8]

The *New York Staats-Zeitung* derided the event as a comedy, noting that Willich was dressed like King Solomon and Weitling was preaching about "Jesus Christ, the first proletarian." Many remembered that Willich himself had conspicuously adopted a Christlike appearance shortly after resigning from the Prussian Army. While Weitling's radicals sang and drank till dawn, Marxist Joseph Weydemeyer was planning his own assembly.[9]

Weydemeyer's March meeting drew more than eight hundred German workers. He and his comrades focused on reforms like the ten-hour workday and improved working conditions. Weydemeyer's rival Allgemeiner Arbeiterbund, or "German Workers League," became an important early organization dedicated to achieving tangible gains for the working class.[10] For Willich, such reforms were inadequate, covert lures that ultimately sustained capitalism. The world needed full-blown revolution. Even as Europe's democratic firmament dimmed and the flame of revolution flickered, the forty-two-year-old warrior was still reaching for the stars.

Near the end of March 1853, Willich called on Carl Schurz to enlist his support in rekindling the revolutions in Europe. The wise young intellectual would have none of it. "I soon saw with what illusions he had come here,"

Schurz wrote to Kinkel, "and realized that he would not be convinced either by arguments or his own observations." He described Willich's activities as "purposeless . . . showy undertakings, all noise-making." The ambitious efforts of the Revolutionary League were all but dead after just six months. Now Willich was pushing for the creation of a German state in America, a notion that was "no less fantastic" to Schurz than attempts to organize an invasion of Germany. Moreover, the idea was "exactly calculated to disappoint the practical American understanding." Schurz believed that the agitation of Willich and other extremists had "used up the enthusiasm for transatlantic affairs," and that events of the past several years, like Louis-Napoleon's coup, had made Americans distrustful of European radicals. Schurz preferred to work quietly behind the scenes to convert American politicians to the rebels' cause while awaiting the next surge in revolutionary activity in Europe. "The people must be given rest and quiet to recover from these disappointments," Schurz told Willich and Kinkel, but Willich was not listening.[11]

Schurz's assessment of the public mood and of Willich's blind spot were accurate. The Prussian former officer clung tenaciously to a revolutionary vision for which he had sacrificed nearly everything. His conscience compelled him to strive for immediate revolution in Europe by proselytizing socialism among his fellow German immigrants in America, young workers, and students. Each constituency presented opportunities for radicalization despite significant challenges.

German Americans, Willich insisted, were having a hard time adjusting to the United States' social mores. Willich noted that America's focus on business and individualism was much stronger than Europe's. When it came to a choice between what was good for business and what was morally right, business usually prevailed at the expense of workers. Workers were beginning to organize and even strike, but a violent worker revolution in America was "out of the question," he concluded. "[There] the wealth still grows from the ground like mushrooms," Willich explained.[12] Despite widespread poverty, the rapid increase in overall prosperity created a burgeoning middle class and lessened the potential for class conflict or systemic change. Few in the educated middling ranks of American society wanted to form alliances with and advocate for wage workers. The growing influence of organized religion, and the Catholic Church in particular, proved a conservative bulwark against the ambitions of reformers and revolutionists in Willich's new home across the sea.

The American "calculates the means of extending the republic," Willich explained, "and he always had as much as he could see." But America's political freedom was a "comedy" without the commensurate social and educational infrastructure to nurture the mind and nourish the body politic. In Willich's view, the Catholic Church was filling that void with "pretensions and burlesque rites." He despaired that it was easier to find fifty poor people to defend the ridiculous doctrines of the church than it was to find just two willing to risk a violent act to improve their own well-being. German American Catholic priests called the revolutionists of 1848 "red republicans with blood on their hands" and also opposed worker strikes. "The Catholic Church has more power over its believers here than in Europe," Willich concluded.[13]

Willich did find hope for the future in some of the young Americans he met. He had lively discussions with students and came away impressed with their political acumen. "They have an awareness that their thoughts become public opinion," Willich noted, "and [they] understand that public opinion translates into state action." He found himself "delighted with their reservation of conscience and had the feeling that opinions formed here would change history." Furthermore, he compared the value of one year's residence in America to ten years' living among the English. Buoyed with such inspiration, Willich hit the road in the late spring of 1853 to help organize radical assemblies among the largest German American communities in the West.[14]

Willich made his way down the Ohio River, visiting Cincinnati and Louisville, before arriving in Saint Louis to reunite with his old commander Friedrich Hecker. Hecker was living in quiet retirement on a farm in the countryside, and it seemed that much of the fiery spirit that made him a leading light in 1848 had faded. When Willich urged him to join Wilhelm Weitling, who had started a German settlement in Iowa, Hecker remained aloof from the project. Willich then traveled to Weitling's model village of Communia in Clayton County, northwest of Dubuque. Twenty-two Communia Workingmen's League members had amassed fourteen hundred acres of property. Weitling was ecstatic after arriving at the colony on Good Friday. "On Saturday we buried the Judas of misunderstanding," he exclaimed, "and on Sunday, the Holy Easter of the *Arbeiterbund*, we had the resurrection to the eternal glory of our good cause." The religious imagery used by his sponsor was wearing a little thin on Willich. Weitling offered him the position of town administrator. Willich declined, stating that to accept would demand "more courage than a charge into a cannon's mouth." By May, the community had grown to sixty-one souls, but Willich left the colony near the end of the month and journeyed to a place where he felt he could achieve real progress. Waiting for him in Milwaukee were longtime friends Fritz and Mathilde Anneke.[15]

Milwaukee boasted one of the most successful and vibrant German sub-cultures in America in 1853. More than 35 percent of its residents had been born in Germany, a greater proportion than in any other US city.[16] By the end of the decade, Milwaukee's population would swell to more than forty-five thousand. Like New York, the community was divided into numerous ideological camps. Longtime residents, called "grays," were liberal in politics but conservative in religion. Newcomers, labeled "greens," included refugees from the failed revolutions of 1848–49. They leaned left, and many were religious independents. Willich and his radical allies were often ostracized as dangerous "reds." At a time when the Milwaukee Germans were attempting to unite these factions into one thriving ethnic community, radicals like the Annekes saw an opportunity to use a revolutionary hero like Willich to tip the scale of social organization in their favor. They already had a significant head start.

Many Forty-Eighters who came to Milwaukee and other American cities in the years following the failed revolutions were well educated. Once settled in their adopted homeland, they yearned for trappings of the middle-class culture they had enjoyed in the most literate region in Europe.[17] They judged American free schools to be barely adequate, for the educational system focused on rote memorization and conspicuously lacked instruction in critical thinking. Instead of being a viable alternative, religious education was part of the problem. Although the Bible was banned from public schools, its "poisonous influence" still entered the minds of children and adults alike "through every crevice," according to local leader Rudolph Koss. The result was that "crass superstition and bottomless ignorance" took the place of thoughtful inquiry and scientific pursuits. In response, liberal Germans longed to create institutions and associations that would germinate the "sprouts of a genuine republican art-life."[18] The Annekes were at the forefront of such efforts. In 1850, Fritz Anneke took charge of the Turner school begun by a fellow Baden insurrectionist, and Mathilde Anneke spoke in a series of lectures there. Mathilde went on to publish the first women's monthly magazine in March 1852, employing women as typesetters. This unusual practice spawned backlash from local male typesetters. In response, conservatives formed a local union to protect this traditionally male profession from incursion by female workers.[19]

Activism among working-class Milwaukeeans grew during the first half of the 1850s. Early efforts to combine worker education with trade unions foundered. Local German intellectuals had a hard time forming intimate bonds with their working-class neighbors. Lectures held to generate interest in higher learning were poorly attended by laborers and other wage workers. Before long, members of the educated middle class abandoned their efforts to elevate the consciousness of their brothers and sisters, who were exhausted from working long hours six days a week. By 1853, workers had returned to forming traditional labor unions with a focus on the immediate well-being of their members and little or no educational component.[20]

Freethinkers among the German "greens" began to infiltrate local religious communities and promote a rationalist approach to social life. Eduard Schroeter, a popular speaker for free congregations in the region, started the short-lived but influential German weekly the *Humanist* in September 1851. Schroeter steered clear of the political infighting so common among other local newspapers and concentrated on education. He also promoted equal rights for women and men of all races. In the words of one local historian, Schroeter "converted many a barbarian to humanism" as he wielded his pen as a weapon against religious superstition.[21]

Gottfried Kinkel's arrival in Milwaukee on November 29, 1851, created a sensation. He spoke to various assemblies each day for a week and raised over $300 for the German National Loan, but enthusiasm for the project was already on the wane. German Americans were much more interested in securing a healthy and prosperous living for their families in their new country than they were in refighting a lost battle against the formidable forces of reaction thousands of miles away. Kinkel's visit did rekindle interest in the vexing issues of education and worker's rights. To address these issues, the German community of Milwaukee had to come together and speak with one loud voice. The Society of Free Men, organized on January 2, 1853, had just such an aim.[22]

The Society of Free Men planned a picnic celebrating the 116th birthday of political philosopher Thomas Paine, who had become an icon of the rationalist movement on both sides of the Atlantic. Just a year earlier, the Socialist Worker's Organization had conducted a successful Paine birthday event attended by thousands. Yet things turned ugly in 1853. Anticlerical rhetoric from the freethinkers had aroused so much uproar that many religious residents avoided the celebration. Catholics boycotted it when they discovered that Jews and atheists had been invited. The day ended with a brawl between Germans and Irish policemen that created ill will in the community. The German Catholic newspaper *Seeboten* was quick to condemn the event. Weeks later, when Saint John's Catholic Church on the city's west side burned, the editor of the *Seeboten* made an outrageous accusation: "Who could have started this fire but they who recently at the Paine celebration cried that the

world cannot be happy until the last cleric has been hanged with the intes-
tines of the last prince." The society was undeterred by such hysterical libel
and continued to grow. Its members planned to celebrate the anniversary
of their founding on July 3. The event's keynote speaker would be popular
revolutionary August Willich.[23]

This was the kind of opportunity Willich had been waiting for since he
landed in America. His fiery speech was more than simply another plea
to stand ready for imminent revolution in Europe. The charismatic leader
suggested that Milwaukee Germans abandon their petty rivalries and unite
under the banner of a new organization called Der Sociale Turnverein von
Milwaukee. This club's founding principles made it different from the pre-
ceding two Turnvereins. It would not be concerned exclusively with physical
exercise. Rather, the new organization would also hold itself accountable
for enriching the intellectual experience of its members. "The Turnverein,"
argued Willich, "should avow themselves explicitly and justly to the Red Banner of Socialism. They should form the Army of the Future, which will be of
the greatest practical importance against the secret collaboration between
Jesuits and reactionaries."

Willich urged every liberal German to join, even if he could not participate
in the physical exercise, to show by example the usefulness of the organization and the correctness of its principles. "Watch the pale, spent figures that
are found among the American youth," he suggested, "whose mirth and innocence are destroyed in the spring of life by the greed of money-making."
Willich called the intent and design of the Turner gymnasium "the direct
opposite of the convents and monasteries," stating, "They promote life and
health and an awareness of personal power and independence." This spirit in
social and civic life, he suggested, "is the foremost adornment of man." In the
weeks following this impassioned appeal, the new Turner society blossomed,
attracting an initial membership in the hundreds and eventually absorbing
the Society of Free Men to become the dominant voice in Milwaukee's liberal
German social and political affairs.[24]

After Willich completed his speech, Dr. Godfrey Aigner of the Society of
Free Men rose and read a "Declaration of Independence" of his own compo-
sition. This clever homage to the iconic 1776 document was peppered with
republican rhetoric. Like the founders, the society's members argued that
nature had endowed man with certain inalienable rights. Critical among
these was the right to form and profess individual religious convictions, as
long as these utterances did not impair the rights of others. This manifesto,
like its famous predecessor, included a list of grievances.

These transgressions included an alleged attempt by the Christian church to control the republican legislature and impose laws not sanctioned by the US Constitution, such as restrictions on Sunday activity and regulations concerning temperance. Clerics suppressed the mind of adult and child alike, the Society of Free Men claimed, by "the denial of [the] right to independent thought and the destruction of . . . liberty of conscience." "When the long list of misuses and wrongful interferences shows the intention of those individuals to enslave the majority of a people and the whole of posterity," the group's treatise read, "then the spiritually free part of the people have the right, indeed the duty, to render these people harmless" and to care for the educational and religious needs of the community in other ways. "A priesthood, who in every action evinces the lowest type of tyranny," Aigner declared, "is unfit to be the leader of a free republican people."[25]

Many citizens were repelled by such radical pronouncements. In response, the Society of Free Men labeled them "blind believers, knaves of priests, enemies of science, truth, virtue and happiness" and stated, "If they wish to be free republicans, we must think of them as hypocrites; if they want to be good believers, as slaves." Members of the group vowed to support this resolution "by word and deed, [their] honor, and, if need be, with [their] lives." This bold declaration of war to free the minds of people from the spiritual bondage of organized religion was another battle Willich and the freethinking minority were destined to lose.[26]

• • • • •

Willich returned to New York to find little enthusiasm for his adventuristic schemes. Weydemeyer had become a mouthpiece for Marx, who also published regularly in Horace Greeley's *New York Tribune*, the first daily to achieve nationwide distribution. Marx, Engels, and American allies like Charles Anderson Dana criticized extremists like Willich, denouncing their provocative rhetoric. Weydemeyer described them as fringe actors who operated in the shadows and conspired to carry out another doomed uprising. Willich, Franz Sigel, and others on the Far Left were portrayed as egomaniacal actors playing at revolution.[27]

As immigrants found safety and economic opportunity that had been denied to them in the Fatherland, the Marxian argument for patience to allow class formation as a prerequisite for revolution gained adherents. Willich penned a defensive, self-serving reply to Marx's attacks in an October 1853 issue of the *Belletristiches Journal*, claiming that his dispute with Marx was merely a personal matter. In reality, their differences ran much deeper. Willich would eventually acknowledge some of Marx's most important contributions to economic theory before the decade was out. As for his own vision of im-minent pan-European revolution, Willich deferred that dream.[28]

· · · · ·

Perhaps Schurz had been right. Willich needed rest and recovery after seven years of nonstop activism. He abruptly canceled a return trip to Germany just two days before he was scheduled to depart. Willich subsequently stayed a few months in New York, where he toiled in the Brooklyn Navy Yard. Friends in the nation's capital then arranged for him to put his mapmaking skills to use with the United States Coast Survey, where he began working in 1854. He labored as a draftsman on hydrographic survey vessels captained by US Navy officer John N. Maffitt, sailing up and down the Atlantic Seaboard. After three years at sea, Willich took a desk job at survey headquarters in February 1857.[29]

A sizable German community in Washington, DC, and an even larger one in Baltimore offered numerous opportunities for social and political engage-ment. To really understand the position and challenges of the American worker, Willich had to become one himself. He settled into life as an ordinary citizen. He commuted daily to a regular job, enjoyed long walks on the broad boulevards, and for the first time in his life, allowed himself to fall in love.[30]

In romance, as in politics, Willich's emotions often trumped his powers of reason. Marriage was on his mind. In a private letter to Kinkel, he gushed about his beloved, calling her a "daughter of the South" and a "tropical flower." These were thinly veiled code words that Kinkel understood at once; his friend Willich had become intimate with a woman of color. Washington's free black population outnumbered local slaves nearly two to one. Although the District of Columbia housed an active abolitionist community, it was still a southern city. Miscegenation laws were crystal clear. Marriage between whites and blacks was expressly forbidden. In any case, the woman quickly vanished from Willich's correspondence. A few years later, when he was accused of secretly marrying his sweetheart, Willich denied it. What he could not deny was that he had made a home for himself in America. He would risk his life trying to help his new country overcome racial and nativist prejudice and live up to its promise and potential as a model republic for the world.[31]

Standing in the way of United States fulfilling its democratic destiny were incongruities that tarnished its republican reputation. The perpetuation of slavery, a compromise forged by the founders to create a federal union, was the greatest of these blemishes. Another stain on the American system was the increasing economic divide between wealthy, educated elites and poor wage workers. While workers had begun banding together for mutual aid and support during the early labor union movement, they were now being pitted against each other by unscrupulous politicians. Some public men aligned with Anglo-Saxon supremacists in a new political party bent on excluding recent immigrants from the privileges of citizenship. "Know-Nothings" stepped into a political vacuum created by the dying Whig Party in the mid-1850s and began promoting an ugly agenda.

A huge influx of immigrants from the Irish famine and the failed European revolutions in the late 1840s crowded into America's largest cities, whose infrastructures were ill prepared for the onslaught. Crime soared as so-called natives, who claimed a superior Anglo-Saxon racial heritage, found themselves competing for work with recent immigrants. Nativists blamed nonnatives for the various woes of urban life. They concocted theories of a secret conspiracy between the Catholic Church and the Democratic Party to subvert liberty by controlling large blocks of immigrant voters. By 1854, the Know-Nothings had scored a series of stunning electoral victories in New England and other regions and had adopted a political brand known as the American Party. In the spring of 1855, the newly elected Know-Nothing mayor of Chicago issued an edict forbidding immigrants from holding city jobs. Cincinnatians witnessed violent battles in the streets between German Americans and nativists. On August 6 in Louisville, similar riots left twenty-two dead and much of the city damaged. More than ten thousand citizens left the city for safer settlements in the months that followed "Bloody Monday."[32]

Americans across the nation were stunned and outraged by such brazen attempts to impede immigrant voting and manipulate elections. In the 1856 presidential election, American Party candidate Millard Fillmore finished third with less than 22 percent of the vote, denying victory to John C. Frémont of the new antislavery Republican Party and handing the election to Democrat James Buchanan, who garnered just 45 percent of the popular vote. Fillmore won only one state, Maryland, where support for the Know-Nothings remained strong. In the District of Columbia, a fusion ticket of Democrats, Republicans, and Free-Soil Party members elected an anti–American Party mayor by just thirteen votes. This set up another violent clash the following year that would reawaken Willich politically and chart the course for an important period in his life.

Determined not to have another mayoral election stolen from them by Roman Catholics and their immigrant allies, the Know-Nothings unleashed their favorite weapons, street violence and voter intimidation. An unknown person with a pocket full of crisp currency bought train tickets for a gang of fourteen hoodlums known as the "Plug Uglies" of Baltimore. The rowdies boarded an early morning train for Washington, DC, on Election Day, June 1, 1857. Upon arrival, they joined other toughs from local gangs the Chunkers and the Rip-Raps and marched to a polling station near Northern Liberty Market. When pushing and shoving a line of Anti-Know-Nothing voters failed to take effect, the gang departed and returned a short time later armed with pistols, knives, and clubs. A melee ensued, injuring more than twenty people, including several policemen. Polls were demolished and voters dispersed, leaving the Plug Uglies and their ghoulish allies free to roam the streets in search of mayhem. Later that morning, Washington's mayor appealed to President Buchanan for help. The president did not hesitate.

Shortly after noon, two companies of US Marines marched from their barracks on Eighth Street and made their way to Northern Liberty Market, where gangsters had set up a six-pound brass cannon purloined from a firehouse. When the marines announced they would reopen the polling station, Plug Uglies threatened to kill all 115 of them if they tried. Armed only with a cotton umbrella, the troops' commander stepped forward, placing his body between the mouth of the cannon and his men. He urged the rowdies to surrender as his force moved forward. The rioters conducted a fighting retreat, spraying bullets in all directions. One hit a marine in the jaw. Soldiers responded without orders by firing wildly into the crowd, killing six innocent bystanders. Public outcry was immediate. "In the name of all that is dear to us as Americans," the editor of the *Evening Star* wailed, "how long is this state of things to be tolerated?" As it turned out, not long. Local authorities forced the Plug Uglies to disband and the American Party faded away. In the aftermath of this tragic event, Willich reemerged as an activist.[33]

Willich's friend Friedrich Kapp had an idea. In such dangerous times, German Americans needed a hero they could relate to. Kapp suggested that an ethnic German who personified fidelity to the American ideal would fit the bill. Nativists argued that their fathers and grandfathers had fought to create this republic, but just how successful would Washington and his officers have been without the expertise of Baron Friedrich Wilhelm von Steuben, one of the finest drillmasters in the world? Kapp decided to pen Steuben's biography, hold a series of festivals in major cities, and raise funds for a monument to the Revolutionary icon. The first such event was held in July 1858 on the outskirts of New York City, and ten thousand people attended. Then Willich helped

organize a similar festival in Washington. It, too, was a great success, drawing an estimated five thousand revelers and raising more than $800 for the
statue. Ironically, nativist attacks helped unify diverse communities of German immigrants. Such immense gatherings reflected the flowering of what
historian Alison Clark Efford calls a new "German language of American
citizenship," leveraging a newly formed German American ethnic identity
as "a cultural minority within a plural nation."[34]

A mile-long line of marchers began assembling early in the morning at
the city hall. By 7:30 a.m. they were on their way to Arlington Spring. The
procession included numerous groups, including more than forty Jäger militiamen, a newly formed men's singing society, and even a society of fresco
painters. Near the head of the parade the Socialist Turnverein carried a banner that read, "Liberty, Brotherhood, Labor." Festival grounds were arrayed
with benches, gymnastic equipment, parallel bars, and various forms of musical entertainment. The speaker's platform, festooned with the US flag, stood
alongside the French tricolor and the black, red, and gold flag of German
unity. A large portrait of Steuben loomed over the stage. The crowd gathered
and sung an ode to their hero and to the goddess of freedom, then settled
in for the program. Two speeches followed, one in English and another in
German. After a brief musical interlude came a third speech in English. A
band and glee club performed "Greetings to the Fatherland" to prepare the
audience for the featured speaker of the day. August Willich rose and walked
to the lectern.[35]

Willich's speech marked a turning point for the former revolutionary
leader. After chronicling repression of his people from the days of the Roman Empire through serfdom and on to the late failed revolution, Willich
predicted that a world court would stand in judgment against the "overbear-
ing nobility and their cleric co-conspirators." For now, however, German
Americans needed to turn their attention to their adopted homeland. Their
duty was to fight corruption and establish social infrastructure necessary for
mutual aid and personal enrichment. The princes of Europe had been served
a summons in 1848. Now was the time to "grasp the spirit of the Constitution
with German honesty, perseverance and ruthless courage" and help America
realize its destiny as the leader of a free and democratic world. Willich's ex-
plicit historical dialectic from the American and French Revolutions, through
the heroic but failed attempts of 1848, and on to a second American revolution that would help ignite sweeping social, economic, and political reforms
worldwide was not lost on the audience. The crowd responded to Willich's

challenge with cheers, then retired to an afternoon of singing, dancing, and drinking. Willich used the event as his impetus to reenter public discourse. He subsequently published several letters in Gustav Struve's *Sociale Republik* that deployed his radical version of German ethnic nationalism from the 1848 revolutions in an American political context.[36]

Willich, the new president of the Steuben Association, argued that German Americans, by virtue of their superior education and history of scientific and literary leadership, had a responsibility to lead reform in the US public educational system. This was their manifest destiny as citizens of the "nation of nations." American movements based solely on class interests were doomed to failure, Willich argued, due to ethnic diversity. Unschooled native and Irish working-class people, for example, had little in common with highly skilled and educated German craftsmen and artisans. "The Anglo-Saxons," Willich further explained, "out of their mere restless, money-making business life" were spiritually adrift, longing for "an unknown home." These lost souls could only realize true happiness by adopting the German national spirit. This meant "a return to the philosophical and scientific life which makes living in Abraham's lap and in the Christian heaven seem miserable." It was a chauvinistic argument, but one that gave Willich purpose as he resumed his life's mission of creating a more just and equitable world. If there was any chance of reaching this audacious goal, it had to start in America. Willich sheathed the sword from Weitling, refilled his inkstand, and left for Cincinnati to "fight the old struggle with a new weapon."[37]

Chapter Nine

• •

A SOCIAL REPUBLIC

CINCINNATI WAS BOTH the largest city in the American West on the eve of the Civil War and the cultural capital of the region. The Queen City was home to nearly a dozen daily newspapers, and it indulged its literate citizens in a diverse milieu of music, theatre, art, and scientific exhibitions. Lectures, debates, and literary societies flourished. The booming industrial economy brought prosperity and social improvement to a population fully engaged in living out the American promise of liberty and happiness. One-third of the residents of this growing metropolis of more than two hundred thousand souls were native Germans who established their own vibrant neighborhood on the north side of a canal in an area that became known as "Over-the-Rhine."

Contemporary writers compared the walk north from Court Street across the canal to stepping into a foreign land. Leaving behind the American and his "everlasting hurry and worry of the insatiate race for wealth," one enters into the environs of a gregarious people "closely wedded to music and the dance, to the song, and life in the bright open air." The local beer garden was the center of social life in Cincinnati's German community. Between 1850 and 1860, the number of breweries in the city mushroomed from thirteen to thirty-six. Yet crime and disorderly behavior were rare in this German American enclave. The local Turnverein, the first in the nation, boasted a commodious hall for its members. Festivals and parades were a regular occurrence as well-educated Germans celebrated everything from their favorite composers and poets to their most revered political heroes. Cincinnati's

German immigrants had a reputation for being hardworking, thrifty, and fiercely proud of their cultural heritage.[1]

Johann Bernard Stallo was the most prominent leader in Cincinnati's German community. The talented attorney, philosopher, and judge delivered the welcoming speech when revolutionary hero Friedrich Hecker visited the Queen City in 1849. Stallo was an idealist and a liberal freethinker. He felt it was the destiny of progressive German Americans like himself to enlighten their new country to Jeffersonian principles and move the republic closer to the founders' ideal model. When nativists attacked Turners in 1856, prompting a violent response from German militias, Stallo successfully defended his ethnic brethren in court. Later that same year, his disgust with the Democratic Party's pandering to slaveholding interests led him to become a founding member of the new Republican Party.

Stallo's sympathy for the plight of workers in a rapidly growing industrial center led him to take an interest in their welfare. He was no socialist, however. He believed strongly in the ability of individuals to own and manage their own property, yet he understood "that society is indeed a community, and that all are responsible for the sustenance of each one." Stallo knew that wage workers, and especially recent immigrants, were in danger of being turned into veritable machines. Worked to the bone for long hours, they had little chance of ever realizing the fruits of their labor. They needed an advocate, someone who cared more for their welfare than he did for himself. On a tour of the East Coast in 1858, Stallo believed he had met such a person. He was a government cartographer and community leader in Washington, DC, named August Willich.[2]

Much had changed in the five-plus years since Willich had immigrated to America. Prolonged economic slumps in 1854 and 1855 hit immigrant workers particularly hard. The world's first global financial crisis in 1857 caused widespread unemployment. Recent immigrants who had left Europe expecting freedom and economic opportunity in their new country faced an American labor-market reality that clashed with their aspirations, leaving many bitter and disappointed. Laissez-faire business and political leaders, already at odds with emerging labor unions over wages and working conditions, had no unemployment insurance or public assistance to offer those living on the margins in poverty. Hampered by what he viewed as the complacent, timid approach of their English-speaking brethren, Willich insisted, "In this republic a beginning [for labor activism] is only possible through the German element."[3]

The opportunity to gain a German-language platform for Willich's radical views under the sponsorship of the German American Social Workingmen's

AUGUST WILLICH, EDITOR,
CINCINNATI *REPUBLIKANER*, C. 1859.
CINCINNATI MUSEUM CENTER.

Club was irresistible. At Stallo's urging, Willich became editor of the *Cincinnati Republikaner*, a former Whig weekly, in December 1858. It became the only daily labor newspaper in America for nearly two and a half years. In his introductory editorial, Willich promised that the paper would help educate local laborers and give them a political voice to combat worker oppression and ethnic prejudice. "We intend to support those reforms that are supposed to make this republic a truth for everyone," he vowed. Willich made a covenant with his readers "to turn [them] into a community of free men" and to work tirelessly to achieve a "republic of labor and intelligence."[4]

Willich and other radical labor leaders aimed for nothing less than a redefinition of the meaning of republican freedom, one of the cherished virtues of the American citizenry. Artisans and laborers, according to scholar Alex Gourevitch, appropriated the historical language of republicanism, exposed its contradictions, and created a new tradition that condemned dependent labor as wage slavery, which was antithetical to the ideal of equality. Unfree labor was also inconsistent with the notion of popular sovereignty, a core value of republican government. Labor activists offered an alternative: the cooperative commonwealth. Grassroots momentum behind these ideas led Willich to rethink his political strategy and develop new tactics for achieving his ultimate goal of universal social justice, beginning within the confines of his adopted land.[5]

Previous calls for violent government overthrow and communism vanished from Willich's rhetoric. America had already taken the first great step toward democracy by declaring the republic and sustaining it, however fragile and imperfect, through several generations of intersectional disputes. The challenge in the United States was to make sure that the great tsunami of capitalism would not so overwhelm the republic in a tide of avarice and individual self-seeking that equality and community would be swept away. By educating the masses about increasing injustice in the current system and marshaling their latent political muscle, Willich hoped to move America closer to its founding ideals and transform it into a true social republic.

The end game for Willich was a worker's republic that would look very different from the existing system of politics and government administration. This reformed society would feature an economic administrative council, do away with traditional political parties, and dismantle the US Congress. Trade unions and a national trades assembly made up of representatives from local and regional trades councils would replace these institutions. To accomplish this end, Willich and his allies would eventually need to use education and activism to reach well beyond a core constituency of German workers and convince them to transcend issues of race, religion, and political affiliation. Exploitation of the working class could be addressed only if competing societal divisions were muted and worker's issues made paramount in the minds of most Americans. This was a daunting if not impossible task, given the deep cleavages that had already appeared in the young republic's social and political relations. It was also a threatening vision in the eyes of conservative elites.[6]

Willich's first step was to get Cincinnati's German laboring class behind him. He made the *Republikaner* a free subscription and assured his working readership that the paper was dedicated to the interests of "the producing class against swindle and betrayal." The daily's masthead featured slogans central to Willich's economic philosophy, including "Value in Return for Value" and "To Each His Own." While Willich still differed with Marx in believing that workers would lead an eventual worldwide socialist revolution, he acknowledged his former communist rival's contributions to the science of economics and particularly applauded Marx's labor theory of value. Willich and Marx agreed that wealth derived from labor. Capital is turned against labor by concentrating it in the hands of the few. Government allows monopolies to form, thus denying the worker the full value of his labor. Willich's remedy was to wrest power from moneyed interests and corrupt government officials and give it to workers. Then individuals could overcome their alienation in a capitalist society and become one with their community. This was the shared interest of all humanity. Only in this scenario would the purest form of republican government be realized. Although Willich's methods had changed, the core of his beliefs still echoed the philosophy of Moses Hess and the socialist ideology he had adopted since the mid-1840s.[7]

Organization and political action were at the heart of Willich's strategy to reform society. He founded local unions for machinists, blacksmiths, and iron molders. He partnered with Frederick Oberkline, a local ironworker, to form the Cincinnati Trades Assembly, a group that gathered union members from different trades and ethnic backgrounds to hold mass meetings and exert political influence. At one such meeting, Willich coaxed his audience to kindle "the desire that every noble American freeman should possess"— namely, "the independence of character to stand firm against all who oppress his condition as a man socially, morally and pecuniary." When Ohio governor David Tod introduced a bill in the state legislature to make strikes against employers a criminal offense, Willich and his allies rallied nearly three thousand workers in Court Street marketplace to express their indignation.[8]

Willich was keenly interested in the work of William Sylvis of Philadelphia, who founded the National Union of Iron Molders in 1860. Willich ally Frederick Oberkline was the corresponding secretary for that organization. Sylvis strove not merely to create a mutual-aid society focused on workers' interests, but also to "promote the moral and social qualities of man, enlarge his intellectual powers, and increase his sphere of usefulness." The union's newspaper, the *United States Mechanics Own*, aspired to be America's first national labor sheet, hiring correspondents from nearly a dozen large cities across the country. Oberkline eventually served on the editorial staff of the *Republikaner*, working as Willich's English-speaking representative in dealings with organized labor. By seeking to broaden the reach of his radical reform program, Willich alienated other German American labor leaders who wanted only an isolated ethnic German national organization. Differences between Willich and his fellow Germans, however, ran deeper than squabbling over ethnic provincialism. Willich found that peers like Joseph Weydemeyer were willing to compromise too readily for limited aims like the ten-hour workday or modest wage increases, rather than focusing on the exponential change necessary to solve the larger problems of worker poverty and powerlessness.[9]

Rather than tearing down the walls of government, Willich admonished working-class Americans to use their political power in a democratic repub- lic to affect change. "The road to the full value of your labor goes through the corridors of the city hall, state legislature, and capitol in Washington," he insisted. He helped create a Labor Party ticket for Cincinnati in 1860 fea- turing future US president Rutherford B. Hayes as the preferred candidate for solicitor. Willich's ultimate goal of a national labor political party was a distant dream, so he rallied Germans to the Republican Party banner in the meantime. Like most of his fellow radicals, he urged the 1860 nomination of John C. Frémont, who had lost the 1856 presidential election to Democrat James Buchanan. When Lincoln was finally nominated as the dark-horse alternative to front-runner William H. Seward in 1860, Willich called on his readers to support the candidate. Lincoln's humble background made him a likely friend of the worker, and his antislavery credentials appeared sound enough to satisfy most abolitionists. In fact, Willich had already put his life and reputation at risk in a bold attempt to reach out to Cincinnati's black community as a partner in the struggle for free labor and racial justice.[10]

· · · · ·

Radicals like Willich hated the institution of chattel slavery not just because it was morally abhorrent. Slavery was the most heinous example of a much broader social issue. Whether worker exploitation was happening on the plantation or on the factory floor, the root of this injustice was the same. Wage laborers in the North were nearly as powerless as black slaves against those few who controlled the capital amassed from their ceaseless toil. "Black and white slavery derive from the same principle," Willich claimed. As long as slavery existed, he told his readers, whites "would not have set foot on the battlefield for the advancement of human rights." In an America where the issue of race had often been a prism through which social, political, and economic relations were viewed, Willich equated slavery with class conflict, making common cause with black and white abolitionists. One event in the winter of 1859 cemented this alliance.[11]

John Brown's daring raid of the US arsenal at Harpers Ferry in October and his subsequent execution in December polarized the border city of Cin- cinnati unlike any single occurrence in its history. Queen City residents had strong economic and social ties to their slaveholding brethren in the southern states. Brown's audacious attempt to incite a slave rebellion created a sensa- tion. Many Cincinnatians viewed the revolt's architect as an insane traitor whose violent actions were likely to tip the scales toward civil war.

Willich and his allies saw Brown as a brave martyr who was prepared to sacrifice everything for a just cause, much like the European revolutionaries of 1848. The man who trained Brown in guerilla tactics and conspired in the raid, Englishman Hugh Forbes, was one of the first people Willich met with after landing in New York in 1853. Forbes had served with Garibaldi in Italy in 1849 and would do so again in 1860. Brown himself had traveled to Europe in 1849, studied guerilla tactics used by rebels like Willich, and met with revolutionaries from various rebellions. Historian Timothy Mason Roberts describes Brown as a cisatlantic revolutionary who observed radical developments in Europe and applied those learnings in America. When news of Brown's hanging reached the city, Willich organized a meeting and led a torchlight parade to protest the execution and laud Brown's bold strike for freedom.[12]

The procession honoring John Brown ended at Arbeiter Hall, where Willich shared the podium with black teacher and activist Peter Clark. A Cincinnati native, Clark was a classically educated grandson of a Kentucky slave woman and her white master. He envisioned a future America where the "distinction of Irishmen, German, or African [would] be lost in the general appellation as American citizens." To accomplish this lofty goal, violence might be used as a last resort. Clark told the crowd that they were "in the midst of a revolution that must be fought to the death." Willich said that Clark's speech "should have been witnessed by all defenders of the trade in human flesh" as an example of the resolve and spirit of a committed revolutionary. Willich insisted that, despite his black skin, Clark was such an accomplished and skilled man that he "would hold an eminent position in any civilized society."[13]

Willich pulled no punches in a fiery address to the large assembly at the Brown rally. Seeing an American civil war as inevitable, he urged his audience to "whet their sabers and nerve their arms for the day of retribution" when despicable slave owners and their crafty abettors "would be crushed into a common grave." He chided ignorant Irish and other deluded Democrats who preached tolerance and compromise while selling out America's cherished republican principles of freedom and justice for all. The thunderous ovation in response to Willich's stirring words reminded him of "a harmonious melody sung by races and nationalities separated by nothing but outward appearance." The meeting broke up with Willich leading the crowd by torchlight through the dark streets amid threats of violence to himself and other activists. He would not be deterred in pushing his agenda to eradicate slavery.[14]

The local press's reaction to this unprecedented assemblage was swift and savage. One witness described his horror at seeing "a motley crowd of both

sexes, diversified by every hue common to the human species" sitting beside one another on benches. The flag of the African Americans was displayed alongside the black, red, and gold of German republicans and the
Star-Spangled Banner draped in mourning crepe. The *Cincinnati Enquirer*
complained that the politics of the German workers had always been "of the
most degraded stamp, and of the most dangerous character to the peace and
welfare of the nation." In addition, the *Enquirer* accused meeting organizers
of promoting racial equality by recognizing "no distinction of color on their
social intercourse." The *Cincinnati Volksfreund* suggested that Willich and
other meeting leaders had disrespected Washington and Jefferson, whose
portraits hung in that very hall, since these founders were slave owners themselves. Willich ignored such criticisms.[15]

Willich and Clark joined forces to push the envelope of interracial collaboration. Two weeks after the Brown rally, Clark and other blacks attended a
Turner fair only to be sent away due to complaints from whites at the gathering.
Willich published a letter from the excluded blacks expressing regret for the
incident and noting that they had entertained hopes of a blossoming friendship between the two races. The editor of the *Republikaner* was among a tiny
minority of white nineteenth-century intellectuals who believed that blacks
were not an inferior race and were entitled to the same rights and privileges
of citizenship as the so-called Anglo-Saxons. Cincinnati whites were appalled
at this heresy against the sacred notion of white racial destiny. The conservative *Volksfreund* called Willich "a German nigger worshiper." Yet such vitriol
only emboldened the old Prussian. He insisted that racist behavior on the part
of some Turners tarnished their credentials as democratic republicans, and
on December 30, the Cincinnati Turnverein passed a resolution renouncing
discrimination along color lines. The Turners would eventually have the opportunity to prove that this oath was more than mere words on a page.[16]

Another obstacle to the education and mobilization of workers for their
own benefit, in Willich's view, was the pernicious influence of organized religion. He particularly decried the influence of the Roman Catholic Church.
The pope's burgeoning masses were being duped into worshiping superstition over science, thus separating physical man from his inner spirit, entities
that were indivisible by nature. Belief in the supernatural and allegiance to
clerics threatened community life and the very essence of a republic, which
was based on self-government by consent of the whole people. German Prot-
estantism, while admittedly preferable to Catholicism, was still counter-
productive, since it ultimately distracted men from focusing their efforts to
alleviate social injustice. True religion, according to Willich, could be found

in Alexander Humboldt's *Cosmos*: one living universe and one human spirit in harmony with nature. "The religion of the future," Willich suggested, was "the religion of science and art."[17]

The *Republikaner* editor made little effort to temper his radical views on religion, but he did reach out to enlightened clergymen rather than focusing his rationalist message solely on fellow humanists. Willich found a kindred spirit in Virginia-born Unitarian preacher Moncure Daniel Conway. Conway's Hegelian views on the unity of man, nature, and religion and his ardent support of abolitionism made him popular among local religious liberals and freethinkers following his appointment to the First Congregational Church of Cincinnati in 1856. Enveloped by a vibrant community that promoted arts and literature, Conway indulged his interests in social reform and philosophical inquiry. The bold preacher's congregation of wealthy liberals like Stallo and Alphonso Taft, father to the future president, listened as he urged them to challenge traditional views of religion and society. Conway reached out to blacks, Jews, utopian socialists, and others with his inclusive, progressive message. "Enlarge the place of thy tent," he preached.[18] Deeply impressed with Willich's leadership of local Germans, Conway remembered later, "In the after years when I saw Garibaldi in London, I felt as if I had met him before in the form of my old friend Willich."[19]

In Cincinnati, Conway was absorbed into the intellectual orbit of Willich, Stallo, and other German rationalists. Many churchgoers indulged Conway to a point, but when their pastor refuted the Bible as the Word of God in the fall of 1858, he split the church in two. Conservatives left to form their own congregation, and Conway's flock became known as the Free Church. Conway went as far as to praise Deist Thomas Paine from the pulpit on the anniversary of Paine's birth, January 29, 1860. Though he would never accept Paine's religious outlook, the preacher admired his role in converting future founders like Washington, Adams, and Jefferson to the cause of American independence. Conway reluctantly joined Willich and Clark on the stage at the John Brown meeting, lauding Brown's principles but not fully supporting his violent methods. Conway's persistent challenges to religious orthodoxies and friendships with transcendentalists like Ralph Waldo Emerson threatened to sow further division at a time when the imminent dissolution of the national Union inspired urgent calls from community leaders to come together. When Conway left Cincinnati in 1860 never to return, Willich lost a key ally in his crusade against religion-sponsored ignorance. The clergyman's departure also marked the end of an exceptional and tenuous triparty alliance of black, Anglo, and German abolitionists.[20]

Celebrated black abolitionist Frederick Douglass wrote in 1859, "A German only has to be a German to be utterly opposed to slavery." Did Douglass sincerely believe this, or was he simply propagating the same myth of ethnic unity that Peter Clark evoked when he called Germans "the only freedom-loving people" in Cincinnati? Willich and most other radical intellectuals realized that while many German Americans tilted toward antislavery, most had little concern for black civil rights, and only a small minority were abolitionists. Yet the intersection of the antislavery and labor movements afforded these leaders an opportunity to change the narrative on republican values, proselytize theories of a "German Spirit," and invoke the revolutionary heritage of 1848 to rally the rank and file. Willich welcomed the prospect of an American civil war on the near horizon as a war of slave liberation, but the ultimate stakes were greater than that. Higher on radicals' priority list was defeating the slave aristocracy in the southern states, preserving democracy and republican government, and, for socialists like Willich, making unprecedented strides toward ending capitalist exploitation of workers in factories and on plantations.[21]

Chapter Ten

• •

REVOLUTION REDUX

IT WAS UNSEASONABLY WARM and sunny as President-Elect Abraham
Lincoln stepped off the train at the railroad depot in Cincinnati on Tuesday
afternoon, February 12, 1861. Lincoln's journey from his home in Springfield,
Illinois, to his inauguration in Washington, DC, stopped in key cities along
the way so he could thank supporters. Cincinnati workers from Over-the-
Rhine precincts voted for Lincoln in large numbers. They were anxious to
welcome the incoming president and ensure that he knew just what they
expected from him as the prospect of civil war loomed.[1]

German American voters in the West were important to Lincoln from the
outset of his presidential aspirations in early 1859. Immediately after suffering
defeat at the hands of Stephen A. Douglas in the US Senate race, influential
Illinois Republicans began devising a path to the highest office in the land
for the rail-splitting, wrestling champion lawyer whose debates with Douglas
had earned him national attention. German-born Republican Party founders
helped pull the strings.

Prominent Germans who jumped on the Lincoln bandwagon included
"Gray Gustav" Koerner, the first German-born member of the Illinois legislature; Milwaukeean Carl Schurz, who had become one of the best-known
German Americans in the country; and Illinois newspaper editor Theodor
Cannisius. These men helped Illinois Republicans conduct a stealth campaign
that kept Lincoln's name out of the headlines while more prominent hopefuls
William Seward of New York, Salmon P. Chase of Ohio, and Edward Bates
of Missouri suffered constant attacks from the press. Seward and Chase were
frequently denounced as radical abolitionists, while Bates's reputation was

besmirched by past dalliances with the Know-Nothings. Lincoln plotted a moderate course to the nomination while working behind the scenes. He also became a secret partner in Cannisius's German-language newspaper.[2]

Schurz initially backed Seward, but once Lincoln emerged from the convention as the Republican nominee, Schurz marshaled his considerable energies and talents to support him. While Lincoln penned position statements for Cannisus's *Illinois Staats-Anzeiger*, Schurz barnstormed the nation from west to east drumming up support for the candidate. A month before the election, Schurz wrote his wife bragging that Lincoln considered him his foremost campaign worker. Schurz and Koerner were rewarded with diplomatic posts. Both served as generals in the Union army, and Schurz eventually became secretary of interior and a United States senator. Historians have debunked myths that the German American vote was the deciding factor in Lincoln's 1860 election, but in a day when political science was still in its infancy, the Republican candidate's gut told him that he needed German Republicans to turn out to win the West versus Douglas. As Lincoln prepared to meet fellow Republicans in Cincinnati, he had political debts to repay.[3]

Thousands in the throng of well-wishers remembered Lincoln's previous Cincinnati speech on September 17, 1859. That two-and-a-half-hour landmark oration, the last stop in an Ohio tour, had launched his bid for the presidency. His Cooper Union speech five months later may have made him president, as Lincoln himself once claimed, but the Cincinnati effort made him a national political player. The masterful address simultaneously seized the higher moral ground in its opposition to slavery and staked out a moderate political position. Lincoln opposed the extension of slavery, but he suggested that Americans tolerate it where it was constitutionally protected. Addressing himself to neighboring Kentuckians, he vowed to stand firm on these principles while promising "to leave [slave states] alone." It was a political tour de force that won Lincoln many converts among fence-sitting moderates.[4]

Lincoln's reception committee during his 1861 visit included Cincinnati mayor Richard M. Bishop, who would later become governor of Ohio. William Haines Lytle, commander of the First Division of the Ohio Militia, and Miles Greenwood, the grand marshal and the owner of Eagle Iron Works, led a grand parade that wound its way to Lincoln's plush accommodations at Burnett House. Later that evening, two thousand German workers from Over-the-Rhine, flambeaux torches in hand, marched to the president-elect's hotel to pay their respects. Delegation spokesperson Frederick H. Oberkline read a prepared statement in English. The message from the pen of August

Willich had been published in English and German that morning. Willich told Lincoln precisely where he and his fellow German Americans stood on the key issues of the day.[5]

Willich reminded the president-elect that he had earned German Americans' votes as a champion of free labor and free homesteads. He criticized Democrats who called for compromise between the interests of free and slave labor as "the despicable device of dishonest men." Moreover, he urged Lincoln to stay true to the Constitution "against secret treachery and avowed treason," a reference to northern Copperheads who expressed sympathy for secessionists and southern governors who were seizing federal armaments and occupying government forts. "If to this end you should be in need of men," Willich promised, "the German free workingmen, with others, will rise as one man at your Call, ready to risk their lives in the effort to maintain the victory already won by freedom over Slavery." It was a presumptive, provocative message. Lincoln, ever the shrewd and calculating statesman-politician, responded cautiously.[6]

Lincoln listened carefully from his balcony as Oberkline read Willich's message. Seven states had seceded from the Union by the time the candidate reached Cincinnati, but he was not yet president, and no war against seceding states had been declared. Thus, Lincoln declined to respond to Willich's offer of martial assistance in the "present national difficulties." He promised to wait until the last moment before divulging his next move. In regard to the Homestead Law and free labor, the Republican nominee pronounced himself happy to concur with most of his German American friends. Then Lincoln went even further, praising workers as "the basis for all governments." It was man's natural duty, the president-elect insisted, "to improve not only his own condition, but to assist in ameliorating mankind." "I am for the means that will give the greatest good to the greatest number," Lincoln declared. This was certainly music to Willich's ears, and it dovetailed neatly with the editor's dream of a future social republic.

Lincoln left no doubt about his distaste for nativist elements in his own party. "In regard to Germans and foreigners," the president-elect affirmed, "I esteem them no better than other people, nor any worse." He pledged to do all in his power to raise the yoke of people encumbered by oppression and tyranny. Lincoln did not see immigrants as a threat; rather, he encouraged people from densely populated Europe "to make this the land of their adoption." It was not in his heart, Lincoln assured his audience, "to throw aught in their way, to prevent them from coming to the United States." This was a ringing endorsement of the value of recent immigrants in the national citizenry. Lincoln was proving to be a leader that Germans and other ethnic groups could rally behind. When the call for troops did come a few months later, the Germans of Cincinnati responded with the enthusiasm that Willich had promised.[7]

• • • • •

News that Maj. Robert Anderson had surrendered Fort Sumter electrified the city of Cincinnati. Lincoln called for seventy-five thousand men to enlist and fight a war against their own countrymen, friends, neighbors, and even family. When the president asked Ohio to recruit thirteen regiments for three months' service, citizens of the Buckeye State responded to the call, filling their quota with ease. Among the millions of European immigrants who had flocked to the New World in the 1840s and 1850s amid social change, economic hardship, and political uncertainty, German Americans were particularly anxious to enlist.[8]

Willich's radical friends were excited to resume both their transatlantic struggle for democracy and their obligation to lead in what Fritz Anneke called America's "second freedom struggle." The Civil War not only amounted to a second American revolution but was also, in Friedrich Kapp's words, part of "the same battle in which European nations are engaged." "This is the *American* 1848!" a Missouri newspaper editor exclaimed. But Northern radicals like Willich were not the only group invoking the legacy of 1848 to motivate their constituency in an upcoming war of revolution.[9]

Europeans and nations around the globe were also caught up in the excitement. In an age of worldwide revolution, debates on issues like democracy, republican governance, and worker's rights flowed in opposite overseas directions simultaneously. Completion of a telegraph cable in 1858 decreased transatlantic communication times from ten days to less than ten minutes. Karl Marx and Friedrich Engels, who had been serving as foreign correspondents for Horace Greeley's *New York Tribune*, followed developments with keen interest and offered prescient insight and a socialist perspective on the conflict to readers in America and around the world.[10]

Southern leaders pivoted from reluctant support of the violent 1848 revolutions in Europe, which undermined slavery in the Caribbean, for example, to embrace a new perspective. Andre Fleche argues that the 1848 revolutions validated universal rights to self-determination, which to slaveholders meant that a Confederate nation had the right to exist as a slave republic. This put defenders of the Union in a rhetorical tight spot. Radicals responded that the right of revolution was justified in the case of Europeans yearning for universal rights, but not for the perpetuation of slavery, an institution inconsistent with moral principles and republican values. The challenge for Willich and other German American leaders was to rally the majority of their ethnic brethren who had dubious allegiance to an ephemeral ideal of "Union" and a diverse array of positions on slavery.[11]

German Americans did not flock to the Union banner simply due to the urging of political émigrés in the United States. Regular pay and a desire to prove themselves as loyal Americans in the face of nativist attacks certainly accounted for part of the phenomenon. Bruce Levine argues that recent immigrants to the United States who rushed to war had been influenced by the events of the 1840s. These newcomers became more highly politicized in the wake of their economic challenges, thereby providing a mass following for leaders like Willich. Mischa Honeck goes a step further, citing a pervasive ethic of German ethnic manhood, a militarized Turner culture, and a crusading "politics of principle" that congealed into a "muscular republicanism." Years of training and drilling created physically and morally superior fighting men—a combat-ready citizenry.[12]

For socialists like Willich, the calls to arms in 1848 and 1861 were virtually identical. His former battle against monarchial rule was for "the same rights of men against a combined conspiracy of a traitorous slave aristocracy with the same powers of the old world." Historian Andrew Zimmerman echoes Willich in claiming that the most compelling parallels between 1848 and 1861 did not revolve so much around definitions of liberalism or nationalism. Instead, they illustrated the issue of social revolution, which Zimmerman calls "the central strategic question of the Civil War." The epic conflict between property rights and democracy, a global issue brought to a head in America by the issue of slavery, precipitated a radical revolution that would ultimately destroy the largest slaveholding economy on the planet.[13]

• • • • •

Gustav Tafel, spokesman for the Cincinnati Turners, posted a sign-up sheet at Turner Hall on Walnut Street on Sunday, April 14, the day that news of Lincoln's call for volunteers reached the city. Hundreds enlisted on the spot. Like Willich, Tafel was a former editor of one of Cincinnati's German-language newspapers. He would go on to command a predominantly German regiment later in the war. Tafel credited the idea of an all-German regiment to Robert Latimer McCook, Johann Bernhard Stallo's law partner. McCook

GERMAN FESTIVAL AT TURNER HALL, CINCINNATI, 1865. ENGRAVING FROM
PHOTOGRAPH BY J.W. WINDER. *FRANK LESLIE'S ILLUSTRATED NEWSPAPER.*

had traveled to Europe in 1860 and observed the armies of its most powerful
regimes. Ultimately, he was most impressed with the Prussian military system. McCook met Tafel the day after the Turner meeting. Though McCook
was a Douglas Democrat, he and most of his party were rallying around the
old flag now that the South had opted to protect slavery at the expense of
the Union. He suggested that "the men who elected Lincoln should now also
step into the ring and fight!" Tafel assured him that Germans stood ready
to do just that.[14]

Stallo and Tafel organized a mass meeting at Turner Hall on Wednesday
evening, April 17. Stallo delivered an impassioned speech, calling for his fellow
Germans to ignore nativist prejudice and "stand up like men to safeguard the
Union and protect the Star-Spangled Banner." Tafel proposed that McCook,
with his family legacy of military accomplishments, was the ideal man to
lead the new regiment. The assembly set up eight recruiting stations. Willich
became an American citizen and enlisted as a private despite his extensive
military training and combat experience. He also lied about his age. Gov.
William Dennison initially precluded men over forty-five from becoming
officers, which was clearly Willich's ambition. Willich held his own rally at
Arbeiter Hall and recruited four companies of volunteers. Ohio's first German regiment was designated the Ninth Ohio Volunteer Infantry, which

Germans called Die Neuner. Neighbors and friends clamored for Willich to be named the regiment's colonel, but Tafel and other influential Germans lined up behind McCook.

Tafel argued that the Ninth needed not just a talented leader, but a man with strong political connections in Columbus, Ohio, and Washington, DC, to ensure that the new regiment would get arms and supplies quickly. When the ten companies voted on April 23, McCook edged out Willich for commander of the regiment six votes to four. To salve the old Prussian's feelings, Willich was nominated for lieutenant colonel by unanimous consent. Willich, however, had set his sights on the adjutant role, thinking that job would make him the de facto leader of the regiment. Tafel, whom McCook had sponsored for adjutant, stepped back, allowing Willich to claim the role. Willich then moved that McCook's appointment be approved by acclamation. The troops elected another former Prussian officer as lieutenant colonel, but Willich became the acknowledged "father of the regiment."[15]

The Ninth Ohio might have been commanded by Col. Robert McCook, but drilling and field leadership fell to Willich. McCook's deference to Willich was apparent when the colonel described himself as "merely the clerk to a thousand Dutchmen."[16] The Ninth was different from most volunteer regiments. Their men were somewhat older with an average age of twenty-six for enlisted men and thirty-five for officers. Many had served in wartime Europe, including all ten company captains. Men volunteered in large numbers from Turner clubs in Cincinnati, Louisville, and surrounding communities. These men participated in militia-style drill exercises as part of the Turner curriculum and were in superior physical condition.[17] More than three hundred men who enlisted in the Ninth were weeded out in late April by intensive physical screening and replaced by more fit recruits. The *Cincinnati Commercial* claimed the Turner recruits were "as solid as heart pine and as supple as antelopes." When the examining surgeon thumped their chests, the reporter continued, "it sounded like so many anvils." Ethnic comradery and self-discipline helped make the Ninth excellent soldier candidates. Their head start on the drill field eventually paid dividends on the battlefield.[18]

The Ninth Ohio boarded trains for their new military home at Camp Harrison, Ohio, a fairground between the towns of Spring Grove and Carthage. They named the streets and rude cabins of their new village after the principal ways and grand edifices of their beloved Over-the-Rhine neighborhood. There they joined other volunteer units preparing for deployment. In the meantime, they drilled incessantly. No one believed in the benefits of frequent, serious drill exercises more than August Willich. The Ninth's training routine became the envy of other regiments and a prime source of entertainment for camp visitors. Cincinnati's *Commercial Gazette* described the scene: "They drill non-stop with tenacity, they know no beginning or end, and have already brought it to an exceptional state of readiness and precision. An old English-speaking officer said recently that the Ninth was one of the best regiments he had ever seen."[19]

On May 10, the ladies of Cincinnati presented Colonel McCook with their regimental colors: a silk flag of thirteen gold stars on a field of blue, with an adjoining pennant that read, "Fight bravely for Freedom and Justice."[20] The Ninth's Maj. Frank Linck received a gift from an unusual source. The Independent National Guards, composed of native-born local citizens, presented Linck with a sword. The major was absent that day, so Willich accepted on his behalf. The gesture signaled that nativist agitation had been put aside in favor of unity and patriotism. "You all bear within you," Willich began, "the painful recollection of the prejudices, which, only a short time ago, goaded the citizens of this Republic to deadly hate against each other." Willich called this gift "a historical omen" and a "healthy action in the establishment of the real freedom of the human race." The ceremony closed with a parade to Wagner's Tavern, where soldiers and citizens, Germans and natives, joined in celebration, singing and drinking into the wee hours. A week later, the Ninth made an eighteen-mile march to new quarters at Camp Dennison, near the village of Miamisville, Ohio.[21]

May drew to a close, bringing with it the end of any illusion that the war would be over in a few months. Lincoln called for more men, asking ninety-day recruits to reenlist for three years. On May 23, Willich drilled the troops as usual, then formed them into a hollow square. He gave an impassioned speech urging them to reenlist. "The country desperately needs us and all the citizens presently in arms," he pleaded. "As you have left home to fight the Rebels, so you should not return until you have matched word with deed. Stand by the Star-Spangled Banner until it is out of danger."[22] When one malcontent announced that he and some of his followers would not serve longer, his company commander placed a sign marked "coward" on his back and drummed him out of camp. The rest of the regiment reenlisted almost to a man. One soldier insisted that he and his comrades had extended their commitment out of a sense of duty and honor, rather than for hundred-dollar bonuses and pension benefits. Thus, the Ninth became the first Ohio regiment to reenlist, and a woman from Columbus subsequently sent the regiment a drum she had made in recognition of the honor. Three days later, Governor Dennison reviewed the troops and pronounced them outstanding. Then Col.

Robert Anderson, hero of Fort Sumter, swore them into service on May 27. That same day, the soldiers received uniforms and rifles to replace their red Garibaldi shirts and makeshift muskets.[23]

As the volunteers spoke little English, Willich used the Prussian drill manual to train them. Over the course of the war, various division and corps commanders would compel German-speaking regiments to adopt tactics from the manuals used at West Point, but at this early stage, many Union colonels and generals in the volunteer army came from civilian life and were learning military science on the job. They were lucky to have drillmasters like Willich. The former Prussian officer knew how to mold and discipline raw recruits, and his superiors could look the other way if the drills did not comport precisely with Scott's *Infantry Tactics*.[24]

Word spread quickly that the Ninth was becoming an elite fighting force, and Germans from throughout the region sought enrollment in the regiment. Two Turners from Lexington, Kentucky traveled to Camp Dennison to enlist. They journeyed from company to company hearing the same reply—the Ninth was full and would not accept additional recruits. Captain Kammerling of Company F had just given the two young men the bad news when one of them remarked, "O.K. then we'll just have to give it a try with the Sixth Regiment." The Sixth was better known as the Guthrie Grays, a local regiment commanded by Harvard graduate Col. Nicholas Anderson, nephew of Col. Robert Anderson. Upon hearing this, a balding man with a long red beard tinged with gray whirled around and stared with steely blue eyes at the volunteers. "What!" the old officer exclaimed. "The Sixth! See that fence? Jump it!" The men easily vaulted over the fence and back again. "You are both accepted," the officer announced. The old man turned to Kammerling, saying, "We'll take these fellows; soon some of those on furlough will not return." The boys enrolled, never forgetting their first meeting with Adjt. August Willich.[25]

Thousands of visitors from Cincinnati streamed into Camp Dennison to watch the Ninth drill. While the Guthrie Grays and the Tenth Ohio Infantry spent time in grand dress parades, the Germans conducted battle simulations, much to the excitement and approbation of the onlookers. The Tenth was a hard-drinking regiment composed mostly of Irish immigrants under the command of Col. William Haines Lytle, a decorated Mexican-American War veteran. A group of Lytle's men, along with some ruffians from the Grays, became so jealous of the attention that Willich's boys were getting that they threatened to "come down and clean [them] out." Willich instructed his men to sleep on their arms and be ready for action at a moment's notice. More than a hundred rowdies showed up one evening around 11:00 p.m. Willich's pickets fired into the air, and a bugle signal called the regiment to fall into line of battle. The troublemakers took one look at the armed Germans, turned about, and ran off amid much catcalling and laughter.[26]

Alongside their national colors and regimental pennants, the companies of the Ninth flew red banners. They drank lager and sang songs of the Fatherland in addition to American patriotic tunes. The troops' favorite marching song was the famous French revolutionary anthem "La Marseillaise." Red republicans from Turner organizations dominated their ranks. Willich, the men's regimental father, made no bones about his desire to crush the slave oligarchy, help German Americans earn their place as full citizens, and play an instrumental role in improving the condition of American workers. Those immigrant soldiers who had been banished from their homeland in a failed attempt to win social justice were not about to see the United States of America lose a war for the very soul of republican government.

The Ninth reorganized on June 11 and elected Willich major.[27] Morale soared as the well-trained regiment of 1,135 men left for active duty in western Virginia at 6:00 a.m. on Sunday, June 16. Their mission was to help expel rebels from the region, which was otherwise a hotbed of Union sympathy. Gen. George B. McClellan, commanding the Department of the Ohio, was eager to use his thirty thousand troops to make a name for himself. To that end, he staged his forces in Parkersburg, Virginia, and probed for the enemy.[28] McClellan placed his favorite brigade commander, Gen. William Starke Rosecrans, at the head of his force. Rosecrans chose the Ninth Ohio as the vanguard of his brigade, which consisted of four Ohio infantry regiments and a Michigan artillery battery. It did not take long before they encountered the enemy outside of Webster, where small videttes of Confederate cavalry appeared out of nowhere to harass them, only to vanish again.[29]

On July 3, McClellan reviewed the Ninth in person, noting that he had never seen, either in America or in Europe, such a robust and well-drilled regiment.[30] He detached the Germans from Rosecrans and placed them under his direct command for a planned assault against Confederate forces led by Brig. Gen. Robert S. Garnett. Garnett had fortified two key passes in order to retain control of transportation routes through western Virginia. The southernmost of these two entrenchments was at Rich Mountain, just west of the town of Beverly. Lieut. Col. John Pegram brought thirteen hundred men and four cannons to the location. It was an exceptionally strong defensive position and protected the Staunton-Parkersburg Turnpike. McClellan transported five thousand troops and eight cannons to Roaring Creek Flats, two miles west of the Confederate camp. Before he could cross Roaring Run Creek on July 10, rebel cavalry set fire to the bridge, halting the Federals' advance and causing them to spend an entire day repairing the crossing. The next morning, McClellan ordered his topographical engineer, 1st Lieut. Orlando M. Poe, to make a reconnaissance of Confederate position and report back. This was to be the Ninth's first significant skirmish in the war.

Poe assembled a makeshift advance brigade commanded by Robert McCook and consisting of the Fourth and Ninth Ohio Regiments and Michigan's Coldwater Artillery. The troops crossed at a ford south of the disabled bridge and advanced to their outer picket lines. Then. Lieut. Col. Sondershoff dispatched six companies of the Ninth Ohio under Willich's command as flankers. Poe was impressed by the way that the Ninth's men did their duty. Despite receiving fire from rebel pickets along with canister and spherical case shot from enemy guns, the Germans made their way through dense forest understory to a position a mere two hundred yards from the rebel entrenchments. They held their position, allowing Poe to gather the information he needed.[31] There, Willich demonstrated a coolness under fire for which he was already famous in Europe. Smiling while instructing his men to stay low to the ground, he assured them that the rebels were firing too high and would not harm them.[32] The Ninth suffered only one dead and two wounded in the fray. In the end, Poe determined that an attempt to carry the enemy works by storm would prove too costly, so McCook pulled the men back to camp.[33]

Early the next morning, Rosecrans left with his brigade on a mission to turn the enemy's flank, while the Ninth spent July 12 in reserve. Rosecrans lost his bearings in the dense woods and rain, but he finally gained the rear of the Confederate defenses late in the afternoon, routing the badly outnumbered rebels. McClellan telegraphed Washington and claimed the small skirmish as a major strategic victory, thus paving his path to command of the Army of the Potomac. Rosecrans also won widespread acclaim for his performance. Even the Ninth's minor engagement became the stuff of legend back in Ohio and helped secure Willich's future promotion. The loyal press was hungry for heroes at this early stage in the war, and the little contest at Rich Mountain fit the bill. McClellan opened a way for the Federals to eventually clear western Virginia of its disloyal elements and carve it into a separate state two years later.[34]

Willich called the regiment together on August 10 to tell them that Gov. Oliver P. Morton of Indiana had given him command of his own all-German regiment, the Thirty-Second Indiana Volunteer Infantry. The old war-horse promised the soldiers membership in a future all-German brigade. "Then," predicted Willich, "we shall show them what German patriots can do!" That scheme never came to pass. Willich's Ohioans would go on to serve with distinction in numerous important battles throughout the war, giving testament to the talent and leadership of their *de facto* commander. The Ninth bade good-bye to their drillmaster, lauding him as a true gentleman and a textbook soldier.[35]

Chapter Eleven

• •

PAPA

HIS MEN CALLED HIM "PAPA." They were his only children. Willich loved his proud German sons of the republic, providing them with the best food and weapons available, praising them when they performed well, and scolding them when they misbehaved. Many Union infantry commanders aspired to be the object of such universal respect and affection among the rank and file. Willich and his Thirty-Second Indiana Volunteer Infantry operated like a family. His men trained and fought for him without reservation, becoming one of the most accomplished Federal infantry regiments in the Western Theatre.

Selecting a leader for Indiana's first all-German infantry regiment might have been a highly politicized affair, but Gov. Oliver P. Morton managed the task with consummate skill. Rather than play favorites among dozens of interest groups who lobbied for their preferred candidates, Morton made a shrewd appointment. He plucked Willich from his position as major in the Ninth Ohio. Few could argue with the choice of such a well-known, experienced military man who had won laurels on the battlefields of two continents. Willich accepted his commission as colonel on August 12, 1861, then hit the recruiting trail. German Americans rushed to enlist.[1]

Willich established headquarters at Union Hall, across from the Indianapolis courthouse at Pennsylvania and Market Streets, and began screening scores of volunteers from throughout Indiana and beyond. Prospective recruits came to Camp Morton from Cincinnati and Louisville. German Union men from Tennessee also made the trek to Indiana to enlist. At least seventeen companies, some already organized and fully manned by various

AUGUST WILLICH, COLONEL 32ND INDIANA
VOL. INFANTRY. CARTE DE VISITE, C. 1861.
LIBRARY OF CONGRESS.

Turner organizations, applied to be one of ten companies in the elite regiment. Willich's selection criteria were rigorous. Men who had served with him in the revolutions of 1848–49 were welcomed into his new fighting force. The Thirty-Second Indiana, like the Ninth Ohio, included men who were older, fitter, and more experienced than the typical volunteer soldier.

The new colonel surrounded himself with proven, capable officers. For drillmaster, Willich chose highly decorated former Prussian infantry major Henry von Trebra, who had fought against Willich in the Fatherland. Carl Schmitt, Willich's trusted aide from the revolutions, was appointed adjutant. Several company captains had European combat experience or had served ninety-day enlistments in other regiments. The vast majority of officers and men, having been recruited from the ranks of Forty-Eighters and Turner societies, were different from American-born regiments in two other respects. Many were freethinkers in religion and socialist in their politics. Willich considered them as men first, then as citizens who had a military obligation. This gave all-German regiments like the Thirty-Second Indiana a distinct camp culture.[2]

COLONEL AUGUST WILLICH, LIEUTENANT COLONEL HENRY VON TREBRA, ADJUTANT
CARL SCHMITT, 32ND INDIANA VOL. INFANTRY (LEFT TO RIGHT). PEN, INK, AND WASH
BY ADOLPH METZNER, 1861. LIBRARY OF CONGRESS.

Willich refused to employ a cleric as chaplain, bestowing the post instead
on former *Evansville Volksbote* editor Emil Bischoff, whose delivery was "free
of all religious humbug" and relied only on "the principle of reasoned morals." Any participant at the regiment's Sunday morning assembly could speak
in opposition to the chaplain or on a topic of his own choosing. The army
caught wind of this unusual arrangement, and Bischoff was never mustered
in. His replacement, Rev. Wilhelm Schmidt of Evansville, resigned after six
weeks. From that point forward, Willich resisted appointing another chaplain.
The colonel himself performed tasks such as presiding at graveside services.
Relations in camp were based on mutual respect. Discipline was enforced
not through fear and intimidation, but rather via a patriarchal family model
with Willich as the father figure directing and caring for his children. "He
is seen as strong on discipline," an admiring soldier wrote, "but at the same
time allows the individual as much freedom as possible."[3]

Willich appointed talented and tenacious quartermaster Edward Mueller of Indianapolis on August 21. It was a brilliant selection; Mueller would prove himself invaluable, particularly in lean times ahead. Before their departure for Kentucky, Willich's men were spoiled with ample coffee, fresh and smoked meats, soups, and potato salad. Mueller made sure they never ran out of beer, a staple of the German diet. "I think I can endure with such fare," a soldier wrote home.[4] A few months later, William T. Sherman, the new commander of the Department of the Cumberland, threatened to cut off the regiment's beer. Willich rushed to Louisville, successfully pleaded his case, and returned triumphantly with ten barrels of the precious lager in his train car. The regiment named it "Colonel Willich's beer," and it tasted better than ever.[5]

Willich's reasons for enlisting went well beyond Lincoln's stated goal of preserving the Union. He believed that the American Civil War was a conflict with immense global ramifications, and he was determined to share this perspective with his troops. Willich's public proclamation on August 25 stressed the need for Germans to prove they were not foreigners and to "protect their new republican homeland against the aristocracy of the South." Lectures to his men revealed broader concerns. "When the war began," Willich explained, "it was viewed merely as a battle about nationality; it also turns out, however, that it is in the interest of all humanity." Defeat of republican government in the United States might doom the rest of the Western world to the rule of aristocracy and privilege for the foreseeable future. Willich would do his part to keep that from happening. Willich told his old friend Anneke that, should the opportunity present itself, he fully expected his men to follow him in an attempt to liberate Germany from monarchial rule after the Civil War's end.[6] That was the pipe dream of an old romantic.

On August 28, Willich established headquarters at Camp Murphy in northwest Indianapolis near the Lafayette Depot and began training his regiment. Maj. Henry von Trebra made astonishing progress in converting new recruits into an orderly and efficient unit. In just days the regiment was performing complex maneuvers by bugle command, forming columns and squares and wheeling with ease. Soldiers from other regiments at Camp Morton were relieved from guard duty so they could watch and learn from the Thirty-Second Indiana's execution on the drill field. A former lieutenant in the Prussian Army observed, "The regiment executes movements that the Americans cannot accomplish after three months of practice."[7] This was not merely a bluster of ethnic pride. The *Indianapolis Journal* claimed that Willich's regiment was, "beyond question the finest regiment that has left our state, and we doubt if any state has sent out a body of volunteers their equal in all respects."[8]

Willich and his regiment grew anxious to fight. Confederate forces under Gen. Simon Bolivar Buckner had occupied Bowling Green, Kentucky, on September 18, then sent more than six hundred men north to Buckner's hometown of Munfordville, a mere seventy-two miles from Louisville. Willich received orders to depart Indianapolis on September 27 and head to Kentucky. Though his troops lacked knapsacks and sufficient ammunition, they marched to the train depot the next day. In addition, the soldiers had not been paid since enlistment. Willich himself could not afford a horse, so he led his men on foot.[9] He also sent urgent telegrams to Morton from Madison, Indiana, begging him for fifty thousand cartridges, as only fifteen per man were available.[10]

The Thirty-Second Indiana left Madison by steamboat on October 1, arriving safely at Louisville wharf around 8:00 p.m. On October 5, Willich accepted an American flag from the wife of a prominent local attorney. He received a pair of fine horses for himself and his major, along with sabers, thanks to a subscription of Indianapolis citizens. The next day, the regiment left to guard a railroad spur at Lebanon Junction, Kentucky.[11] Willich telegraphed Morton again upon arrival and pleaded for his wagon train, remarking, "The movements of the regt. will be embarrassed [without it]."[12] Willich and his boys spent two weeks encamped in a beautiful valley near New Haven, Kentucky, where they continued to drill and enjoy pleasant times at a place they dubbed "Camp Hope." They sang songs, drank lager, and circulated a camp newspaper they called "The Blockhead," after their leader's sobriquet for his children who misbehaved.[13]

Robert Anderson's resignation prompted new commander William T. Sherman to reorganize and consolidate the Department of the Cumberland. Sherman ordered Willich to march south to Camp Nevin, near Nolin, Kentucky, where he arrived on October 20. The general staff was so impressed by the spirit and deportment of the regiment's marching that they posted the Thirty-Second Indiana far south as an advance guard against the enemy. Here the first German regiment from Indiana established a camp that was the envy of its soldiers' American-born compatriots.

The reputation of the Thirty-Second Indiana grew due to its soldiers' excellence on the drill field and their superior health and positive attitude. Qm. Sgt. Emanuel Wassenich designed and built a portable oven for baking bread in the field. The regiment lost far fewer men to disease and illness than other regiments at Camp Nevin, where more than thirteen thousand Union soldiers lived in close quarters. Regimental physician Dr. Ferdinand Krauth believed in preventative health care, maintaining "that it was ten times more important in camp life to prevent diseases as to cure them." Krauth insisted on personal and camp cleanliness. Moreover, various Turner organizations erected makeshift gymnastic apparatus in the field to help maintain physical fitness. Willich's men further benefited from the fact that many of them came from urban environments and had acquired resistance to communicable diseases that ravaged regiments from the countryside.[14]

The Thirty-Second Indiana became part of Gen. Richard W. Johnson's Sixth Brigade in Brig. Gen. Alexander M. McCook's Second Division in early November. To celebrate the new organization, Willich invited McCook and his brigade commanders to camp to enjoy his superior food and well-stocked wine selection. The guests imbibed freely—Colonel Lovell H. Rousseau was so tipsy he fell over, and Johnson was even worse off. The next day, Willich delivered a speech to his troops, cautioning them to follow military protocol when brigade and division commanders were present. "Children! Until now, neither me nor my officers have demanded typical military honors from you and will not in the future. Given that we now belong to a specific department of the army, you must at least salute the generals, and especially the brigadier general, if he enters camp. You know the man, don't you?" A voice from the regiment called out in reply, "Was it perhaps the general who was completely sloshed?" Willich suppressed a grin, then waved a finger at the offender and ordered him to his quarters.[15]

Another humorous incident involved Governor Morton's announcement that he would visit the troops. Willich asked General Johnson what he should do with his baggage at the review. Johnson told him that it would not be necessary to bring wagons and teams. "Oh general," replied Willich, "I do not mean wagons, but I want to know what to do with my baggage, the doctor and the chaplain."[16]

The monotony of camp life ended in early November as Willich's men practiced on the parade ground. No sooner had Colonel Willich ordered the bugler to sound "deploy" then a hail of spent bullets dropped harmlessly among the troops. Soldiers of the Thirty-Fourth Illinois Infantry under Rousseau's command had mistakenly set their practice targets in line with Willich's camp.[17] A few days later, the news arrived that Brig. Gen. Don Carlos Buell had assumed Sherman's command and folded his department into a new Department of the Ohio. Buell was under tremendous pressure from Washington to act, so drilling among other regiments at Camp Nevin

PONTONIERS OF 9TH COMPANY, 32ND INDIANA VOL. INFANTRY.
ENGRAVING BY HENRY MOSLER, 1861. *HARPER'S WEEKLY.*

accelerated to a frequency that the Thirty-Second Indiana was already accustomed to.

Willich leveraged his engineering expertise during this period, assembling the regiment's best mechanics into the first dedicated pioneer company in the Union army. Capt. William Sievers of Company I and his master engineer Lieut. Joseph Pietzuch led forty skilled laborers in the specialized work of bridging. Willich designed a wagon that converted to a floating pier, creating a pontoon bridge that made crossing small streams with heavy equipment easier. The company erected a prototype on a fork of the Nolin River in less than two days. Before they finished, heavy rains washed out the Elizabethtown Bridge near Red Mills, disrupting the division's supply route and putting the entire army on short rations. Willich offered the services of his pontoniers to repair the bridge, but a disorganized chain of command meant that the offer was accepted after the army had departed the area. In the meantime, Quartermaster Mueller made sure Willich's troops were well nourished. He skirted normal channels and obtained fare for the regiment through creative foraging.[18]

Early December snows found Willich's regiment constructing log cabins in anticipation of spending the winter at Camp Nevin. Work was barely underway when Buell decided to move. He ordered McCook to head south and join the rest of Buell's army on the road to Bowling Green. More than fifty thousand Union soldiers of the Army of the Ohio marched to oust the Confederates from Kentucky. Colonel Willich and the Thirty-Second Indiana formed the vanguard of Johnson's Sixth Brigade, leaving Camp Nevin bound for Munfordville at 8:30 a.m. on December 10. A planned march of eight miles turned into twelve, as the regiment needed a place with sufficient water. Troops ultimately selected the south bank of Bacon Creek, twelve miles from their destination. Meanwhile, the Confederates were doing their best to slow the progress of Buell's huge army.[19]

Willich sent two companies out on picket duty that evening, only to discover that John Hunt Morgan's Confederate cavalry had destroyed a bridge over the creek. Willich's pontoniers rebuilt it. Of greater concern was the Louisville and Nashville Railroad Bridge over a deep gorge at Green River. If that span was destroyed, Buell's supply line would be degraded and the advance delayed for weeks or even months. Buell ordered McCook to send a brigade to Munfordville immediately, and the task fell to Johnson, who was bogged down at Bacon Creek. Johnson instructed Willich to send two companies under Lieutenant Colonel von Trebra ahead of the brigade to reconnoiter. Von Trebra reached the town in time to flush out a small detail of Confederates who had already blown up one of the massive stone support piers and destroyed one hundred feet of track at the south end of the railroad bridge. The lieutenant colonel's men took a defensive position and waited until the rest of Johnson's brigade and Brig. Gen. Thomas J. Wood's Fifth Brigade arrived on Thursday, December 12.[20]

Willich's pioneers faced a daunting assignment. They established camp on the south side of the Green River and planned to construct a temporary pontoon bridge over the waterway. They would also make repairs to the damaged bridge in full view of Confederate cavalry. A mile forward of the bridge, Willich established picket posts immediately harassed by elements of Col. Benjamin Terry's Eighth Texas Cavalry. Willich's men suffered two wounded in the brief skirmish but managed to kill four enemy riders. The pontoon bridge was completed in less than three days. Willich then ordered two additional companies across the river while posting four companies to the south as skirmishers. The remaining two companies stayed in reserve on the north side of the river. Albert Fink, a talented German civil engineer, arrived from Louisville the evening of September 16 to begin repairs on the remarkable span that he himself had designed and built just two years earlier.[21]

The following morning, soldiers and work crews awoke to perfect bridge-building weather. It was unusually warm and clear, and the area was a bustle of activity. Willich was at division headquarters at midday, leaving Lieutenant Colonel von Trebra in temporary command of the regiment. Capt. Jacob Glass's Company B formed the right wing of the picket chain about a mile southeast of the bridge. Glass's patrol engaged rebel skirmishers near a place called Rowlett's Station around noon, driving them back with support from the balance of the company. Suddenly, a large Confederate force came into view. Glass had stumbled upon Confederate brigadier general Thomas Hindman's thirteen hundred men another mile to the south; this force included soldiers from the Second and Sixth Arkansas Infantry Regiments in addition to Terry's Texas Rangers. While Glass promptly pulled back, Lieut. Max Sachs, in temporary command of Company C on the Union left, was not as prudent.[22]

Sachs ordered his bugler to sound general alarm as Terry's Rangers swarmed them. Reserve companies north of the river rushed across the pontoon bridge to support their comrades. Von Trebra formed the troops in close column and assigned Companies K, G, and F to reinforce Glass on the right. Companies A and I supported Sachs on the left. Confederate infantry hesitated, but Texas cavalrymen were emboldened by the opportunity to rout the Federals. They attacked all along the Union line in a headlong dash, firing with pistol and shotgun from as close as fifteen yards away. Union soldiers kept their cool, allowing the Texans to close in before letting off a withering reply that killed and unhorsed a large number of attackers.

Fifty rangers surrounded Sachs and one of his platoons that had foolishly advanced into an open plain. Sachs refused to surrender, and he and his comrades were riddled with bullets. The lieutenant and three of his men were killed. Seven others were wounded. The injured men were barely saved when Capt. Frank Erdelmeyer arrived on the scene with Company A. "The wild riders were thrown back," Erdelmeyer later recalled, "but again and again they returned." The battle raged for nearly two hours with Willich's 450 men attempting to hold firm against a force nearly three times their size.[23]

Artillery batteries from both sides engaged briefly, but changing troop positions on the field exposed Union infantrymen to friendly fire from their own gunners. Aided by a flanking maneuver from Erdelmeyer, Cotter's Battery A of the First Ohio Artillery was effective in silencing four guns of Mississippi

HOLLOW SQUARE REPELS TEXAS CAVALRY AT BATTLE OF ROWLETT'S STATION,
DECEMBER 17, 1861. *HARPER'S WEEKLY.*

captain Charles Swett's Warren County Light Artillery Battery. Von Trebra
led an advance on the rebel left center, drawing a furious response from the
Texans, who recklessly drove their horses into and through the Union ranks,
only to be chopped down by reserves led by Adjt. Carl Schmitt.

The situation was desperate on the Union right. The Texans attacked relentlessly, taking down ten men of Company F in one charge and driving
them back behind the reserves of Capt. Peter Welschbillig's Company G.
The Union captain deployed his fifty men in a hollow square and awaited
another attack by the Confederate horsemen, now numbering more than two
hundred. Rebels first assaulted the front and left flank of the square but were
repulsed by disciplined firing at short range. The Texans re-formed and came
at Company G again, this time from three sides. The square held and more
Confederate cavalrymen lay prostrate on the field. A third charge resulted
in fierce hand-to-hand combat, with a number of Confederates unhorsed by
bayonet. Colonel Terry was killed. The remaining Confederate cavalrymen
rode off in wild disorder, dismayed at their inability to overwhelm such a
small force. In their place, Hindman's infantrymen appeared on the scene.[24]

Willich arrived on the field and took command of the right wing just as
Welschbillig was shuttling his wounded to the rear. Fearing that Arkansas
troops might turn his right flank, Willich withdrew to a safe position. The
rebel infantry also pulled back. Both sides claimed victory in what became
known as the Battle of Rowlett's Station, but the Union army held the field,

successfully defending a critical bridge and killing one of the rising stars of the
Confederate cavalry. Willich lost thirteen men killed or mortally wounded.
Estimates of the Confederate dead vary widely, but rebel losses were signifi-
cantly greater. Willich's troops demonstrated how infantry could repel an
attack from a larger force of enemy cavalry using classic infantry formations
learned at the Prussian military academy, like the hollow square, combined
with disciplined troop management.[25]

The victory at Rowlett's Station was a small but badly needed triumph in
a year when Union defeats at Bull Run, Ball's Bluff, and Wilson's Creek damaged morale in the North. In a burst of hyperbole, the *New York Times* called
Rowlett's Station "the most brilliant National victory yet achieved." The battle
resulted in widespread acclaim for the Thirty-Second Indiana. Buell bragged
to McClellan that "the little affair in front of Munfordville was really one of
the handsomest things of the season." In General Order Number 23, Buell
applauded the Indianans "as a study and example to all other troops under
his command," asking them to "emulate the discipline and instruction which
insure such results."[26]

Willich was proud of the coolness and bravery his men exhibited in their
first big fight but annoyed at the actions of some of his officers. He praised
von Trebra for his skill and gallantry while chiding him for exceeding his
authority and bringing on a general engagement while Willich was absent.
This was Willich's ego talking. He mourned the death of Sachs but also blamed
him for advancing too hastily and too soon, resulting in the needless deaths
of other brave soldiers. Finally, Willich gave credit to Lieutenant Pietzuch
and his pontoniers. Without their efforts, the regiment would have been
stranded on the opposite side of the river, leaving pickets without support
and ensuring their annihilation.[27] Willich sent a saddle from one of the dead
Texas Rangers to Governor Morton as a keepsake, suggesting that his men
could have "emptied twice the number [of enemy saddles]" had they been
equipped with Springfield rifles in place of the inferior guns produced by
Miles Greenwood of Cincinnati.[28]

Willich led a graveside service atop a knoll near the battlefield for ten
of his fallen men. He said of these soldiers, "[They have] paid the highest
price that a citizen of the Republic can pay, which he, however, also must
be prepared to pay, when the Republic is in danger." No prayers were said.
Instead, Willich then read portions of a poem by William Cullen Bryant:
"Ah! Never shall the land forget, / How Gushed the life-blood of her brave—/
Gushed warm with the hope and courage yet, / Upon the soil they fought to
save."[29] The eulogy moved men to tears. Each soldier was handed a bouquet of

COLONEL AUGUST WILLICH RECEIVES CONFEDERATE PRISONERS AT GREEN RIVER,
KENTUCKY, 1862. PEN, INK, AND WATERCOLOR BY ADOLPH METZNER.
LIBRARY OF CONGRESS.

evergreen, and as the band played "La Marseillaise," they filed by the graves, dropping evergreen sprigs onto the bodies of their dead comrades. Willich then asked those present to give three cheers for the men who "had fallen in the struggle for human rights and liberty, and were now on their journey to eternity." The ceremony ended with hurrahs. Afterward, the colonel led his regiment through the skirmish drill. It was a peculiar burial service for the Christians present.[30]

As a final tribute to the slain patriots, Pvt. Adolph Bloettner of Company F chose a piece of local limestone and sculpted a beautiful monument in their honor. Bloettner carved an eagle with outstretched wings in relief on the top of the marker, adorning the face of the stone with cannons, American flags, an oak sprig, and an olive branch. Names of the dead and their birth dates were inscribed on the tablet along with an inscription in German that translated into English read: "Here rest the first martyrs of the Thirty-second, the first German regiment of Indiana. They were fighting nobly in defense of the free Constitution of the United States of America. They fell on the 17th day of December, 1861, in the battle at Rowlett's Station, in which one regiment of Texas Rangers, two regiments of infantry, and six pieces of artillery, in all over three thousand men, were defeated by five hundred German soldiers." The stone survives as the oldest Civil War memorial marker.[31]

• • • • •

Willich and his men remained at Camp George Wood for two months after the battle. Repairs to the Green River Bridge were completed on January 9. Members of the Thirty-Second Indiana cheered as they watched the first trainload of supplies reach the south bank.[32] Colonel Willich wished his men luck in the New Year. "What is needed in the current emergency," he cautioned, "is a sharp eye, a strong hand, composure, good discipline and citizen-like state of mind that proves itself on the battlefield." His men were eager to accept the challenge, not knowing that the balance of the year would bring them unimaginable hurdles and horrors.[33]

One particularly frosty February morning, Willich marched the regiment to the gravesite where ten of their fallen brothers rested. The troops presented arms, and the band played an appropriate tune. Ignoring the frigid temperature, Willich launched into one of his typical long orations, bent on educating and inspiring his troops. "He began by saying that now a decisive moment of the war had come," a soldier remembered, and then reeled off proof of a dialectical continuum from the Peasants War in 1525, through the Thirty Years War, the French Revolution, and the Revolution of 1848. Willich described how the people, despite their initial victories, had always given in to "the longing for their women and children, or the domestic hearth." The result, Willich argued, was that "instead of reaping a blessing, they reaped curses." Willich then launched into his rote speech on the cause of the war, but according to one soldier, "involuntarily his all too vivid sense of fantasy strayed from this small earth up into the higher regions." The Prussian began lecturing on astronomy and science. Men stomped their feet to stay warm and show their displeasure at the lengthy soliloquy under such harsh conditions. The colonel took their cue, ended his address abruptly, and marched his stiff, perturbed men back to camp. "These are interesting subjects to enjoy with a glass of beer," one soldier wrote, "however, not [with] a regiment in 10-degree cold."[34]

A few days later, the Thirty-Second Indiana received orders to march. Instead of having them follow the rest of the army south toward Bowling Green, McCook ordered his Second Division north to the Ohio River. There, the soldiers would board steamboats and reinforce Grant, who was besieging Fort Donelson on the Cumberland River in Tennessee. The Confederate surrender there on February 16 made that mission unnecessary, so McCook retraced his steps and headed back to Bowling Green. Confederate general Albert Sidney Johnston continued the cat-and-mouse game by abandoning Bowling Green and taking his force to Nashville, Tennessee, leaving a swath of destroyed rail lines and burned bridges in his wake.[35]

Willich's pioneers were instrumental in training other units to construct pontoons to support large numbers of troops and supply trains over swollen rivers and streams. When Gen. Richard W. Johnson ordered him to disband his dedicated pioneer company because it conflicted with the new Pioneer Corps, Willich refused and was relieved of command for a few days. Then the two men came to an understanding. From that time forward, Willich simply ordered "pioneers to the front" when they were needed, and the pontoon builders complied.[36]

Confederate general Johnston's stay at Nashville was brief. Buell's Army of the Ohio pursued as rapidly as bad roads and winter rains allowed. The Thirty-Second Indiana finally marched through Nashville to take a position near Franklin on March 2, but the Confederates were long gone. Over the next two weeks, the newly promoted Major General Buell gathered five divisions for his next offensive. Maj. Gen. Henry Halleck, the new overall commander in the West, commanded three armies led by Buell, John Pope, and U. S. Grant. Halleck had ambitious plans to "split secession in twain in one month," as he boasted to Gen. George McClellan. To accomplish this feat, Halleck needed to control the critical rail juncture at Corinth, Mississippi. The stage was set for an epic collision that would elevate the war's violence beyond the threshold of imagination.[37]

Chapter Twelve

• • • • • • • • • • • • • • • • • • •

MAELSTROM

A LARGE ROUND SHOT screamed past Maj. Gen. Lew Wallace at saddle height, making his terrified horse wheel to his left. A dull thud like a maul pounding sand echoed across the battlefield. Wallace watched in horror as an arm ripped from the shoulder of a Union infantry soldier, "stiffened like a stick, fingers outspread, revolving end over end in the air," flew away from him.[1] Welcome to Shiloh, which means "the peaceful one" in Hebrew.

By early afternoon on April 7, 1862, Wallace's division on the extreme right wing of the Union army was wavering. Rebel forces were heavily concentrated at the Corinth Road, their front sheltered by a dense stand of water oaks. Confederates under the command of Gen. Patrick Cleburne were pushing back the divisions of Maj. Gen. John A. McClernand and William T. Sherman, exposing Wallace's left flank. Some of Wallace's soldiers retreated into the woods, reminding him of "blackbirds in their migratory fall flight."[2] Wallace advised Col. George F. McGinnis, commander of the Eleventh Indiana, to fall back if things got too hot. He even contemplated a retreat when a movement to the southeast caught his attention.[3]

A body of unidentified men began to file out of the forest and onto the Woolf Field in a near-perfect double-column formation. As Wallace squinted through his field glasses to determine if this unexpected entry was friend or enemy, he breathed a sigh of relief. The wind shifted to reveal white stars on a field of Union blue, held aloft by the color-bearer. The rebels, despite facing only a solitary regiment, yielded and sought cover in the oak forest. The Union regiment re-formed into line of battle and commenced firing.[4]

Wallace marveled as he watched the blue-clad regiment resume its double-column formation and enter the water oak swamp. Gen. W. T. Sherman also watched the drama play out. "Here I saw for the first time the well-ordered and compact columns Of General Buell's Kentucky forces," he remarked, "whose soldierly movements at once gave confidence to our newer and less-disciplined forces. Here I saw Willich's regiment advance upon a point of water-oaks and thicket, behind which I knew the enemy was in great strength and enter it in beautiful style."[5]

In a last-ditch effort to rally his Confederate reserves, Gen. P. G. T. Beauregard had decided to attack the center of the Union line in hopes of penetrating it where the Army of the Ohio and the Army of the Tennessee connected. As a Confederate brigade under the command of Sterling A. M. Wood advanced to the stand of oaks near a pond to the right of Brig. Gen. Alexander D. McCook's Second Division, they encountered Willich and his regiment.[6] Sherman described the action at this moment as "the severest musketry fire [he] ever heard." For about twenty minutes Willich and the rebels exchanged lead. By this time, the Indianans had outrun support on their flanks and were receiving canister, shell, and musket balls from three sides, including friendly fire. They faltered and began to show signs of distress. Skirmishers eventually fled through the lines; "This splendid regiment had to fall back," Sherman reported.[7] The troops retreated into a ravine, regrouped, and charged the enemy again in double-column formation. After driving the Confederates for several hundred yards, the regiment deployed in line of battle and opened fire, then reverted to double column and advanced farther. The unit's soldiers also began firing wildly at too great a distance from the enemy. Wallace could hardly believe what happened next.[8]

An officer on horseback suddenly appeared, riding around his left flank and stopping in front of the regiment. His back was to the enemy. Wallace described the scene: "What he said I could not hear, but from the motions of the men he was putting them through the manual of arms—notwithstanding some of the men were dropping in the ranks. Taken all in all, that I think was the most audacious thing that came under my observation during the war." The effect of restoring order to the regiment was "magical," according to Wallace. The drillmaster rode back to the rear of the column after conducting this unusual exercise for about ten minutes. The column then advanced as if on parade.

Wallace dispatched an orderly to ride to the commander of the regiment, present his compliments, and ask him to reveal his identity. "August Willich of the Thirty-Second Indiana Volunteers," came the reply. Wallace had been on the battlefield since dawn, but he did not realize that reinforcements from Buell's Army of the Ohio had arrived on the scene. Willich was part of a replenished force that helped Grant secure victory for the Union army when only twenty-four hours earlier the bluecoats had been on the verge of defeat.[9]

•••••

Willich and his troops had left Nashville on a 120-mile march to Savannah, Tennessee, on the morning of March 16, 1862, forming the vanguard of McCook's division. Several burnt bridges slowed the progress of Buell's army just three days later. Willich took on the important task of repairing the span over Duck River north of Columbia. In the meantime, Buell ordered the divisions of Brig. Gen. William "Bull" Nelson and Thomas L. Crittenden to ford the stream, as the work was expected to take nearly two weeks. Nelson arrived at Savannah on April 5, but Willich and the rest of McCook's division were still on the road the morning of April 6 when they heard rumbling in the west.[10] Willich drew his sword, dug a small hole in the ground, and lay prone, his ear pressed to the earth. Upon rising, he announced the noise to be cannon fire. Soon afterward, a messenger from Buell arrived with word that Grant had been attacked near Pittsburg Landing.[11]

That day, McCook rushed his division to Savannah for twenty muddy, grueling miles as the roar of battle grew deafening. Willich rode to other regiments in the brigade to cheer them on. When he returned to his boys, he announced, "The regiments are in good spirits." His troops replied, "Us too!" "Of course, you blockheads," the old man sounded back. "You do not need to tell me that."[12] Pvt. Henry W. Shuman of the Fifty-Seventh Indiana was marching alongside his ten-year-old son and drummer boy when Willich stormed by on one of the finest horses the father had ever seen. Shuman yanked his son out of the way, fearing he might be run over by the steed. The colonel, realizing what had happened, looked Shuman square in the eyes and apologized. "I beg your pardon, sir," he said. "I would not for the world injure that little boy."[13] By the time McCook's division reached the banks of the Tennessee River opposite Pittsburg Landing, the town of Savannah was full of dazed and wounded Union soldiers, victims of the onslaught of forty thousand Confederates.

Grant was forced to fight a battle before he was ready; he had not planned to engage the enemy until the arrival of Buell's army. The Confederates pushed Grant back into successive defensive positions in a fierce firestorm, producing heavy casualties on both sides. Confederate general Albert Sidney Johnston died on the field on the first day of battle. Grant was successful in exchanging territory for hours. By the end of the day, he had assumed a strong defensive stance atop a tall ridge overlooking Dill Branch on his left and Tilghman Branch of Owl Creek to his right. Confederate general P. G. T. Beauregard, assuming overall command following Johnston's death, made a final assault with two brigades against Grant's line. However, his troops confronted fifty pieces of Federal artillery. The sun sank in the west while the rebels dodged shells from Union gunboats. A dozen companies from Buell's lead brigades managed to arrive on the battlefield near the end of the day, but by then Grant had matters well in hand. Beauregard withdrew for the evening, returning newly won ground to the Union.[14]

The tables turned on Beauregard overnight as the bulk of Buell's nineteen thousand men arrived, bolstering total Union forces to nearly forty-five thousand. The Confederates could count on only about twenty thousand effectives after the previous day's casualties. Grant began his counterattack at dawn. By midmorning, the Federals had pushed Confederate lines back about three-quarters of a mile from Pittsburg Landing.[15] Col. William H. Gibson, in temporary command of the Sixth Brigade due to Gen. Richard W. Johnson's sudden illness, loaded his entire force onto the steamer John J. Roe in Savannah, steamed upriver, then floated across, arriving at the landing around 10:00 a.m.[16] Willich rushed his men off the ship. General Grant ordered him to head immediately for the battlefield ahead of the rest of the brigade. The Thirty-Second Indiana was to serve in reserve of Gen. Alexander McCook's other two brigades who were already engaged with the enemy near the center of the Union line.

Willich led his men to the Stacy Field, where he found McCook about two hundred yards to the rear of the second line of battle. Chafing at the idea of being held in reserve, Willich requested permission to pass to the front and make a bayonet charge.[17] McCook replied, "Just pitch right in wherever you see fit, you know how to manage these affairs."[18] It was the kind of license that Willich was accustomed to having. Before they advanced, Willich addressed his men briefly. "Little children," the colonel began, "today decides the fate of America." The speech was interrupted by a shell flying overhead. "Gentlemen, I must first pray for my little children. If we are beaten today everything is lost; let us do our duty as a free man does. Forward, march!"[19]

Willich led his men ahead in double column for about two hundred yards between the brigades of Brig. Gen. Lovell H. Rousseau and Col. Edward N. Kirk. The action about five hundred yards northeast of Shiloh Church progressed just as Lew Wallace and Sherman described it. Willich's men attacked, then fell back in disarray, their colonel regrouping them for successive charges

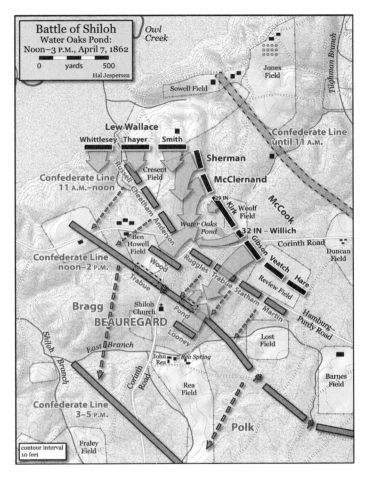

SHILOH: WATER OAKS POND

and even pausing to steady their nerves by drilling them in the midst of enemy fire. With the Seventy-Seventh Pennsylvania supporting him on his left, Willich and his regiment rushed forward to prevent the Confederates from outflanking Wallace.[20]

Col. George F. McGinnis, commanding the Eleventh Indiana Infantry in Col. Morgan L. Smith's First Brigade on Wallace's far left, reported that this was "the most trying moment" of the day. "Fortunately," McGinnis continued, "and much to our relief, at this critical moment, the Thirty-Second Indiana, Colonel Willich, came up on our left, and with their assistance the advancing army was compelled to retire."[21] The Fifth Kentucky's Louisville Legion, part of Rousseau's brigade, performed similar service for McClernand's First Division, as both he and Sherman had been overlapped by McCook's lines. While Willich's men regrouped again after their third charge of the afternoon, "Rousseau's brigade moved in splendid order steadily to the front," Sherman said, "sweeping everything before it."[22] Kirk's brigade was also conspicuous in its bravery in that hotly contested sector of the field.

By the time Willich's men made a fourth charge, tattered remnants of the Twenty-Seventh Tennessee Infantry and Ninth Arkansas Infantry put up limited resistance and were easily flushed out of the woods. Willich and his men pursued the retreating rebels for another mile until they had run themselves ragged, then halted.[23] At this point, Willich felt a stinging sensation in his breast close to the heart. He removed his coat to find that he had been wounded during one of the charges. Fortunately, though, the spent ball had lodged in his wallet and prevented a serious injury. One of the lucky ones, Willich emerged from the fight with only a few broken ribs.[24] At the same time, nineteen of his men died from wounds received that day, and the regiment suffered more than a hundred additional casualties.[25] McCook ordered Willich to rejoin the division at Pittsburg Landing, but the old colonel could not locate Gibson's Sixth Brigade and elected to bivouac in an open field near east Shiloh Branch and join the troops in the morning.[26] The bloodiest battle in the history of the continent to date had just ended. Nearly twenty-four thousand casualties suffered by the two armies served as an ominous portent of even greater carnage in the months and years ahead.[27]

• • • • •

His worst nightmares could not have prepared Lieut. Adolph Metzner for this hell on earth. The Louisville, Kentucky, druggist had responded to the call of his fellow Germans in August 1861 and became part of Capt. Frank Erdelmeyer's First Company in the Thirty-Second Indiana. A gifted artist, Metzner used an abundance of free time in camp to create more than a hundred sketches, finished drawings, and watercolors documenting his three years of volunteer service in the Union army. Most images drawn by Metzner before Shiloh reflect the mood prevalent during the romantic early months of the war. His works, mostly portraits, were finely rendered, some of them in vibrant colors. More often than not, Metzner modeled his art to

DECAPITATED CORPSES OF SOLDIERS FOLLOWING THE BATTLE OF SHILOH, 1862.
WATERCOLOR BY ADOLPH METZNER. LIBRARY OF CONGRESS.

emphasize the humorous aspects of his subjects. That art changed in the aftermath of April 7, 1862.

Metzner replaced bright, triumphal paintings of officers on horseback and enlisted men cavorting in camp shenanigans with dark, hurried, and gruesome sketches. In these images, dead men and horses contort into macabre sculptures. Corpses whose limbs are intact lie in every conceivable position, frozen arms and legs jutting into the fetid air with screaming or groaning expressions permanently etched on their ashen faces. Decapitated soldiers appear to be resting under a tree amid discarded accoutrements in an unnatural landscape denuded by hideous weapons of destruction.[28]

Innocence and optimism vanished. The two massive armies had suffered nearly five times as many casualties as at Manassas, the next costliest battle of the war to that date. Going forward, the Civil War would be a drawn-out bloodbath. After Shiloh, Grant remembered that he relinquished "all idea of saving the Union except by complete conquest."[29] Sherman was characteristically blunt, stating, "The scenes on this field would have cured anyone of war."[30]

Despite the awful struggle, Corinth remained in rebel hands. Beauregard pulled his shell-shocked army back to entrenchments around the city and vowed to hold it at all costs. "If defeated here," the Confederate general wrote two weeks after Shiloh, "we lose the whole Mississippi valley and probably our cause." By the first week in May, reinforcements swelled his ranks to more than seventy thousand men, though many of these were recovering from wounds or were bedridden as typhoid and dysentery raged through their camps.

Henry W. Halleck, Grant's commander, turned cautious. After covering nearly eighteen miles in less than three days, he slowed upon reaching Farmington on May 9, entrenching frequently as he neared Corinth. Halleck adopted a siege mentality as opposed to Grant's aggressive strategy of inflicting maximum damage on the enemy. He skirmished with the rebels but did not attempt to join them in another major battle.[31] Willich and his men, along with the Thirty-Fourth Illinois, helped repel an enemy charge on May 28, then took Serrat's Hill, a key eminence where the Federals placed siege guns a mere thousand yards from Confederate defenses. The next day Union troops dug more than twelve hundred yards of earthworks in anticipation of an attack that never materialized.

Beauregard had changed his mind. The crafty general created a series of diversions to convince the Union army that battle was imminent. Roving cavalry kept the night ablaze by maintaining the campfires of phantom regiments, and buglers sounded customary garrison calls to empty campsites. Sharpshooters and skirmishers engaged Halleck's army up and down the line on May 29. Train cars arriving at the depot were met by loud cheering, as if reinforcements were arriving steadily, but the cars were empty and Halleck was hoodwinked. Beauregard had come to the unhappy conclusion that his force lacked sufficient guns, water, and food while facing overwhelming numbers. He evacuated Corinth, setting part of the town ablaze. Abandoning the important rail junction was a tough blow to the Confederacy, but Beauregard made a sound judgment. This was neither the time nor the place for such a huge wager of war. By July, Halleck had been promoted to general-in-chief, and Braxton Bragg had replaced Beauregard in command of the Army of Mississippi.[32]

Before he left for Washington, Halleck reasoned that he needed to divide his army in three in order to conquer Tennessee and the rest of the Confederate breadbasket. He sent Maj. Gen. John Pope on a halfhearted pursuit of retreating rebels while Grant secured Corinth and repaired railroad lines to his north. At the same time, Buell moved his Army of the Ohio east to connect with Maj. Gen. Ormsby M. Mitchel in northern Alabama. If all went as planned, Buell and Mitchel would take Chattanooga and drive Maj. Gen.

BRIGADIER GENERAL AUGUST WILLICH, 1862.
PENCIL AND WASH BY ADOLPH METZNER.
LIBRARY OF CONGRESS.

Edmund Kirby and his rebel troops out of East Tennessee. That ambition was soon discarded, however, and Buell and Mitchel found themselves responding to the Confederate war agenda.[33]

Willich's regiment and the balance of McCook's division left Corinth June 11, 1862. This departure marked the beginning of five months of hardship and frustration. The summer heat was unrelenting, and many men dropped from sunstroke or dehydration during a thirty-seven-day march across Alabama to within thirty miles of Chattanooga. Willich received his brigadier general's star on July 17. Von Trebra was promoted to colonel and took command of the regiment. In addition to the Thirty-Second Indiana, Willich's Sixth Brigade included the Thirty-Ninth Indiana, along with the Fifteenth and Forty-Ninth Ohio Regiments and the First Ohio Light Artillery. Willich continued the practice of using bugle signals in place of verbal commands, and his troops became known as "the horn brigade."[34]

General Willich reviewed his brigade the next morning at 6:00 a.m., riding by with his cap doffed while regiments presented arms and dipped their banners. The newly minted brigadier struggled through a speech in English, apologizing for his faulty pronunciation. Realizing that troop morale needed a boost, Willich admonished his men to lose their desire to shake off a soldier's life. The old man explained to the audience why such efforts would prove fruitless: "The women at home will drive you back with the slipper!" The entire assembly erupted in laughter. Willich also emphasized the fact that neglect of small details, such as carelessness in advance post duty, had destroyed entire armies. "If we have bad shoes," he said, "we cannot march. If we cannot march, we cannot fight. If we are unable to fight, we shall all go to the devil." He dismissed the brigade to thunderous applause.[35]

Rebel generals Braxton Bragg and Kirby Smith took the initiative in the middle of August. More than fifty-two thousand Confederates invaded Kentucky, setting up a wild race through the commonwealth that ended up accomplishing little for either side. McCook's Second Division was the last to depart for Kentucky, forming the rear to guard against Bragg, who was charging north from Chattanooga to rendezvous with Smith and wreak havoc. For ninety days, McCook tramped all over the state, camping on the battlefield of Rowlett's Station and retracing previous marches. Rations were short and water scarce. The ranks of Willich's brigade dwindled. They missed the big fight at Perryville on October 8 when command errors kept Buell from utilizing all of his forces in the battle. Then Buell's uneven performance in Kentucky cost him his job. The dusty, weary men of the Sixth Brigade, Second Division of the Army of the Ohio made camp seven miles south of Nashville on November 6 to await the arrival of Buell's replacement, the highly regarded and popular Maj. Gen. William Starke Rosecrans.[36]

Rosecrans went to work immediately, personally meeting each officer down to the brigade level while spending the majority of his time rebuilding the infrastructure of his depleted army. Soldiers were fed well and paid for the first time in six months. Rosecrans established an elite medical corps wherein dedicated ambulances and field hospitals became standard operating procedure. He also dismissed unfit officers. In the newly renamed Fourteenth Army Corps, Department of the Cumberland, most soldiers stopped grumbling. As pressure to act from Lincoln mounted, Rosecrans fended it off until he was ready to begin the next great campaign. That day came on December 26, 1862.[37]

Rosecrans and his forty-two thousand troops moved against Bragg's army of thirty-seven thousand men, eventually entrenching in a strong defensive position near the town of Murfreesboro, Tennessee. McCook commanded

Rosecrans's right wing, which included Richard W. Johnson's Second Division. Johnson's three brigades were commanded by Willich, newly promoted brigadier general Edward Kirk, and Col. Philemon P. Baldwin. For four soggy days, Rosecrans's Army of the Cumberland, as it came to be called, slogged south in mud that occasionally reached the men's knees.[38]

Willich's aides were not above having a little fun at their commander's expense on the march south from Nashville. One day when the general was in a particularly buoyant mood, Captain Allen rode up to headquarters after a reconnaissance. "Well, captain," Willich inquired anxiously, "what is the news from the front?" Allen appeared nonchalant. "Oh, not much of any news, general," he reported, "just a little shelling going on." Willich bounded to his feet. Staff and orderlies gathered to hear the important news. "Shelling? What shelling?" the old man demanded in a thunderous voice. "What is the damage?" "Oh, not much damage," Allen replied with a straight face. "It was only the boys out there shelling a little corn for their horses." The whole assembly broke out in raucous laughter. No one laughed louder than the general himself. "That is good! That is some fun!" he managed to say amid the merriment.

Despite his genial disposition, Willich himself was no comedian. Later that same day, Col. Charles Harker rode to Willich's headquarters. The brigadier thought it would be a good time to try his new joke out on his visitor. When Harker inquired about the news of the day, Willich fired his salvo. "Oh well, Colonel, there be not much news; only the boys been shelling a little corn for the horses." Willich's glance darted from man to man, as if to say, "Now is the time for laughter," but his staff stood silent. He then broke into a boisterous laugh that terminated shortly after it began, as no one else joined in. As more men were drawn to the scene by the general's outburst, a perplexed Willich scratched his head and exclaimed, "By jinx, there was something funny about that when I heard it." Such light moments were about to end.[39]

The afternoon of December 30, McCook's division arrived about three miles northwest of Murfreesboro, within hailing distance of Confederate lines. Willich's brigade took up a position on McCook's right flank. The night was bitterly cold, and the men, who had eaten just four crackers in four days, had hardly slept.[40] Few slumbered that evening as adrenaline levels ran high in anticipation of the titanic struggle that would surely come the next day. McCook's right wing occupied a high ridge interspersed with cedar groves and facing fields of cotton and corn. Kirk's brigade to Willich's left faced east, parallel to the rest of the Union line stretching three miles to the northeast, where the Federal left abutted Stones River.[41]

Some Union division commanders were concerned about potential enemy movements on their extreme right, as there was no natural barrier on that flank. Willich refused his brigade perpendicular to Kirk's right flank, with the Thirty-Ninth and Thirty-Second Indiana abutting Kirk and facing due south. Behind Kirk's brigade and Willich's Indiana regiments to the west, the Eighty-Ninth Illinois, Forty-Ninth Ohio, and Fifteenth Ohio formed a protective three-sided rectangle on the east, south, and west of a battery of the Ohio First Artillery. Rosecrans planned to launch an early morning offensive against the Confederate right, and he instructed McCook to hold his position if attacked. If no rebel assault came, McCook should "attack him, not vigorously, but warmly," to keep the Confederates from moving troops to the Union left. Coincidentally, Bragg had a similar plan.[42]

The rebels began silently massing troops opposite McCook's division, an action that continued throughout the night and was concealed by a line of cedars. Bragg planned to turn the Union right flank via a huge wheeling maneuver involving as many as seven infantry brigades. He would then drive the Federals back past the Nashville Pike to the Stones River, encircle them, and cut off their supply lines. The plan was audacious and nearly perfect. Bragg was counting on the element of surprise to launch his attack. He got it, thanks to an inexplicable lapse of readiness on the part of McCook and his generals.[43]

Maj. Gen. George H. Thomas, commanding the Union center, was the first corps leader to suspect that McCook was vulnerable and to relate those concerns to the commanding general. Rosecrans responded with a ruse that did not work. He instructed McCook to build fires west of his right flank to deceive the enemy as to the strength and disposition of the Union line. McCook assured his commander that he could hold his ground for at least three hours if attacked. It was a promise he could not keep.[44]

Signs of danger on the Union right persisted into the early morning hours. Several officers heard the distinct sounds of artillery limbers rumbling through the cedar forest. Third Division commander Brig. Gen. Phillip H. Sheridan hurried to McCook's headquarters around 2:15 a.m. to warn him. He found his boss asleep on a bed of straw, woke him, and expressed his concerns. McCook shrugged them off, claiming that the impending Federal attack on the Confederate right would stifle any planned attack on his position.[45] In the meantime, Richard Johnson did nothing to fortify the Second Division's lines. He placed Baldwin's reserve brigade and his own headquarters a mile and a half behind his front lines. Kirk asked Johnson to bring the reserves up closer to his own brigade, but Johnson refused. Willich visited Johnson's headquarters multiple times during the night to convey his apprehension regarding the division's alignment, but Johnson continued to follow McCook's lead.[46]

Willich wore a rubber coat, cap, and boots to protect him from the incessant rains.[47] Foregoing sleep, he skittered here and there like a mother hen sensing a nearby fox. Willich begged Johnson to allow the brigade's soldiers to load their guns that evening, but Johnson disagreed, suggesting that the brigadier return to his quarters and await orders.[48] Willich and Kirk sent pickets out all night. The sentinels saw nothing, heard nothing, only unsettling Willich further. His troops noticed. While the old man usually adopted a calm and quiet manner when battle drew near, it was now as if he was watching the impending fight take place in his mind. He considered probable scenarios. How would he adapt to changing tactical imperatives in the chaos and confusion to come? The more nervous Willich became, the more his men worried.

Around three o'clock in the morning, Willich ordered Lieut. Col. Fielder A. Jones of the Thirty-Ninth Indiana to throw forward a company to patrol the woods about six hundred yards in the Federals' front. They found no evidence of enemy troops there. Willich had his men up in arms by 4:00 a.m., but shortly before dawn they received permission to build fires and make coffee.[49] In Kirk's brigade, a similar air of indifference had taken hold. Horses were unlimbered and taken to a stream a short distance to the rear for watering. Meanwhile, McCook enjoyed a luxurious shave at headquarters.[50] McCook's behavior was puzzling, since he had told Rosecrans just hours before that he suspected the entire rebel army was massed in his front and would attack him that morning. But Rosecrans was determined to stick to his original plan. The thin line of the Union right wing was about to pay a heavy price for lack of vigilance.[51]

Willich and his brigade brewed coffee and cooked what was left of their bacon shortly before dawn on December 31, but the old man was still uneasy. He ordered Jones to advance the picket lines farther south to the woods in their front.[52] He also instructed Col. William H. Gibson of the Forty-Ninth Ohio to call on reserves of the Thirty-Ninth and Thirty-Second Indiana should the pickets become engaged. Willich then rode north to confer with Johnson at division headquarters on Gresham Lane.[53] He intended to renew his protest regarding the alignment of the division, which he believed to be faulty.[54] Had Willich expected an immediate attack, he would never have left his brigade at that moment.[55]

Kirk and Willich hardly suspected the degree of danger they were in at dawn on December 31. Two divisions of rebel soldiers under the commands

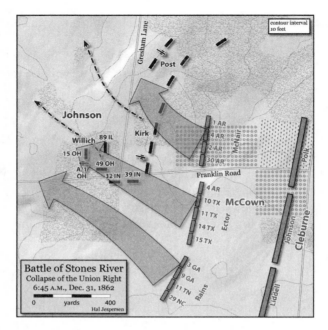

STONES RIVER: COLLAPSE OF THE UNION RIGHT

of Maj. Gens. Patrick R. Cleburne and John P. McCown had silently assembled directly opposite Kirk. While Union soldiers enjoyed breakfast, the Confederates primed their troops with a few swigs of whiskey and awaited orders to attack. At 6:22 a.m. Willich and Johnson were conferring while Fielder Jones continued to probe with his skirmish lines. Suddenly, Jones heard shots. Then he saw them coming.[56] Skirmishers from Kirk's brigade described the onslaught of tens of thousands of rebels on their thin lines as resembling a "tornado" with hordes of gray-clad soldiers "yelling and shooting like demons."[57] Aligned from south to north, McCown's frontline brigades of Gens. James Rains, Matthew D. Ector, and Evander McNair overran the skirmishers and crashed into Kirk's main lines in mere minutes, disabling the general and sweeping his brigade from the field. As they fled northwest, Kirk's regiments careened directly through Willich's brigade, creating confusion and panic.[58]

In the meantime, Ector's Texans were rolling over the Thirty-Ninth and Thirty-Second Indiana with ease, as Kirk's remnants had already scattered them. They prepared to vanquish the Forty-Ninth Ohio while Rains and his

CAPTURE OF GENERAL WILLICH AT STONES RIVER, DECEMBER 31, 1862.
WATERCOLOR BY ADOLPH METZNER. IT IS UNLIKELY THAT METZNER
WITNESSED THE EVENT DEPICTED. LIBRARY OF CONGRESS.

Georgia, North Carolina, and Tennessee troops gained the rear. The Eighty-Ninth Illinois vanished, leaving only the Fifteenth Ohio to make a brief, futile stand before its men, too, took to their heels and skedaddled. Disaster unfolded. Colonel Gibson eventually assumed command of the brigade, but all sense of organization disintegrated as Union soldiers ran for their lives.[59]

Willich heard the commotion and leapt onto his horse, desperate to rejoin his command. He was accompanied by brigade surgeon Dr. Gustavus A. Kunkler. Johnson also mounted, but a wise aide advised him not to follow lest he be captured.[60] Amid the smoke and confusion, Willich and Kunkler galloped directly into McNair's Arkansans, who were mopping up what was left of Kirk's broken brigade. James Stone, a volunteer aide to General McNair, confronted Willich and demanded his surrender, but Willich and Kunkler turned their horses and fled. Both mounts were brought down. Kunkler's horse was killed instantly as grapeshot pierced his heart and a spent ball wounded the doctor in the chest.[61] A cannonball shattered the hind leg of Willich's horse, but the general was not injured. Stone took Willich's sword and led him away.[62]

The battle raged on. The Union right folded back almost to the Nashville Turnpike until the rebels, winded from driving them nearly three miles on no sleep and little food, finally exhausted themselves.[63] The next day, the two armies mostly rested and tended to many thousands wounded, only to take up the battle again on January 2. Despite their near annihilation on New Year's Eve Day, Willich's boys of the Thirty-Second Indiana played a contributing role in the ultimate triumph of Rosecrans's army.

Gibson moved Willich's brigade into reserve position near the center of the Union line. The rebel attack commenced at 4:00 p.m., and a Union artillery barrage from the fifty-seven guns of Capt. John Mendenhall's battery on an eminence near McFadden's Ford stymied the enemy advance. A determined counterattack by the Union left wing succeeded in driving the rebels back. While most of the Union left had crossed Stones River in pursuit, Brig. Gen. John M. Palmer's Second Division of Maj. Gen. Thomas L. Crittenden's corps was in trouble. The unit's right flank was harassed by elements of the Second and Sixth Kentucky and by two Louisiana regiments who emerged from shelter in a belt of timber on the west side of the river.[64] Palmer ordered Gibson to detach a regiment to the fray and dislodge them with the bayonet. The Thirty-Second Indiana responded with typical enthusiasm, helping to drive the rebels across the river despite heavy casualties. Bragg's army was in full flight. Papa Willich would have been proud.

The two great armies suffered more than twenty-four thousand casualties. Willich's brigade sustained a horrendous loss. Nearly a hundred men died on the field, and another 365 were wounded. Moreover, at least 682 soldiers in Willich's brigade were missing.[65] Most of the missing had been captured. Following the carnage at Shiloh and Stones River, the Sixth Brigade of the Second Division could muster only 30 percent of its former strength as soldiers dug in for the winter at Murfreesboro. The maelstrom of war in unimaginable scale had invaded the lives of the soldiers under Willich's command. "Six hundred German patriots have sealed their love for their adoptive country with their blood," Capt. William G. Mank of the Thirty-Second Indiana wrote in early 1863. "Enough for a regiment in one year!"[66]

Chapter Thirteen

• •

CAPTIVE

WILLICH JOINED THOUSANDS of captured Union soldiers marching to the rear of the Confederate lines. They crossed the railroad bridge and caught a glimpse of Braxton Bragg directing operations from an eminence east of Stones River. Jubilant guards herded the captives into the walled courthouse yard in Murfreesboro. They told prisoners that they were lucky, since rebels would raise the black flag and kill those captured the following day, when Lincoln's Emancipation Proclamation was to take effect.[1] A fellow prisoner observed Willich wringing his hands and moaning, "My poor boys! My poor boys!"[2]

Some fifty commissioned officers were moved upstairs to make room for more Yankee prisoners. Willich's remorse turned to anger. He launched into a withering criticism of division commander Richard W. Johnson, blaming him for the rout of the Union right wing. Johnson certainly deserved censure, but so did McCook and all brigade commanders on the right. Even the experienced Willich had ignored his instincts and left his command at a critical moment. His brigade decimated, Willich and his comrades were forced to sign a parole of honor, promising not to fight the Confederates until exchanged. Their day of deliverance was much further in the future than they anticipated.[3]

Willich gazed out the courthouse window at smoke from the battle two miles to the northwest. His ears told him that the initial rout had turned into a desperate struggle. His eyes convinced him that rebel reports of Rosecrans in full retreat toward Nashville were false. The deluge of prisoners into the courthouse yard slowed to a mere trickle.[4]

Near nightfall, cannons still thundered. Willich and his famished, exhausted comrades marched to the rail station, loaded themselves into boxcars, and began their journey south. The prisoners demanded rations, which were promised upon arrival at Tullahoma late in the evening. When they finally arrived, the prisoners were given a single hard biscuit. The next day, they received only water until they reached Chattanooga late in the evening of January 1, 1863. Willich and his companions were shuttled to a warehouse on the outskirts of town, then back to the cars for a night ride into Georgia. By early morning, the men had reached Atlanta for what most figured would be a short stay. It turned out to last several weeks.[5]

Just days after Willich's arrival in Atlanta, Confederate president Jefferson Davis issued a proclamation declaring that captured Union officers should be considered complicit in fomenting slave rebellion, delivered up to local authorities, and jailed in civil prisons with common criminals. Willich believed this fate was just slightly better than being handed over to a lynch mob.

The captives walked mere steps to their place of confinement, a fine three-story brick building at the corner of Whitehall and Alabama Streets. It looked clean and spacious from the outside, and it was close by the railroad car shed, where prisoners could watch troops and supplies being sent to the front. The building had been the local Masonic hall until 1860. Merchants Brown and Fleming occupied the bottom two floors. On the third floor, where prisoners were housed, various stands and platforms remained, along with two grand crystal chandeliers. The filthy interior looked deserted. In fact, it was crowded with tiny neighbors who would make days unbearable and nights devoid of slumber. The makeshift prison was infested with lice.[6]

Willich's fair, thin skin made him an easy mark for the ravenous insects. The fifty-two-year-old general was so pestered by unwelcome bedmates he thought they, rather than the rebel army, would end his time on earth. He procured large quantities of mercurial ointment from well-meaning local citizens, but the medicine made him ill and did little to alleviate his suffering. After a hospital stay of several days, an emaciated Willich returned to his friends complaining, "If I stay here, the little vermin will kill me. If I use medicine, the medicine kills me. So, I think boys," he whimpered, "I am done for."[7]

Even so, Willich did survive his ordeal, and life in the prison was not all pain and drudgery. Captives enjoyed an unlimited supply of gas for the chandeliers, using their bright light to enliven cheery stag dances and other amusements. General Willich gave lectures on military tactics. Another officer recited Shakespeare, and a third led prisoners in exercise routines. In-

FORMER MASONIC HALL IN ATLANTA THAT HOUSED WILLICH
AND OTHER UNION OFFICER PRISONERS FOLLOWING THEIR CAPTURE
AT STONES RIVER. LIBRARY OF CONGRESS.

mates enjoyed chess, checkers, and cards. In addition, curious citizens and other visitors paid calls on the captives frequently. Pretty Atlanta girls walking by made fun of the Union soldiers. Novelist and dedicated supporter of the Confederacy Augusta Evans looked in on the prisoners one day. Visits from Confederate officers revealed rumors of a planned Northwest Confederacy. Later investigations would prove such schemes were a real threat. James Whelan, the Catholic bishop of Nashville, also stopped in to chat. Whelan was a stalwart Union man who would eventually be driven from his pulpit due to his political sympathies. He and other like-minded people looked for ways to comfort the captured soldiers.[8]

Following the horrific battle at Shiloh Church in Tennessee, prisoners began arriving in Atlanta in significant numbers during the spring and summer of 1862. Atlanta's secret circle of Union supporters did whatever they could safely do to help Federal prisoners as they passed through town. Local Union men, women, and even children took great risks to assist captured soldiers by placing money in newspapers, books, and pies on clandestine visits to railcars and prisons. One Atlanta newspaper reported with frustration that respectable ladies of the community brought bouquets of flowers and strawberries to the Yankee prisoners.[9]

Food supplied to the prisoners in Atlanta barely sufficed to keep them alive. Once a day, a slave entered the prison with a small supply of boiled beef and cornbread. "Here's your meat! Here's your cornbread!" the man exclaimed. Paroled officers were allowed to keep money and personal possessions, creating a thriving underground economy in edible contraband. Greenbacks were worth twice their face value in Confederate currency, so captives traded their cash for sweet potatoes, onions, and butter. They combined these items with meat to concoct a tasty stew cooked in an oyster can in one of three small fireplaces, using green pine logs as fuel. One or two prisoners at a time were allowed to shop at the market accompanied by a guard. They paid exorbitant prices for basic foodstuffs. On one such trip, a Union prisoner got into serious trouble.[10]

Lady luck had smiled on Lieut. John F. Elliott of the Thirty-Sixth Illinois Infantry in the weeks before the Murfreesboro Campaign. He was flush with gambling winnings when captured, and he managed to conceal this fact from his captors. One day in early February, Elliott tried to purchase supplies with a large stash of counterfeit Confederate bills. An Atlanta citizen came to the prison and accused Elliott of trafficking in bogus currency. He was searched, then whisked away to a judge who indicted him. Elliott was told that he would be tried in civil court on the fourth Monday in March. His friends feared for his life and immediately began planning his escape.[11] They got their chance a few weeks later.

On February 25, a Confederate officer entered the prison with welcome news. Willich and his comrades would finally leave for Richmond and be exchanged. The prisoners were in good spirits as they scrambled into boxcars that evening and headed east. Seventy-five officers crammed into one car, including Willich and Lieutenant Elliott. They immediately executed

Elliott's escape plan. The lieutenant changed clothes with Capt. D. A. Briggs of the Second Indiana Cavalry, who had somehow acquired a Confederate uniform. Willich gave him a field map. Others supplied Elliott with a pocket compass, a few dry biscuits, and nine dollars in genuine Confederate currency. When the train stopped for water at Conyers, Georgia, he slipped out the boxcar door and vanished into the night. Thirty days later, after walking three hundred miles, fording streams, and hiding out, Elliott limped into the Union army's Camp Davis near Corinth, Mississippi, still wearing the purloined rebel uniform. Officers of the Fourth Ohio were rightly suspicious of his story, but Elliott's brother Charles was fortunately in camp with the Seventh Ohio and vouched for his sibling.[12]

Willich and the balance of the Union prisoners reached Augusta the day after Elliot's escape, lodging in a large warehouse. That evening, Willich found a German inn and enjoyed a brief respite from his troubles with a dozen German musicians and a German professor.[13] The next day they hopped aboard passenger cars for the journey across South Carolina. Prisoners foraged for their own vittles when the trains stopped. At Weldon, North Carolina, the captives' patience finally ran out, and they demanded and received food. Morale improved as they pulled into Richmond. Freedom appeared close at hand. Hopes were dashed, however, as the men marched to their new home, the infamous Libby Prison.[14]

· · · · ·

The "Hotel de Libby," as Union prisoners dubbed it, had a well-earned reputation for its lack of basic amenities. The building was built in 1860 by Luther Libby, a wealthy ship captain from Maine. He and his son had operated a grocery and ship chandler business in town beginning in 1854. Libby's storehouse lay in "Tobacco Row," close to the railroad and the James River in a neighborhood of warehouses, shanties, and vacant lots. It was remote from downtown and an ideal location for receiving and safeguarding prisoners. When war broke out, Confederate authorities seized Libby's warehouse and the property of other suspected Union sympathizers and converted it to military use. Flat iron bars were installed over the windows to suit the building's new purpose. The large wooden sign lettered "Libby and Son" was retained as a subtle reminder to Richmond citizens that disloyalty to the new Confederacy would not be tolerated.

The three-story prison fronted Cary Street. Because the land sloped down to the Lynchburg Canal in the rear, a fourth room in the building was

LIBBY PRISON, RICHMOND, VIRGINIA, IN 1863. LIBRARY OF CONGRESS.

situated below ground level. This area functioned as a dank, filthy dungeon for those unfortunate prisoners to whom Confederate authorities meted out especially harsh punishment.[15] Libby's first and second stories housed prisoners in three walled-off forty-five-by-ninety-foot rooms on each floor. The middle room on the ground floor was reserved for cooking. Prisoners had limited access to the kitchen, and Union soldiers handed bread to comrades in the dungeon through holes in the floor. The prison's running water, a foul liquid piped directly from the river, allowed for a makeshift water closet in the upper two stories. Libby Prison was designed to house seven hundred prisoners. By the time Willich arrived, nearly twice that number occupied the building.[16]

Libby Prison had an infamous reputation. The Confederate officer in charge, Maj. Thomas P. Turner, was renowned for his cruel treatment of prisoners.[17] Of the jailer's cadre of guards, none was more feared than a vicious Russian bloodhound named Hero. This imposing creature stood three feet, two inches tall at the shoulder and weighed nearly two hundred pounds. Gaunt, weak prisoners were no match for the muscular beast, so Hero was a strong deterrent to the frequent escape attempts that plagued most Civil

War prisons.[18] Although a significant escape did take place later in the war, in the spring of 1863 Libby was considered one of the toughest jailbreaks in the Confederacy.

Willich and his fellow inmates stepped off the stone sidewalk through the prison door and emptied their pockets. "Fresh fish," as new prisoners were called, were segregated by rank. Officers enjoyed slightly better air in the upper stories, while enlisted men occupied lower floors or were shipped out to other locales. Guards issued worn, soiled blankets crawling with lice. Men slept packed together in a six-by-two-foot space on the floor, much like the ancestors of the African slaves Willich was fighting to liberate. Prisoners were kept at least three feet away from the small windows, which left nearly half the room in semidarkness. The only music came from the clattering of rain on the tin roof, a hollow song like a funeral dirge. Libby's air was putrid and still, and every conceivable variety of vermin crawled from its cracks and crevices. Its inmates were tortured day and night.[19] Willich shared his favorite remedy, a "blue precipitate," with Lieut. Col. James Shanklin. When Shanklin died soon after his release, Willich admitted that the medicine probably accelerated his demise.[20] Lying on the hard floor with his head resting on his arm, the brigadier general had ample time to reflect on mistakes made in the Battle of Stones River and to ponder his future. He put that time to good use.

One thing that frustrated Willich was armies' inability to transport troops across rivers and large streams quickly and efficiently. He had helped introduce the idea of "pioneer" companies constructing wagons that converted to pontoon bridges. But this significant innovation still delayed an army for hours or even days. Willich had a better solution. He designed an amphibious vehicle that used removable wheels and a water-tight outer shell to convert from a wagon to a boat quickly and safely. Each conveyance held twenty men. Willich constructed a prototype after his release from prison, promoting the idea with Rosecrans and other senior Union military leaders. Yet the new design was never adopted.[21] Despite his engineering education and accomplishments in the field, Willich had a hard time convincing his superiors that a lowly "Dutchman" could ideate better than a West Point graduate. He had another scheme up his sleeve, however, that he would implement on his own.

The old man understood that rate of fire was a critical part of success on the battlefield, especially when combined with adroit tactical maneuvering. Recent innovations like the rifled musket held some promise of extended range and improved accuracy at a distance, but infantry still had to stop after each shot; grab, tear, and charge the cartridge; ram the ball; and then prime, aim, and shoot. This took precious time, about twenty seconds on average.

In certain situations, sharpshooters were furnished with an assistant who would hand them a freshly loaded weapon. Such an arrangement worked only when the firing line was entrenched or in a stationary position behind a wall. The technique also took guns out of the hands of able soldiers. The new Spencer repeating rifle was a terrific innovation but expensive and scarce. How could a line sustain firing while advancing against an enemy? Willich believed he had the answer.

Willich's technique featured what he called "advance firing." Instead of approaching in one long line, stopping to fire, and then taking time to reload, troops employing advance firing created a continuous hail of lead during a sustained movement toward the foe. Here's how it worked: Soldiers formed a line of battle in four ranks. In succession, each rank advanced a few paces beyond the rank ahead of it after the front rank had fired. Each man passed to the left of the fellow in front of him. By the time that the fourth rank had discharged a volley, the first rank again advanced to the front line and fired again, the soldiers having had plenty of time to reload and prepare their weapons. The concept was simple and adapted from earlier iterations Willich recalled from his military school training. Willich remembered a technique known as "hedgerow fire" that had been used successfully with European skirmishers, and believed it could be adapted to the company and regimental level during combat. He would use it sparingly but with great success.[22]

By the end of his stay at Hotel de Libby, Willich hardly resembled the hale and hearty man that many had come to know as one of the finest leaders in the army. Threadbare clothes hung loosely on his withered frame. Willich was so worn from worry, cold, and starvation that his usual cheerful, warm disposition turned cross and cranky. Fellow prisoners allotted him a corner where he paced back and forth like a caged lion.[23] One day, a group of God-fearing Union soldiers requested that a chaplain visit the prison and conduct a prayer service. Willich stood quietly as captives sung hymns and prayed for the unfortunate, including the piteous prisoners themselves. The rebel chaplain then recited a prayer for President Davis and his cabinet, the Confederate army, and the rebel cause. The old Prussian could abide it no longer. "Stop Mr. chaplain!" Willich cried out in a booming voice. "Stop the damned prayer!" The preacher did not say another word and headed for the door.[24]

Willich's long incarceration ended in early May 1863. He and a few dozen fellow prisoners marched to the railroad depot and boarded cars bound for Petersburg. Their next stop was City Point, where the formal exchange was made on May 5. Willich, the oldest and highest-ranking prisoner, led Union soldiers as they climbed aboard the truce ship *State of Maine*. They proceeded to the vessel's stern, uncovered their heads, and gazed on the American flag for the first time in months. Tears streamed down the old man's face as he saluted the flag once, paused, then repeated the gesture with a long, reverent raise of his hand. Finally, he doffed his cap and made a deep, prolonged bow before the Star-Spangled Banner. Capt. Jefferson E. Brant of the Eighty-Fifth Indiana witnessed the moment and forgave Willich "for all his fretfulness and profanity while in prison." The group stood and stared at their flag in silence, waiting for the ship to depart.

The *State of Maine* steamed down the James River, passing rebel batteries and the spot in Hampton Roads where the sailing frigate USS *Cumberland* had been sunk by the CSS *Virginia*. The *Cumberland*'s flag still fluttered on the masthead of the half-submerged warship. Willich arrived in the harbor at Annapolis early the following morning.[25] When he traveled to Washington City, he had a difficult time securing a meeting with the War Department. According to Willich, the president himself was the only man who seemed to share his passion in defeating the rebellion, so he requested an interview with the commander in chief. He met with President Lincoln two days later on May 8.[26]

The president listened carefully as Willich described the condition of Richmond and other intelligence he had gathered on his sojourn across the Deep South. Willich called the region "a graveyard of walking corpses," explaining how boys and men of all ages were "placed in irons and dragged like wild animals from prison to prison because they refuse[d] to enter the army." Rebel officers approached Union prisoners offering to exchange three, four, or even five dollars in Confederate currency for one dollar in US greenbacks.[27] Willich also compared the Confederacy to "a little bladder filled with very bad air," remarking, "Once you prick it, it sinks with a great stink."[28] Furthermore, the old man told Lincoln that "there was not a sound pair of legs" in Richmond, suggesting that had US troops known how poorly defended the city was, they "could have fetched Jeff Davis and his consorts out of the city."[29]

Willich had plenty of advice for the president. He and Mr. Lincoln held similar ideas when it came to politics and war, and they also shared a love for colorful imagery in their storytelling. Willich described the war as a battle between a Union elephant and a Confederate dog. The dog constantly harassed the elephant, biting at his feet, while the elephant kicked back, trying to knock him down. Willich told the president that the war would end when "the elephant gets mad, drives the dog into a corner, and tramples the life out of the damn beast."³⁰ If only Lincoln could get his top generals to act like raging bull elephants rather than plodding, annoyed pachyderms, the republican Union could be saved.

The gaunt, careworn old general made his way back to Cincinnati, where Judge Johann B. Stallo and friends cared for him during his recuperation. By May 13, Willich was well enough to attend a reception in his honor in the courtyard of Turner Hall. The building itself was too small to accommodate the four thousand well-wishers. Veterans of the Ninth Ohio Infantry band played a familiar marching tune as Willich and Stallo appeared on the balcony, whereupon the judge delivered a brief address. The crowd erupted in cheers as Willich stepped forward to speak. He thanked the community for their support. "Every handshake has been in part an expression of thanks," Willich began, "for the humble service I have given to the republic." He then related his experiences as a prisoner in the South, just as he had done with President Lincoln. His most important message, however, focused on how the need to win the war had taken on greater significance and urgency during the watershed year of 1863.³¹

Willich explained that "when the war began it was viewed merely as a battle about nationality." He admitted that he wanted to prove to the nativists that Germans were worthy citizens. Those efforts were not as successful as he had hoped, as prejudice against immigrants lingered in the army and on the home front. German regiments like the Ninth Ohio and Thirty-Second Indiana "have always brought honor to the German name," Willich insisted with pride, "and through them the insulting words 'Damned Dutchmen' have become words of honor." "We Germans are also republicans," the general exclaimed while the crowd cheered.³²

Mr. Lincoln had transformed the limited aims of the war in his Emancipation Proclamation. "As it turns out," the old general continued, this war was "in the interest of all humanity." Willich concluded his speech with a call to action. He urged "all Northern friends of the South" to take a look at the true condition of the Confederate States, rather than the mythical image of a noble Southern society they had fabricated in their own minds. The South was an educational and cultural wasteland, Willich argued. Poor, illiterate white families "live in the woods in the outlying regions and among the swine," he observed. When Willich asked a literate black slave why poor whites supported rich slaveholders in this conflict, the slave said he took pity on them for their ignorance. The war had severed "the old and rotten relationship" between Southern agriculture and Northern industry, Willich claimed. Its successful conclusion promised "a new immigration" that would transform the South into a vibrant and productive region for all citizens, not just the wealthy. "We must break down the rich Southern planters who form the aristocracy," the brigadier pleaded, and prosecute the war "with all our might." The gathering broke up amid hurrahs and patriotic music from the military band.[33]

Willich's former comrades Karl Marx and Friedrich Engels followed progress of the American Civil War daily, given its critical importance to democratic aspirations across the globe. Marx lauded Lincoln's Emancipation Proclamation as "the most important document in American history, tantamount to tearing up the old American Constitution." Engels, unlike Marx, was an expert on military strategy. He understood, perhaps earlier and better than many Union military leaders, that control of the key railroad junctions in Chattanooga and Atlanta was critical to defeating the Confederacy. It must have cheered them to see Willich returning to active duty in the Western Theatre of the war, for despite past feuds, neither doubted the old warrior's proven talent for military leadership or his commitment to radical revolution.[34]

Willich's homecoming tour continued as he made his way back to his command. On May 20, three male singing clubs serenaded him in Louisville, performing songs from the Fatherland. He and Adjt. Carl Schmitt, himself recently released from Confederate prison, journeyed to Indianapolis, where Willich spoke in Woodland Garden.[35] The old man was anxious to reunite with his boys, but he had not missed much while he was away. Rosecrans and his army had spent the last several months licking their wounds and preparing for a bold assault that would finally drive the rebels out of Middle Tennessee and force them to abandon Chattanooga. For Willich and his brigade, a year that started so ingloriously would culminate with their leader burnishing his reputation as one of the most accomplished brigadiers in the Union army.

Chapter Fourteen

• •

BLOW FIGHT!

COL. WILLIAM HARVEY GIBSON was a busy man during the first five months of 1863. The senior regimental commander in Willich's Second Brigade, Gibson was accustomed to filling in for his brigade leader. While Willich languished in Confederate prison, Gibson ensured that the Old One's high standards were upheld.[1] To keep troops healthy and fit, Willich insisted they be kept active in camp lest they fall victim to illness and grumbling. To maintain combat readiness, Willich drilled his men incessantly. One of Willich's favorite adages was "A drop of sweat on the drill-ground will save many drops of blood on the battlefield."[2] The stand-in brigade commander made sure that his charges lived by that maxim. The resulting discipline ended up paying big dividends.

Willich returned to his boys in Murfreesboro, Tennessee, on May 25, 1863. His staff presented him with a new sword purchased by the men of the brigade. Willich clutched the weapon, reminding those with him that the aims of the war had expanded to include liberation of two-thirds of America's four million slaves. "I fought for liberty in the old country," he began. "I fight for liberty in this country. If I thought that in this war I was helping to bind the chains on one little negro," he asserted, "I would not strike one blow with this little thing."[3] Later, the men of the Fifteenth Ohio assembled in front of Papa's tent. "I am so glad to see you; I could just take you in my arms and kiss you!" the general gushed. Before riding off to greet another regiment, Willich told them he had "some little things" to tell them once he got the brigade together.[4]

Drilling intensified under Willich's watchful eye—squad drills, company drills, battalion drills. Every day that did not include pouring rain witnessed the brigadier's troops sweating it out on the practice field. Willich paid special attention to the brigade drill, personally directing and reviewing large, complex maneuvers that often started at 5:00 a.m. and lasted more than three hours. One afternoon, the entire brigade practiced combat simulation. Their objective was to capture the Franklin Road Bridge across Stones River. Willich outlined an elaborate mock battle situation including enemy positions, line of attack, and movements designed to deal with various contingencies. His men found this type of drilling "interesting and instructive," as opposed to parade marching from a military manual.[5] The general believed that the main obstacle to successful military training was "the professional canonization of mere useless and stupid formalities."[6]

One of the "little things" that Willich promised his brigade was the new maneuver he had perfected while imprisoned. The old man believed that skirmishers played an essential role in combat, and he advocated "main firing . . . done by skirmish lines" rather than by the "weak lines of the regulations." Only after skirmishers have been driven back, or only in the case of a forward charge, should the main line of infantry engage the enemy. These beliefs, along with his fondness for small column formations, were consistent with Prussian tactical theory going back to Frederick the Great. In fact, Willich believed that the best tactics used by effective skirmishing should be applied to line troops when the time was ripe.[7] Foremost among these was the technique of advance firing. Willich adapted this technique and employed it with each regiment under his command. After a bit of confusion, his soldiers took to it with ease.

Willich described advance firing as if he were watching it unfold before his eyes. The regiment formed a line of battle in four ranks. The first rank fired, then stopped to load while the other ranks advanced a few paces, fired, and allowed the next rank to advance. "The whole line advances rapidly, sending volley after volley—a stream of lead—into the wavering lines of the enemy," Willich explained.[8] At first, some soldiers botched the exercise by passing to the right of the men in their front, instead of on the left as prescribed. "Two men must not try to go through the same hole!" the old man shouted with irritation and amusement. After a little practice, each regiment grasped the maneuver and executed the drill with precision. It would not be long before they used it on a real battlefield in a critical situation.[9]

• • • • •

President Lincoln and general-in-chief Henry Halleck were losing patience with William S. Rosecrans. Though he barely avoided disaster at Stones River, Rosecrans was nonetheless lauded as a hero. The Northern press transformed a bloody, inconclusive tactical draw into a sorely needed Union strategic victory. Now Lincoln wanted Rosecrans to go after Bragg, drive him from Tennessee, and destroy his battered army. However, Rosecrans refused to budge. He vowed not to traverse the thousand-foot rise of the Cumberland Plateau without a huge train of arms and supplies needed to ensure success. He pleaded for more horses and mules despite the fact that he already had more than forty thousand animals. Had they been at Rosecrans's disposal, all the gun factories in country could not have supplied the number of repeating rifles the general insisted he needed to complete his mission. A fleet of gunboats to patrol the Cumberland River would also be nice, Rosecrans added wishfully.

Lincoln struggled to control his temper. "I would not push you to any rashness," the president wrote Rosecrans on May 28. Lincoln added that he was "very anxious" that Rosecrans get going to keep Bragg from reinforcing Johnston against Grant. "Dispatch received," Rosecrans replied curtly. "I will attend to it." He then developed a brilliant plan. Rosecrans aimed to dislodge Confederate forces from entrenched positions north of Duck River and about twenty miles north of the railroad junction at Tullahoma and drive them back to the doorstep of Chattanooga. The gateway to the Deep South would then be his for the taking.[10]

Rosecrans's complex, audacious scheme involved challenging Bragg's strong defensive positions along the imposing Highland Rim in the heart of Middle Tennessee. Rosecrans would first send Brig. Gen. David S. Stanley's cavalry and Maj. Gen. Gordon Grainger's two divisions to feint an attempt to turn the Confederate left managed by Lieut. Gen. Leonidas Polk near the town of Shelbyville. That would hold Polk in position. After making contact, the balance of Rosecrans's huge army would wheel right and attack the rebel center held by Lieut. Gen. William J. Hardee, holding those two divisions in place. This was no mean feat. Maj. Gen. Alexander McCook's Twentieth Corps would blast through Liberty Gap in the middle of Hardee's lines while Maj. Gen. George Thomas's Fourteenth Corps fought its way through Hoover's Gap to the east on Hardee's right flank. Rosecrans left the principal assault in the hands of Twenty-First Corps commander Thomas L. Crittenden, who positioned his troops beyond Bragg's right flank. If all went as planned, Crittenden would plow through Gillie's Gap and occupy the town of Manchester northeast of Tullahoma. At precisely 3:00 a.m. on June 24, the Union army advanced.[11]

Willich received orders to march at 5:00 a.m., but he had to wait three hours in torrential rain for other commands to move out of his way before beginning a trudge through the mud. Once Gen. Phil Sheridan's Third Division had cleared his front, Willich's First Brigade led Richard W. Johnson's Second Division down a slippery dirt road toward Old Millersburg, where they rested at noon. As of that time, the Federals had seen no sign of the enemy. Willich sent five companies of Col. Thomas J. Harrison's newly mounted Thirty-Ninth Indiana ahead to reconnoiter. Harrison's men were brimming with confidence, having recently been issued the same new Spencer repeating rifles that would make Col. John T. Wilder's mounted "Lightning Brigade" famous. Harrison's troops had a good look at the imposing obstacle they faced.

Hardee chose a formidable defensive position at a defile between two steep 350-foot hills at the entrance to Liberty Gap, four miles north of Bell Buckle, Tennessee. He stationed reserves on the crests of these knobs, which were bare on the bottom halves but covered with trees and large rocks in the upper regions. If Willich was not careful he might lead his brigade into a shooting gallery in a narrow, cleared valley just beyond the entrance to the gap. Harrison probed forward, skirmishing with about eight hundred rebels. The two Confederate regiments occupying the gap, the Fifth Arkansas on the rebel left and the consolidated Thirteenth/Fifteenth Arkansas on the right, belonged to Brig. Gen. St. John Liddell's brigade in Cleburne's division. Around 2:00 p.m., Willich brought the rest of the brigade up to the skirmish line, prompting rebel skirmishers to fall back to their reserves in the hills. A frontal attack would be suicide. The only way to take the gap, Willich determined, would be to outflank the Confederates on both sides. This risky ploy would stretch Willich's brigade thin, leaving it susceptible to puncture. Union general Johnson understood the predicament, so he placed the Second Brigade at Willich's disposal. Both armies hurried men to their flanks in the opening hours of a two-day contest to control Liberty Gap.[12]

Willich ordered the Forty-Ninth Ohio to deploy eight companies to the east of Liberty Pike, but Colonel Gibson reported that he was still outflanked. Two reserve companies from the Thirty-Second Indiana marched on the double-quick to his aid. Colonel Harrison and his five mounted companies galloped at full speed to Willich's left flank, arriving just in time to repel two hundred rebel infantrymen. Gibson then seized the initiative, sending three companies dashing up the hill amid a furious hail of enemy projectiles. Willich ordered the two Indiana companies forward in support. At one point, the advancing Union troops halted briefly, stunned by flanking fire on their

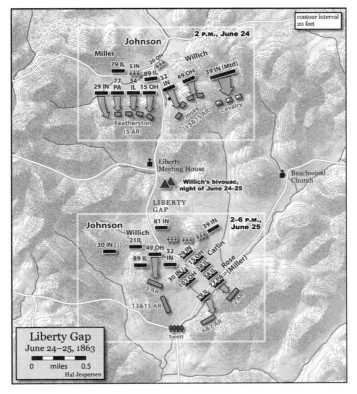

LIBERTY GAP

left, but Harrison and his Spencer rifles took care of that threat.[13] The rebels fled and the bluecoats took their hilltop camp, replete with tables set for the afternoon meal. Meanwhile, on Willich's right, another fierce struggle was taking place.[14]

Lieut. Frank Askew, commander of the Fifteenth Ohio Infantry, faced a similar challenge. A convex open slope of seven hundred yards lay between Askew and his goal, a rebel force sheltered by innumerable rocks and a long fence fronting a dense stand of timber. The enemy's left flank extended past the end of the Ohioan's line, rounding the brow of the hill. Willich sent the Twenty-Ninth Indiana and Seventy-Seventh Pennsylvania from the Second Brigade to Askew's right, instructing them to flank the enemy, change front perpendicular to the Ohioans, and attack up the hill in the rear of the enemy's lines. At the same time, Askew's men struggled up a steep slope, grasping bushes and saplings to pull themselves forward. The Fifteenth Ohio received most enemy fire, losing fifteen men.

By the time Second Brigade regiments arrived in support, they encountered little resistance as surprised rebels abandoned their camps and ran down the opposite side of the hill. Union troops chased them for a mile, then broke off the pursuit. Late that afternoon, Confederate general Liddell received false intelligence of a Union withdrawal back through the gap, so he sent skirmishers forward to investigate. Instead of abandoned campsites, Liddell's men ran into Willich's skirmishers and pulled back. General Johnson called a halt to the action and ordered his division to bivouac in the vicinity of Liberty Meeting House. Superior numbers and tactics had trumped strong defensive position. Despite driving rain, weary Union soldiers slept soundly through the night.[15]

The day had been a success for the Federals, just not in the way that Rosecrans had planned. Incessant rain and bloated baggage trains so delayed Crittenden that he was unable to execute his primary attack. So Rosecrans improvised, shifting his focus to Hoover's Gap, where Col. John Wilder's mounted brigade had blasted through the gap's southern terminus. This set the table for Thomas, who was also unable to get his corps in position. Willich would need to hold Liberty Gap throughout the next day while Bragg scrambled to stop the Federal advance toward Tullahoma.

Convinced that Cleburne's Confederate division had been reinforced overnight, Johnson had his Union division up and at arms at 3:00 a.m. on June 25 to guard against surprise attack. There would be no repeat of Stones River that day. Willich deployed skirmishers from the Thirty-Second Indiana to the left of the picket line across a valley bisected by the road to Bell Buckle. There the line connected with pickets and the skirmish line of the Eighty-Ninth Illinois on the right. Willich positioned the Illinois men between two hills, west to east. Instead of using his pickets as "a mere line of observation" as was customary, the brigadier general reinforced them with support companies in reserve, creating a long skirmish line that could fend off enemy feints "without alarming the camp." Willich wanted to fight the next phase of the struggle over Liberty Gap on his terms.[16]

Throughout the morning, small patrols of Confederate skirmishers and cavalry advanced from positions less than a thousand yards away to probe Willich's line. The old Prussian kept his men steady and out of range of rebel batteries posted on the opposite hills. A few brief, ineffectual skirmishes achieved nothing but presaged the hot contest to come. Around two in the afternoon, fighting began in earnest. Rebel troops advanced in line against

GENERAL WILLICH COMMANDING HIS BUGLER TO 'BLOW FIGHT!'
LIBERTY GAP, TENNESSEE, JUNE 1863. PENCIL AND WATERCOLOR
BY ADOLPH METZNER. LIBRARY OF CONGRESS.

the Union center. Another Confederate infantry brigade stood behind them in reserve.[17] Willich turned to his bugler and shouted, "Hornist, why don't you blow?" The bugler was confused. "What shall I blow?" The general replied, "Don't you see how the fight goes on? Don't you see the rebels getting away from that fence? Blow fight! Blow fight!"[18] Willich's fortified skirmish lines repelled several bold charges. Confederate and Union lines traded blows and positions, forward and back. After an hour-long firefight, Willich's frontline troops were nearly out of ammunition, so the old general called up reserves from the Fifteenth Ohio to relieve them. The rebels were desperate to dislodge Union troops from heights they had abandoned only twenty-four hours earlier, so they threw everything they had against the men in blue.

Willich placed Goodspeed's battery on a hundred-foot-high hill in the rear of his lines and opened fire against enemy batteries and rebel infantry. It was a dangerous ploy, as Union gunners had to fire low over their own troops to reach rebel targets. Some shells met their marks, but others fell as friendly fire despite precautions. As the afternoon wore on, dozens of dead and wounded soldiers littered the field as a hot skirmish morphed into full-fledged battle. By 5:00 p.m., Willich's front lines were running low on ammunition, and the rebels clung stubbornly to assault positions at the base of the hills. The old man sensed an opportunity to transition from defense to offense at this stage of the battle. He called on his last reserve regiment to inflict the killer blow. What happened next, according to Willich, was "a view not many are favored to witness."[19]

Colonel Gibson rushed his Forty-Ninth Ohio Regiment from reserve position in the forest to the base of a wooded hill behind the Thirty-Second Indiana. The soldiers wheeled right and passed through the ranks of cheering frontline troops amid heavy musket and artillery fire. A number of Indianans caught up in the excitement broke ranks and followed the Ohioans forward. Gibson advanced down a ridge in the woods and toward a low fence bordering a cornfield. One hundred yards away, rebels who had advanced under cover of their artillery formed a strong line in a gully behind some farm buildings and an orchard. At this critical juncture, Willich ordered Gibson to attack the enemy. "He directed me to try our drill," Gibson reported, "recently originated and introduced into the brigade."

Gibson issued the command: "Advance, firing!" The regiment formed in four ranks "as if on drill" and unleashed a withering, continuous fire that was delivered "with a regularity and rapidity that no veterans could withstand." A volley from the first rank had barely taken effect when the men of the fourth rank stepped forward and took their shots. The third rank followed in quick succession. As the second rank stepped up to fire, enemy bullets stopped arriving. Rebels retreated to a wooded hill beyond the cornfield. When the Forty-Ninth Ohio reached a low fence, Willich ordered the troops to halt. They could not pursue the enemy fast enough to avoid being raked by canister over four hundred yards of open ground.[20] A captured Confederate sergeant was stunned by Gibson's high rate of fire. "Lord Almighty, who can stand against that?" he asked. "Four lines of battle and every one of them firing?"[21] As Goodspeed's battery pounded away at the rebels, Gen. R. W. Johnson ordered his Second Brigade to relieve Willich and drive the Confederates down the Bell Buckle Road. The rebels were utterly routed. Willich's brigade lost fifty men but the enemy's losses were far greater. The gap was in Union hands.[22]

Willich's performance at Liberty Gap drew praise from all levels in the Army of the Cumberland. Rosecrans was quick to credit Johnson's division with the victory.[23] McCook pronounced himself "delighted" with their performance, calling it "worthy of Shiloh." He went on to say that he "had never witnessed such gallantry and heroism."[24] Willich, too, lauded his boys. "The highest ambition of a commander must be satisfied," the old warrior crowed, "by being associated with such men, who, through patriotism and love for the free institutions of their country, have attained a degree of efficiency which professional soldiers seldom, if ever, reach."[25] Lieut. Col. Frank Askew, commander of the Fifteenth Ohio, put his finger on the key reason for the brigade's success. "I think the general may flatter himself," Askew concluded, "that his unwearied exertions in drilling and disciplining his brigade were on these days to some extent rewarded."[26] Rosecrans outthought his enemy in this first stage of the new campaign. Willich outmaneuvered and outfought him.

Rosecrans and his large army moved cautiously south toward Chattanooga. They expected Bragg to turn at some point and fight a decisive battle, most likely at Tullahoma, where rebel entrenchments were strong. Smelling blood in the water, some Union generals urged their commander to press their opponent and destroy the Army of Tennessee. Willich claimed that "the tide of the rebellion [had] turned," and he argued that disheartened "evil spirits" of the Confederacy were "doomed to their just fate."[27] The Prussian's instincts about the state of Bragg's command were correct. Several of his highest-ranking subordinates had lost confidence in his leadership. Willich blamed poor weather for the Union's inability to finish the job. "Had it not been for the nearly impassable roads and fields," he speculated, "Bragg's army would have been destroyed."[28] Rosecrans's slow pursuit enabled Bragg to determine where and when he would make his next stand, so the rebels continued their retreat out of Middle Tennessee all the way to Chattanooga. On the evening of July 7, Bragg and his large army camped in the long shadow of Lookout Mountain and prepared for a battle that would turn the tables on the Federals and nearly annihilate them.

Chapter Fifteen

• • • • • • • • • • • • • • • • • • • •

IRON BRIGADE

LINCOLN COVETED CHATTANOOGA. Capturing the key railroad juncture was, in the president's own words, "fully as important as the taking and holding of Richmond."[1] The small but strategically located town was vital to maintaining supply lines as the Federals pushed farther into the Confederate heartland. "If we can hold Chattanooga and East Tennessee," Lincoln told Rosecrans, "I think the rebellion must dwindle and die."[2]

Rosecrans was typically cautious following a triumphal nine-day campaign that banished Bragg's army from the environs of Tullahoma. Frustrated by weeks of inaction, Halleck ordered the Army of the Cumberland to advance on Chattanooga immediately. Rosecrans ignored him. He would move when ready. Maj. Gen. George H. Thomas supported his commander's obstinance. Rosecrans wanted Chattanooga, but he also wanted to remove the only blemish from his brilliant Tullahoma Campaign. He yearned to destroy Bragg's army once and for all.

Rosecrans decided that the time was right on August 16, 1863. He set troops in motion, implementing a complex, risky plan to deceive Bragg. Rosecrans divided his three corps to speed his march through narrow mountain passes. As Bragg's intelligence was sketchy, the ruse worked. Rosecrans sent Col. John T. Wilder's mounted First Brigade of Maj. Gen. Joseph J. Reynolds's Fourth Division well north of Chattanooga to distract Bragg while the bulk of his army took three days to cross the Tennessee River. Confederates abandoned the city to avoid being trapped with no line of retreat. On September 9, Federals marched into Chattanooga. The balance of Rosecrans's force dispersed north and south of the town.[3]

GENERAL WILLICH IN CAMP WITH PET RACOON AND CIGAR NEAR LOOKOUT
MOUNTAIN, SEPT. 1863. WATERCOLOR BY ADOLPH METZNER. LIBRARY OF CONGRESS.

Rosecrans, too, had faulty intelligence; the information was created by
well-briefed Confederate soldiers posing as deserters. The Union commander
believed that Bragg was either retreating into Georgia toward Dalton and
Rome or was making his way to Atlanta. He ordered a pursuit, dismissing
the counsel of Thomas, who argued that the three corps were spread thin
and vulnerable should Bragg mount a concentrated attack. Rosecrans lacked
a critical piece of information that nearly proved fatal. Bragg had halted his
entire army only twenty miles south of Chattanooga at LaFayette, Georgia. Pigeon Mountain screened the large force from most of Gen. Thomas's
Fourteenth Corps, who were stationed in the vicinity of Lookout Mountain,
a day's ride to the west.

The cloud of disinformation lifted on both sides of the conflict during
the second week of September. Though Bragg discovered opportunities to
throw masses of men against advance divisions of two isolated Union army
corps, dissension and confusion within his senior leadership foiled those

plans. Bragg's generals were unable to execute his orders promptly in both instances, robbing him of probable victory. Rosecrans finally realized that the Confederate commander was not fleeing but had turned and concentrated his forces dangerously close to Thomas's lonely corps. "It was a matter of life and death," Rosecrans reported. He rushed Maj. Gen. Alexander McCook's Twentieth Corps from its base at Alpine, Georgia, to close up on Thomas's right. Unfamiliar with the road network, McCook chose a circuitous fifty-seven-mile route, taking three days to make the journey. He arrived just in time to save Thomas from disaster.[4]

The stage was set for a bloody, disjointed, and chaotic collision. Terrain near Chickamauga Creek was an army commander's nightmare. Large expanses of woodland defined the landscape from the LaFayette Road to the creek on the west. Scattered farm fields broke the monotony of rolling, wooded hills. Parts of the forest were open and afforded visibility of up to a hundred yards, but other places were so clogged with thickets and underbrush that soldiers could see little before them. Corps and division commanders had virtually no opportunity to view their entire force. Brigade leaders had trouble seeing the ends of their lines, much less the precise location of the enemy. Add smoke, noise, and general confusion to the mix, and the fog of war approached blackout conditions. Bragg and Rosecrans might have had strategic aims for the slugfest, but the outcome of this tumultuous affair would be determined largely by tactical decisions at the brigade and regimental level, as well as the fickle caprice of lady luck.[5]

•••••

Maj. Gen. George H. Thomas was convinced that Bragg intended to attack him in force from the north, turn his left flank, and place the Army of Tennessee between his corps and Chattanooga, effectively cutting off his retreat line to Rossville. That was precisely Bragg's intent. Rosecrans moved to counter that plan on September 18. Overnight, he shifted Thomas from the Union center to the extreme left, extending his line past the Confederate right. Thomas spent the late afternoon and evening of September 18 moving his corps about five miles to his left along Chickamauga Creek to Crawfish Springs. He then took a position near Kelly's farm on the LaFayette Road. Thomas's lead division, commanded by Absalom Baird, reached the location at daybreak. Bragg's plan would fail as long as Thomas held the Union left. Past midnight, Thomas requested support from McCook to help plug any gaps in his line that might appear due to the nocturnal maneuvers.

McCook detached Richard W. Johnson's Second Division, including Willich's First Brigade, to report to Thomas for the duration of the upcoming battle.[6]

Johnson arrived on the Poe field just south of the Kelly house around noon. By this time, a pitched battle on the Union left near Jay's Mill had already begun. Thomas and Johnson rode to the south end of Kelly field and imagined an unseen enemy they knew was there in force. Thomas instructed Johnson to move up in line of battle and engage the enemy wherever he found them. Johnson placed Philemon Baldwin's Third Brigade on the left and Willich on the right, with Col. Joseph Dodge's Second Brigade in reserve. The silence in that sector was surreal. Sgt. I. K. Young of Dodge's brigade recalled a bucolic scene with birds chirping and butterflies flitting about while a cow lazily chewed its cud. Ten minutes later it became "a raging hell."[7]

Willich arranged his regiments in a two-line formation that was double-column massed on center.[8] The Forty-Ninth Ohio and Thirty-Second Indiana formed the first line, left to right. Behind them Willich placed the Fifteenth Ohio and Eighty-Ninth Illinois. North of the Brock field three hundred yards away, Confederate brigadier general John Jackson of Cheatham's division awaited them. Jackson's Georgia and Mississippi troops had just spent five hours driving off the weary brigade of Col. John T. Croxton, whose men had been up all night. Advancing a few hundred yards, Willich's brigade was raked by shell and canister fire from Scogin's Georgia battery. Willich's men dropped to a prone position while Wilbur Goodspeed's battery of the First Ohio Light Artillery was brought forward to silence the rebel gunners. Opposing batteries dueled for a short time before the old Prussian executed a bold move.

Willich ordered a bayonet charge by his entire brigade front line on the double-quick shortly before 1:00 p.m. Jackson's rebels were almost out of ammunition, and they began retiring before Willich's troops gained their position. Willich's men reclaimed several guns that Baird had abandoned earlier in the day.[9] Jackson pleaded for relief, and Cheatham responded with the reserve brigade of Gen. George Maney, consisting of four Tennessee regiments. Maney's nine hundred men took position on a small ridge littered with dead rebels and peered over the crest. What they saw alarmed them.

Willich's two frontline regiments, the Forty-Ninth Ohio on the left and the Thirty-Second Indiana on the right, formed in four ranks and sounded the command: "Advance, firing!" Willich's excited troops raced headlong toward Maney's right, while Dodge's brigade closed on their left. Maney had no support on either side and not enough troops to cover the ridge.[10] In the midst of their second successful charge of the afternoon, some companies of

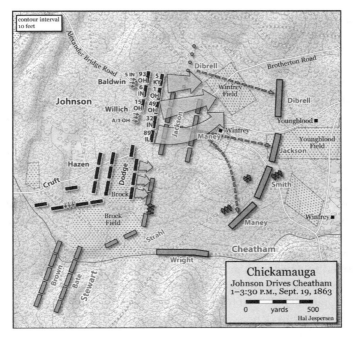

CHICKAMAUGA: JOHNSON DRIVES CHEATHAM

the Eighty-Ninth Illinois scrambled over one another to lay claim to artillery pieces rather than pursuing the enemy. Lieut. Col. Duncan Hall halted the regiment, pulled the men back twenty yards, and restored order. General Willich then arrived on the scene. Just as he had done with his Indianans at Shiloh, Willich turned his back to enemy fire, congratulated the Illinois boys on their success, and chided them for their exuberance. He refreshed Hall's troops on the technique of advance firing, drilled them for a short time in the manual of arms, re-formed them in four ranks, and ordered them to execute advance firing.[11] "I trust the time will come," Maj. William D. Williams wrote in his report, "when we can all sit by our peaceful firesides (when great command shall have been awarded him [Willich]) and recount the time when he was our brigade commander, standing in front of the regiment, amid the rain of bullets and shells, and drilling us into steadiness and confidence."[12]

Willich and Dodge swept Maney from the area. At 2:45 p.m., Willich halted near the west end of Winfrey field. Baldwin's brigade on Johnson's left flank had not been able to keep up with Willich, as the woods in the soldiers' path were dense. To the left of Baldwin was a gap more than a mile wide.

Willich told Johnson that Baldwin's left was hanging in the air. Johnson assured him that Brig. Gen. Absalom Baird's First Division of Thomas's Fourteenth Corps would be there soon. Yet hours passed with no sign of Baird.[13] Willich later complained that the absence of a frontline division on Johnson's left foiled the opportunity of the day. The Federals could have turned the Confederate right and won the battle, the frustrated Prussian speculated.[14] In the meantime, the rebels were regrouping for one last charge before the daylight disappeared.

On Cheatham's right, Lieut. Gen. Leonidas Polk dispatched the Confederates in Saint John Liddell's division, who were still recovering from intense firefights earlier in the day, to flank Baldwin from the north. Liddell's troops were also to harass Willich head on. Willich anticipated the move, suggesting that Baldwin face his second-line regiments, the Ninety-Third Ohio and Sixth Indiana, north to defend his left flank. Baldwin took his advice. A brigade of Arkansans commanded by Col. Daniel Govan overlapped Baldwin, ideally positioned to envelop them from the rear, but they could not see the opportunity through dense forest. The sun dipped below the treetops, creating random shafts of light that further obscured their vision. In such conditions, real-time decisions depended on instinct and experience. Willich had both in ample measure.

The rebels made their move shortly after 3:30 p.m. Mississippians under Brig. Gen. Edward Cary Walthall emerged from the timber, advancing gingerly across the Winfrey field to avoid dead and wounded comrades. Federals met them with muskets and artillery across an open field of fire. At the first volleys from Willich and Baldwin, the entire rebel brigade dropped to the earth. Fifteen minutes later they withdrew.

On Baldwin's left flank, Govan attacked the men in blue, briefly stunning them and mortally wounding Col. Hiram Strong, commander of the Ninety-Third Ohio. Baldwin grabbed the colors himself and urged the Ohioans to charge, shouting, "Rally round the flag, boys!" Willich galloped over to Baldwin's Sixth Indiana to spur them on. Rolling his hat into a tight club, the old general dashed among the Indianans, pausing every so often to "hit a fellow a crack over the back," all the while cursing in German and yelling in English, "Go in boys, and give 'em hell!" Willich's fine horse, a gift from the citizens of Cincinnati, was shot through the eye and shoulder.[15] Govan ultimately retreated into the twilight. Soldiers in this sector of the battlefield breathed a sigh of relief, anticipating sorely needed sleep. Instead, they got a dreadful nightmare.[16]

Liddell was far from done. Unsuccessful charges against Willich and Baldwin convinced him that the Union left was still vulnerable if fresh troops

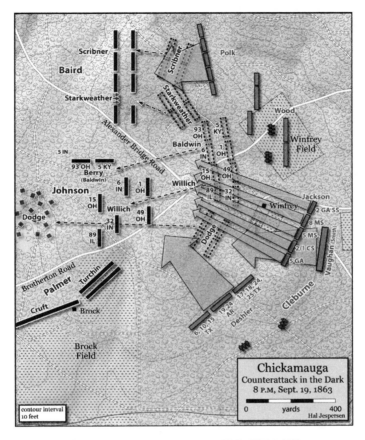

Chickamauga
Counterattack in the Dark
8 P.M, Sept. 19, 1863

contour interval
10 feet

0   yards   400
Hal Jespersen

CHICKAMAUGA: COUNTERATTACK IN THE DARK

could be thrown against it. He begged Maj. Gen. Patrick R. Cleburne to take
another shot at the Yankees, but the wily Irishman refused. Liddell then
went over his head. Corps commander Lieut. Gen. Daniel H. Hill agreed
with Liddell and ordered Cleburne's three brigades, numbering more than
five thousand men, to assemble in a mile-long line of battle facing Johnson's
division, which was concentrated in a crescent shape with its open end to the
rear. Cleburne's line extended past the enemy on both flanks. Johnson was
therefore in a precarious situation. To make matters worse, at the moment
that Cleburne deployed his line, General Thomas ordered Johnson to pull
back from his advance position to a ridge near the Kelly field. Baird's Union
division then began moving to its right to close up on Johnson. Thomas,
Baird, and Johnson left the area to survey their new position as daylight

diminished. Ten minutes before sunset, Cleburne's troops stepped forward to the eastern edge of Winfrey field.

The confusion of daytime battle paled when compared to the utter chaos of a night fight. Johnson's entire front was enveloped in a firestorm. The intensity of the exchange exceeded anything the Second Division had witnessed at Shiloh or Stones River. Gen. S. A. M. Wood's Confederate charge was barely visible in the gloaming. Only sounds and flashes from the dark forest gave soldiers an inkling of enemy positions. As Cleburne noted in his report, "Accurate firing was impossible." Friendly fire was rife on both sides as combatants groped their way forward, changed front, and fell back in a blind dervish of death and dismemberment. Officers strode blithely into enemy lines and were captured or shot. Tragically, this nocturnal horror accomplished little besides denuding each army's best divisions, resulting in casualties approaching 30 percent of effective strength.

The rebels hit Baldwin's brigade first, striking it at an oblique angle. The First Ohio shuddered and fell back. Baldwin, who was with his boys from the Sixth Indiana in the second line, grabbed the regimental colors and shouted, "Follow me!" When he turned his horse to face the enemy, he was shot dead. The fighting subsequently became hand to hand. Baldwin's shattered troops fell back.[17] Willich confronted the swarming rebels with two regiments and was swept aside. On Willich's right, Dodge was overrun, retiring in disarray. Willich's men retreated, firing as they withdrew, but the rebels kept coming. At a brief pause in the melee, Willich halted his troops and tried to settle them.

Three hundred yards to the rear of his original position, Willich formed his brigade into a semicircle as the soldiers received fire from three sides. "Dress on your colors," he commanded. After a few minutes, the men's adrenaline levels dropped to a manageable level.[18] During this lull, a rebel yelled to them that they were surrounded. "Surrender and you'll be safe," he screamed. "Never!" Union troops replied in unison. Then the members of Goodspeed's Battery A, First Ohio Light Artillery opened up with shot and shell on what they presumed was Confederate general John Jackson's reserve brigade.[19] Willich had dispatched Jackson near Brock field earlier in the day, and the rebel general wanted revenge. Cleburne concluded, however, that pitch-black darkness made further pursuit too dangerous, so Jackson and the balance of his division withdrew to the forest. Johnson's and Baird's divisions limped back to their bivouacs north of Brock field.[20] Exhausted soldiers dropped into slumber where they stood, but there would be little sleep for the officers in Rosecrans's army that evening.

Ambulance crews rescued wounded men from the battlefield amid sniper fire and the occasional solid shot. Surgeons worked all night amputating limbs during the season's first frost.[21] Rosecrans called his generals to the widow Glenn's house. The commanding general and his corps leaders decided not to retreat that evening. Instead, they would hold Thomas's left wing at all costs and look for opportunities to turn the tide against the rebels on September 20. The day had been a mixed bag of technical blunders and heroic defenses, just what one might expect on terrain where visibility was so limited. Rosecrans drew comfort from the fact that he had avoided disaster on his left, foiling Bragg's stubborn repeated attempts to turn Thomas's flank. Besides, Rosecrans still had an open line of retreat back to Chattanooga.[22] Willich himself was far from satisfied with the outcome of the day's morbid adventure. He was particularly sore with Absalom Baird, who had failed to appear at a critical moment.

Willich was not bashful when speaking his mind about his fellow officers' mistakes. Many of his superiors were products of West Point, an institution he neither honored nor respected. He was even less charitable when assessing the performance of peers appointed for political reasons and not because of their experience, talent, and intelligence.[23] However, despite the incompetence of some with stars on their shoulders, Willich ultimately respected the chain of command as integral to military discipline. After a frustrating day of botched maneuvers and missed opportunities left his cherished brigade nearly decimated, he tried to control his temper and prepare to do battle the next day.[24]

• • • • •

September 20 dawned with the opposing commanders focused on the same sector of the battlefield. Rosecrans fretted about his left. He began moving additional support to Thomas, to extend his line as far north as the McDonald house and Reed's Bridge Road. Meanwhile, Bragg's intelligence told of golden opportunity on his right, and the rebel commander envisioned a repeat of the first day of Stones River with a happier conclusion. Confederates would mass troops on an exposed Union flank, attack in overwhelming numbers at dawn, roll up the bluecoats north to south, and trap them in bottlenecks like McLemore's Cove. Rosecrans's entire army could be destroyed if all escape routes to the north were blocked. In what was becoming a familiar pattern, however, Bragg's communications failed him, and several of his key generals obfuscated. By three hours after daybreak, nothing had happened. Bragg's window of opportunity was closing.[25]

Rosecrans used the reprieve wisely, lengthening his line to the north and building breastworks to defend against a rebel attack that he expected at any moment. When former US vice president John C. Breckenridge finally marched his Confederate division onto Reed's Bridge Road, the Federals were prepared but not strong enough to hold the enemy back. Rebel brigades led by Marcellus Stovall and Dan Adams swept aside the brigade of Gen. John C. Beatty, who had overextended his line in an attempt to bridge a gap between the breastworks and the junction of the LaFayette and Reed's Bridge Roads. Breckenridge then turned his center and right brigades to the south and advanced against Thomas's left flank. Benjamin Hardin Helm, brother-in-law to President Lincoln, was having a tougher time assailing the Union breastworks near Kelly field. Desperate fighting erupted at close range, and Helm fell mortally wounded just a few yards from Union defenses. Thomas sent the reserve brigade of Col. William Grose to arrest the advance of Stovall and Adams. Yet these troops were routed, dissolving "like a rope of sand." Confederates were perilously close to gaining the Union rear at Kelly field.[26]

In the meantime, Cleburne's division attacked on Thomas's right. Willich's brigade, massed in column formation and facing east, stood in reserve behind Baldwin's former brigade, now commanded by Col. William W. Berry of the Fifth Kentucky Union Volunteers. Johnson ordered Willich to "resist to the last extremity." Willich moved two of his regiments into line alongside Berry's men, creating a stout defense. The rebels could not penetrate the Union breastworks, and Federal troops mowed them down. Thirteen hundred of the Confederacy's finest infantrymen lay dead on the field, while several Union brigades lost scarcely a dozen men each. Willich had another two regiments plus Goodspeed's artillery battery at his disposal to deal with impending disaster on Thomas's left flank. The general ordered that battery and the Fifteenth Ohio to change front to the north, join with his former comrades from the Ninth Ohio and the rest of Col. Ferdinand Van Derveer's brigade, and stop Stovall and Adams just in the nick of time.[27]

Fortunately for Thomas, Polk and Hill on the Confederate right wing demonstrated poor leadership and a lack of initiative. No one moved behind Stovall's and Adams's elated, exhausted troops to consolidate their gains until it was too late. Portions of Beatty's shattered brigade and another under the command of Col. Timothy Stanley added firepower to the Federal defense. Willich's Forty-Ninth Ohio, which had been detached earlier in support of Baird, returned to lend a few hundred bayonets to the effort on the enemy's left flank.

Stovall and Adams were overmatched and routed. The rebels fell back half a mile to the McDonald farm, where the wounded General Adams was captured. Willich removed the Thirty-Second Indiana from its position in Berry's line and pursued Stovall for more than a mile before reassembling his brigade near McDonald field. From the Union point of view, Willich and other reserves had saved the day for the army on its left flank.[28] Breckenridge could only mutter in disgust over yet another missed opportunity. Neither side could reasonably expect that the outcome of battle was about to be determined not by tactical skill and valor, but by fatal misunderstanding and a large dose of luck.

• • • • •

Rosecrans was still preoccupied with his left. In one sense this was a good thing. Thomas's relentless cries for help and his commander's acquiescence ensured a stubborn defense and a clear line of retreat to Chattanooga. On the other hand, Rosecrans's zeal in saving Thomas, combined with his lack of sleep amid extraordinary confusion and stress, meant that mistakes were bound to occur. Most tactical blunders could be salvaged by quick-thinking officers on the front lines, but Rosecrans made one colossal error at 10:45 a.m. on September 20 that led directly to Union defeat.

Rosecrans ordered the entire division of Brig. Gen. Thomas J. Wood, positioned on the Union right behind breastworks opposite the Brotherton field, to move north and close what he thought was a gap in the line to the right of Maj. Gen. Joseph Reynolds's division of Thomas's corps. The void did not exist. Wood was aware of this fact, but Rosecrans had recently censured him for not promptly following orders. Knowing that this was potentially "the fatal order of the day," Wood reluctantly obeyed it and asked McCook to fill the huge gap he was about to create. Unfortunately for Rosecrans, Lieut. Gen. James Longstreet had massed nearly eleven thousand Confederate troops in the forest six hundred yards east of the LaFayette Road opposite Wood. Ten minutes after Wood read the order from Rosecrans, Longstreet received permission from Bragg to begin his attack at 11:10 a.m. The timing was sheer coincidence. In a matter of minutes, the rebel column gained the rear of the Union army. Pandemonium ensued. Rosecrans watched the unfolding disaster, gazed up at the sky, and made the sign of the cross.[29]

McCook's divisions, commanded by Brig. Gen. Jefferson C. Davis and Maj. Gen. Phillip Sheridan, were overrun. Longstreet's troops wheeled right to inflict as much damage as possible before the Union army could retreat to its base in Chattanooga. Trailing elements of Thomas J. Wood's division of Crittenden's Twenty-First Corps had not yet cleared the gap on their way north and were vanquished by the rebels. As the rout accelerated, Wood's center brigade under Col. Charles G. Harker turned to confront Brig. Gen. Evander M. Law's rampaging Texans. Col. Emerson Opdyke and his 125th Ohio led the counterattack, surprising the enemy and halting his advance. Then Harker took the offensive. The 125th and 64th Ohio Regiments borrowed a page from Willich's playbook and used advance firing to decimate the rebels. "See the Tigers go in!" Wood shouted. Confederate major general John Bell Hood was gravely wounded in the attack while attempting to rally his former brigade, and he ended up losing a leg.[30] The stage was set for the final phase of the battle. Thomas shifted his attention from a successful defense of the Union left to preventing the utter destruction of large parts of Rosecrans's army as troops fled north to safety.

While Thomas was holding the enemy at bay near Kelly field, rebels kept coming from the south. Harker fell back to a strong defensive position on a series of hills known as Horseshoe Ridge, where he joined reinforcements from Brannan's division who had been dislodged from the Union line in Longstreet's attack. Together with the remnants of other commands, the Federals conducted a stubborn defense against wave after wave of rebel assaults. Thomas eventually joined them. It was not until 3:45 p.m. that he learned the entire right wing of the army was in retreat at Rossville. At 4:30 p.m. Thomas was ordered to retreat.[31] The timing could not have been worse.

Willich moved his brigade to the southwest corner of Kelly field to cover the retreat of John M. Palmer's and Joseph J. Reynolds's divisions. Union general Richard W. Johnson received the order to withdraw but elected to delay, as the brigades of Dodge and Berry were already heavily engaged. Confederate General Leonidas Polk had launched a massive artillery barrage to soften up Union defenses at Kelly field, then had sent the divisions of Breckenridge, Cheatham, Hill, and Cleburne forward.[32] Willich described what happened next.

"The storm broke loose," the old general reported, stating that Union defenders "rushed without organization over the open field, partly over and through [his] brigade."[33] When an alarmed staff officer reported that the enemy had passed his flank and was now in their rear, Willich replied coolly, "Well, what of that? When he is in my rear, ain't I in his rear?"[34] Another eyewitness reported Willich smiling cunningly as he conducted a series of intricate maneuvers despite the chaos surrounding him, creating "a show of strength four times greater" than he actually possessed.[35] Goodspeed's battery turned to face south and silence the Eufaula Artillery. The Thirty-Second Indiana and Eighty-Ninth Illinois wheeled right, checking rebels from Gen. Henry D. Clayton's brigade of Alexander Stewart's division while other brigades in Johnson's command made their way to the woods. "By hav-

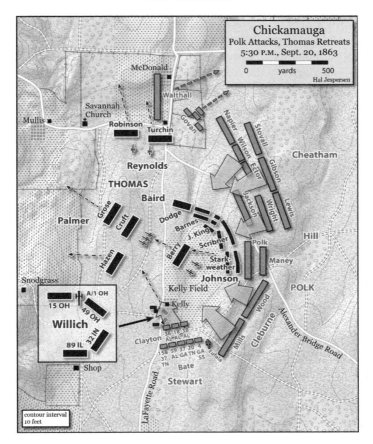

CHICKAMAUGA: POLK ATTACKS, THOMAS RETREATS

ing Willich in reserve," Johnson reported, "he [Willich] was able to engage the enemy in four different directions, and by his prompt movements he saved the troops from annihilation and capture."[36] During these critical moments, reported William D. Williams commanding the Eighty-Ninth Illinois, Willich's brigade "earned its sobriquet as the 'Iron Brigade of the Cumberland Army.'"[37]

General Thomas ordered Willich to fall back and cover the retreat of the army. Willich's brigade was so successful in implementing "retreat firing," halting and fronting every fifty yards to deliver a succession of volleys, that it enabled remnants of the army to retreat in good order.[38] Willich sustained no further losses as his men forced stragglers to join them on the three-hour eight-mile march north from the battlefield. Just after midnight, the troops finally rejoined the rest of their division in camp, where they received their rations and tried to process their stunning defeat.[39]

Senior Union officers praised Willich's performance. Johnson insisted that Willich "was always in the right place," citing his "individual daring." "This gallant old veteran deserves promotion," he pleaded.[40] Thomas also urged promotion for Willich, noting that "he most nobly sustained his reputation as a soldier."[41] McCook and Rosecrans joined the chorus. Willich, however, shrugged such plaudits aside. He placed more value on earning the devotion of his own troops. Commander of the Forty-Ninth Ohio Samuel F. Gray spoke for officers and enlisted men of the brigade when he lauded Willich's leadership on the field of Chickamauga. Gray pointed to the general's "perfect organization from the beginning to the end of the fight" and declared, "We owe to his superior courage and skill our preservation and any honor we may have won."[42]

Willich's brilliant performance at Chickamauga was cold comfort. His brigade suffered 539 casualties, more than a third of its effective force.[43] In the general's view, the fight was just one of several examples of a "battle gained by the soldiers and lost by the leaders." He maintained that the rout of the right wing came about "in consequence of inexcusable and criminal tactical blunders." Willich insisted that Union soldiers "were ready to return, but the Generals were not ready to lead them back to the battle-field."[44] It pained the old general to see "[his] best troops melt away to a mere nothing." The brigade had been reduced from more than 3,500 men to fewer than 800 since he had taken command.[45]

Willich made sure his men understood that their sacrifice had meaning and significance. His boys had once again proved their worth and he described them as "true sons of the Republic, who value life only so long as it is the life of freemen, and who are determined to make the neck of every power, slaveratic [sic] or monarchical, bend." Willich further warned that the traitor and Copperhead in the North who tried to "make their glorious deaths useless to the cause of humanity" should be forced to stand over the graves of the dead soldiers "and learn penitence."[46] In the meantime, the Army of the Cumberland pulled back into Chattanooga, where it was safe from enemy bullets, bayonets, and ordnance but vulnerable to hunger.

• • • • •

Rosecrans's battered army teetered on the verge of starvation for much of October as Bragg laid siege to the town from the heights of Lookout Mountain and Missionary Ridge. Halleck ordered Ulysses S. Grant and his Army of the Tennessee to send reinforcements to Chattanooga immediately. In response, Grant sent William T. Sherman and elements of two corps. Grant then assumed overall command of a new Military Department of the Mississippi, consisting of his army, the Army of the Cumberland under Rosecrans, and the Army of the Ohio under Ambrose Burnside. Sherman succeeded Grant as commander of the Army of the Tennessee. At this point Grant sacked Rosecrans, replacing him with Thomas, whom he admonished to "hold Chattanooga at all hazards." The steadfast Thomas replied, "I will hold the town till we starve."[47]

In the meantime, the reduced ranks of the once-proud Cumberlanders were reorganized. Willich's new division leader was Thomas J. Wood, whose Third Division was part of Maj. Gen. Gordon Granger's Fourth Army Corps. Soldiers from the Twenty-Fifth and Thirty-Fifth Illinois joined Willich's command, along with men from the Sixty-Eighth Indiana, the Eighth Kansas, and the Fifteenth Wisconsin.[48] The Fifteenth was the decimated regiment of Hans Heg, who was mortally wounded near Viniard farm at Chickamauga. Heg's regiment suffered great loss at Stones River, entering the Battle of Chickamauga with just 176 men. The regiment emerged two days later numbering only sixty-five troops.[49]

Willich loved all his boys, but the soldiers of what he called "the little Fifteenth" Wisconsin held a special place in his heart. Like the Thirty-Second Indiana, the regiment was composed almost entirely of immigrants. One evening, hunger drove them to mischief. The little Fifteenth appropriated General Willich's favorite milk cow, cooked it, and ate it. "God damn the Fifteenth!" Willich cried when he learned of the pilferage. No one else had the courage to commit such an act, he then reasoned, his anger subsiding. After all, the old man's primary concern was the welfare of his troops. Nothing was done about the matter.[50]

Grant arrived on October 23 and prepared to go on the offensive against Bragg, who was spread thin bottling up the Federals in Chattanooga. Five days later, Grant sent Maj. Gen. Joseph Hooker on a daring mission to seize Brown's Ferry west of Chattanooga to open what he called "the cracker line" railroad connection to the supply depot at Bridgeport, Alabama. Once the supply line was secured, Grant waited for Sherman to arrive with twenty thousand men. Sherman planned to take a position screened by a range of hills north of town, then lead an offensive south along the crest of Missionary Ridge, folding the rebels back on themselves. Thomas would finish them off from the west with a frontal attack.[51]

Bragg was outnumbered and outmaneuvered, and his options were limited. His only good move was a flanking action toward East Tennessee. On November 4, Bragg sent Longstreet north on a mission to dislodge Burnside's twenty thousand troops from the vicinity of Knoxville. Bragg was then left with a mere forty-two thousand men for a potential face-off with a force 50 percent greater than his own. By November 22 however, Sherman's army was still en route to Chattanooga. Longstreet begged for more men, so Bragg gambled and ordered Patrick Cleburne's and Bushrod Johnson's divisions to the train station bound for Knoxville.[52]

Bragg's movements puzzled Grant. Were the rebels withdrawing? He needed to know. Grant asked Thomas to seize Orchard Knob, a hundred-foot eminence on the flats between Chattanooga and Missionary Ridge. This position would provide a better view of Bragg's army and push Confederate advance positions back to the base of the ridge. Thomas arranged a spectacle on November 23 unlike anything either side had ever witnessed. Twenty-three thousand men led by Wood's division marched out of the Union breastworks and onto the plain in perfect parade-ground order. The rebels watched and admired what they assumed was a grand review, yet the bluecoats kept coming.[53] At the tip of the spear were the brigades of August Willich on the left and William B. Hazen on the right. They placed their troops in an unusual arrangement with line of battle in front and double column closed en masse in the rear.[54] Hazen focused his attention on the Twenty-Eighth Alabama, which defended a ridge alongside the conical hill. Willich's brigade stormed the knob where the entrenched Twenty-Fourth Alabama waited three hundred yards to Hazen's left.

Willich's skirmishers from the Eighth Kansas made quick work of their opposites in gray. Willich's brigade advanced in quick time, taking the hill with a loss of only four killed and ten wounded. Hazen's opponents were more stubborn. A fierce firefight raged along the adjoining ridge for more than an hour. Enfilading fire raked Hazen's right while his men used bayonets in hand-to-hand combat with the rebels. Two of Hazen's regiments, the Forty-First and Ninety-Third Ohio, suffered 167 casualties before the Alabamians escaped, leaving their colors and 146 captured rebel infantrymen behind. Willich's men erected an epaulement on the crest of the knob and built breastworks around its perimeter.[55] Having selected the Eighth Kansas to lead the charge, Willich established "a feeling of companionship and mutual confidence" between old and new regiments in his brigade. That rapport proved essential to their success two days later.[56]

The chess match continued. Bragg recalled Cleburne's troops from the train station when the fighting at Orchard Knob broke out. Soldiers raced back to defend the north end of Missionary Ridge. Pleased with his demonstration at Orchard Knob and knowing that Sherman was bogged down trying to cross the Tennessee River, Grant decided to press his advantage elsewhere. Maj. Gen. Joseph P. Hooker had arrived with fifteen thousand men from the Eleventh and Twelfth Corps of the Army of the Potomac. Willich had a bird's-eye view as three Hooker divisions made an audacious assault on rebel positions at Lookout Mountain eight miles to the south. These troops drove the Confederates off of the huge eminence with relative ease, sending them scurrying across the valley to Missionary Ridge to prepare for the penultimate battle.[57]

Bragg anticipated Grant's next move and was ready for it. The morning of November 25 dawned cloudless and cold. Sherman began an assault on the north end of Missionary Ridge at 10:30 a.m. but ran into stiff resistance. Cleburne used superior knowledge of the terrain to his advantage, outfoxing his Union counterpart. As a panoply of frustration unfolded in the early afternoon, Grant and Thomas peered through their field glasses from the summit of Orchard Knob. Then Grant accelerated phase two of his plan, worked out with Thomas the prior evening. He would not wait for the dwindling prospect of a Confederate pullback to the south but instead attack Bragg's center to relieve pressure on the stalled Sherman.[58]

Grant intended to charge across the open plain to the east of Chattanooga and take the rebel rifle pits at the foot of Missionary Ridge, pause to regroup, then storm the ridge itself. When he finally barked orders to Thomas, however, Grant ordered him to "advance and take the enemy's first line of rifle pits." Grant's ultimate intentions were lost in translation as orders moved through the chain of command. Some division commanders understood his directive to mean that they should advance and take the ridge. Others were convinced they should stop at the rifle pits. By the time word trickled down to brigade level, the orders were anything but clear.[59] Willich admitted later that he learned of Wood's direction to stop at the rifle pits only after the battle was over. "By what accident, I am unable to say," the old general confessed. "I did not understand it so; I only understood the order to advance."[60] Willich looked up at the seemingly impregnable ridge with more than fifty cannons aimed downward and muttered to Wood, "Well, I makes my will."[61]

Six cannon shots boomed in rapid succession, signaling more than twenty-three thousand Union soldiers arranged in tight ranks with colors waving to step onto the plain. Confederates in the rifle pits at the base of Missionary Ridge watched with mixed feelings of awe and dread. Rebel gunners poured a heavy hail of shell and case into the double line of Federals, dropping hundreds of men. Union attackers increased their speed to double-quick time and

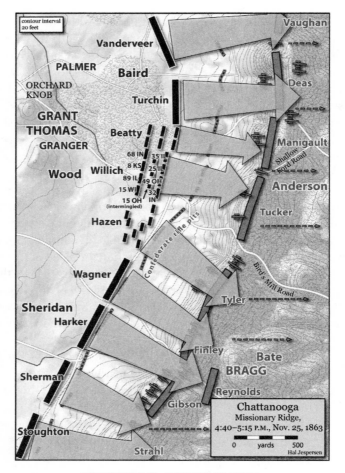

CHATTANOOGA: MISSIONARY RIDGE

rushed the rifle pits, giving and receiving fire as they charged. Most defenders ran, but many were captured. Lieut. Col. Jacob Glass of Willich's beloved Thirty-Second Indiana Infantry was killed on the spot. He had written his brother Fritz just a few days previous, enclosing his last wishes should he "find death in the next battle." He pleaded with his mother, "[Do not] mourn my death as long as this Republic lives."[62]

Jubilant Federals found themselves in a precarious position as rebel artillery and marksmen trained their guns on the pits at the base of the hill. "It was evident to everyone," Willich reported, "that to stay in this position would be certain destruction and final defeat."[63] Col. John Martin, commanding the Eighth Kansas, said to his brigadier, "Here we are general. What more?" Willich replied, "Forward, storm. We have to take the works on the ridge."[64] Lieut. Col. John McClenahan of the Fifteenth Ohio on the division's skirmish line asked Willich where his men should stop. "I don't know," the Prussian replied. "At Hell, I guess."[65] Skirmishers from various regiments were already climbing the hill as the command to advance sounded.

Willich's men ran up the hill as quickly as they could for half a mile, reaching a place where the extreme angle of the slope sheltered them from enemy guns that could not fire low enough to menace them. The soldiers rested behind stumps, logs, or small rises to catch their breath. Willich's brigade resumed its advance after a few minutes, the troops deftly picking their way up the slope and avoiding exposed avenues of approach where artillery could sight them. The Old One ran behind his second line, hat in hand. At one point, he encountered a straggler hiding behind a stump. "I jumped on him and kicked him," the general remembered with a laugh, "and see, I broke all my spurs."[66] Just below a crest in the center of the ridge, the men of Willich's and Hazen's brigades paused to affix bayonets, then charged over the brow of the hill. This sequence was repeated up and down the long line of bluecoats assaulting the steep ridge. More than a few Union attackers yelled, "Chickamauga!" before meeting the enemy in fierce hand-to-hand combat. The fight was over in minutes. Overwhelmed rebels fled down the rear slope of the ridge, leaving entire artillery batteries behind as trophies of war. A correspondent from the New York World who witnessed Willich's charge gushed, "I don't believe that history can furnish a parallel to this feat . . . The most brilliant dash ever made by a French army has been eclipsed."[67]

Once action died down atop the ridge, soldiers from Company F of the Fifteenth Ohio returned with rebel prisoners and broke into a tremendous shout. Willich ran over to them and asked, "What! What is the matter now?" Great news, they replied. They had captured two large kettles of coffee. Minutes later, soldiers from Company G rode up and presented Willich with two captured horses. The delighted general cried, "My boys, you kills me with joy, you kills me with joy!"[68]

Days later, Willich's mood was somber. The brigade had suffered 337 casualties in the assaults on Missionary Ridge and Orchard Knob. "The regiments of my command have been reduced to less than one-fourth their strength," bemoaned the brigadier. He pleaded with his superiors, "Fill up the regiments, so that our invaluable veterans do not waste away altogether."[69] There was little time for celebration or reflection, however. Willich's weary men were

CAPTAIN LOUIS VON TREBRA AND SOLDIERS OF THE 32ND INDIANA VOL. INFANTRY
STORM A CONFEDERATE ARTILLERY POSITION ATOP MISSIONARY RIDGE ON NOV. 22,
1863. WATERCOLOR BY ADOLPH METZNER. LIBRARY OF CONGRESS.

now part of Grant's army, a force that never stood still. Three days after the
stunning victory at Missionary Ridge, they were on the move again; Grant
sent Thomas and Sherman to Knoxville to support a beleaguered Burnside.
The men marched off on their 120-mile journey not knowing that the mission would be a wasted effort and the beginning of the worst winter of their
lives.

Chapter Sixteen

• •

LEADING FROM THE FRONT

IN THEIR RUSH to relieve the Confederate siege of Knoxville, William T. Sherman and his twenty-five thousand men pushed relentlessly through cold and rain, thereby hampering the Union army's effort to pursue and finish Bragg. Sherman expected to find Burnside and his men without food and barely holding out against Confederate general James Longstreet's siege. He was in for a rude surprise.

Sherman stood a mere fifteen miles from Knoxville on December 5 when he received a note from Burnside telling him that a rescue was no longer needed. Longstreet had been repelled when he had made an ill-advised frontal attack on Burnside's lines on November 29. The day before Sherman's force arrived, Longstreet retreated into the hills of East Tennessee. Sherman rode into Knoxville ahead of the column the following day and found Burnside comfortably ensconced in a beautiful mansion. Sherman and his staff were then served a lavish turkey dinner with all the trimmings. "I had seen nothing of this kind in my field service," a disgusted Sherman remarked, "and could not help exclaiming that I thought they were starving." There was little left to do but march the troops back to Chattanooga. Sherman left two of Grainger's divisions behind, including Thomas J. Wood's Third Division, led by Willich's First Brigade. Their mission was to pursue and neutralize Longstreet.[1]

Willich's men sported the same soiled and bloody uniforms they had worn when they scaled Missionary Ridge. As there was no time to properly provision them for the march, the troops endured harsh wintry weather for ten days with disintegrating shoes and insufficient rations.[2] When his brigade finally arrived in Knoxville, Willich promised his men that their suffering would end. Before the soldiers pitched their tents, the old Prussian forced area millers into his service so that the regiment would be supplied with fresh bread. Willich's troops ate well early that winter while other brigades had to eke by on sparse fare.[3]

Instead of engaging Longstreet in battle, Wood's division wandered from place to place, rebuilding railroad bridges and growing more disenchanted as the months dragged on. Most of Willich's brigade answered the call to reenlist in January 1864, but not many in his old Thirty-Second Indiana did so. The vast majority elected to serve out the last six months of their commitment and return home. The proud Germans resented duties "better suited to a team of mules," and they complained frequently of nativist prejudice. Their tents, shoes, and clothing were threadbare, offering little protection against the cold winter winds.[4]

Willich himself missed much of the winter hardships. The fifty-three-year-old general left his command for Cincinnati, where he underwent an operation to remove a cancerous growth from his lip. Upon his return, cheering men swarmed him, some holding his stirrups and bridle reins while he joked with them. Willich gave a typical humorous yet inspiring speech, saying that he had arrived just in time to pilot soldiers on another grand adventure.[5] As it turned out, the spring of 1864 would be the last time he would lead troops into battle.

On April 8, Willich's brigade began a march back to Chattanooga to prepare for the summer campaign. With Grant now in Virginia, Sherman took command of the western armies. He planned to face off against Gen. Joseph E. Johnston, who had replaced Bragg in command of the Confederacy's Army of Tennessee. Willich's brigade received new uniforms, clothing, and shoes while camped at McDonald's Station near Cleveland, Tennessee.[6] His men also resumed their drill regimen of three hours per day: one hour each with company, regiment, and brigade. On May 3, they set out toward the rebel army's winter camp at Dalton, Georgia, as part of Sherman's one hundred thousand soldiers, twice as many as Johnston had available for combat. Sherman's Atlanta Campaign would be a classic cat-and-mouse affair, with Johnston retreating to favorable defensive positions while Sherman attempted to outflank his opponent and use his numerical superiority to best advantage. The rivals' initial confrontation would be at a place of Johnston's choosing called Rocky Face Ridge.[7]

Johnston entrenched part of his army on a long eminence that ran north to south five hundred feet above the Crow Valley. He placed the balance of his force along a series of hills east of the northern terminus of the ridge, anchoring his right at Potato Hill. This formation allowed Johnston to control Buzzard Roost Gap and defend access to the Western and Atlantic Railroad. Capping the ridge were sheer vertical walls of sandstone and shale varying between twenty and sixty feet in height. Storming Missionary Ridge had been a momentous achievement, but a frontal assault against the heights of Rocky Face Ridge appeared to be certain suicide.

Johnston's entrenched position at his center was impregnable. Sherman understood this. He opted to demonstrate against the ridge with skirmish lines as a diversion while he sent Maj. Gen. James Birdseye McPherson's Army of the Tennessee through Snake Creek Gap and around Johnston's left flank. Sherman also planned to gain the Confederate rear and take the town of Resaca. Wood's division kicked off Sherman's feints east of Tunnel Hill near Buzzard Roost Gap on May 8.[8]

Wood sent skirmishers out the night before the fighting began. Four companies of Willich's Fifteenth Wisconsin and troops from Hazen's brigade received orders to move forward at 6:00 a.m. and take the ridge if possible. Confederates from Maj. Gen. Carter Stevenson's division trained muskets on the advancing soldiers from the heights. During the night, the rebels had rolled boulders down on the Federals while shouting, "Yankees, here's your road to Atlanta!" They hardly expected the bluecoats to attempt to take the crest, but Willich's "little Fifteenth" did exactly that. The men discarded their haversacks, took off their caps, and clawed their way up the mountain, using trees and crevices as handholds and pulling their comrades up the slope in complete silence. Led by Sgt. John O. Wrolstad of Company I, the Norsemen drove the enemy off their portion of the crest and held it until relieved by troops from Gen. John Newton's division. This stunning achievement accomplished little besides keeping Johnston's troops occupied on his right flank.[9] Willich's brigade suffered thirty-eight casualties in repeated demonstrations against Rocky Face Ridge.

Various divisions of Maj. Gen. Oliver O. Howard's Fourth Corps skirmished with the enemy for five days while McPherson executed his flanking maneuver. When he finally reached the outskirts of Resaca on May 9, McPherson found part of Johnston's army waiting for him in force. He pulled back to Snake Creek Gap and waited for reinforcements. Sherman elected to send most of his army to join McPherson the next day, allowing Johnston to abandon the ridge and mass his army at Resaca for the next test of wills between the two commanding generals.

During the early morning hours of May 13, Wood moved his division into Dalton, east of Rocky Face Ridge, then joined the rest of the Fourth

Corps and marched south. The next morning, Union soldiers encountered Johnston's entire army dug in north and west of Resaca. Sherman ordered an immediate attack.[10] Wood placed Willich's First Brigade on the right and the Second Brigade under William G. Hazen on the left at the bottom of a fish-hook where the rebel line began to bend off its north–south axis and refused its right flank facing north. Willich assembled his brigade into his favorite formation, double column closed en masse, with the Fifteenth Ohio on his left front line next to the Forty-Ninth Ohio on the right. The Thirty-Second Indiana and Eighty-Ninth Illinois formed behind them, with the Thirty-Fifth Illinois and Fifteenth Wisconsin in the third line. Willich advanced on the enemy over broken landscape and dense undergrowth.

Willich's brigade met rebel skirmishers from Brig. Gen. Edward Cary Walthall's brigade of Maj. Gen. Thomas Hindman's division about six hundred yards into the advance. In concert with Hazen's brigade, Willich's troops drove the Confederates back violently, encountering little resistance. By 1:00 p.m., the Federals gained a ridgeline between the enemy's abandoned rifle pits and an imposing set of rebel works across an open field 250 yards away. General Wood surveyed the enemy's entrenchments, concluding that they could not be carried without sustaining unacceptable losses. He ordered Hazen's men to build barricades on the crest of the ridge and await further orders. Willich sent the Fifteenth Wisconsin and Fifteenth Ohio to relieve regiments from Col. Francis T. Sherman's brigade occupying the abandoned rebel first line of defense along the ridge. Brisk exchanges between the opposing armies continued throughout the day, with neither side making significant headway.

Late that afternoon, Maj. Gen. William T. Sherman began moving most of Hooker's Twentieth Corps and Schofield's Twenty-Third Corps to the Confederate right flank, where they planned to launch a massive assault the following day. Howard shifted the Fourth Corps to his right to fill the gap created by Schofield's departure. Willich occupied an eminence above Camp Creek vacated by Col. James W. Reilley's brigade of Brig. Gen. Jacob D. Cox's Third Division. Before nightfall Willich's brigade dug trenches, expecting a furious battle the next morning.[11]

At dawn on May 15, Wood's division prepared to launch an offensive, but orders to attack never arrived. Instead, Howard waited as Hooker launched his attack. Hooker was unsuccessful and the armies slugged it out to a bloody draw, sustaining heavy casualties. In the meantime, Wood and the rest of Howard's corps were instructed to attack the rebel center only if they perceived weakness. By 4:00 p.m. Wood's patience ran out, so he ordered his

CAPTAIN HUBERT DILGER OF THE 1ST OHIO LIGHT ARTILLERY SURVEYS CONFEDERATE
EARTHWORKS FROM ATOP AN EMPLACEMENT WHILE A SNIPER'S BULLET STRIKES AT
HIS FEET. DISREGARD OF SHARPSHOOTERS LED TO WILLICH'S WOUNDING ON MAY 15,
1864. WATERCOLOR BY ADOLPH METZNER. LIBRARY OF CONGRESS.

skirmishers to reconnoiter the enemy's front. Before Willich's and Hazen's
skirmishers could advance a hundred yards, they met a galling fire of musketry and artillery that sent them scurrying back to their regiments. If there
were weak points in the rebel line, this was not one of them. Willich rode
forward to the rude breastworks of the Thirty-Fifth Illinois with no inkling
that his luck was about to run out.[12]

The old general dismounted and climbed to the top of the parapet, field glasses in hand, to take stock of the stalemate. He was dressed in his full brigadier general's uniform, replete with a yellow sash that waved in the breeze like a handkerchief taunting an angry bull.[13] A rebel sharpshooter less than two hundred yards away crouched low, took upward aim at his quarry, and pulled the trigger. A single ball ripped through Willich's upper right arm near the shoulder, glanced off the bone, and exited his back below the shoulder blade, barely missing his spine.[14] The blow knocked him off his feet, and Adjt. Gen. Carl Schmitt helped place his wounded commander on a stretcher, then carry him to an ambulance which rushed him to a dedicated hospital tent two miles behind the lines. When men crowded around Willich, a young officer ordered them back, but the general rebuked him. Despite the pain, Willich implored his boys to do their duty as if he were still with them. Colonel Gibson of the Forty-Ninth Ohio took command of the brigade, and the battle raged on.[15]

The rebels made an assault against the Federal center around 11:00 p.m. but were easily repulsed. This was nothing more than a diversion, as Johnston learned that Sherman had sent Gen. Thomas W. Sweeny across the Oostanaula River at Lay's Ferry and was threatening his supply lines. Johnston abandoned Resaca the evening of May 15, burning the railroad bridge over the Oostanaula. In this first major battle of Sherman's Atlanta Campaign, the Federals had lost more than four thousand soldiers, while the greatly outnumbered Confederates had suffered fewer than three thousand casualties.[16] Willich's brigade lost eighty-seven men.

The Atlanta Campaign continued without Willich. In early September, Col. Charles Hotchkiss assumed command of Willich's storied First Brigade after Gibson mustered out and returned to Ohio. Hotchkiss noted that the brigade had lost half its strength since Shiloh.[17] Joy at the fall of Atlanta and the seemingly imminent collapse of the Confederate army was tempered by the fact that Willich's men had paid such a dear price and lost their beloved leader. Hotchkiss claimed that in two years under the general, the men never doubted his commands, even when he placed them in danger. "No officer or enlisted man mars the records of our courts-martial with a cowardly charge against his name," Hotchkiss insisted, and "no flag has received a stain or been lost because its keepers shrunk in the hour of action." The brigade was so well trained and disciplined that it could almost "fight itself."[18] The First Brigade would sustain that reputation to the end of the war.

Willich, on the other hand, would never fight again. The rebel ball that pierced his shoulder severed a nerve in his right arm, rendering that limb and hand nearly useless for the rest of his life. On his trip through Nash-ville, the wounded warrior spoke with pride about his boys. Comparing the Eighty-Ninth Illinois to his own Thirty-Second Indiana, Willich insisted, "My Illinois boys are just as brave and composed."[19] He recalled a conversation with Count Mercier, the French foreign minister, as the diplomat droned on about the greatness of the French army. "Monsieur," Willich addressed the count, "I was educated at the military school. I have known the armies of France, Austria, England, and Switzerland, and I tell you that you may carefully select the best of your French troops, the crack regiment of your Zouaves, and then take by lot any one of our Western regiments, and plac-ing them face to face on trial, your boys will quickly find there is nothing between them and the firmament."[20]

Willich traveled back to Cincinnati to recover among friends and former comrades but had no thoughts of leaving the army. He had no family, no other career. The army was his home. The slave aristocracy in the Confeder-ate States had not yet capitulated, and Willich vowed to stay in service until that mission was accomplished.

Chapter Seventeen

● ● ● ● ● ● ● ● ● ● ● ● ● ● ● ● ● ● ●

ONE ARM IS ENOUGH

THE OLD MAN spent three restless months recuperating from an injury that could have ended his military career. Gens. Phil Kearney, John Bell Hood, and others had lost the use of an arm, yet they still managed to achieve distinction on the battlefield. Willich was eager to get back to the field to prove once again that brains trumped brawn. His superiors did not see it that way. On August 13, 1864, Willich assumed post command at Cincinnati in the Northern Department, reporting to Maj. Gen. Samuel P. Heintzelman.[1] Heintzelman was a fifty-nine-year-old Black Hawk War veteran. A corps commander early in the Civil War, he was capable but cautious. Heintzelman was relieved of his field command in late 1862, and Cincinnati was his last career assignment. He retired a few months after Willich's arrival.[2] This was the kind of position that many accomplished field commanders dreaded, but Willich threw himself into the work with zeal and determination.

Willich received seven companies of soldiers to serve as guards. Part of the Thirty-Seventh Iowa Infantry and known as "the Greybeard Regiment," these troops became very special to him. Iowa obtained special permission from Secretary of War Edwin Stanton to enroll men over the age of forty-five for garrison duty, thereby freeing up younger soldiers for more active service in the field. Many of these men were older than Willich himself and fierce patriots by reputation. The sturdy seniors arrived in Cincinnati in early September 1864. Willich assigned several Greybeard officers special duties. A front had opened behind battle lines that endangered the safety of border state residents and the success of the overall war effort.[3]

Defeating the Confederate army on the battlefield was difficult enough. Having to contend with enemies among his own people in the North, however, angered Willich. Ohio was the home of Democrats who had nominated convicted traitor Clement Vallandigham, the leader of the so-called Peace Democrats, as their candidate for governor in 1863. That same year, Confederate cavalry led by Brig. Gen. John Hunt Morgan terrified southern Indiana and Ohio with daring raids. Morgan had plenty of local help. Heintzelman received numerous reports from Ohio civilians of large quantities of arms and ammunition arriving at local train depots throughout the border North. Willich resolved not to allow dangerous Copperheads to cause trouble. The more he assessed the threat, the more serious it appeared.

Vallandigham was back in Ohio in 1864, but Lincoln tolerated that unusual fact. He did not want Vallandigham made a martyr yet again, as Gen. Ambrose Burnside had done by arresting him at home in his nightclothes. Instead, Lincoln merely kept a close eye on the infamous antiwar advocate. Vallandigham led a secret society known as the Sons of Liberty. One of his acolytes, Harrison H. Dodd, advocated violent overthrow of the governments of Indiana, Illinois, Kentucky, and Missouri. Dodd had a stockpile of guns in a warehouse in Indianapolis, and he and his accomplices planned to set Confederate prisoners at Camp Morton free and incite rebellion in Indiana. One of Willich's first administrative tasks was to help investigate the smuggling of arms and munitions to Copperhead insurgents.[4]

Willich found large quantities of pistols and carbines in the hands of Confederate sympathizers in Indiana, Kentucky, and Ohio. One dealer had sold more than five thousand cavalry pistols to such nefarious customers. The general made a detailed report to R. Kittridge and Company, an investigator employed by the federal government.[5] Heintzelman acted by issuing General Orders Number 5 prohibiting the transport of firearms and ammunition without the express permission of the United States Army.[6] Several leaders of the Sons of Liberty were arrested in October 1864, tried, convicted of treason, and sentenced to death. More convictions followed into 1865, but the executions were delayed and the sentences eventually commuted.[7] Willich spent nine months in the stifling purgatory of a military desk job, hoping to return to the field one day. When that day finally arrived, it came as the result of an unusual and tragic circumstance.

• • • • •

It all started in routine fashion. On January 8, 1864, a teenage boy named Thomas Martin was arrested in Kentucky and charged with being Confederate guerilla. On February 12, Martin arrived at McLean Barracks military prison in downtown Cincinnati. Martin was convicted by a military court and sentenced to be executed by firing squad between the hours of 12:00 p.m. and 2:00 p.m. on Friday, May 5, 1865.[8] With Union victory seemingly on the horizon, few suspected that the sentence would be carried out and that Martin would become the last rebel prisoner executed in the Civil War. His death would remain burrowed deep in Willich's conscience for the rest of his life.

By the time Willich took command of the post at Cincinnati in August 1864, Martin had been imprisoned at McLean Barracks for six months. The affable youngster had also become popular with a number of the guards and staff officers. Willich adopted the lad as his personal errand boy, allowing him limited freedom of movement and trusting him with routine tasks. The poor, ignorant young man hardly seemed a threat to anyone. Martin and his captors expected that he would return to his family in Kentucky once the war ended, his brief stint as a Confederate guerilla forgiven. Instead, cruel fate intervened.[9]

Gen. Joseph Hooker, who had assumed Heintzelman's post after the old veteran retired, still had axes to grind. Despite a reputation for aggressiveness that had earned him the nickname "Fighting Joe" early in the war, Hooker's poor performance at Chancellorsville cast a pall over his record and embittered him. Being replaced by Gen. George Meade as commander of the Army of the Potomac just three days before the critical battle at Gettysburg only stoked his discontent. Moreover, Hooker's success in the Chattanooga Campaign was marred by a tiff over William T. Sherman's promotion of Gen. Oliver O. Howard, whom Hooker outranked, to command the Army of the Tennessee. Hooker left Chattanooga in a huff and assumed the job in Cincinnati. That stint lasted seventeen months.[10]

Hooker prepared for his imminent departure in late April 1865; he had been reassigned to command the Department of the East. His aide was assigned to review reams of papers that had accumulated during his command of the Northern Department. During this review, the general and his staffer came across Martin's case. Hooker had completely forgotten it, and when he was told that the boy's sentence had not been carried out, he sent for Willich and demanded an explanation. Willich related the facts of the case and told of Martin's exemplary conduct. Later that afternoon, the Prussian received an order from Hooker to shoot the boy May 5. Willich could not believe it.[11]

What purpose would such a merciless act serve now that the Confederates had surrendered? Willich wrote Gen. George H. Thomas asking for transfer to his command. With tears in his eyes, the Old One also rushed to Judge Stallo, his mentor and best friend, and pleaded with him to do something to save the boy. Stallo hurried to see Judge William M. Dickson and requested his assistance. Judge Dickson was a founding member of the Ohio Republican Party and a close associate of Lincoln, Edwin M. Stanton, and Salmon P. Chase. Aghast that Hooker would commit such a cruel act, Dickson took action immediately.

When Dickson learned that Hooker had left to attend Lincoln's funeral in Springfield, he decided to go over his head.[12] The judge rushed to Alfred Gaither, superintendent of the Adams Express Company. They fired off a telegram at 10:20 a.m. on May 5 urging Maj. Thomas T. Eckert to lay the matter before Secretary of War Edwin M. Stanton. Colonel Hart of Hooker's staff telegrammed his commander, who said that the matter was out of his hands. An anxious morning passed with no reply from Stanton.[13]

Young Thomas Martin dressed for death. Fr. Frederick Garesché, a Catholic priest and the brother of Gen. William S. Rosecrans's chief of staff who had been killed at Stones River, baptized the boy and gave him Holy Communion. Martin wore light pants, a collarless white shirt, a steel-colored vest, a black frock coat, a small necktie, white stockings, and brogans. A ball and chain clung to his ankle, and a crucifix adorned his belt. A light-colored slouch hat shaded his calm, pale countenance.[14]

The killing field was about 150 square feet of ground near a twenty-foot-high cliff on a hill overlooking Deer Creek Valley to the east. To get there from downtown Cincinnati, the firing squad traversed a rough and winding route. Despite efforts to keep the time of the execution secret, word leaked out, and a large crowd gathered near Kempton Barracks, where the soldiers were stationed. At noon seven companies of the Thirty-Seventh Iowa Infantry and Company A of the 192nd Pennsylvania Infantry assembled in the yard outside the barracks. At 1:10 p.m. Willich's adjutant, Charles A. Booth, gave orders to move out. The soldiers arrived at the designated spot, formed a hollow square, and awaited the arrival of the prisoner. Martin rose from his bed, grabbed his hat, and walked to a waiting carriage. To the soldiers gathered near McLean Barracks, the condemned youngster simply said, "Boys, I will die like a brave man."[15] The procession ambled slowly and deliberately down the old Walnut Hills Road toward the ravine where executions were held. Willich and Chief Clerk Lawrence Sands stayed behind in the office, in case a last-minute telegram from Stanton might arrive to stay the execution. As they approached the ravine, the soldiers looked back and saw a cloud of dust. It was just ten minutes from the appointed hour.

Could it be true? Indeed, it was! The clerk galloped furiously up the road, and his horse slid to a stop. Willich arrived moments later. Sands read a telegram from Stanton sent at 1:45 p.m. and addressed to Hooker. "Suspend the execution of Thomas Martin, to be executed in Cincinnati on this day, until further orders" the missive directed, "by order of the President." Soldiers who were minutes away from shooting the boy now congratulated him on his narrow escape. They were just as happy to be spared the gruesome duty they were about to perform. The party re-formed and marched with light step back to the city, buoyed with joy and relief. After four long years of slaughter, perhaps the better angels of man's nature would prevail as their martyred president had hoped. Few understood the depth of bitterness that General Hooker held in his own heart.[16]

Willich's conscience told him he could no longer work for Hooker. He appealed directly to General Grant, asking to be transferred. Grant agreed on May 9 and directed Willich to report to General Thomas, commander of the Army of the Cumberland, without delay.[17] Hooker learned of Martin's reprieve from an aide upon returning from Lincoln's funeral. He pressured Stanton into cancelling the stay of execution and Martin was shot the following day.[18] Willich declined to attend the execution. His heart was broken. He had seen many young men butchered on the battlefield, but most of them had died for a cause they either believed in or one that was imprinted in their brains by ambitious politicians. Martin's death seemed senseless.

On May 13, Willich asked Gen. Lorenzo Thomas to muster the Greybeards out of service. This was done promptly. Willich claimed that these men, many of whom were more than sixty years old, had sent thirteen hundred sons and grandsons into the Union army. "At this post," Willich said of the old men under his command, "they have performed very heavy duties, which to perform them would even have been difficult for an equal number of young men." Mental anguish could be as debilitating as physical suffering.[19]

Willich resigned his command in the Northern Department on May 18, 1865, only a week after young Martin was executed. He yearned to be back in the field with his boys, forget this terrible incident, and lead his brigade with dignity and respect. That wish was granted, although the assignment turned out to be much different than he could have imagined.

Chapter Eighteen

• •

MOPPING UP

THE NEWS STRUCK the Fourth Corps like a thunderbolt out of a cloudless June sky. *They are sending us where? Texas? For God's sake, why?* The war was over. Men were anxious to get back to their families, their jobs, and their farms after four years of hardship and sacrifice. Department of Texas commander Phil Sheridan felt he had plenty of troops to secure the area from resurgent Confederate troublemakers. Then he spoke to his superior. Grant was concerned about Mexico, where another civil war had been raging for years. France took advantage of the Union's preoccupation with the Confederate rebellion and invaded Mexico in 1864. Now defeated ex-rebel officers were streaming into the French puppet state and getting cozy with its new leader, Maximilian. The last thing the United States needed was a resumption of war over Texas.[1]

General Willich, on the other hand, held a personal grudge against Louis-Napoleon, whose sudden coup had helped end the revolutionary dreams of many European republicans thirteen years earlier. If Maximilian was rash enough to start something in Texas, Willich would be thrilled to crush him and embarrass the French emperor. Merely being back out in the field with his boys gave the old war-horse a rush of adrenaline and a renewed purpose. He was indeed where he belonged.

The reunion began taking shape at the end of April, as various brigades of the Fourth Corps made their way to Nashville. On May 2 the soldiers cleaned their camps for inspection by General George H. Thomas the following day. Officers wore black crepe insignias in mourning for their martyred president. On May 19 Thomas led a review of the entire corps, galloping up on horseback accompanied by his staff amid great cheering from soldiers and citizens. Enlisted men were excited. Surely the vast majority of them would be mustered out of service and on their way home in no time. Such thoughts consumed every waking hour. Those who observed carefully, however, had cause for concern.[2]

A week after the review, large quantities of camp supplies and clothing arrived for receipt by the quartermaster. Would all these supplies be for any other purpose than a major campaign? Soldiers grumbled. Their mood brightened, however, when rumors swirled on May 28 that their former brigade commander had returned to his troops. Officers and men of the Eighty-Ninth Illinois gazed intently at the brigade commander's tent. They were rewarded with a glimpse of their former leader emerging from the trees on his favorite steel-gray charger. Willich rode from one regiment to the next, stopping to tell a few jokes and give brief addresses to his comrades. He promised he would be back in a few days to "turn himself inside out" with stories from his year away from them. "I am sure there is no other man living," Pvt. Joel Chambers remarked, "the sight of whom would cause the same amount of excitement, enthusiasm and real heartfelt joy."

On June 1, Willich resumed command of a brigade composed of the Fifteenth and Forty-Ninth Ohio, the Eighty-Ninth Illinois, the Eighth Kansas, and the Fifty-First Indiana. The next day, the entire brigade marched in a torchlight procession carrying banners in Willich's honor. "Lafayette in '76—in '65 Willich," read one. Others exclaimed, "With Willich We Defy the World," and "Willich We Love as a Father." The parade halted in front of the general's tent, where the chaplain of the Eighth Kansas conducted formal exercises that brought the old man to tears. Willich gave a long, emotional speech. "We welcome back our old commander," Chambers gushed. "He fell to rise again. Long may he live to drink Rhine wine and lager beer."[3]

After most soldiers from the Eighty-Ninth Illinois were mustered out of service on June 5, the remaining regiments in Willich's brigade speculated that they would be next. Those hopes were dashed later that day. Thomas ordered the Fourth Corps to move south, first to New Orleans, then across the Gulf to Texas. Men whose term of enlistment would expire by October 1, 1865, were mustered out, forcing another reorganization of the corps. The new structure consisted of three divisions composed of two brigades each. Willich's brigade became part of the Third Division under Gen. Thomas J. Wood. In place of the Eighty-Ninth Illinois, the brigade's soldiers welcomed two new regiments, the Seventy-First Ohio and the Fifty-Ninth Illinois, into their military family. Many men, especially those who had fought since 1861, expressed astonishment with this order and pleaded for a general mustering-out. It was no use. By June 16, they were boarding railcars to Johnsonville on the Tennessee River, where they would catch steamers bound for New Orleans.[4]

Willich established a floating headquarters on the steamer *Anna*, accompanied by the Forty-Ninth Ohio and the Eighth Kansas. The boarded at 11:00 p.m., more than twenty hours after reveille. The ship sat at dock until 10:00 a.m. the next day, when five steamers transporting the Fourth Corps began their journey. They arrived at Paducah, Kentucky, around 8:00 that evening. The sour mood of the troops worsened from hunger, as the danger of fire prohibited cooking on board. The men devoured a huge breakfast on shore the next day and made their way south, arriving at Cairo, Illinois, early in the morning, June 19. Moving large numbers of troops on the river was an exercise rife with complexity and danger. Willich, commanding the flotilla, ordered the ships to form a procession in single file to avoid potentially fatal collisions. Despite such precautions, it happened.

Soldiers of the Thirteenth and Forty-First Ohio felt a jolt, followed by the ominous sound of wood scraping metal as their steamer, *Echo No. 2*, rammed the monitor *Oneida*, which was anchored in the Ohio River. The steamship began taking on water. Willich guided the *Anna* alongside the crippled ship and worked feverishly to offload troops onto his vessel. All soldiers made it except two from the Forty-First Ohio, who perished along with some horses. Rumors swirled that the captain of the *Echo* was a former rebel and had wrecked the ship intentionally, but authorities soon found that whiskey was the real culprit. Tragedy revisited them a few days later at Vicksburg, when two soldiers enjoying a swim in the Mississippi were overcome by the strong current and drowned.[5] By the time they reached New Orleans on June 24, the men were eager to spend some time drying their sodden uniforms. No such luck. Their camp was a swampy piece of land seven miles south of the city at Chalmette Bottoms. For the history buffs in the corps, this was the same place where Andrew Jackson had defeated the British in the War of 1812. It was a hellish place of intense heat and humidity augmented with zero shade and no dry fuel for fires. The only creatures happy upon their arrival were millions of mosquitoes whose insect brains were not large enough to comprehend how such a delicious feast had dropped into their laps.

The only good thing about spending twelve grueling days camped in Louisiana was that it made the men eager to embark on their voyage across the Gulf of Mexico to Texas. Following a subdued Independence Day celebration, troops boarded steamers bound for Indianola, Texas. Many soldiers had never seen such an immense body of water or witnessed schools of turtles, sharks, and other sea creatures. The novelty of nature's bounty soon gave way to another new experience, seasickness. "The vessel is rolling considerable and many of the boys are getting pretty white," one soldier commented. More than a few were "heaving Jonah and making all sorts of hideous noises." On July 9 the soldiers disembarked at Matagorda Bay. Before they left the steamers and headed for Indianola, officers ordered them to fill their canteens. Fresh water was scarce in this part of Texas. Some did not heed the warning and suffered terribly.[6]

• • • • •

Indianola was deserted. Hopes for a good night's rest in an abandoned building were shattered when the troops marched through the town in late afternoon, stopping for supper about a mile away. Their next day's challenge was a twenty-mile march to Green Lake. Baking in the stagnant heat, they moved southwest through a barren landscape. Men still on their sea legs struggled with exhaustion. Nearly one-third fell out along the trail. Some fixed bayonets, drove them into the prairie, and hung a bit of tenting on the butt end of their rifles, lying in what little shade they could manufacture until the sun finally set. Mosquitoes were so thick they obscured the moon. Mosquito netting, the most valuable commodity in camp, was wrapped around the heads of the horses to keep them calm. Most stragglers were rounded up by nightfall. Hapless soldiers trudged into Green Lake wondering whether things could get much worse. Then they realized that they were short on rations. A few hardy officers who had survived the ordeal with residual energy rode back to Indianola to requisition supplies. Thankfully, food and other necessities arrived on July 16. Green Lake would be their home for the next month, so they tried to make the best of it.[7]

Willich kept his troops busy with drills and other exercises so they would not dwell on their homesickness. This worked for a time. Mail service resumed, which pleased the men, despite an incessant question asked in nearly every letter. *When will you return home?* Watermelons and wild grapes grew in abundance nearby. Fishing was good, and soldiers shot alligators for sport. Slowly the troops became accustomed to the heat. Some ventured out to appropriate steers, recording cattle brands so the army could reimburse ranchers. Others resorted to poaching and looting, which Willich would not tolerate. After one such incident, the general gave his boys a stern speech, confiscated their arms, and had the guns put under guard for three days. After that, alligator shooting resumed under the supervision of a commissioned officer. Despite Willich's best efforts to keep the men occupied, disgruntled soldiers deserted in droves.[8]

Two men from the Forty-Ninth Ohio sneaked away from camp on their second night at Green Lake. Nine more deserted the following evening, including a sergeant and a corporal. Thomas McGann of Company C called such men "a disgrace to their posterity." Men who had won enduring fame by their brave deeds on the battlefield "in one moment lost it all," keened McGann. "Sooner die here and let the worms consume my body," he vowed. On August 7, Willich ordered his men to march to San Antonio. There was no truth to the abundant rumors that the Forty-Ninth Ohio would be mustered out any day. Instead, ill soldiers were sent to Victoria. The Fifteenth Ohio circulated a petition and refused to move. After Willich pleaded with them, the men shouldered their haversacks and marched ahead.[9]

Several soldiers driven to desperation in the unrelenting Texas sun dashed their guns to pieces in protest. Willich tried to lighten their loads by transporting knapsacks in supply wagons whenever possible. A Mexican guide led the troops to a stream bed on August 13, but it was so fouled with animal waste that they could taste it in their coffee. Willich subsequently began sending cooks and mess wagons ahead of the main body of his brigade so that supper would be waiting for them at the end of a long day's march. After nine days, the men finally arrived at Calaveras Creek near the San Antonio River, where they remained for two months. The camp had no shade.[10]

Willich was weary of aimless marching with no military purpose. A rainstorm on August 17 lightened the brigade's mood. When the showers stopped, a rainbow formed. Willich and his adjutant rode through it, chatting. The general wished that he could "take the old First Brigade, land on the shore of northern Germany and declare a republic." These were the fantasies of a tired old romantic. It was all Willich could do just to hold his unit together as its numbers dwindled from exhaustion, disease, and desertion.[11]

By late August, Willich could no longer bear to see his men suffer. He rode to San Antonio to meet with Sheridan to persuade him to accelerate the mustering-out of Union volunteers in the Fourth Corps. On August 26, General Wood left for a new assignment in Little Rock, Arkansas, leaving Willich in command of the division. It would be a short commission. One evening, the brigade lost its way and a number of soldiers turned on Willich, "deriding him, using opprobrious epithets." His adjutant concluded that this incident "broke his heart." The old man developed a fever upon arrival in San Antonio, and he was so sick by August 31 that he was relieved of duty. On

September 7 Willich was granted thirty days' leave. The division reorganized and was renamed the Third Division of the Central District of Texas. All of this maneuvering only emboldened the disaffected men. Members of each regiment in the brigade formed a committee of inquiry. On September 15 they submitted a petition to the War Department, asking to return home. The plea was read to all regiments. Rumors swirled daily, but it was not until late October that the soldiers finally received orders mustering them out of service.[12]

Willich was breveted a major general on October 21, 1865. On November 9, he reported to Brig. Gen. Lorenzo Thomas that he was fully recovered. "With the exception of my right arm which was permanently disabled at Resaca," Willich argued, "I am in good health and fit for any duty the Department may be pleased to order me upon." Thomas might have been impressed with the old man's devotion, but he urged Willich to resign his commission while he still had his health. The fifty-five-year-old warrior reluctantly agreed and mustered out of service in January 1866.[13]

• • • • •

Now that he was out of the army, the old general could speak his mind. The future of America's armed forces was of great concern to Willich. "The extravagant sacrifices in human life and money that were required to subdue a relatively small rebellious fraction of our nation," he argued, "can be attributed only to the inadequacy of the military knowledge and art displayed in the organization, education and handling of our northern armies." He maintained that America should pursue the "emancipation of the national genius from the bonds of military-class rule" in order to protect and defend the country. Shortly after his resignation, Willich published a pamphlet outlining his prescription for moving forward. He had plenty to say, but was anyone listening?[14]

Americans' aversion to a standing army dated back to the founding days of the republic. Having just won their liberty from a sovereign power with a large military force, former English colonists bristled at the idea of subjecting themselves to martial dominance in their new country. The Framers of the Constitution needed to balance such concerns with a duty to protect the United States from foreign aggression. The Revolutionary War proved that local militias were not enough to defend against anything more than small riots and Indian attacks. The combination of a Continental army and local militias ultimately proved successful, so the Framers formed a small Regular

Army backed by a reserve aggregate of state militias. They inserted a clause in the Constitution that allowed the federal government to "raise and support armies" in times of national emergency. As conflicts grew in scope and size throughout the first half of the new century, the need to raise, train, and equip large numbers of Americans for war became critical. The War of 1812 and the Mexican-American War proved successful models of the new system. Yet even with civil war threatening in the 1850s, political leaders remained ambivalent and divided over the future organization of the US military. When the scale of war grew to epic proportions in 1861, the president and Congress had to mobilize huge numbers of soldiers quickly, deferring the question of the future state of US military organization to peacetime.[15]

A year after the Civil War's end, enrollment in the US armed forces plummeted from more than one million men to fewer than seventy-seven thousand. Even so, this figure was still three times the size of the antebellum military.[16] Various statesmen made proposals to Congress regarding the future of the nation's military, thus reviving the old debate between those who favored a professional standing army and others who advocated for an alternate model.

Willich's position was clear. Personal experience and knowledge of history convinced him that a standing army was "a contrivance of monarchies." America's great experiment with an exclusive professional military system had utterly failed. Solutions to structural issues surrounding the postwar American army could be found in the original vision of early nineteenth-century Prussian Army reformers. They had attempted to remake the Prussian military system into a citizen army in the wake of disastrous defeats by Napoleon. A German aristocracy accustomed to exerting special privilege ultimately corrupted that model. In an American republic, however, the dream of a true people's army stood a greater chance of becoming a reality.[17]

In order to sell his plan to key political and military influencers, Willich had to first enumerate the shortcomings of the current system. This was a tricky task, as many of the people he needed to convince were products of West Point. In the upcoming election cycle, many regular army veterans moved into political leadership, riding a tide of Radical Republican hegemony. Willich was hardly the right man to make the case for fundamental change in the nation's military system.

Nevertheless, the aged volunteer veteran launched into a withering assault on the professional officer corps. He asserted that intelligent citizens found themselves "used as a mere bundle of sinews, muscles and bones" when led by "the lurid intellect of a regular corporal or the scraps picked up from a half-digested compendium of a military school." Just as he had argued to the king of Prussia twenty years previous, Willich maintained that an exclusive class of privileged elites alienated military leaders from the citizenry. The American military system had come to resemble that of England, "only substituting for a hereditary or well-established moneyed aristocracy, a temporary electioneering aristocracy." Any military talent these professional officers might have possessed was soon "destroyed by an idle garrison life, and by an exalted social position." Reorganizing America's military required a shift in mind-set back to America's founding ethos. Standing armies were created, according to Willich, as a "royal prerogative against the national efforts for the establishment of common rights." We must "emancipate the nation from military class rule," he argued, because of its "incongruity with the republican principle of self-government." A national citizen militia was the best way to accomplish this.[18]

Willich borrowed heavily from the Prussian Landwehr system introduced in 1808. In his plan for the American military, he envisioned replacing the standing army with a national militia composed of citizens from all walks of life. Military service would be compulsory and a requirement for enfranchisement. Three classes of militia would be segregated by age, beginning with twenty- to twenty-five-year-old men. The youngest men would be called out first in a time of war. Invalids would manage military arsenals and stores. A modest national police force would handle small-scale scale disturbances and other peacetime duties. If a crisis called for more manpower than police could provide, the first-class militia could be called out for that purpose. Willich's plan also presumed changes to America's educational system, since citizen-soldiers needed training and instruction in the military arts to achieve readiness.

Military instruction would become part of the regular curriculum at all schools in Willich's scheme. Younger lads would spend two or three afternoons a week working on their physique and conducting mock military exercises. High school boys would practice rifle and cannon. Children would show off their skills at national festivals. For citizens who aspired to teaching, seminaries would be established where high school graduates would study for a year. In addition, each state would establish military camps that all twenty-year-old men could attend for a three-month term to drill and train. Upon completion of camp training, young men would receive the franchise and join the militia. An educated citizenry would furnish a well-rounded pool of officer candidates selected for diverse talents and skills acquired in civilian life, rather than from the stifling, exclusive atmosphere of a military academy.[19]

A national citizen militia would correct shortcomings in recruitment evident during the Civil War. The volunteer system, according to Willich, enabled the disloyal and indifferent to avoid military service by staying home to "betray, with the ballot, those that fought on the battlefield." The bounty system encouraged a mercenary spirit. Draft rules were simply unjust. Substitution was Punic and resulted in criminals rather than able soldiers filling the ranks. These systems combined to create "an exemption law for the richer classes and the establishment of a market for the blood of the poor." "The tax for the preservation of the Republic," in Willich's view, was due from *every* citizen and "paid in kind, i.e. in blood."[20]

Willich criticized professionally trained military leaders who had conflicting and "monstrous" ideas regarding the organization of the army. Some officers wanted to nearly eliminate cavalry, which would inhibit pursuit of a beaten enemy and imperil both the army's rear guard and their lines of communication. Others saw war as essentially a contest of artillery, which would create a ponderous and inflexible fighting force. The country was better off without such theorists. Willich bemoaned military doctrine that favored smoothbore muskets and other outdated technology over the latest innovations. He had experienced resistance to new ideas during the war. In his extensive postwar review, Willich cited examples of the government's repeated failures to properly equip, feed, train, and deploy troops. Only the medical corps escaped his scathing critique.[21]

The biggest problem with the existing professional military system, in Willich's opinion, was that it created incompetent leaders. Implicit obedience to orders meant that intelligent men subjected themselves to "imbecility and brutality" due to the threat of punishment, rather than exhibiting cheerful obedience to men of moral and intellectual superiority. America needed military leaders who had proved their leadership talents in private life and who had been promoted through the ranks. Great leaders with real practical knowledge and experience and who were dedicated to the national interest instead of their own self-promotion, made the best guardians of liberty. When the entire genius of the nation is available to the government, argued Willich, there is no excuse for limiting the selection of senior officers to a small number of professional soldiers whose training does not produce tactical skills, much less strategic aptitude. Worse still were many leaders who were simply not bright enough for the task. The Civil War provided numerous examples of lost battles that might have been won had it not been for generals' egregious mistakes.[22]

Willich warned against complacency now that the war was over and the slave aristocracy was defeated. "Other intellectual, social and moral abnormalities still exist in our midst," he stated. These relied on threats of violence for their continued existence. The general predicted that "this brute force [was] bound to be marshalled" sooner or later "against the genius of human liberty." To confront this danger, American society needed a contingency of acquired intelligence. Only careful planning and preparation, Willich said, would "enable us to tame the wild beast, which otherwise may tear the Republic to pieces."[23]

Willich stopped short of naming this threat. Was it the unbridled greed of monopolists or the false doctrines of organized religion that imperiled liberty? No matter. Most people in power saw no imminent threat, particularly on the military horizon. Despite the devastating loss in blood and treasure, the United States emerged from the war as a formidable military power without peer in the Americas. Conquest of Indian tribes was nearly complete. Military occupation of the South ended by 1877.[24] Americans focused on fueling the industrial juggernaut with a workforce eager to get back to the job of supporting their families. Willich's ambitious proposals were not seriously considered.

Meanwhile, friends in Cincinnati had plans for their hometown hero. Willich's next adventure would take him away from his martial comfort zone and thrust him into the political arena, where he had never shown much aptitude. The result was predictable.

Chapter Nineteen

•••••••••••••••••••••

SCANDAL

WILLICH WAS BORN and bred to be a military man. His leadership talents had thrust him into positions of prominence among communist radicals and labor activists, yet these efforts did nothing to help him survive financially. With the war over, the disabled veteran spent time on the speaking circuit pushing his reform agenda without a plan for his future. Friends tried to secure him a position in the regular army, but he had burned many of those bridges with his scathing criticism of the institution and its West Point–trained officer class. Willich initially refused to apply for a pension. He would not be convinced to do so until December 1866. Friends could not bear seeing him live on the edge of poverty with a meager allowance fixed at thirty dollars per month. They had an idea that would honor the retired general's service while enabling him to support himself for the rest of his life. Willich would enter electoral politics with considerable hesitation. It was a path he should have resisted.

Judge Stallo proposed that Willich run for auditor of Hamilton County, Ohio, boasting that "a one-armed soldier could do this as well as a two-armed local politician."[1] The job was pure patronage. It required no special skills and came with a large staff to do most of the work. On July 9, 1866, an editorial written by Willich's supporters called his impending nomination "a fitting recognition of gallantry and a proper reward to a faithful old soldier."[2] The compensation was generous. Tradition held that the county auditor received no fixed salary; instead, he was allowed to keep the portion of the collections above actual expenses. The job was not about civil service. It was a boondoggle, and the old veteran would be set for life.

Once Union Party political operatives had tapped Willich for the lucrative post, they scheduled a series of events to laud their military hero across the region. The first rally, attended by more than twenty thousand enthusiastic supporters, was held in Indianapolis on July 31, 1866. Indiana governor Oliver P. Morton, who had his eye on a US Senate seat, used the reception to endorse Willich and to remind people that it was he who had given the old hero his first command. Morton called Willich a patriot, scholar, and statesman, even though the old general had neither attended university nor practiced the art of diplomacy. Morton went on to praise his protégé as an international figure on par with Lafayette, DeKalb, Steuben, and Kosciuszko. It was an address that strained credibility with all but Willich's most ardent fans.[3]

Four days after Morton's speech, Willich was nominated as the Union Party candidate for Hamilton County auditor on the third ballot. Democrats countered by nominating German American bondsman Adolph Ahlers. With a coalition of erstwhile Republicans and pro-war Democrats still holding sway a year after the war's end, there was little doubt that the Union Party would triumph.

The Union Party campaign kicked off on September 8, 1866, with a huge rally at Court Street Market in downtown Cincinnati. Willich shared the speaker's podium and the ticket with future governor and president Rutherford B. Hayes and Edward F. Noyes, who was also destined to become Ohio's chief executive. Willich spoke in German, gesturing with his left hand to remind people that war wounds had rendered his right arm useless. He chastised the Democrats as the party of slavery and spoke out strongly in favor of the Fourteenth Amendment to the Constitution guaranteeing all citizens, including newly freed slaves, equal protection under the law. Banners made fun of President Andrew Johnson as "His Accidency." The Eleventh Ward opted for humor with a play on the retired general's surname, boasting, "We will lick the Rebels."[4]

Cincinnati's two largest German-language newspapers, the *Volksfreund* and the *Volksblatt* supported the Democratic ticket. Invective raged between the competing parties, but in the end, Hayes, Noyes, and Willich were elected by comfortable margins. To Willich's friends, his election was poetic justice. To his enemies, however, Willich's cozy situation was not a well-earned safe haven. It was an example of a corrupt civil service system run amok. One opponent, *Volksblatt* editor Frederick Hassaurek, would wait until Willich's term ended in 1869 to seek his revenge.

• • • • •

Hassaurek had emigrated from Vienna as a teenager, and he became a successful newspaper editor. Until Willich arrived on the scene, he had been
the leading German journalist in the city. Like the general, Hassaurek once
railed against Catholic influence and capitalist excess. He was a delegate to
the 1860 Republican National Convention in Chicago. As co-publisher of
the rival newspaper the *Volksblatt*, Hassaurek was frequently at odds with
Willich. Willich felt that the journalist adopted and discarded personal principles on a whim, relying only on "the market price of his political influence"
as his guide. "I regarded this man as dangerous," Willich remembered, "and
productive of corruption among the Germans and I tried to neutralize it."[5]

At the outset of the Civil War, the twenty-nine-year-old Hassaurek sailed
for the comfort and safety of the American embassy in Ecuador, where he
served as minister. This position was Lincoln's repayment of a political debt
he owed for the German's support in the 1860 election. Hassaurek earned a
salary of $7,500 a year paid in gold. The fifty-one-year-old Willich, in con-
trast, took up gun and sword in defense of his adopted homeland and was
rewarded with a pittance of a pension and a lame right arm. While Willich
returned to Cincinnati a hero and the "representative German," Hassaurek
receded into the background. This was more than the younger man could
stand.[6]

The elections of 1867 and 1868 offered Hassaurek an opportunity to use
his talent as a political chameleon to regain his prominence in Ohio political circles. Yet he bungled it. He initially aligned with conservatives to keep
black suffrage off the state Republican platform. Then he reversed field a
month before Ohio's 1867 referendum, parroting the language of Schurz and
Willich, only to see the measure fail. This behavior marked him as a dubious
liberal, or simply a political opportunist.[7]

Sincere German American radicals like Willich had been cultivating an
ethos that conflated ethnic nationalism with racial justice since the mid-
1850s. Although Willich's alliance with leading Cincinnati blacks had been
exceptional, historian Alison Clark Efford asserts that he and his peers drew
direct parallels between immigrant male citizenship and black male enfranchisement as the "capstones" of a transnational mission to create free nation-
states.[8] Willich stumped for Grant at various gatherings across the Midwest,
using the well-oiled mechanism of the social festival to reinforce the duty of
American Volk to use the German national spirit to perfect their adopted
republic.

At Chicago's annual Saengerfest, Willich urged singing societies to battle
"impure demons" intent on clipping the wings of the free German spirit and
arresting its progress. "Our German *Vereine*," Willich argued, "have only a

right to exist if they clear the way for civilization." Willich's demons "were the very same that [he] had to battle against before [he] left the Fatherland," namely "brutality and stupidity." He cautioned the singers not only to stay vigilant against nativism and "suppress the evil spirit among Anglo-Saxons and Irishmen," but also to resist similar prejudices among themselves. "You will not only esteem a principle when it is German," he cautioned, "but when it is human."

Willich reserved his choicest barbs for organized religion. To clerics who threatened to take away lager beer, send Sabbath breakers to Hell, and deny workers their one day of family enjoyment, Willich cried, "Never will we submit to it!" If religious fanatics wanted to "walk around, ghost-like, wrapped in a sack-cloth," so be it, the general said. "We will leave the devil undisturbed in the possession of Hell, and God in possession of his Heavens," Willich assured his audience, "but we will have the earth to ourselves." The freedoms won with republican government and universal suffrage are not guaranteed by law or the Constitution, he argued, but by the humane spirit of man within himself. Only men who do not tremble in front of Hell or live for Heaven can be truly free.[9] Hassaurek and other conservative Germans were fed up with Willich's unceasing attacks on faith and the Catholic Church. Hassaurek decided to strike back.

Criticism of politicians and public officials was a favorite sport of the nineteenth-century partisan press. Hassaurek was a frequent combatant in these dustups. In Willich' s case, however, his interests were more personal than political. Hassaurek reserved his choicest venom in 1869 for the express purpose of ruining the reputation of the old general. He accused the former auditor of paying a bookkeeper's salary out of county coffers instead of funding it from his own enormous income. He further suggested that Willich and the assessors had intentionally overlooked property so that it could be listed as omitted from the tax rolls. This presumably allowed Willich and his deputy to list the property as "omitted" and earn a 10 percent fee for collecting taxes on said properties. The charge involving the bookkeeper's salary had merit. The second charge was an outright fabrication.[10]

Hassaurek painted Willich as a two-faced opportunist who had abandoned his socialist principles and was beholden to the same corrupt system he had once denounced. On February 7, 1869, Hassaurek's editorial in the *Volksblatt* was reprinted in English in the *Cincinnati Enquirer*. The journalist mocked Willich as a fallen savior of the workers who was content to pocket money earned by his staff rather than sharing the proceeds value for value as he had long preached. "Not satisfied with throwing overboard his old principles at the first opportunity of putting them into practice," Hassaurek chided, "he reaches for the pieces of silver not belonging to the perquisites of office, and burdens the tax-payers." Under the guise of reform, Hassaurek called for an investigation by the board of the county commissioners and the county solicitor. He kept the pressure on for more than two months until he finally got what he wanted.[11]

Willich and his supporters ignored Hassaurek's accusations until public pressure mounted. John B. Jeup, editor of the *Cincinnati Volksfreund*, responded to Willich's frequent criticisms of Democrats and the Catholic Church, threatening to overwhelm him "ten feet high" and put a "too sudden quietus" to his charmed existence. County officials dismissed omissions clerk Daniel W. Thrasher, who had served under Willich and his predecessor. A clerk in the auditor's office reported to the commissioners on the unusually high number of new buildings on the omission list for the year 1867. Only then did Willich break his silence.[12]

Willich's defense was weak. He said that he had simply followed the customs of former auditors, practices that the commissioners had blessed. "I did not ask the people" for the auditor's office, Willich reminded them. "It was known as one of the offices," he claimed, "the emolument of which exceeded the equivalent for the labor to be performed." This was as good as admitting that he was merely a figurehead, an idea he reinforced by acknowledging that he was not involved in the omissions. Thrasher performed this function on his own, according to Willich, and received the 10 percent fee. When Willich learned of the unusually high number of omissions, he reported that fact to the commissioners and asked to have Thrasher investigated.[13] At the very least, Willich was disconnected in his role. Critics called him incompetent. But was he a criminal?

On April 16, 1869, a committee appointed by the Court of Common Pleas examined the records of the auditor's office and the county commissioners. Willich had already admitted that he paid his bookkeeper out of county funds. Thrasher was found to have been paid more than $24,000 in omission fees. The committee ruled that that the payments in both instances were illegal and that the county was entitled to recover the money.[14]

A month later, the county solicitor filed suit against Willich, Thrasher, and three other former auditors. This action sought to recover sixty thousand dollars from Willich and thirty-five thousand dollars from Thrasher.[15] The local press was less than enthusiastic about the lawsuit, which some viewed as politically motivated. Someone changed an Associated Press report about Willich's farewell banquet in late March to imply that Willich had taken his illegal rewards and fled the country. In reality, Willich had announced his intention to visit Germany months earlier and had left Cincinnati to take water therapy on his injured arm at Cleveland. His supporters cried foul.[16] Democrats responded just a week after the original lawsuit was filed by bringing similar charges against two wartime auditors from their own party. In the *Volksblatt*, however, Hassaurek ignored the other defendants and continued his verbal assaults on Willich.[17]

As the months dragged on, reformers reminded the public of the long tradition of bestowing this lucrative position on various worthies. Few doubted that this was a civic sin needing correction, but many saw the attack on Willich as a personal vendetta. Judge Stallo resigned from a local Turner society in protest of Hassaurek's membership.[18] Even newspapers like the *Volksfreund*, which had opposed Willich's election, questioned Hassaurek's integrity, accusing him of fleecing the county treasury by charging nearly three times the going rate for city advertising. Frank Erdelmeyer, the last colonel of Willich's old Thirty-Second Indiana Regiment, held a rally in support of his former commander. "Fred Hassaurek is well known," one meeting resolution stated, "as a man who has made it a business, for a number of years, to defame the principles of other men's creeds." The *Cincinnati Commercial* chimed in: "Certainly no informed person believes that the gallant old general is a dishonest man."[19]

Rather than run from his troubles as critics suggested, Willich postponed his European visit for a year while the scandal played out. On June 21, 1869, Stallo's junior law partner urged dismissal of suits against all five defendants. A judge declined the motion.[20] As the 1869 election season neared, the public lost interest in the case, and other motives behind the publicity became clear. Hassaurek had formed a reform ticket that fused Democrats and Republicans to capture county offices in the October elections. Hassaurek played both sides against the middle, endorsing Republican Rutherford B. Hayes for governor on the state ticket, while pushing the reform party in the county ticket. Although Hayes still won the governor's chair, Hassaurek's action helped split the Republican vote in Hamilton County, allowing Democrat George Pendleton to outpoll Hayes.

The *Cincinnati Commercial* charged that Hassaurek had made a deal with Andrew Johnson. If the reform ticket carried Hamilton County, thus embarrassing the Radical Republicans, Johnson would use his influence with Pres. Ulysses S. Grant to appoint Hassaurek's half-brother Leopold Markbreit to a diplomatic post. Mission accomplished—Markbreit became minister to Bolivia. Willich condemned the winning county ticket as a "hermaphrodite" scheme meant to pave the way for Hassaurek to conspire with US Supreme Court chief justice Salmon P. Chase. In exchange for Hassaurek delivering German support to Chase for a Democratic run for the presidency in 1872, Chase would support Hassaurek for the US Senate. When Chase's bid for that nomination failed three years later, Hassaurek's ambitions also ended, and he resigned as editor.[21]

By the time Willich left for Germany in June 1870, interest in the lawsuit was at a low ebb. Defense attorneys challenged the legal basis for the two-year-old charges. The judge overruled them, stating that "there is no question of fraud, but a pure question of legality." The ruling partially vindicated Willich and his co-defendants. As to the legal question, the judge recounted the recent history of county auditor practices. When the Civil War broke out, the county auditor had been under pressure to come up with monies to fund bounty payments for enlisting volunteer soldiers. Commissioners devised the scheme to seek out property previously omitted from the tax rolls and pay the tax omission clerk a 10 percent finder's fee for these collections. The auditor hired a bookkeeper at county expense to manage the extra workload. Willich and his predecessors simply followed those same practices.

The judge ruled that the hiring of an omissions clerk and a bookkeeper were illegal acts and that all related fees and salaries were therefore illegal. After the ruling, the state legislature passed bills that legalized these payments for the years 1861–69, effectively ending the matter. Willich's reputation was bruised, but not ruined. By the time the trial ended, Willich was already overseas trying to patch up a relationship he had set aside twenty-three years earlier.[22]

• • • • •

The prospect of two reunions made Willich yearn to revisit his native land in 1870. The first was personal. By renouncing his nobility and resigning from the Prussian Army in 1847, Willich had alienated his family and become an outcast. He and his older brother Julius, a retired Prussian Army lieutenant in his midsixties, had not been on speaking terms since. The younger brother was unsure of the reception he would get from Julius, but he now had the means and the time to attempt a reconciliation.

World events also called Willich back to the Fatherland. Prussia, whose power had ebbed and flowed throughout his lifetime, was ascending. The year after the American Civil War ended, war broke out between Austria, which led a confederation of independent ethnic German states, and a reinvigorated

Prussia, whose foreign policy was engineered and led by Minister-President Otto von Bismarck. Bismarck believed that the great cause of German unity, not achieved in 1848–49, would only come about through cunning diplomacy partnered with the application of iron and blood. Austria was crushed in nine weeks. Prussia annexed Austria's German allies and formed the North German Confederation. Bismarck's ultimate goal was in sight. By wresting the southern German states away from the influence of France, his dream of a reunited German empire would become reality.[23]

Willich had an emotional stake in the final stage of Bismarck's scheme. After all, he had fought to liberate the Prussian people from monarchial oppression. He still had a personal score to settle with French emperor Louis-Napoleon, whose sudden coup nearly twenty years previous had effectively ended the hopes of Willich and his fellow exiles for a pan-European republican revolution. Willich's dream of a communist society was as distant as ever, but the romantic notion that Germany could finally take its rightful place as a world power in an international system of nation-states had broad appeal among Forty-Eighters. The recent Union victory in the United States was more than a repudiation of the slave aristocracy. It was a vindication of nationalism and strong central government. This triumph encouraged Bismarck and excited many German Americans. Whether Willich sensed it or not, he was about to witness the final step in the reunification of Germany as he sailed to Bremen in June 1870.

The family reunion was not a happy one. Julius von Willich had been living in the town of Torgau, northeast of Leipzig, since his retirement from the army in 1857. Despite his younger brother's sincere overtures, Julius's heart was hardened. He never understood how August could give up so much for such a fruitless adventure, not to mention the damage his brother had caused to his own career and family. He had turned his back on them and taken up arms against his own comrades. Julius could not forgive treason.[24] He allowed his brother to stay with him, but events soon led August back to Berlin.

Bismarck knew he could goad the French into war. France felt threatened by the North German Confederation, which had destabilized a tenuous balance of European powers forged at the end of the Napoleonic Wars. In order to ensure that the southern German states sided with him, Bismarck needed France to be seen as the aggressor. He accomplished that goal with ease. After the Spanish overthrew Queen Isabella in 1868, they offered the crown to Prussia's Prince Leopold. This was a nightmare scenario for France, which feared encirclement by Prussia and her Spanish ally. French diplomatic pressure forced Leopold to refuse the offer, but Bismarck would not let such an opportunity pass. He altered and published a telegram from his king to a French envoy that substituted demeaning language for conciliation, thus humiliating France. The forgery worked and France declared war on Prussia on July 16, 1870. Southern German states immediately sided with their northern ethnic brethren.[25]

That same day, Willich was in Dresden and sent an excited letter back to friends in Cincinnati. "This morning at three o'clock," he began, "the order to mobilize the troops was received." Willich depicted Louis-Napoleon as a murderous adventurer intent on committing a buccaneer raid on Germany. On false rumors that the French had already blown up the railroad bridge at Mayence and had advanced into the Rhineland, Willich boasted, "Let them come. . . . The further the French penetrate, the more surely they will be welcomed into hospitable graves." In reality, the French strategy was defensive. Any ethnic German who sided with the French in this contest, warned Willich, "should be eradicated from the earth." He promised that he would travel to Berlin in a few days and offer his services to the king. "I will do so, with the hearty readiness with which I fought against the slave power of the South," he promised.[26]

Prussian field marshal Helmuth von Moltke had been planning his strategy for war with France for thirteen years. He was ten years older than Willich and had served in the Danish and Swedish Armies before being admitted to the Prussian military academy at the age of twenty-two. He graduated in 1826 when Willich was still a student there. Like Willich, Moltke was a lover of literature, art, and history. Unlike Willich, he remained a staunch supporter of the monarchy. He had successfully planned and executed the triumph over Austria four years earlier. Moltke had a winning plan, a superior army, and a righteous cause. He had little patience for foreigners who wanted to jump on the Prussian bandwagon. Willich was one of the throngs of volunteers Moltke turned away at the outset of the war with France. The Prussian field marshal reluctantly allowed American general Phillip Sheridan to hang around as an official observer with no combat role.[27]

The deck was stacked in Moltke's favor. The French had fewer than three hundred thousand trained regulars ready for service. The balance of their total force of approximately eight hundred thousand was a hastily formed aggregation of conscripted reserves who lacked organization and discipline. Not only was the German fighting force at least 30 percent larger, but the Prussian system of compulsory military service also meant that their troops were better trained and highly motivated to defend their homeland.[28]

Willich returned to his brother's house in Torgau to watch the spectacle unfold as the Prussians mobilized over a million men for the offensive. He described the scene in a letter to Indiana senator Oliver P. Morton on

July 19. "The whole nation," Willich noted, "men, women and even children, appear to be happy that the crisis has come." He also predicted, "After this murderous gambler, Louis Napoleon, called by the Pope 'the most Christian Monarch,' shall have finished his abominable career, the time for reforms in Europe will begin."

Willich believed that the defeat of France would also have a positive effect in America. "The political power of the Catholic hierarchy will be broken with the power of France," he forecasted. Prussian victory represented "defeat of those dark powers in the United States, which try to alienate our Catholic fellow citizens from those institutions which form the very basis for our republic." Willich called for US support of the Germans as America's only true ally in Europe. If the war dragged on, he recommended that the United States intervene on Prussia's behalf.[29] Such help was neither welcome nor necessary.

After nine months of fierce fighting, it was over. Paris fell, Louis-Napoleon was imprisoned, and the French founded the Third Republic. A united Germany emerged as a dominant power in continental Europe alongside imperial Russia. German methods of universal conscription and war planning were lauded and imitated by other nations. For Willich, Germany was on its way toward fulfilling its destiny. "The Germans stand proudly and respected among other nations," he gushed, "which have until then looked down on them with arrogance."[30] While Willich basked in the warm pride of the Fatherland, he turned his attention to one of his great regrets, his lack of a first-class university education.

Willich did not wait for the war's end to enroll in the University of Berlin. On October 18, 1870, he matriculated, pursuing a liberal arts education in one of the model universities of Europe. The university's renown had grown even larger since the days when Friedrich Schleiermacher sat on the faculty. Willich took courses in physics, economics, Roman history, and natural law, taught by some of the most eminent professors on the Continent. It was one of the happiest periods of his life. He received his departure certificate on March 31, 1871, but was in no great hurry to return to America. He enrolled in trade school to study mineralogy and other sciences, but the militarized atmosphere of Berlin eventually wore on him.[31] News that the lawsuits against him and other former auditors had been dismissed prompted Willich to plan a return voyage in the fall. The flame of labor reform still burned deep in his heart, but the auditor scandal had robbed him of an effective platform for his socialist views. Nevertheless, America was his home. After visiting friends,

Willich left Prussia for the final time, arriving in New York in early October 1871.[32]

Once settled back in Ohio, Willich resumed lecturing at various patriotic meetings and societies. On one of these occasions in October 1873, he presented a talk titled "The Origin, History, and Destiny of Man in Light of Humboldt's Cosmos." Despite enthusiastic advance billing, few attended the event. The former officer used words his audience was unfamiliar with, and he made no attempt to explain their meaning. One local newspaper described the lecture by reminding its readers of a well-known anecdote regarding one of Willich's early influences, the German philosopher Hegel. "Only one of his students understood him and that one misunderstood."[33] In teaching, as in politics, Willich lacked the talent necessary for a career that did not involve the martial arts. It was time for the old soldier to slow down and enjoy the time he had left in the company of his friends, his books, and his music.

Chapter Twenty

• • • • • • • • • • • • • • • • • • • •

READING SHAKESPEARE IN AUGLAIZE

THE STEAMER *DEUTSCHLAND*, with nearly eight hundred souls aboard, belched plumes of deadly black ash as it inched into its berth at Castle Garden Depot in New York Harbor on October 9, 1871. Few noticed. After all, the waters of the harbor were teeming with all manner of floating conveyances. More than 60 percent of US exports flowed through the bustling port. New York's population had doubled since 1850, and more than a million residents crowded the huge metropolis. German immigrants streamed into the city in record numbers following the Franco-Prussian War, outnumbering Irish arrivals by a factor of two. Many immigrant ships carried smallpox, but fortunately that scourge skipped the *Deutschland* on this particular voyage.[1]

Willich walked down the gangplank alone. His quiet return hardly resembled his arrival from London eighteen years earlier. No jubilant crowds assembled to cheer him. No celebratory banquets were held in his honor. For most German Americans, the Revolution of 1848 was a distant memory. Their immediate concern was building a secure future for their families. A united Germany was now a fact, though its imperial form of government did not resemble the citizen republic that socialists had dreamt of. The American Civil War was six years in the rear view. Willich's adopted country faced new and vexing challenges as it tried to reconstruct the old Union.

Immediately following the war, Radical Republicans dominated government and dictated strict terms to the South for reunion. Democrats pushed back. Willich believed in universal manhood suffrage and identified himself with the Republican Party. He had been swept into political office and financial security by the victors, only to see rival reformers attempt to destroy

DIEKER HOUSE, ST. MARYS, OHIO, C. 1875. COURTESY OF KRAIG NOBLE.

his reputation. Although the lawsuit against him and his predecessors had been dismissed, his integrity had been questioned. This wounded Willich to his core. Resuming his former life in Cincinnati was unthinkable. Before long, the reform impulse that had assailed Willich in his county auditor role would reach to the highest office in the land, and he would be compelled to make a choice between party loyalty and personal principles.

A man with no family and scant possessions save an organ and some books could settle anywhere. After a brief residence in Cleveland for further treatment on his lame right arm, Willich accepted the invitation of army comrade Maj. Charles Hipp to move to Saint Marys, a German settlement of seventeen hundred residents in Auglaize County, Ohio, where he could spend the rest of his days surrounded by peace and polite society. Hipp was an officer in the Thirty-Seventh Ohio Volunteer Infantry who had been with Willich at Resaca. The major was wounded twice at Ezra Church near Atlanta, and he had had his own shattered arm amputated. Just as J. B. Stallo had served as Willich's best friend and advocate before the war, Hipp assumed that role in the general's twilight years.[2]

Willich rented a corner room on the second floor of the Dieker House, the best hotel in town. Each morning before breakfast, he walked for miles along the towpaths of the Miami and Erie Canal. Railroad expansion slowed canal traffic, creating a relaxing environment for exercise and contemplation. The lack of feeling in his right hand frustrated his efforts at quail hunting, but reading and music remained a daily routine in his life. Willich's humble, ragged attire proved challenging to a local seamstress. "I sew and patch and patch his shirts and his underclothes," the washerwoman complained, "and I can hardly keep the general together." Saint Marys was the kind of welcoming, social place to settle into and enjoy one's golden years, but the old warrior still had a few battles left to fight.[3]

Throughout his many adventures, victories, and disappointments, the issue of social justice remained the pole star of Willich's life. The ultimate dream of a communist society in Germany or America seemed as distant as ever. Willich and other champions of American labor reform had reason for both optimism and concern by the early 1870s. On the one hand, new national organizations like the National Labor Union and the Knights of Crispin, whose membership topped fifty thousand by 1870, gave workers hope for basic rights such as the eight-hour workday. That cause was taken up by the International Workingmen's Association in Geneva in 1866. While shoemakers and other tradesmen were organizing, however, their very livelihoods were being threatened by an influx of unskilled immigrant labor and increased mechanization in the workplace. On May 19, 1869, President Grant issued his National Eight Hour Law Proclamation for all federal workers. Instead of cheering the nation's chief executive, some former allies began to distance themselves from him. Rampant corruption in the Grant administration and what some viewed as a carte blanche attitude toward wealthy industrialists led some Republicans to oppose the president for reelection in 1872.[4]

The revolt within the Republican Party was started by Willich's old comrade Carl Schurz. This most celebrated German American Forty-Eighter had another motive in revolting against the Grant administration. During a three-hour speech in Congress, Schurz detailed a sensational scandal. The War Department had violated neutrality law during the Franco-Prussian War by selling guns and ammunition to the French, who were using these supplies to kill Germans. Denials by the president, accusations of bribery, and hard evidence of gun cases stamped with the addresses of various US armies enraged German Americans.[5]

Schurz began forming the Liberal Republican Party, an offshoot of the political machine that had dominated national politics since the end of the war. Liberal Republicans argued that corruption and graft in the civil service system were making a mockery of the Grant administration, and they also maintained that the basic ends of Reconstruction had been met. The rebellion was over, and blacks had been guaranteed fundamental rights of citizenship. It was therefore time to end the military occupation of the South, restore the franchise to all males of age, and get on with the business of rebuilding the nation.[6]

Big names jumped on Schurz's bandwagon. Charles Sumner and Charles Francis Adams pledged support for the new party. Willich, too, got caught up in the excitement and joined the splinter group, creating an odd political alliance. Although Liberal Republican support of laissez-faire economics was an anathema to him, Willich still viewed the Democrats as traitors and the Republicans as having abandoned the principles of free labor and catered to monopolists. Getting rid of Grant would be a positive step, and Schurz was the only German American with the political clout to pull it off. Schurz's effort, however, more closely resembled a drunken stumble.

The Liberal Republican convention in May 1872 turned into a fiasco. Instead of nominating a proven political leader, the convention chose eccentric newspaper magnate Horace Greeley as its candidate to unseat Grant. Democrats had been wooed to the Liberal Republican banner as part of a fusion ticket strategy. Dumbfounded and unable to agree on a viable alternative, they nominated Greeley as well. President Grant crushed Greeley in the general election. Schurz's experiment with third-party politics ended. Victory in the Civil War and the subsequent German unification had helped transform a German American political philosophy that supported black citizenship into an illiberal nationalism that effectively abandoned African Americans struggling for equality and social justice.[7]

Rather than being humiliated by his association with such a comical enterprise, Willich was inspired. Schurz had strayed far from his old principles; he would later oppose the eight-hour day for federal workers. What the nation needed was a political party that would advocate for the lowly wage worker, save the country from the grasp of greedy industrialists, and restore power to the people.[8]

Willich and like-minded friends from both major parties went to work. In January 1873, he and other Union veterans presented a petition to Ohio senator John Sherman opposing a bill passed by the US House of Representatives offering federal land grants for retired soldiers. The petition claimed that the bill would do more harm than good, as its true purpose was to benefit land speculators. Petitioners valued the good of the whole country more than any benefit they would accrue from such a law. Special legislation that favored one group of citizens over others was patently unjust. Furthermore, as worthy as veterans were, special interests were corrupting the American republic.[9] On July 31, 1873, delegates to a Columbus, Ohio, convention formed a new party, presented a platform, and ran a full slate of candidates for statewide office. They called themselves the People's Party. It was yet another attempt at forging an alliance between renegade Republicans and disaffected Democrats. At a campaign rally in Batavia, Ohio, on October 3, Willich argued the need for a third party and detailed its platform.

Willich sounded his familiar refrain. The great issue at stake was the survival of free labor. The recent war had culminated in victory over the slave aristocracy, but other formidable foes, namely monopolists, privileges, and special legislation, threatened to subvert Jefferson's promise of equal and exact justice for all. Repeating themes from his years as editor of the *Cincinnati Republikaner*, Willich argued that American farmers had to compete with low-cost producers on the world market in grain, while exclusive patents and import tariffs protected monopolies. When a farmer went to buy a plow or a sewing machine, this special legislation inflated prices and profits, causing the farmer to lose as much as 30 percent of the value of his production. This was not a fair value for value exchange. This was a corrupt system designed to benefit the wealthy few at the expense of the people who actually did the work.

Such an arrangement, Willich implored his audience to understand, was "the root of all economical and moral evils growing in our country." Special-interest legislation was essentially a tax levied on the working class and cloaked by the sham of protecting national industries. Allowing railroad conglomerates to buy up the best land at a bargain meant that the next best locations would be snapped up by speculators and sold at inflated prices. Steamboat monopolies garnered subsidies of the people's money under the false pretense of increasing the lucrative business of the country. In Willich's view, both major political parties were complicit in the con game.[10]

Northern Democrats were a party in crisis, still reeling from their antiwar platforms during the final three years of the conflict. Politics does make strange bedfellows, however. George Pugh came out as a strong advocate for the People's Party. As Clement Vallandigham's running mate in the Ohio gubernatorial election of 1863, Pugh had advocated for an immediate armistice with the Confederacy. Convicted of treason by a military court and exiled to Canada, Vallandigham was hanged in effigy in Union soldier camps during the election campaign.[11] Willich and other Union veterans listened to Pugh's speeches in 1873 with clenched teeth.[12] Just seven years earlier, Willich had assailed Pugh, accusing him of converting to Catholicism for political and personal gain.[13]

In a move that shocked many, Willich laid blame for Republican collusion with monopolists on his former sponsor, Indiana senator Oliver P. Morton.

According to the retired general, Morton found the current system perfect, extolling the virtues of a burgeoning industrial economy while the working class experienced few tangible benefits. Of Republicans, Willich insisted, "We have nothing to expect from [them] except bitter feud against every step towards equal rights and free labor."

Willich believed that Ohio and the country at large were prepared to listen to and act on the People's Party message. The party's platform advocated four critical reforms: ending land grants and special privileges to private corporations, shrinking the size of the federal government by abandoning the spoils system, limiting import duties to spur revenue production, and repealing laws favoring capital at the expense of labor. Willich tried to enlist women in the movement, predicting, "The struggle of women for social and political independence will enter another phase as soon as the monopolists do not pry any more of the value from their labor." He did not advocate violent government overthrow, but his proposals were still radical, even to those most impacted by runaway capitalism. If citizens would only understand the values of free labor and free exchange, he argued, they would "cease to serve as voting power to the enemies of their own interest."[14] The old general's dream of a society where monopolies were abolished and special interest legislation did not exist frightened many. The People's Party was a political pipe dream.

The new party was no more successful than the Liberal Republicans had been. The People's Party candidate for Ohio governor polled barely 10,000 votes, about the same as the Prohibition Party candidate. Democrat William Allen captured the governor's chair by slightly more than 800 votes out of nearly 450,000 ballots cast.[15] Most American citizens were not eager to abandon a two-party system that had coalesced just prior to the Civil War, and they certainly were not ready for anything that smacked of socialism. August Willich was a man of big ideas, fervent commitment, and little talent for politics.

From that point forward, Willich withdrew from active participation on the Ohio political scene. On occasion, as when his old friend Rutherford B. Hayes was running for president in 1876, Willich could be coaxed into an endorsement. "Down with the traitor—up with the stars," Willich exclaimed to a Kansas Republican newspaper in support of Hayes's candidacy.[16] The two had shared the trials of the battlefield and had suffered public criticism in the past for their liberal views on race and labor rights. But Hayes, like Schurz, had moved far from Willich politically. When the Great Strike of 1877 sent unprecedented numbers of German American workers to the streets to oppose wage cuts, Hayes's secretary of the interior, Carl Schurz, advocated for a much larger standing army to quell such dangerous insurrections. Schurz ally E. L. Godkin, editor of the *Nation*, issued a warning to the "well-to-do and intelligent classes of the population," stating, "[Be wary of those] who carry in their very blood traditions which give universal suffrage an air of menace to many of the things civilized men hold dear."[17]

In his final years, the old general spent much of his time on the great pleasures of his life. Fellow guests at the Dieker House tolerated his midnight singing of Schubert's songs for one voice and piano and listened attentively as he regaled them with anecdotes of his wartime exploits.[18] The town schoolmarm made him a small pouch for salt, as his old wound had deprived him of his sense of taste. Willich instructed young ladies in proper posture. His pockets were always full of candy, which he distributed liberally to youngsters he met on his daily walks. "Alle amerikanischen Kinder sind auch meine Kinder," was how he described his love for the children he never had. He indulged his passion for Shakespeare with the community, leading study circles and reciting lines from the bard's best-known plays. Nearly three decades after Willich's death, local women formed a Shakespeare Club in his memory. The club was the forerunner of the Saint Marys Community Public Library.[19]

• • • • •

Willich did not come downstairs for supper on Tuesday night, January 22, 1878. The boy who blacked his boots opened the general's door and peeked into the dark room. All he could make out was a lampshade on the floor and the general's coat on his bed. Perhaps the old man was at a friend's house. The next morning, the boy's brother, who worked as a clerk at the hotel, climbed the stairs to wake the general. As he entered the room, he found Willich lying on the floor. He had been dead for many hours. The corpse was partially dressed and the bed strewn with medical instruments used to allay chronic pain from war wounds that never fully healed. Likely the victim of a heart attack, Willich had complained of shortness of breath a few days before his death.[20] He was sixty-seven years old.

News of Willich's demise caught everyone by surprise, as the retired general had been in good health. Friends and former comrades streamed into the little town of Saint Marys. The undertaker worked feverishly to prepare the corpse for display. Willich's body, guarded by sentinels at the front and back doors, lay in the front parlor of the Dieker House from Wednesday until the planned Friday funeral. In the meantime, rival groups from Indiana and

Ohio lobbied for the honor of burying the former general's remains in their community. The delegation from Willich's Thirty-Second Indiana Infantry regiment wanted him to lie in state in the Indiana State House, then be interred in the soldier's cemetery. Since the deceased left no family in America, a meeting was held at Major Hipp's house where his closest friends decided that Willich would be interred in a nearby burial ground. By this time, thousands of mourners had converged on the town from the Ohio Valley region and beyond.

The enormous funeral was unlike any event Saint Marys had ever witnessed. Beginning at 10:00 a.m., guests lined up to say their final good-byes at the Dieker House. After five hours the casket was closed, Rev. W. A. Yingling recited a brief prayer and the body was carried to a waiting hearse. The pallbearers included Willich's most loyal and dear friends. Judge Stallo was there for him, as he always had been. Charles Hipp helped guide his old friend to his final resting place, along with William C. Margedant, the Hamilton machinist who had served on the staffs of Rosecrans and Sigel in the war. Henry Mosler of Wapakoneta, a Prussian-born artist who had befriended Willich in Cincinnati, helped carry the body. Adolph Metzner, the talented, quirky artist who had documented the history of the Thirty-Second Indiana with intimate scenes of camp life, came from Indianapolis to pay his respects. Unitarian minister Rev. Thomas Vickers, the most liberal clergyman in Cincinnati, labeled an atheist by some critics, along with fellow Queen City resident Fritz Dieter, completed the honored list.[21]

Schools closed for the day and special trains ran so that residents from surrounding towns and villages could attend the memorial services. Nearly twenty-five hundred people formed a funeral caravan that slogged a mile through mud and muck to Elm Grove Cemetery. A band from nearby Lima led the procession, playing a somber death march. Three local militia companies followed, trailed by the New Bremen town band, directly in front of the hearse and pallbearers. Behind the body marched other close friends, followed by large delegations from the Ninth Ohio, Thirty-Second Indiana, and Thirty-Seventh Ohio Volunteer Regiments carrying the tattered battle flags of Willich's brigade. A sizable column of Union veterans from other regiments made up the seventh group in the long procession. Local citizens followed the soldiers on foot, with dignitaries in twenty-seven horse-drawn carriages bringing up the rear. The elaborate spectacle would have embarrassed Willich, but by celebrating his life, mourners were also honoring the sacrifices made by hundreds of thousands who did not survive the war.

Once the immense crowd had assembled at the gravesite, militia companies

FUNERAL MONUMENT OF AUGUST
WILLICH, WHO DIED JAN. 22, 1878.
COURTESY OF KRAIG NOBLE.

formed a cordon around each delegation, and the formal service commenced. A German singing society from New Bremen performed as the corpse was lowered into the earth. William H. Gibson then stepped forward to deliver the eulogy in English. Gibson had served alongside Willich for much of the war. He lauded Willich's character and his lifelong struggle for universal liberty. After Gibson had finished his moving tribute, Ferdinand Vogeler, the 1877 nominee for Ohio lieutenant governor on the losing Republican ticket, gave the German-language eulogy. He had served under Willich in the Thirty-Second Indiana, and he praised his late commander for his caring, inspirational leadership.[22]

Tributes to Willich poured in from all corners of the nation and the world at large. Most cited his war record, his advocacy for workers, and his military leadership in the failed German republican revolutions of 1848–49. The *New York Times* penned an extraordinary tribute to the dead general, calling him "undoubtedly the ablest and bravest officer of German descent engaged in the war of the rebellion." The paper attributed Willich's success to "his untiring energy, bravery in the field, and marked abilities."[23]

The old general left no will. He had little interest in money or worldly possessions. After Willich's estate was examined and Hipp was appointed administrator, Auglaize County officials found that besides his meager personal effects, Willich had saved some of the money he had garnered from his auditor position and invested it in railroad stocks and bonds. He had lent more than $20,000 to his many friends, yet the wealthy former general spent his final years living like a pauper. The court concluded that Willich's only surviving blood relation, older brother Julius von Willich, should inherit the estate, save the sizable sum of $300 to erect a suitable grave monument. At the insistence of Willich's brother, the marble marker was topped by the von Willich family coat of arms.[24] Citizen August Willich would never have approved of such a bold display of the privilege and title he had renounced more than thirty years previous.

The Prussian nobleman turned communist revolutionary became an unlikely American hero. His military training, combat experience, and leadership skills made him a critical asset for the Union army. His commitment to the cause of the American worker was unflinching, though his efforts in that vein have been largely forgotten. In addition, he was a lifelong advocate for social justice. August Willich and other Forty-Eighters risked everything to ensure that democratic republics survived, both for the American people and on behalf of their fellow citizens throughout the Western world.

Conclusion

• •

THE REDDEST OF THE RED

IN APRIL 1862, Carl Schurz successfully lobbied President Lincoln to promote two German immigrants, Cols. Peter Osterhaus and August Willich, to
the rank of brigadier general.[1] Osterhaus had already commanded a division
under Franz Sigel and would later join Schurz and Sigel as the only native
Germans to achieve the rank of major general during the Civil War. Following
Willich's performance at Chickamauga in late 1863, Gen. George H. Thomas
formally recommended him for promotion to major general. Nothing happened. Early in 1865, Indiana governor Oliver P. Morton reminded Lincoln
of Willich's proposed advancement. "I think well of it myself," Lincoln remarked, "on more grounds than one." Despite the president's endorsement,
the matter was forgotten.[2]

Despite their superior military talent and accomplishments, Willich and
other native Germans were unable to gain higher rank and make a larger
impact during the Civil War. This fact raises critical questions about the
recognition of German American Civil War officers and hints at deficiencies
in Willich's own character and qualifications. The Prussian's radical reputation and halting English certainly limited his career prospects. Schurz and
Osterhaus were liberals and fluent English-speakers. Sigel was a radical, but
he was politically valuable to Lincoln as a German American icon besides
being a shameless self-promoter. Although numerous friends and comrades
made pleas for his further advancement, Johann Stallo pronounced Willich
wholly indifferent to promotion.[3]

Willich might have achieved even more in the military realm, where his
talents shone the brightest, had he assimilated more fully into American

culture, been more ambitious, and remembered the adage of his former military academy director, Carl von Clausewitz, that war was a continuation of politics by other means.[4] Some who surpassed him in rank, like Schurz and Sigel, played the political game with as much skill and finesse as Willich displayed on the battlefield. Willich proved himself politically inept in army circles by demeaning West Point training and in civilian life through disinterest and negligence in his sole elective office.

Given that Willich's exemplary Civil War service has been largely forgotten, what about the overall reputation of German American Union soldiers in historical memory? Such remembrance was twisted and tainted by blame laid on the half-German Eleventh Corps, commanded at various times by Schurz and Sigel, after Union defeat at Chancellorsville in 1863. When nativist media labeled German Union soldiers "flying Dutchmen," they damaged Germans' pride and dampened their enthusiasm for the war effort. German Americans fought bravely on numerous fields for the balance of the war, but they never got over the scapegoating following Chancellorsville.[5]

Historian Christian Keller challenges traditional melting pot theses, contending that immigrants' service in the Civil War inhibited and delayed their assimilation into American culture.[6] Nevertheless, German Forty-Eighters made an outsized impact on American society. Despite numbering fewer than ten thousand, many in this special group became progressive leaders in education, journalism, arts, science, and politics.[7] Add two world wars to the narrative, however, and one discerns a long-term historiographical bias against the German American experience, including during the Civil War. The fact that so few American historians read archaic German print and script also inhibits scholarship. Obstacles and prejudices aside, two hundred thousand German Americans fought for the United States and deserve more recognition for their role in attaining Union victory.[8]

Willich was a skillful, brave, and ingenious military leader who could occasionally be stubborn, impulsive, even foolhardy, risking his life unnecessarily in the face of overwhelming odds. He and his men were habitually at the tip of the spear, whether leading the assaults at Liberty Gap and Missionary Ridge or covering the retreat of Union forces at Chickamauga. The fact that he escaped death on the battlefield is remarkable given the personal risks he took in leading his troops. But Willich did survive—in fact, he thrived. He overcame defeat and disappointment in Europe to become one of the finest generals in the Union army.

● ● ● ● ●

Understanding why Germans risked their lives to fight for their new country expands our view of the Civil War as America's second great revolution, part of a global struggle for social justice and political freedom. Willich's life story provides insight into the role of transatlantic radical leaders in that revolution.

In an immediate sense, Willich failed in two of the three great causes of his life. He and his fellow revolutionaries did not overthrow the monarchs and princes of the various German states, nor did they create a unified German democratic republic. Willich's unceasing efforts to transform the American political system into a social republic where workers controlled the means of production and received full value for their labor never gained serious traction. His efforts to recruit and lead immigrant volunteers helped defeat the slave-owning aristocracy in the Confederate States, but the vision that Willich and Lincoln shared of a more perfect republican nation was a lofty goal that would probably take generations to realize.

Historian Eric Foner argues that the enduring challenge for radicals is that they must be "willing to fight and lose for a long time before achieving even partial success."[9] Military men like Willich and statesmen like Friedrich Hecker came from the well-educated German middle class. They grew to resent aristocratic dominance and forces of rapid industrialization that robbed working people of their independence and dignity and threatened to consign them to a permanent underclass. Both supported reform within the existing system initially, only to see momentary gains erased by hardline reaction time and again. Their commitment to change and frustration with intractable rulers pushed them into radicalism and rebellion. If their unwillingness to accept compromise and unite with liberals for gradual reform imperiled their cause, their inability to rally the masses to join them in violent revolution doomed it.

The "reddest of the red," as Willich was known by friend and foe alike, clung stubbornly to radical prescriptions and violent means even after such measures had failed.[10] Existing power structures in the German Confederation under Prussian leadership were too strong to be threatened or bullied by a loosely organized gang of rebels. German liberals, along with Marx and Engels, counseled patience, but Willich was unwilling to wait generations for the fulfillment of his dreams.

Rather than give up on cherished democratic socialist principles, Willich and other rebel leaders emigrated from Germany in the hope that they would find a warmer reception for their ideas across the ocean. Export of German revolutionists and their ideology to America made sense. After all, radicals throughout Europe had been working in concert for a republican vision that, at least in theory, transcended national borders. The multicultural United States of America seemed an ideal place to continue that struggle. Willich changed course from system overthrow to extensive reform through existing legislative channels.

The general argued that America needed to place workers in control of republican government. Collective management of production by workers themselves would restore human dignity and end unfree labor. People who did the work would reap the full value of their labor, not a minimal wage designed to keep workers subservient while lining owners' pockets with outsized profits. Willich's original scheme anticipated the short-lived Paris Commune of 1871 and the industrial socialism of Daniel De Leon decades later.[11] Labor activists did have some success. Workers organized as never before, winning small concessions in working hours and using strikes to protect their interests, but the more ambitious reform goals of Willich and others remained elusive.

The juggernaut of capitalism combined with a flood tide of immigration to increase competition among workers and create unprecedented economic prosperity for the country as a whole. Life might have been challenging for many immigrants, but they still had more opportunity in America than in their homeland. Then the Civil War stalled the labor movement. Leaders like Willich transformed labor republican messaging into a compelling enlistment plea to destroy the slaveholder aristocracy. German American men, already bonded by nativist prejudice, forged a strong common identity as German-born sons of the republic who were fighting for issues of global importance.[12]

Willich positioned German American sacrifice in the Civil War as an international human rights crusade during frequent speeches to his troops. The general advised Union veterans to remain vigilant in the wake of victory, and he urged them to support democratic revolutions in the Old World. "No temporary peace will undo the revelations of the times," he insisted. "Soon the voice of the people will be heard claiming the rights of men." Willich urged listeners to wave the American "banner of human liberty above the storm" as "a pilot light for the struggling nations."[13]

Willich and his peers came full circle in an epic global contest over the future of free popular government. Many ideas that had inspired Germans to rebel against their monarchs in 1848 first gained legitimacy with the triumph of the American Revolution. Hundreds of political exiles throughout Europe had followed Thomas Paine to America to freely imbibe the early republic's egalitarian elixir.[14] Willich finally achieved success by helping to preserve that same imperfect nation, hoping to impact its transformation into an example for the world. Ambitious dreams of a model republic, however, fell victim to dominant forces beyond his sphere of influence.

Willich expected to lead his boys back to the Fatherland and establish democratic government. Like many of his ambitious schemes, that one never came to pass. In fact, when France declared war on Prussia in 1870, Willich deferred republican dreams in favor of German unity. He offered his services to King Wilhelm Friedrich I of Prussia, the same man he had opposed on the battlefield in 1849. A united Germany was a small win for the embattled radical, but it was progress nonetheless.

Understanding the legacy of revolutions takes time and historical perspective. In his lifetime, Willich witnessed the brief ascent of the Radical Republicans who achieved immediate, uncompensated abolition and universal male suffrage, only to yield to southern interests and counterrevolution with the end of Reconstruction. He observed the birth and death of international worker organizations like the First International and attempts to create socialist political parties. Hostile reaction from reformed revolutionists like Carl Schurz to events like the Great Strike of 1877 must have deepened his concerns over the plight of the American worker. But Willich believed in Hegel's theory that history itself was proof of rational progress toward a perfect society. He never relinquished hope that the unfinished revolution would be fulfilled in due course.[15]

Pioneering German sociologist Max Weber wrote, "What is possible would have never been achieved if, in this world, people had not reached for the impossible."[16] Nineteenth-century proposals like an eight-hour workday, unemployment benefits, and child labor laws, once maligned as radical assaults on American institutions, became mainstream public policy in the twentieth century. Activists like Willich who promote far-reaching reform may be forced to wait decades or even centuries for favorable moments and conditions to emerge. Moreover, most extreme ideas never come to fruition.

Willich also reminds us that emotions play a critical role in leadership. His conflicts with Karl Marx were not solely based on philosophy. Whereas Marx was aloof, erudite, and condescending, Willich was a charismatic, passionate activist. Willich eclipsed Marx as the popular leader of London's German refugee community and became a beloved military commander on two continents by leveraging feelings to inspire people to form lasting affective commitments.[17]

Willich's conscious and competent use of emotional triggers to incite action shone in both diction and deed. Symbolic politics were hallmarks of Willich's leadership style, whether he was parading in carpenter garb before ex-comrades in the Prussian Army, addressing Union soldiers as "citizens" and "little children," or using emotionally loaded words like "freedom," "republic," and "democracy" to evoke feelings of patriotism among trade union members. He used music and song to sustain hope and build collective efficacy in Besançon, on the battlefield, and beyond. He encouraged singing societies to see themselves as reflections of a German national spirit, building group identity and fostering German American ethnic nationalism. The general used moral suasion to convince Germans that they were striving for a cause greater than simply overthrowing monarchy, garnering higher wages, or holding their adopted country together. In every instance, Willich assured his followers that they were struggling for nothing less than universal rights, good versus evil, and human dignity.

Like Karl Marx, Moses Hess was a philosopher, not a soldier, but he understood the mentality of social justice warriors. Hess called Willich an apostle of a new secular evangelism who was seeking martyrdom for his beliefs. Even if one no longer believes in God, Hess reasoned, "nevertheless our entire life and aspirations are far more apostolic than philosophic."[18] Hess argued for permanent revolution until final victory of the working class was achieved.

Willich remained loyal to that call from 1848 to the end of his life. Circumstance and environment forced him to adjust his tactics at times, but his core principles never changed. Indeed, they formed a prism through which he viewed everything, including the American Civil War. "Encouraging and promoting a solution to the social question," Willich confessed to Fritz Anneke in 1862, "is and will remain the only task of my life; this work alone not only makes life more challenging for me, but in my view also gives it value."[19]

Notes

INTRODUCTION

1. *Penny Press* (Cincinnati), January 30, 1860.

2. Harvey J. Kaye, *Thomas Paine: Firebrand of the Revolution* (New York: Oxford University Press, 2000), 43.

3. Robert J. Ingersoll, "Thomas Paine," *North American Review* 155 (July 1892): 195.

4. Richard Carwardine, "'Simply a Theist': Herndon on Lincoln's Religion," *Journal of the Abraham Lincoln Association* 35, no. 2 (Summer 2014): 20–21.

5. Moncure D. Conway, *Thomas Paine: A Celebration* (Cincinnati: Dial, 1860), 14.

6. Thomas Paine, *Common Sense* (Philadelphia: W. and T. Bradford, 1776), 87.

7. Mike Rapport, *1848: Year of Revolution* (New York: Basic Books, 2008), 47–59, 117–29, 211–226, 277–79, 290–301, 336–48.

8. Partial treatments of August Willich's life story abound in biographical summaries, book chapters, journal articles, theses, and online blog postings. The most important of these are: Loyd D. Easton, *Hegel's First American Followers* (Athens: Ohio University Press, 1966); Rolf Dlubek, "August Willich (1810–1878): Vom preußischen Offizier zum Streiter für die Arbeiteremanzipation auf zwei Kontinenten, "in *Akteure eines Umbruchs. Männer und Frauen der Revolution von 1848/49*, ed. Helmut Bleiber, Walter Schmidt, Susanne Schötz, (Berlin: Trafo Verlag 2003), 923–1004; Joseph R. Reinhart, ed., *August Willich's Gallant Dutchmen: Civil War Letters from the 32nd Indiana Infantry* (Kent, OH: Kent State University Press, 2006).

9. My perspective that the US Civil War was part of an ongoing international revolution for social justice draws from three important works: Andre M. Fleche, *The Revolution of 1861: The American Civil War in the Age of Nationalist Conflict* (Chapel Hill: University of North Carolina Press, 2012); Timothy Mason Roberts, *Distant Revolutions: 1848 and the Challenge to American Exceptionalism* (Charlottesville: University of Virginia Press, 2009); and Don H. Doyle, *The Cause of All Nations: An International History of the American Civil War* (New York: Basic Books, 2015). See also James M. McPherson, *Abraham Lincoln and the Second American Revolution* (New York: Oxford University Press, 1991).

10. *Evansville (IN) Journal*, August 2, 1866; Andrew Zimmerman, "From the Rhine to the Mississippi: Property, Democracy, and Socialism in the American Civil War," *Journal of the Civil War Era* 5, no. 1 (March 2015): 3–37.

11. English-language biographies of prominent German Forty-Eighters who became American Civil War Union officers include: Stephen D. Engle, *Yankee Dutchman: The Life of Franz Sigel* (Baton Rouge: Louisiana State University Press, 1993); Hans L. Trefousse, *Carl Schurz: A Biography* (Knoxville: University of Tennessee Press, 1982); Sabine Freitag, *Friedrich Hecker: Two Lives for Liberty*, trans. Steven Rowan (Saint Louis: University of Missouri Press, 2006); Mary Bobbitt Townsend, *Yankee Warhorse: A Biography of Major General Peter Osterhaus* (Columbia: University of Missouri Press, 2010).

12. Albert B. Faust, *The German Element in the United States* (Boston: Houghton Mifflin, 1909), 523–25.

13. For the best overview on German Forty-Eighters in America, see Bruce Levine, *The Spirit of 1848: German Immigrants, Labor Conflict, and the Coming of the Civil War* (Chicago: University of Illinois Press, 1992). Carl Wittke, *Refugees of Revolution: The German Forty-Eighters in America* (Philadelphia: University of Pennsylvania Press, 1952) is dated but useful. A. E. Zucker, ed. *The Forty-Eighters: Political Refugees of the German Revolution of 1848* (New York: Columbia University Press, 1950) is hagiographic, but it contains important biographical information on dozens of German Forty-Eighters.

14. Walter D. Kamphoefner and Wolfgang Helbich, eds., *Germans in the Civil War: The Letters They Wrote Home* (Chapel Hill: University of North Carolina Press, 2006), 1–7. Kamphoefner makes a strong case for Forty-Eighter leaders advancing social and cultural life among nineteenth-century German Americans but admits that historians debate the extent of the Forty-Eighters' influence on the masses of their less educated ethnic brethren. Stanley Nadel, *Little Germany: Ethnicity, Religion, and Class in New York City, 1845–80* (Chicago: University of Illinois Press, 1990); Martin W. Öfele, *German-Speaking Officers in the U.S. Colored Troops, 1863–1867* (Gainesville: University Press of Florida, 2004); and Kathleen Neils Conzen, *Immigrant Milwaukee* (Cambridge, MA: Harvard University Press, 1976).

15. Kathleen Neils Conzen, "German Americans and the Invention of Ethnicity," in *America and the Germans: An Assessment of a Three-Hundred-Year History*, ed. Frank Trommler and Joseph McVeigh (Philadelphia: University of Pennsylvania Press, 1985), 1:131–47; and Alison Clark Efford, *German Immigrants, Race, and Citizenship in the Civil War Era* (Cambridge: Cambridge University Press, 2013), 17–41.

16. Two important books that shape my understanding of political alliances among German Forty-Eighters, blacks, and abolitionists are Mischa Honeck, *We Are the Revolutionists: German-Speaking Immigrants and American Abolitionists after 1848* (Athens: University of Georgia Press, 2011); and Efford, *German Immigrants*. For an understanding of transatlantic antislavery alliances and the intersection between abolitionism and global democratic revolution, see W. Caleb McDaniel, *The Problem of Democracy in the Age of Slavery: Garrisonian Abolitionists and Transatlantic Reform* (Baton Rouge: Louisiana State University Press, 2013).

17. To understand the links between labor activism and republican political theory during the Civil War period, see Alex Gourevitch, *From Slavery to the Cooperative Commonwealth: Labor and Republican Liberty in the Nineteenth Century* (Cambridge: Cambridge University Press, 2014); and Mark A. Lause, *Free Labor: The Civil War and the Making of an American Working Class* (Chicago: University of Illinois Press, 2015).

18. William T. Sherman, *Memoirs of General William T. Sherman* (New York: D. Appleton, 1875), 1:239.

19. Paine, *Common Sense*, 36.

20. Paine, *Common Sense*, 4.

21. Thomas Paine, *Rights of Man* (London: J. S. Jordan, 1791), 59.

22. Gustav Tafel, *The Cincinnati Germans in the Civil War*, ed. and trans. Don Heinrich Tolzmann (Milford, OH: Little Miami, 2010), 81–82.

CHAPTER ONE

1. Edmund Burke, *Reflections on the Revolution in France* (London: J. Dodsley, 1790), 9.

2. Jean-Jacques Rousseau, *The Social Contract; or, The Principles of Political Rights* (New York: G. P. Putnam's Sons, 1893), 26. Originally published in 1762.

3. Gouverneur Morris, *The Diary and Letters of Gouverneur Morris, Minister of the United States to France; Member of the Constitutional Convention,* ed. Anne Cary Morris (New York: Charles Scribner's Sons, 1888), 1:344.

4. Dlubek, "August Willich," 925. Dlubek found genealogical records from 1932 that confirm Willich's baptism in the Lutheran Evangelical Church near Braunsberg. The original baptismal records were destroyed by Allied bombing during World War II.

5. James A. Moncure, *Research Guide to European Historical Biography, 1450–Present* (Washington, DC: Beacham, 1992), 2:704.

6. Dlubek, "August Willich," 925–26.

7. Salary Compensation Commissions for the Eastern Provinces, Johann Georg von Willich, 1814–1816, HA Rep. 147, no. 447, Prussian Privy State Archives, Berlin.

8. Easton, *Hegel's First American Followers,* 160–62; Virtually all Willich biographers include Schleiermacher as his foster father. Numerous Schleiermacher daybook entries confirm Willich's presence in Schleiermacher's family during the years 1825–27. See "Schleiermacher in Berlin 1808–1834," *Schleiermacher Digital* (digital archive), Berlin-Brandenburg Academy of Sciences. https://schleiermacher-digital.de/.

9. Friedrich Schleiermacher, *Aus Schleiermacher's Leben in Briefen* (Berlin: Georg Reimer, 1858), 307–10.

10. Schleiermacher, *Aus Schleiermacher's Leben in Briefen,* 393–95.

11. Dawn DeVries, "'Be Converted and Become as Little Children': Friedrich Schleiermacher on the Religious Significance of Childhood," in *The Child in Christian Thought,* ed. Marcia J. Bunge (Grand Rapids, MI: William B. Eerdmans, 2001), 329–49.

12. Alfred Diesbach, "August von Willich," *Badische Heimat* 58 (1978): 481–98. The extent of Willich's alienation from his mother is apparent from a report Diesbach found in the Swiss Archives at Bern. When questioned by Swiss authorities, Willich reported that his birthplace was either "Braunsberg, in Prussia, or the Isle of Rügen."

13. Easton, *Hegel's First American Followers,* 160–61. The rumor first appeared in the *Regensburg Zeitung* (Bavaria), August 2, 1849. Both Karl Marx and Friedrich Engels believed that Willich was the son of a Hohenzollern prince. Engels suggested that Willich had inherited the "treacherous Hohenzollern eyes."

14. George Cross, *The Theology of Schleiermacher* (Chicago: University of Chicago Press, 1911), 3–66.

15. Schleiermacher, *Aus Schleiermacher's Leben in Briefen,* 352–53.

16. August von Willich, *Im preußischen Heere! Ein Disciplinarverfahren gegen Premier-Lieutenant v. Willich* (Mannheim, Germany: Verlag von Heinrich Hoff, 1848), iii.

17. Roger Parkinson, *Clausewitz: A Biography* (New York: Cooper Square, 2002), 292–309.

18. Otto von Corvin, *Aus dem Leben eines Volkskämpfers* (Amsterdam: Binger, 1861), 76–82.

19. Corvin, *Aus dem Leben eines Volkskämpfers,* 92–93; Helen Roche, "'Go Tell the Prussians . . .': The Spartan Paradigm in Prussian Military Thought during the Long Nineteenth Century," *New Voices in Classical Reception Studies* 7 (2012): 25–27.

20. Great Britain, *Report of the Commissioners Appointed to Consider the Best Mode of Reorganizing the System for Training Officers for the Scientific Corps* (London: Eyre and Spottiswood, 1857), 100–105.

21. Great Britain, *Report of the Commissioners*, 90–98.

22. Dlubek, "August Willich," 926.

CHAPTER TWO

1. Friedrich von Sallet, *Gesammelte Gedichte* (Königsberg, Prussia: Im Verlage des Verfassers, 1843), 2:383–84.

2. Jonathan Sperber, *Rhineland Radicals: The Democratic Movement and the Revolution of 1848–1849* (Princeton: Princeton University Press, 1991), 15–52, 196–201, 224–25, 232; List of German Refugees, Besançon, France, 1848, August Willich Papers 1848–1850, International Institute for Social History, Amsterdam, Netherlands.

3. Rapport, *1848*, 2–41; Heinz-Gerhard Haupt and Friedrich Lenger, "Bourgeoisie, Petit Bourgeoisie, Workers: Class Formation and Social Reform in Germany and France," in *Europe in 1848: Revolution and Reform*, ed. Dieter Dowe et al., trans. David Higgins (New York: Berghahn Books, 2001), 619–22.

4. Sperber, *Rhineland Radicals*, 53–91; Christof Dipper, "Rural Revolutionary Movements: Germany, France, Italy," in Dowe, *Europe in 1848*, 421–25.

5. Sperber, *Rhineland Radicals*, 110–13; Wolfram Siemann, "Public Meeting Democracy in 1848," in Dowe, *Europe in 1848*, 767–70.

6. Willich, *Im preußischen Heere!*, ix.

7. Sina Farzin, "Sallet, Friedrich von," *New German Biography* 22 (2005): 379–80, https://www.deutsche-biographie.de/pnd118605089.html#ndbcontenthttps://www.deutsche-biographie.de/pnd118605089.html#ndbcontent.

8. August Willich, "Final Declaration," *Cincinnati Republikaner*, March 19, 1860; Dlubek, "August Willich," 927.

9. Sperber, *Rhineland Radicals*, 113–18; Michael Wettengel, "Party Formation in Germany: Political Associations in the Revolution of 1848," in Dowe, *Europe in 1848*, 529–30.

10. Warren Breckman, *Marx, the Young Hegelians, and the Origins of Radical Social Theory: Dethroning the Self* (Cambridge: Cambridge University Press, 1999).

11. Willich, "Final Declaration."

12. Breckman, *Marx*, 90–130, 214–20; Ludwig Feuerbach, *The Essence of Christianity*, trans. Marian Evans (New York: Calvin Blanchard, 1855); Easton, *Hegel's First American Followers*, 183–84, 191.

13. Easton, *Hegel's First American Followers*, 166.

14. Helmut Langhoff, "August von Willich in Wesel—Königlich Preußischer Offizier und 'Communist,'" *Wesel and Lower Rhine Historical Association* 6 (2018): 5–10, reprint.

15. Easton, *Hegel's First American Followers*, 162–67.

16. Moses Hess, *The Holy History of Mankind and Other Writings*, trans. and ed. Shlomo Avineri (Cambridge: Cambridge University Press, 2004), xx–xxvii, 97–115. Originally published in 1837; Auguste Cornu, "German Utopianism: 'True Socialism,'" *Science & Society* 12, no. 1 (Winter 1948): 97–112.

17. Sperber, *Rhineland Radicals*, 118–26; Langhoff, "August von Willich," 7–8.

18. Willich, *Im preußischen Heere!*, viii; Langhoff, "August von Willich," 11.

19. Heinrich Heine, "Die armen Weber," *Vorwärts!* (Paris) July 10, 1844; Todd Chretien, "Marx and the Silesian Strikers," *SocialistWorker.org* (blog), International *Socialist Organization*, October 3, 2012, https://socialistworker.org/2012/10/03/marx-and-the-silesian-strikers/.

20. Willich, *Im preußischen Heere!*, vii.

CHAPTER THREE

1. Friedrich Anneke, *Ein ehrengerichtlichtler Proceß* (Leipzig, Germany: Otto Wigand, 1846), 78–79.

2. Anneke, *Ein ehrengerichtlichtler Proceß*, 10.

3. Anneke, *Ein ehrengerichtlichtler Proceß*, 56–57; Langhoff, "August von Willich," 12–14.

4. Anneke, *Ein ehrengerichtlichtler Proceß*, 63–69; Easton, *Hegel's First American Followers*, 163.

5. Anneke, *Ein ehrengerichtlichtler Proceß*, 16–24.

6. Willich, *Im preußischen Heere!*, 3.

7. Willich, *Im preußischen Heere!*, 4; Langhoff, "August von Willich," 14–15; Friedrich Anneke to Friedrich Hammacher, August 18, 25, 1846, in Friedrich Anneke, *"Wäre ich auch zufällig ein Millionär geworden, meine Gesinnungen und Überzeugungen würden dadurch nicht gelitten haben . . . ": Friedrich Annekes Briefe an Friedrich Hammacher, 1846–1859* (Wuppertal, Germany: Friedrich Engels Haus, 1998), 4–6.

8. Willich, *Im preußischen Heere!*, 10–11.

9. Willich, *Im preußischen Heere!*, 12–13; Langhoff, "August von Willich," 17; Friedrich Anneke to Friedrich Hammacher, November 2, 4, 1846, in Anneke, *"Wäre ich auch zufällig ein Millionär,"* 26–34.

10. Willich, *Im preußischen Heere!*, 14.

11. Willich, *Im preußischen Heere!*, 16–18; Langhoff, "August von Willich," 18.

12. Willich, *Im preußischen Heere!*, 18–19; Easton, *Hegel's First American Followers*, 164–65.

13. Willich, *Im preußischen Heere!*, 19–20; Friedrich Anneke to Friedrich Hammacher, March 31, 1847, in Anneke, *"Wäre ich auch zufällig ein Millionär,"* 41.

14. Adolph Kohut, "Eine der ältesten und einflußreichen Familien Deutschlands," *Der Salon für Literatur, Kunst und Gesellschaft,* no.2 (1890): 129–36.

15. Willich, *Im preußischen Heere!*, 39–40. August Willich to Eduard Sack, February 14, 1847, in *Zeitgenossen von Marx und Engels*, ed. Kurt Koszyk and Karl Oberman (Amsterdam: Van Gorcum, 1975), 108.

16. Willich, *Im preußischen Heere!*, 20–23; August Willich to Eduard Sack, March 13, 1847, in Koszyk and Oberman, *Zeitgenossen von Marx und Engels*, 111–12; Langhoff, "August von Willich," 16.

17. Willich, *Im preußischen Heere!*, 23–24.

18. Willich, *Im preußischen Heere!*, 25–26. Personal requests to the king were highly unusual and lends circumstantial evidence to support Willich's royal birth.

19. Willich, *Im preußischen Heere!*, 27–30.

20. Willich, *Im preußischen Heere!*, 30–33.

21. August Willich to Eduard Sack, July 30, 1847, in Koszyk and Oberman, *Zeitgenossen von Marx und Engels*, 123; Friedrich Anneke to Friedrich Hammacher, July 29 and 31, August 9, 10, 25, 27, 1847, in Anneke, *"Wäre ich auch zufällig ein Millionär,"* 78–87.

22. Willich, *Im preußischen Heere!*, 33–35; Langhoff, "August von Willich," 19.

CHAPTER FOUR

1. August Willich to Eduard Sack, November 1847, in Koszyk and Oberman, *Zeitgenossen von Marx und Engels*, 130–32; Willich, *Im preußischen Heere!*, 41.

2. Friedrich Anneke to Friedrich Hammacher, December 23, 25, 1847, in Anneke, *"Wäre ich auch zufällig ein Millionär,"* 94, 96.

3. Willich, *Im preußischen Heere!*, 36; Friedrich Anneke to Friedrich Hammacher, January 2, 3, 1848, in Anneke, *"Wäre ich auch zufällig ein Millionär,"* 98–99.

4. Easton, *Hegel's First American Followers*, 167–68.

5. Sperber, *Rhineland Radicals*, 102; Dlubek, "August Willich," 930; Boris I. Nicolaevsky and Otto Maenchen-Helfen, *Karl Marx: Man and Fighter*, trans. Gwenda David and Eric Mosbocher (London: Methuen, 1936), 156.

6. Willich, *Im preußischen Heere!*, 43–45.

7. Willich, *Im preußischen Heere!*, 49–51; Wilhelm Weitling to Moses Hess, March 31, 1846, "The Communist League," *Marx/Engels Internet Archive* https://www.marxists.org/archive/marx /works/1847/communist-league/1846let1.htm.

8. Rapport, *1848*, 42–47; Heinz-Gerhard Haupt and Dieter Langewiesche, "The European Revolutions of 1848," in Dowe, *Europe in 1848*, 1–23.

9. Rapport, *1848*, 47–57; Pierre Lévêque, "The Revolutionary Crisis of 1848/51 in France," in Dowe, *Europe in 1848*, 91–99.

10. Carl Schurz, *The Reminiscences of Carl Schurz* (London: John Murray, 1909), 1:111–16.

11. Easton, *Hegel's First American Followers*, 168; Nicolaevsky and Maenchen-Helfen, *Karl Marx*, 167; Dlubek, "August Willich," 931–33.

12. Rapport, *1848*, 72–79; Friedrich Hecker, *Erhebung des Volkes in Baden für die deutsche Republik im Frühjahr 1848* (Basel, Switzerland, 1848), 1–17.

13. Rapport, *1848*, 117–20.

14. Freitag, *Friedrich Hecker*, 102–111; Justine Davis Randers-Pehrson, *Germans and the Revolution of 1848–1849* (New York: Peter Lang, 2001), 319–344; Hecker, *Erhebung des Volkes*, 18–22.

15. Randers-Pehrson, *Germans and the Revolution*, 319–21; Hecker, *Erhebung des Volkes*, 23–25; Charlotte Tacke, "Revolutionary Festivals in Germany and Italy," in Dowe, *Europe in 1848*, 804–8.

16. Randers-Pehrson, *Germans and the Revolution*, 321–23.

17. Randers-Pehrson, *Germans and the Revolution*, 321–23; Hecker, *Erhebung des Volkes*, 26–28; Diesbach, "August von Willich," 481–86.

18. Randers-Pehrson, *Germans and the Revolution*, 324–27; Hecker, *Erhebung des Volkes*, 29–30.

19. Randers-Pehrson, *Germans and the Revolution*, 331; Dlubek, "August Willich," 934–35.

20. Randers-Pehrson, *Germans and the Revolution*, 331–35; August Willich to editor of *Die Gartenlaube*, July 20, 1872, National Library, Coburg, Germany; Hecker, *Erhebung des Volkes*, 31–45.

21. Randers-Pehrson, *Germans and the Revolution*, 332–36; Hecker, *Erhebung des Volkes*, 46–52.

22. Randers-Pehrson, *Germans and the Revolution*, 337; Hecker, *Erhebung des Volkes*, 83–89.

23. Willich to editor of *Die Gartenlaube*, July 20, 1872.

24. Randers-Pehrson, *Germans and the Revolution*, 338–39; Hecker, *Erhebung des Volkes*, 53–67.

25. Willich to editor of *Die Gartenlaube*, July 20, 1872.

26. Willich to editor of *Die Gartenlaube*, July 20, 1872; G. Kramer, "Die Warheit von der Kanderner affair," *Die Gartenlaube* 29 (1872): 477–78.

27. Randers-Pehrson, *Germans and the Revolution*, 338–39; Willich to editor of *Die Gartenlaube*, July 20, 1872; G. Kramer, "Die Warheit von der Kanderner affair," *Die Gartenlaube* 29 (1872): 477–78; Hecker, *Erhebung des Volkes*, 77–93; Dlubek, "August Willich," 936.

28. Randers-Pehrson, *Germans and the Revolution*, 339–40.

29. Randers-Pehrson, *Germans and the Revolution*, 341.

30. Dlubek, "August Willich," 937; Hecker, *Erhebung des Volkes*, 69; Diesbach, "August von Willich," 486–87.

CHAPTER FIVE

1. Le théâtre de Besançon: architecture de la musique #1, *Mediamus* (blog), October 18, 2007, https://mediamus.blogspot.com/2007/10/le-thtre-de-besancon-architecture-de-la.html.

2. Fernand Rude, *Les Réfugiés Allemand a Besançon sous la Dexième République* (Besançon, France: Millot, 1939), 13.

3. Rude, *Les Réfugiés Allemand*, 6–7.

4. Rude, *Les Réfugiés Allemand*, 7–8, 10; Dlubek, "August Willich," 937.

5. Rude, *Les Réfugiés Allemand*, 10.

6. Rude, *Les Réfugiés Allemand*, 11; Easton, *Hegel's First American Followers*, 168–69.

7. Rude, Les Réfugiés Allemand, 12.

8. Rude, *Les Réfugiés Allemand*, 12.

9. Rapport, *1848*, 222–26; Dieter Langeweische, "Revolution in Germany," in Dowe, *Europe in 1848*, 122–24.

10. August Willich to Johann Phillip Becker, June 8, 1848, in Koszyk and Oberman, *Zeitgenossen von Marx und Engels*, 162–63.

11. Georg Steiger to August Willich, June 13, 1848, in Koszyk and Oberman, *Zeitgenossen von Marx und Engels*, 163–64.

12. Rapport, *1848*, 18–20.

13. Rapport, *1848*, 90–93, 156–69; C. A. Bayly and Eugenio F. Biagini, eds., *Giuseppe Mazzini and the Globalization of Democratic Nationalism 1830–1920* (New York: Oxford University Press, 2009).

14. August Willich to Johann Phillip Becker, June 22, 1848, in Koszyk and Oberman, *Zeitgenossen von Marx und Engels*, 167–68; Dlubek, "August Willich," 949.

15. Willich to Becker, June 22, 1848, 168–70.

16. Rapport, *1848*, 191–211; Dlubek, "August Willich," 938.

17. August Willich to Fritz Anneke, July 6, 1848, in Koszyk and Oberman, *Zeitgenossen von Marx und Engels*, 182.

18. Willich to Anneke, July 6, 1848, in Koszyk and Oberman, *Zeitgenossen von Marx und Engels*, 179–84.

19. Mathilde Betham-Edwards, "Holidays in Eastern France," *Fraser's Magazine* 18 (September 1878): 636–41.

20. Phillip Wagner, *Ein Achtundvierziger. Erlebtes und Gedachtes* (Leipzig, Germany: Otto Wigand, 1882), 183.

21. Rude, *Les Réfugiés Allemand*, 15.

22. Willich to Anneke, July 6, 1848, 183.

23. August Willich to a High Meeting of German People's Representatives at Frankfurt A.M., July 28, 1848, in Koszyk and Oberman, *Zeitgenossen von Marx und Engels*, 184–86.

24. Theodor Mögling, *Briefe an seine Freunde* (Solothurn, Switzerland: J. Gassmann, 1858), 134; Dlubek, "August Willich," 940.

25. Rude, *Les Réfugiés Allemand*, 16–18.

26. Dlubek, "August Willich," 941.

27. Dlubek, "August Willich," 941–42; Rude, *Les Réfugiés Allemand*, 18–19; Friedrich Engels to Karl Marx, November 23, 1853, in Karl Marx, *The Knight of Noble Consciousness*, in Karl Marx and Friedrich Engels, *Marx and Engels Collected Works*, (London: Lawrence and Wishart, 1979), 12:479.

28. Rude, *Les Réfugiés Allemand*, 20.

29. Rapport, *1848*, 263–344.

30. Registre des décès, 1849, 1E715, Besançon Municipal Archives, Besançon, France.

31. Wagner, *Ein Achtundvierziger*, 181–83.

CHAPTER SIX

1. Dlubek, "August Willich," 943–44.

2. August Willich to editor of *Die Gartenlaube*, July 20, 1872.

3. Willich to editor of *Die Gartenlaube*, July 20, 1872.

4. Rude, *Les Réfugiés Allemand*, 27–28; Dlubek, "August Willich," 943; Diesbach, "August von Willich," 488.

5. Sperber, *Rhineland Radicals*, 319–37.

6. Langeweische "Revolution in Germany," in Dowe, *Europe in 1848*, 126–28.

7. Rapport, *1848*, 336–43.

8. Rapport, *1848*, 343–45.

9. Friedrich Engels, "The Campaign for the Imperial German Constitution," in *Marx and Engels Collected Works* (London: Lawrence and Wishart, 1978), 10:147–239.

10. David McLellan, *Karl Marx: His Life and Thought* (New York: Harper and Row, 1973), 154–70; Engels, "Campaign," 171–73.

11. Randers-Pehrson, *Germans and the Revolution*, 498–99. Engels, "Campaign," 198–99; Dlubek, "August Willich," 945; Johann Phillip Becker and Christian Essellen, *Geschihte der Süd-deutschen Mai-Revolution* (Geneva, 1849), 224–26; Daniel Staroste, *Tagebuch über die Ereignisse in der Pfalz und Baden im Jahre 1849* (Potsdam, Germany: Riegel, 1853), 1:22.

12. Sperber, *Rhineland Radicals*, 423–24; Engels, "Campaign," 193–94; Becker and Essellen, *Geschihte der Süddeutschen Mai-Revolution*, 161–62.

13. Justine Davis Randers-Pehrson, *Adolf Douai, 1819–1888: The Turbulent Life of a German Forty-Eighter in the Homeland and in the United States* (New York: Peter Lang, 2000), 152; Engels, "Campaign," 195–96.

14. Otto Fleischmann, *Geschichte des Pfälzischen Aufstandes im Jahre 1849: Nach den zugän-glichen Quellen geschildert* (Kaiserlautern, Germany: E. Thieme, 1899), 142; Ludwik Mieroslawski, *Berichte des Generals Mieroslawski über den Feldzug in Baden* (Bern, Switzerland: Jenni, 1849), 4.

15. Staroste, *Tagebuch über die Ereignisse*, 2:266–67.

16. Langeweische, "Revolution in Germany," in Dowe, *Europe in 1848*, 130–42. Langeweische describes parallel unsuccessful German revolutions: a German national revolution supported by liberal bourgeoisie and a primal revolution supported by radical socialists like Willich.

17. Fleischmann, *Geschichte des Pfälzischen Aufstandes*,264–69; Engels, "Campaign," 196–97; Dlubek, "August Willich," 946; Staroste, *Tagebuch über die Ereignisse*, 1:27–31.

18. Dlubek, "August Willich," 948–49; Engels, "Campaign," 197.

19. Staroste, *Tagebuch über die Ereignisse*, 1:177–79.

20. Mathilde Anneke, *Memoiren einer Frau aus dem badisch-pfaelzischen Feldzuge* (Newark, NJ, 1853), 100–102.

21. Anneke, *Memoiren einer Frau*, 103–6.

22. Engels, "Campaign," 209–12.

23. Engels, "Campaign," 212–14.

24. Engels, "Campaign," 214; Staroste, *Tagebuch über die Ereignisse*, 1:191–94.

25. Rapport, *1848*, 345–46; Engels, "Campaign," 214–15.

26. Anneke, *Memoiren einer Frau*, 110; Engels, "Campaign," 215.

27. Anneke, *Memoiren einer Frau*, 112–13; Fleischmann, *Geschichte des Pfälzischen Aufstandes*, 275–76; Staroste, *Tagebuch über die Ereignisse*, 1:272–82.

28. Engels, "Campaign," 215–16.

29. Anneke, *Memoiren einer Frau*, 115–16.

30. Engels, "Campaign," 219–20; Fleischmann, *Geschichte des Pfälzischen Aufstandes*, 339–41; Staroste, *Tagebuch über die Ereignisse*, 1:320.

31. Engels, "Campaign," 220; Becker and Essellen, *Geschihte der Süddeutschen Mai-Revolution*, 305–14.

32. Mieroslawski, *Berichte des generals*, 13–19.

33. Engels, "Campaign," 220–21.

34. Anneke, *Memoiren einer Frau*, 119–20; Engels, "Campaign," 221–22.

35. Engels, "Campaign," 223–27; Anneke, *Memoiren einer Frau*, 121–23.

36. Charles W. Dahlinger, *The German Revolution of 1849* (New York: G. P. Putnam's Sons, 1903), 236–38.

37. Engels, "Campaign," 227; Dahlinger, *German Revolution*, 231–32; Staroste, *Tagebuch über die Ereignisse*, 1:381–82.

38. Engels, "Campaign," 228–30; Dahlinger, *German Revolution*, 251–52.

39. Staroste, *Tagebuch über die Ereignisse*, 2:19–22. Dlubek, "August Willich," 950.

40. Mieroslawski, *Berichte des generals*, 32–35; Engels, "Campaign," 231–32; Staroste, *Tagebuch über die Ereignisse*, 2:109–10. The town of Oos was renamed "Baden-Baden."

41. Engels, "Campaign," 232–34; Dahlinger, *German Revolution*, 253–57.

42. Franz Sigel to August Willich, July 4, 1849, in Koszyk and Oberman, *Zeitgenossen von Marx und Engels*, 259; Engels, "Campaign," 235–36; Dahlinger, *German Revolution*, 265; Staroste, *Tagebuch über die Ereignisse*, Vol. 2, 121–24.

43. Engels, "Campaign," 237; Dahlinger, *German Revolution*, 266–67; Staroste, *Tagebuch über die Ereignisse*, 2:125–28.

44. Randers-Pehrson, *Germans*, 517–20; Engels, "Campaign," 238–39; Dahlinger, *German Revolution*, 268–70.

45. For the idea that lessons and memories of the 1848 revolutions in Europe influenced Willich and other Americans on their path to Civil War, see Roberts, *Distant Revolutions*.

CHAPTER SEVEN

1. August Willich to editor of *Westdeutsche Zeitung*, November 26, 1849, Boris I. Nicolaevsky collection, Hoover Institution Archives, Stanford, CA.

2. Christine Lattek, *Revolutionary Refugees: German Socialism in Britain, 1840–1860* (London: Routledge, 2006), 23–37. Lattek's extensive research and analysis of Willich and other refugees is the definitive work on the community of German émigrés in London in the 1850s. Keith Taylor, *The Political Ideas of the Utopian Socialists* (London: Frank Cass, 1982), 186–208.

3. Lattek, *Revolutionary Refugees*, 25–33; David Felix, *Marx as Politician* (Carbondale: University of Southern Illinois Press, 1982), 94–96.

4. *Sydney Morning Herald*, September 12, 1848; *Daily Union* (Washington, DC), July 8; 1849; *Times* (London), July 9,1849.

5. Lattek, *Revolutionary Refugees*, 123–24; *Census Returns of England and Wales, 1851* (Kew, Surrey, England: National Archives of the UK, 1851).

6. Lattek, *Revolutionary Refugees*, 12.

7. Lattek, *Revolutionary Refugees*, 61–69; Easton, *Hegel's First American Followers*, 170–72; Jonathan Sperber, *Karl Marx: A Nineteenth-Century Life* (New York: Liveright, 2013), 246–49.

8. McLellan, *Karl Marx*, 246.

9. Lattek, *Revolutionary Refugees*, 68; Easton, *Hegel's First American Followers*, 172–73.

10. Schurz, *Reminiscences*, 1:394.

11. Lattek, *Revolutionary Refugees*, 70–71; Nicolaevsky and Maenchen-Helfen, *Karl Marx*, 127.

12. Lattek, *Revolutionary Refugees*, 262n98.

13. Lattek, *Revolutionary Refugees*, 71–72.

14. Lattek, *Revolutionary Refugees*, 73; Easton, *Hegel's First American Followers*, 173.

15. Wilhelm Liebknecht, "Reminiscences of Marx," in *Reminiscences of Marx and Engels*, trans. by Ernest Untermann (Moscow: Foreign Language Publishing House, 1957), 113. Originally published in 1896.

16. August Willich, "Doctor Karl Marx und seine Enthüllungen," *Belletristisches Journal und New-Yorker Criminal-Zeitung*, October 28, 1853; Easton, *Hegel's First American Followers*, 173–74.

17. Lattek, *Revolutionary Refugees*, 132–36.

18. August Willich to Hermann Becker, December 6, 1850, Boris I. Nicolaevsky Collection; Easton, *Hegel's First American Followers*, 172–73.

19. August Willich to Hermann Becker, December 24, 1850, Boris I. Nicolaevsky Collection.

20. Hermann Becker to Karl Marx, January 27, 1851, in Karl Marx and Friedrich Engels, *Collected Works* (London: Lawrence and Wishart, 1983), 11:403. Hereinafter, this work is cited as *MECW*.

21. Jenny Marx to Friedrich Engels, December 19, 1850, in *MECW*, 38:560.

22. August Willich to Hermann Becker, undated (February 1851), Boris I. Nicolaevsky Collection.

23. Lattek, *Revolutionary Refugees*, 126–27.

24. Karl Marx to Friedrich Engels, February 24, 1851, in *MECW*, 38:298.

25. Lattek, *Revolutionary Refugees*, 135–36; Karl Marx to Friedrich Engels, March 17, 22, 1851, in *MECW*, 38:318, 321.

26. Lattek, *Revolutionary Refugees*, 95–99; Alfred De Jonge, *Gottfried Kinkel as Political and Social Thinker* (New York: Columbia University Press, 1926), 117–28.

27. Lattek, *Revolutionary Refugees*, 99–109.

28. Easton, *Hegel's First American Followers*, 175–76. For exile appeals to renew revolutions in Europe, see Sabine Freitag, "The Begging Bowl of Revolution: The Fund-Raising Tours of German and Hungarian Exiles to North America, 1851–1852," in *Exiles from European Revolutions: Refugees in Mid-Victorian England*, ed. Sabine Freitag (New York: Berghahn Books, 2003), 164–86.

29. *Portage (OH) Sentinel*, January 19, 1852.

30. Carl Schurz, *Reminiscences*, 1:399–400.

31. Lattek, *Revolutionary Refugees*, 146.

32. Lattek, *Revolutionary Refugees*, 147.

33. Lattek, *Revolutionary Refugees*, 153.

34. Lattek, *Revolutionary Refugees*, 147–52; Easton, *Hegel's First American Followers*, 176–77.

35. Schurz, *Reminiscences*, 1:388–93.

36. Karl Marx to Friedrich Engels, May 22, 1852, in *MECW*, 39:112–13.

37. Friedrich Engels to Karl Marx, May 24, 1852, in *MECW*, 39:113-14.

38. Karl Marx to Joseph Weydemeyer, May 28, 1852, in *MECW*, 39:114.

39. Friedrich Engels to Joseph Weydemeyer, June 11, 1852, in *MECW*, 39:118-22.

40. Lattek, *Revolutionary Refugees*, 152; Karl Marx to Adolph Cluss, October 5 and December 14, 1852, in *MECW*, 39:204, 265.

41. Karl Marx and Friedrich Engels, "The Great Men of the Exile," in *MECW*, 11:312-16.

42. Sperber, *Karl Marx*, 272, 277. In the absence of other evidence and in the face of numerous examples of Willich's sexual relations with women, Sperber claims that "Willich's homosexuality was an open secret."

43. Lattek, *Revolutionary Refugees*, 151-52.

44. Emmanuel Barthelémy to August Willich, undated (September 1852), Boris I. Nicolaevsky Collection.

45. Victor Hugo, *Les Misérables* (New York: Little, Brown, 1887), 4:67-69. Originally published in 1862.

46. Robert Walsh, "England's Last Fatal Duel," *Sword and Scale*, June 6, 2015, http://swordandscale.com/englands-last-fatal-duel.

47. Alexander Herzen, *My Past and Thoughts*, trans. Constance Garnett (New York: Knopf, 1968), 3:1086. Originally published in 1870.

48. Karl Marx to Friedrich Engels, August 30, 1852, in *MECW*, 39:168-72.

49. Karl Marx to Adolph Cluss, January 21, 1853, in *MECW*, 39:273-74; Sperber, *Karl Marx*, 272-78; Felix, *Marx as Politician*, 103-5.

CHAPTER EIGHT

1. Passenger Lists of Vessels Arriving at New York, New York, 1820-1897, Microfilm Publication M237, Records of the U.S. Customs Service, Record Group 36, Roll 123, National Archives, Washington, DC.

2. Nadel, *Little Germany*, 1-8, 18-22, 41-42, 62-74.

3. Zimmerman, "From the Rhine to the Mississippi," 3-5; Ralf Wagner, "Turner Societies and the Socialist Tradition," in *German Workers' Culture in the United States, 1850 to 1920*, ed. Harmut Keil (Washington, DC: Smithsonian Institution Press, 1988), 224-29.

4. Lattek, *Revolutionary Refugees*, 106-9; Levine, *Spirit of 1848*, 85-87; Roberts, *Distant Revolutions*, 14-15.

5. Thomas R. Whitney, *A Defence of the American Policy, as Opposed to the Encroachments of Foreign Influence* (New York: De Witt and Davenport, 1856), 343-48.

6. Nadel, *Little Germany*, 123-28; Lattek, *Revolutionary Refugees*, 105-7, 146.

7. August Willich to Alexander Herzen, March 9, 1853, Bonn University Manuscripts Collection, Bonn, Germany.

8. Carl Wittke, *The Utopian Communist: A Biography of Wilhelm Weitling, Nineteenth Century Reformer* (Baton Rouge: Louisiana State University Press, 1950), 213-14.

9. Wittke, *Utopian Communist*, 214.

10. Levine, *Spirit of 1848*, 99-102.

11. Carl Schurz to Gottfried Kinkel, April 12, 1853, in Carl Schurz, *Intimate Letters of Carl Schurz, 1841-1869*, ed. and trans. Joseph Schafer (Madison, WI: Wisconsin Historical Society, 1928), 118-21; *New York Staats-Zeitung*, May 4, 1853; Trefousse, *Carl Schurz*, 48; Levine, *Spirit of 1848*, 110.

12. Willich to Herzen, March 9, 1853, Bonn University Manuscripts Collection; Nadel, *Little Germany*, 94-95.

13. Willich to Herzen, March 9, 1853, Bonn University Manuscripts Collection.

14. Willich to Herzen, March 9, 1853, Bonn University Manuscripts Collection.

15. Wittke, *Utopian Communist*, 257.

16. Nadel, *Little Germany*, 22.

17. Conzen, *Immigrant Milwaukee*, 155–56, 176–79.

18. Rudolph Koss, *Milwaukee*, trans. Hans Ibsen (Milwaukee: Milwaukee *Herald*, 1871), 318–19, 332–33.

19. Theodore Mueller, "Mathilde Franziska Anneke: Reformer, Suffragette, Author," *Historical Messenger of the Milwaukee County Historical Society* 23, no. 4 (December 1967): 125–30.

20. Conzen, *Immigrant Milwaukee*, 177.

21. J. J. Schlicher, "Eduard Schroeter the Humanist," *Wisconsin Magazine of History* 28, no. 4 (March 1945): 307–8.

22. Koss, *Milwaukee*, 342–49; Bettina Goldberg, "Radical German-American Freethinkers and the Socialist Labor Movement: The *Free Gemeinde* in Milwaukee, Wisconsin," in *German Workers' Culture in the United States, 1850 to 1920*, ed. Harmut Keil (Washington, DC: Smithsonian Institution Press, 1988), 241–60.

23. Koss, *Milwaukee*, 394.

24. Koss, *Milwaukee*, 401; Schlicher, "Eduard Schroeter," 309–10; Milwaukee's Socialist Turnverein was modeled on the successful New York City chapter. Nadel, *Little Germany*, 120–21; Charles Reitz, "Socialist Turners of New York City, 1853: Archival Materials Warrant Further Research," *Yearbook of German-American Studies* 45 (2010): 95–106.

25. Koss, *Milwaukee*, 395–401.

26. Schlicher, "Eduard Schroeter," 310–11.

27. William Frederic Kamman, *Socialism in German American Literature* (Philadelphia: Americana Germanica, 1917), 34–50.

28. August Willich, "Doctor Karl Marx und seine Enthüllungen," *Belletristisches Journal und New-Yorker Criminal-Zeitung*, October 28, 1853; *Weekly Express* (Chicago), July 27, 1853.

29. Maffitt later became a Confederate naval officer and blockade-runner. Royce Shingleton, *High Seas Confederate: The Life and Times of John Newland Maffitt* (Columbia: University of South Carolina Press, 1994), 22–25; J. N. Maffitt to Alexander D. Bache, February 6, 1857, August Willich to Alexander D. Bache, February 17, 1857, Records of the Coast and Geodetic Survey, RG 23, National Archives, College Park, MD.

30. August Willich, "Final Declaration," *Cincinnati Republikaner*, March 19, 1860.

31. August Willich to Gottfried Kinkel, December 8, 1857, Bonn University Manuscripts Collection; *Cincinnati Republikaner*, June 23, 1860.

32. William E. Gienapp, "Nativism and the Creation of a Republican Majority in the North before the Civil War," *Journal of American History* 72, no. 3 (December 1985): 529–59.

33. Washington Topham, "Northern Liberty Market," *Records of the Columbia Historical Society, Washington, D.C.* 24 (1922): 43–66; Klaus G. Wust, "German Immigrants and their Newspapers in the District of Columbia," in *Thirtieth Report, Society for the History of the Germans in Maryland* (Baltimore: Society for the History of the Germans in Maryland, 1959), 36–65.

34. Ansgar Reiss, *Radikalismus und Exil: Gustav Struve und die Demokratie in Deutschland und Amerika* (Stuttgart, Germany: Steiner, 2004), 334; Efford, *German Immigrants*, 13, 40–47, 51.

35. Reiss, *Radikalismus und Exil*, 334–35.

36. *Washington Union*, July 27, 1858.

37. *Daily Exchange* (Baltimore), August 24, September 3, 1858; *Sociale Republik* (New York), Sept. 25, 1858; *Cincinnati Republikaner*, March 19, 1860.

CHAPTER NINE

1. Charles Cist, *Sketches and Statistics of Cincinnati in 1859* (Cincinnati, 1859), 164–15; D. J. Kenny, *Illustrated Cincinnati: A Pictorial Hand-Book of the Queen City* (Cincinnati: Robert Clarke, 1875), 129–36.

2. Easton, *Hegel's First American Followers*, 49–57.

3. Levine, *Spirit of 1848*, 111–45. Bruce Levine, "Who Were the Real Forty-Eighters in the United States?," in *Exiles from European Revolutions: Refugees in Mid-Victorian England*, ed. Sabine Freitag, (New York: Berghahn Books, 2003), 234–50.

4. *Cincinnati Republikaner*, December 8, 1858. Willich rented a room in Switzer Hall, a boardinghouse in the Over-the-Rhine neighborhood. "1860 United States Federal Census," Ancestry.com, 1997.

5. Gourevitch, *From Slavery to the Cooperative Commonwealth*, 97–137, 182–90. Felix Zimmermann argues that Marxists equated free labor with wage labor, whereas Willich and other republican socialists had a more inclusive definition of free labor as part of the republican tradition. Felix Zimmermann, "Als die Lohnarbeit 'frei' wurde. Zum Verständnis der 'freien Arbeit' bei republikanischen und marxistischen Achtundvierzigern in den USA." *Arbeit—Bewegung—Geschichte. Zeitschrift für Historische Studien* no. 1 (2019): 94–110.

6. Easton, *Hegel's First American Followers*, 185–88.

7. Efford, *German Immigrants*, 63–64; Honeck, *We Are the Revolutionists*, 94–98.

8. Felix Zimmermann, "A Different Republicanism: August Willich and the Trade Unions in Antebellum Cincinnati," transcript of talk delivered April 1, 2017, at "The Legacy of 1848 through Today" conference, Northfield, MN. Zimmermann argues that Willich created a unique vision of a socialist political system for his adopted country, using republican language to connect a practical American trade union movement with German principled politics.

9. *United States Mechanics Own* (Philadelphia), March 24, 1860; *Constitution and By-Laws of the Iron Molder's Union of Albany, New York* (New York: Cassin and Fincher, 1860).

10. Easton, *Hegel's First American Followers*, 189–91.

11. *Cincinnati Republikaner*, October 3, 1859.

12. Honeck, *We Are the Revolutionists*, 71–72; August Willich to Alexander Herzen, March 9, 1853, Bonn University Manuscripts Collection; Lida L. Greene, "Hugh Forbes, Soldier of Fortune," *Annals of Iowa* 38 (1967): 610–11; *Cincinnati Enquirer*, December 6, 1859; Roberts, *Distant Revolutions*, 187–89.

13. Honeck, *We Are the Revolutionists*, 93–95; *Cincinnati Republikaner*, October 3, 1859.

14. Honeck, *We Are the Revolutionists*, 72–74.

15. *Cincinnati Republikaner*, December 2, 3, 5, 1859.

16. Honeck, *We Are the Revolutionists*, 95–97; Nikki M. Taylor, *America's First Black Socialist: The Radical Life of Peter H. Clark* (Lexington: University Press of Kentucky, 2013), 76–79, 98–101; *Cincinnati Republikaner*, December 20, 25, 26, 1859; *Cincinnati Volksfreund*, December 25, 1859.

17. Easton, *Hegel's First American Followers*, 184.

18. Honeck, *We Are the Revolutionists*, 85–93; *Cincinnati Republikaner*, December 8, 1859.

19. Moncure Daniel Conway, *Autobiography, Memories and Experiences* (New York: Houghton and Mifflin, 1904), 1:269.

20. Honeck, *We Are the Revolutionists*, 94–95; Conway, *Autobiography*, 300; *Cincinnati Commercial*, December 6, 1859.

21. Honeck, *We Are the Revolutionists*, 73; Levine, *Spirit of 1848*, 9; Öfele, *German-Speaking Officers*, 1–15.

CHAPTER TEN

1. R. Gerald McMurtry, ed., "Lincoln Visited by a German Delegation of Workingmen in Cincinnati, Ohio, February 12, 1861." *Lincoln Lore* 1575 (May 1969): 1.

2. Harold Holzer, *Lincoln and the Power of the Press* (New York: Simon and Schuster, 2014), 186–94.

3. Alison Clark Efford, "Abraham Lincoln, German-Born Republicans, and American Citizenship," *Marquette Law Review* 93, no. 4 (Summer 2010): 1375–81; *Cincinnati Republikaner*, May 16, 1860. For a refutation of the myth that German Americans defected en masse to the Republicans, handing the 1860 election to Lincoln, see Öfele, *German-Speaking Officers*, 1–10.

4. Gary Ecelbarger, "Before Cooper Union: Abraham Lincoln's 1859 Cincinnati Speech and Its Impact on His Nomination," *Journal of the Abraham Lincoln Association* 30, no. 1 (2009): 1–17.

5. McMurtry, "Lincoln Visited by a German Delegation," 1–2; Levine, *Spirit of 1848*, 255.

6. McMurtry, "Lincoln Visited by a German Delegation," 2; Levine, *Spirit of 1848*, 255.

7. McMurtry, "Lincoln Visited by a German Delegation," 3; Abraham Lincoln, *The Collected Works of Abraham Lincoln*, ed. Roy Basler (New Brunswick, NJ: Rutgers University Press, 1953), 4:201–3; *Belleviller Zeitung* (Belleville, IL), April 11, 1861.

8. Robert S. Harper, *Ohio Handbook of the Civil War* (Columbus: Ohio Historical Society, 1961).

9. Friedrich Anneke, *Der Zweite Freiheitskampf der Vereignigten Staaten von Amerika* (Frankfurt am Main: J. D. Sauerlander, 1861); Levine, *Spirit of 1848*, 256; Fleche, *Revolution of 1861*, 44.

10. Karl Marx and Friedrich Engels, *The Civil War in the United States*, ed. Andrew Zimmerman (New York: International Publishers, 2018).

11. Fleche, *Revolution of 1861*, 1–37.

12. Levine, "Who Were the Real Forty-Eighters," 234–50; Mischa Honeck, "Men of Principle: The German American War for the Union," talk delivered May 4, 2012, at the US Capitol Historical Society Civil War Symposium.

13. *Evansville (IN) Journal*, August 2, 1866; Zimmerman, "From the Rhine to the Mississippi, 3–7, 13–17, 24–37.

14. Constantin Grebner, *We Were the Ninth: A History of the Ninth Regiment, Ohio Volunteer Infantry, April 17, 1861 to June 7, 1864*, translated and edited by Frederic Trautmann (Kent, OH: Kent State University Press, 1987), 3–13. Originally published in 1897; Tafel, *Cincinnati Germans*, 27–28.

15. Grebner, *We Were the Ninth*, 7–8; Tafel, *Cincinnati Germans*, 29.

16. Jacob D. Cox, "War Preparations in the North," in *Battles and Leaders of the Civil War*, ed. Robert U. Johnson and Clarence C. Buell (New York: Century., 1887), 1:97–98.

17. Grebner, *We Were the Ninth*, 199.

18. James Barnett, "August Willich, Soldier Extraordinary," *Bulletin of the Historical and Philosophical Society of Ohio* 20, no. 1 (January 1962): 62.

19. Grebner, *We Were the Ninth*, 45–51.

20. Grebner, *We Were the Ninth*, 54.

21. *Cincinnati Commercial*, May 21, 1861.

22. Grebner, *We Were the Ninth*, 52–53.

23. Frederick Finnup, *The Story of My Life* (Garden City, KS: Finnup Foundation, 1996), 23.

24. Judson W. Bishop, *The Story of a Regiment, Being a Narrative of the Service of the Second Regiment, Minnesota Veteran Volunteer Infantry* (Saint Paul, MN, 1890), 31; Brent Nosworthy, *The Bloody Crucible of Courage: Fighting Methods and Combat Experience of the Civil War* (New York: Carrol and Graf, 2003), 142–43. By August 1861, ethnic regiments were admonished to "conform rigidly" to the West Point manuals, but this edict was not always enforced. *Indianapolis Journal*, August 14, 1861.

25. Grebner, *We Were the Ninth*, 53.

26. Finnup, *Story of My Life*, 24; J. D. Cox relates a similar story, claiming that the Thirteenth Ohio Infantry was also a target of the "Bloody Ninth's" ire. Cox, "War Preparations in the North," 98.

27. *Cincinnati Daily Press*, June 12, 1861.

28. Grebner, *We Were the Ninth*, 61–62.

29. *War of the Rebellion: A Compilation of the Official Records of the Union and Confederate Armies* (Washington, DC: Government Printing Office, 1880–1901), series 1, vol. 51, pt. 1, p. 12. Hereinafter this work is cited as *OR*.

30. Grebner, *We Were the Ninth*, 61.

31. *OR*, vol. 51, pt. 1, pp. 13–17.

32. Finnup, *Story of My Life*, 29.

33. Grebner, *We Were the Ninth*, 62–63; Tafel, *Cincinnati Germans*, 32.

34. Jacob D. Cox, "McClellan in West Virginia," in *Battles and Leaders of the Civil War*, ed. Robert U. Johnson and Clarence C. Buell (New York: Century, 1887), 1:131–37.

35. Grebner, *We Were the Ninth*, 67.

CHAPTER ELEVEN

1. Reinhart, *August Willich's Gallant Dutchmen*, 9-10, 18.

2. Michael A. Peake, *Blood Shed in This War: Civil War Illustrations by Captain Adolph Metzner, 32nd Indiana* (Indianapolis: Indiana Historical Society Press, 2010), 11–12.

3. Reinhart, *August Willich's Gallant Dutchmen*, 24.

4. Reinhart, *August Willich's Gallant Dutchmen*, 25–26.

5. Reinhart, *August Willich's Gallant Dutchmen*, 34–35.

6. August Willich to Fritz Anneke, January 31, 1862, Fritz and Mathilde Anneke Papers, State Historical Society of Wisconsin, Madison.

7. Reinhart, *August Willich's Gallant Dutchmen*, 25.

8. *Indianapolis Journal*, September 30, 1861

9. Michael A. Peake, *Indiana's German Sons: A History of the 1st German 32nd Regiment Indiana Volunteer Infantry* (Indianapolis: Max Kade German-American Center, 1995), 12–13.

10. August Willich to Oliver P. Morton, September 30, October 1, 2, 1861, Governor Morton Telegraph Books, Indiana State Archives, Indianapolis.

11. Peake, *Indiana's German Sons*, 13–14.

12. August Willich to Oliver P. Morton, October 5, 1861, Governor Morton Telegraph Books.

13. Reinhart, *August Willich's Gallant Dutchmen*, 30–31.

14. Peake, *Blood Shed in This War*, 15–16.

15. *Der Nordstern* (Saint Cloud, MN), June 19, 1879.

16. Richard W. Johnson, *A Soldier's Reminiscences in Peace and War* (Philadelphia: J. B. Lippincott, 1886), 181.

17. Reinhart, *August Willich's Gallant Dutchmen*, 40.

18. Reinhart, *August Willich's Gallant Dutchmen*, 40–41; Peake, *Blood Shed In This War*, 16; William Sumner Dodge, *History of the Old Second Division, Army of the Cumberland* (Chicago: Church and Goodman, 1864), 89–91.

19. Peake, *Indiana's German Sons*, 22–24.

20. Peake, *Indiana's German Sons*, 24–26; Reinhart, *August Willich's Gallant Dutchmen*, 40–41.

21. Peake, *Indiana's German Sons*, 26–27; Dodge, *History of the Old Second Division*, 89–90.

22. Peake, *Indiana's German Sons*, 29; Dodge, *History of the Old Second Division*, 92–95.

23. Peake, *Indiana's German Sons*, 31, 36; Dodge, *History of the Old Second Division*, 96–98.

24. Peake, *Indiana's German Sons*, 37–41; Dodge, *History of the Old Second Division*, 98–100.

25. *OR*, series 1, vol. 7, pp. 16–19; Frank Moore, ed., *The Civil War in Song and Story* (New York: P. F. Collier, 1889), 252–53.

26. Gerald J. Prokopowicz, *All for the Regiment: The Army of the Ohio, 1861–1862* (Chapel Hill: University of North Carolina Press, 2001), 54–59; Dodge, *History of the Old Second Division*, 100–105.

27. *OR*, series 1, vol. 7, pp. 16–19; Reinhart, *August Willich's Gallant Dutchmen*, 43–44.

28. August Willich to Oliver P. Morton, December 21, 1861, Oliver P. Morton Papers Indiana State Archives, Indianapolis; *Cincinnati Daily Enquirer*, July 9, 1861.

29. William Cullen Bryant, *Poems by William Cullen Bryant* (New York: D. Appleton, 1855), 208.

30. Peake, *Indiana's German Sons*, 44; Reinhart, *August Willich's Gallant Dutchmen*, 52; Dodge, *History of the Old Second Division*, 103–4; Moore, *Civil War in Song and Story*, 253.

31. Peake, *Indiana's German Sons*, 53–55.

32. Peake, *Indiana's German Sons*, 48; Reinhart, *August Willich's Gallant Dutchmen*, 52.

33. Reinhart, *August Willich's Gallant Dutchmen*, 55.

34. Reinhart, *August Willich's Gallant Dutchmen*, 59–60.

35. Dodge, *History of the Old Second Division*, 126–30; Peake, *Indiana's German Sons*, 51–52.

36. Reinhart, *August Willich's Gallant Dutchmen*, 60–70; Dodge, *History of the Old Second Division*, 113–14; Peake, *Indiana's German Sons*, 50.

37. *OR*, series 1, vol. 17, p. 636.

CHAPTER TWELVE

1. Lew Wallace, *An Autobiography* (New York: Harper and Brothers, 1906), 2:550.

2. Wallace, *Autobiography*, 2:560–61.

3. *OR*, series 1, vol. 10, pt. 1, pp. 173, 191.

4. Wallace, *Autobiography*, 2:561.

5. *OR*, series 1, vol. 10, pt. 1, p. 251.

6. Timothy B. Smith, *Shiloh: Conquer or Perish* (Lawrence: University Press of Kansas, 2014), 385–86.

7. *OR*, series 1, vol. 10, pt. 1, p. 251.

8. *OR*, series 1, vol. 10, pt. 1, pp. 317–18. Larry Daniel is critical of Willich's column formation, calling it "ridiculous" and "blunderous." Larry J. Daniel, *Shiloh: The Battle That Changed the Civil War* (New York: Simon and Schuster, 1997), 199, 284–86.

9. Wallace, *Autobiography*, 2:562; James Barnett, "Willich's Thirty-Second Indiana Volunteers," *Cincinnati Historical Society Bulletin* 20 (Spring 1979): 57–58. Barnett claims that Willich was the model for the character of Valerius Gratus in *Ben Hur*. Larry J. Daniel, *Days of Glory: The Army of the Cumberland, 1861–1865* (Baton Rouge: Louisiana State University Press, 2004), 83–87.

10. Reinhart, *August Willich's Gallant Dutchmen*, 71.

11. Alexis Cope, *The Fifteenth Ohio Volunteers and Its Campaigns* (Columbus, OH: Alexis Cope, 1916), 108.

12. Reinhart, *August Willich's Gallant Dutchmen*, 78.

13. James Barnett, "The Vilification of August Willich," *Cincinnati Historical Society Bulletin*, 24 (January 1966): 39–40.

14. Smith, *Shiloh*, 1–251; Don Carlos Buell, "Shiloh Reviewed," in *Battles and Leaders of the Civil War*, ed., Robert U. Johnson and Clarence C. Buell (New York: Century, 1887), 1:525–33.

15. Smith, *Shiloh*, 252–366; Wiley Sword, *Shiloh: Bloody April* (New York: William Morrow, 1974), 403–4.

16. *OR*, series 1, vol. 10, pt. 1, p. 315.

17. *OR*, series 1, vol. 10, pt. 1, p. 317.

18. Reinhart, *August Willich's Gallant Dutchmen*, 87.

19. Reinhart, *August Willich's Gallant Dutchmen*, 76.

20. Smith, *Shiloh*, 372; Sword, *Shiloh*, 407–8.

21. *OR*, series 1, vol. 10, pt. 1, p. 191.

22. *OR*, series 1, vol. 10, pt. 1, p. 252; James L. McDonough, *Shiloh in Hell before Night* (Knoxville: University of Tennessee Press, 1977), 205–8.

23. Dodge, *History of the Old Second Division*, 193–205; Earl Hess, *Civil War Infantry Tactics: Training, Combat, and Small Unit Effectiveness* (Baton Rouge: Louisiana State University Press, 2015), 165–66; Sword, *Shiloh*, 412.

24. Reinhart, *August Willich's Gallant Dutchmen*, 81.

25. Peake, *Blood Shed in This War*, 25.

26. *OR*, series 1, vol. 10, pt. 1, p. 318.

27. Smith, *Shiloh*, 401–2.

28. Peake, *Blood Shed in This War*.

29. Ulysses S. Grant, *Personal Memoirs of U. S. Grant* (New York: Charles L. Webster, 1885), 218.

30. William T. Sherman to Ellen Sherman, April 11, 1862, Sherman Family Papers, University of Notre Dame, South Bend, IN.

31. Smith, *Shiloh*, 405–19.

32. Dodge, *History of the Old Second Division*, 225–28.

33. Peake, *Blood Shed in This War*, 26.

34. Reinhart, *August Willich's Gallant Dutchmen*, 106; Cope, *Fifteenth Ohio Volunteers*, 180.

35. Reinhart, *August Willich's Gallant Dutchmen*, 117–18.

36. Peake, *Blood Shed in This War*, 28.

37. Peake, *Blood Shed in This War*, 28.

38. Peter Cozzens, *No Better Place to Die* (Chicago: University of Illinois Press, 1990), 48–63; Dodge, *History of the Old Second Division*, 381–97.

39. *Western Reserve Chronicle* (Warren, OH), January 17, 1872.

40. Jacob Buck to Mother, February 1, 1863, Buck Family Papers, Abraham Lincoln Presidential Library, Springfield, IL.

41. Cozzens, *No Better Place to Die*, 70–80; Dodge, *History of the Old Second Division*, 398–401; Richard F. Mann, *The Buckeye Vanguard: The Forty-Ninth Ohio Veteran Volunteer Infantry, 1861–1865* (Milford, OH: Little Miami, 2010), 58–59.

42. Cope, *Fifteenth Ohio Volunteers*, 233; Dodge, *History of the Old Second Division*, 399–403.

43. Cozzens, *No Better Place to Die*, 73–76.

44. Cozzens, *No Better Place to Die*, 77.

45. Cozzens, *No Better Place to Die*, 79.

46. Henry M. Cist, *The Army of the Cumberland* (New York: Scribner's, 1882), 133; Dodge, *History of the Old Second Division*, 404.

47. Cope, *Fifteenth Ohio Volunteers*, 230.

48. David Wynn to John Griffeth, March 3, 1863, Filson Historical Society, Louisville, KY.

49. *OR*, series 1, vol. 20, pt. 1, p. 304.

50. Cozzens, *No Better Place to Die*, 82.

51. Johnson, *Soldier's Reminiscences*, 212; *OR*, series 1, vol. 20, pt. 1, 296; Dodge, *History of the Old Second Division*, 406.

52. *OR*, series 1, vol. 20, pt. 1, p. 313.

53. *OR*, series 1, vol. 20, pt. 1, p. 304.

54. Cist, *Army of the Cumberland*, 133.

55. In 1892, Lieut. J. H. Woodward claimed that Willich had "no apprehension of an attack on his front." Woodward cites Willich remarking, "They are so quiet out there that I think they are all no more here." Woodward paraphrases Willich correctly but confuses the date. Willich made these remarks in response to an inquiry from Rosecrans on December 28, 1862. The entire quote reads, "The enemy is no more here; all gone to Murfreesboro." *OR*, series 1, vol. 20, pt. 1, p. 254. James H. Woodward, "General A. McD. McCook at Stone River," *A Paper Read Before the California Commandery of the Military Order of the Loyal Legion of the United States at Los Angeles, Cal., Feb. 22, 1892* (Los Angeles: Times-Mirror, 1892).

56. *OR*, series 1, vol. 20, pt. 1, pp. 313–14.

57. David R. Logsdon, ed., *Eyewitnesses at the Battle of Stones River* (Nashville: Kettle Mills Press, 2002), 17–19.

58. Cozzens, *No Better Place to Die*, 83–87; Dodge, *History of the Old Second Division*, 407–10.

59. Cozzens, *No Better Place to Die*, 87–90; Mann, *Buckeye Vanguard*, 59–60.

60. Johnson, *Soldier's Reminiscences*, 212–13.

61. Gustavus Kunkler to Rosalie Kunkler, January 9, 1863, Gustavus Kunkler Papers, Navarro College Archives, Corsicana, TX; *Atlanta Intelligencer*, September 22, 1863 mentions Capt. James Stone, an aide to Confederate brigadier general Evander McNair, as the man who captured Willich and presumably took his sword. Stone might have lost Willich's sword months later at Chickamauga, as it was found on that battlefield on September 27, 1863. *Society of the Army of the Cumberland: Twenty-First Reunion, Toledo, Ohio* (Cincinnati: Robert Clarke, 1891), 49. The sword is currently displayed in the battlefield museum at Chickamauga and Chattanooga National Military Park.

62. *OR*, series 1, vol. 20, pt. 1, pp. 912, 946–48; *Madison (IN) Daily Evening Courier*, January 17, 1863; Dodge, *History of the Old Second Division*, 411–12.

63. Dodge, *History of the Old Second Division*, 412–38.

64. Cozzens, *No Better Place to Die*, 193–94.

65. *OR*, series 1, vol. 20, pt. 1, p. 307.

66. Reinhart, *August Willich's Gallant Dutchmen*, 136.

CHAPTER THIRTEEN

1. W. H. Newlin, David F. Lawler, and John W. Sherrick, *A History of the Seventy-Third Regiment of Illinois Infantry Volunteers, 1861–65: Including a Sketch of the Services Rendered by Opdycke's First Brigade, Second Division, Fourth Army Corps in Tennessee in 1864 and the Battles of Spring Hill and Franklin* (1890), 563.

2. Cope, *Fifteenth Ohio Volunteers*, 250.

3. Newlin, Lawler, and Sherrick, *History of the Seventy-Third*, 563.

4. Newlin, Lawler, and Sherrick, *History of the Seventy-Third*, 563–64.

5. Newlin, Lawler, and Sherrick, *History of the Seventy-Third*, 564.

6. Newlin, Lawler, and Sherrick, *History of the Seventy-Third*, 565.

7. Newlin, Lawler, and Sherrick, *History of the Seventy-Third*, 566. William Wirt Calkins, *The History of the One Hundred and Fourth Regiment of Illinois Volunteer Infantry* (Chicago: Donahue and Henneberry, 1895), 509.

8. Calkins, *History of the One Hundred and Fourth Regiment*, 509–11.

9. Thomas G. Dyer, *Secret Yankees: The Union Circle in Confederate Atlanta* (Baltimore: Johns Hopkins University Press, 1999), 82–96.

10. Newlin, Lawler, and Sherrick, *History of the Seventy-Third*, 564–67.

11. Newlin, Lawler, and Sherrick, *History of the Seventy-Third*, 565–66.

12. *Soldiers' and Patriots' Biographical Album Containing Biographies and Portraits of Soldiers and Loyal Citizens in the American Conflict, Together with the Great Commanders of the Union Army; Also a History of the Organizations Growing Out of the War* [. . .] (Chicago: Union Veteran Publishing Company, 1892), 102–5; *Nashville Union*, Apr. 5, 1863; *St. Charles Chronicle*, September 21, 1916.

13. Reinhart, *August Willich's Gallant Dutchmen*, 143.

14. Newlin, Lawler, and Sherrick, *History of the Seventy-Third*, 567.

15. Calkins, *History of the One Hundred and Fourth Regiment*, 511.

16. Will Parmiter Kent, *The Story of Libby Prison, Also Some Perils and Sufferings of Certain of its Inmates* (Chicago: Libby Prison War Museum Association, 1890), 14–17; Cope, *Fifteenth Ohio Volunteers*, 251.

17. *The Libby Chronicle. Devoted to Facts and Fun. A True Copy of the Libby Chronicle as Written by the Prisoners of Libby in 1863* (Albany, NY: Louis N. Beaudry, 1889), 16; Kent, *Story of Libby Prison*, 34.

18. *Hero, Russian Bloodhound, Used for Guarding Union Prisoners at Libby Prison and Castle Thunder, Richmond, Va.*, photographed by J. W. Turner, No. 47 Hanover Street, Boston, Liljenquist Family Collection, Library of Congress, Washington, DC.

19. Kent, *Story of Libby Prison*, 14–17, 54–57.

20. James M. Shanklin Pension File, no. 36426, Civil War Pension Files and Compiled Service Records, RG 94, National Archives, Washington, DC.

21. Cope, *Fifteenth Ohio Volunteers*, 278.

22. Cope, *Fifteenth Ohio Volunteers*, 279. In Europe, skirmishers had used similar tactics since at least the early nineteenth century. C. Leslie, *Instructions for the Application of Light Drill to Skirmishing in the Field: With Observations on Advanced and Rear Guards, and Flank Patrols* (Dublin: Pettigrew and Oulton, 1831), vii, 8, 17–18. This manual also details bugle signals to direct skirmishers and recommends the hollow-square formation for use by infantry defending against cavalry attack. Both of these practices were hallmarks of Willich's tactical repertoire.

23. Jefferson E. Brant, *History of the Eighty-Fifth Indiana Volunteer Infantry* (Bloomington, IN: Craven Brothers, 1902), 25.

24. John Coburn Papers 1870–1885, Indiana Historical Society, Indianapolis.

25. Brant, *History of the Eighty-Fifth*, 30; Cope, *Fifteenth Ohio Volunteers*, 252.

26. Abraham Lincoln to Joseph Hooker, May 8, 1863, in Lincoln, *Collected Works*, 6:202–3.

27. Reinhart, *August Willich's Gallant Dutchmen*, 141–42.

28. *Easton (MD) Gazette*, June 27, 1863.

29. Reinhart, *August Willich's Gallant Dutchmen*, 144.

30. *Easton (MD) Gazette*, June 27, 1863.

31. Reinhart, *August Willich's Gallant Dutchmen*, 141.

32. Reinhart, *August Willich's Gallant Dutchmen*, 141–42.

33. Reinhart, *August Willich's Gallant Dutchmen*, 141–44.

34. Marx and Engels, *Civil War in the United States*, 91–100, 133.

35. Reinhart, *August Willich's Gallant Dutchmen*, 144.

CHAPTER FOURTEEN

1. David Dwight Bigger, *Ohio's Silver-Tongued Orator: Life and Speeches of General William H. Gibson* (Dayton, OH: United Brethren Publishing House, 1901).

2. August Willich, *The Army, Standing Army or National Army?* (Cincinnati: A. Frey, 1866), 23; Mann, *Buckeye Vanguard*, 69.

3. *Miami Helmet* (Piqua, OH), August 14, 1890.

4. Cope, *Fifteenth Ohio Volunteers*, 278.

5. Cope, *Fifteenth Ohio Volunteers*, 280.

6. Willich, *Army*, 10.

7. Willich, *Army*, 17; Nosworthy, *Bloody Crucible of Courage*, 633–38.

8. Willich, *Army*, 19.

9. Cope, *Fifteenth Ohio Volunteers*, 279.

10. Steven E. Woodworth, *Six Armies in Tennessee: The Chickamauga and Chattanooga Campaigns* (Lincoln: University of Nebraska Press, 1998), 1–18.

11. Michael R. Bradley, *Tullahoma: The 1863 Campaign for the Control of Middle Tennessee* (Shippensburg, PA: Burd Street, 2000), 32–53; Cist, *Army of the Cumberland*, 154–58.

12. *OR*, series 1, vol. 23, pt. 1, 486–87.

13. *OR*, vol. 23, pt. 1, 495–96; Mann, *Buckeye Vanguard*, 75–76.

14. Dodge, *History of the Old Second Division*, 476–83; Bradley, *Tullahoma*, 55–57; Reinhart, *August Willich's Gallant Dutchmen*, 146.

15. *OR*, vol. 23, pt. 1, 493–94; Bradley, *Tullahoma*, 57–59.

16. *OR*, vol. 23, pt. 1, 487–88; Bradley, *Tullahoma*, 68.

17. *OR*, vol. 23, pt. 1, 484, 487; Mann, *Buckeye Vanguard*, 76.

18. *Tiffin (OH) Weekly Tribune*, August 28, 1863; Peake, *Blood Shed in This War*, 107; Reinhart, *August Willich's Gallant Dutchmen*, 146–47.

19. *OR*, vol. 23, pt. 1, 488; Bradley, *Tullahoma*, 71–73.

20. *OR*, vol. 23, pt. 1, 488, 496–97; Dodge, *History of the Old Second Division*, 490–92. Mann, *Buckeye Vanguard*, 77.

21. *Tiffin (OH) Weekly Tribune*, August 28, 1863; Bradley, *Tullahoma*, 69.

22. *OR*, vol. 23, pt. 1, 488; Cist, *Army of the Cumberland*, 158–59; Dodge, *History of the Old Second Division*, 498–99.

23. *OR*, vol. 23, pt. 1, 406.

24. *OR*, vol. 23, pt. 1, 468.

25. *OR*, vol. 23, pt. 1, 489.

26. *OR*, vol. 23, pt. 1, 495.

27. *OR*, vol. 23, pt. 1, 489; Bradley, *Tullahoma*, 74–89; Cist, *Army of the Cumberland*, 160–68.

28. Willich, *Army*, 15; Bradley, *Tullahoma*, 95.

CHAPTER FIFTEEN

1. Abraham Lincoln to Henry Halleck, June 30, 1862, in Lincoln, *Collected Works*, 5:295.

2. Abraham Lincoln to William S. Rosecrans, October 4, 1863, in Lincoln, *Collected Works*, 6:498.

3. Woodworth, *Six Armies in Tennessee*, 47–78.

4. Peter Cozzens, *This Terrible Sound: The Battle of Chickamauga* (Chicago: University of Illinois Press, 1994), 33–79.

5. Peter Cozzens, *This Terrible Sound: The Battle of Chickamauga* (Chicago: University of Illinois Press, 1994), 80–100.

6. Cozzens, *This Terrible Sound*, 118–19; Henry Villard, *Memoirs of Henry Villard* (Boston: Houghton, Mifflin, 1904), 2:106–7.

7. Cozzens, *This Terrible Sound*, 152–53.

8. *Willich at Chickamauga* (1863), 2, Newberry Library, Chicago. The anonymous author of this source was likely a Chicago newspaper correspondent following Willich's brigade.

9. *Willich at Chickamauga*, 3; OR, series 1, vol. 30, pt. 1, 538–39, 542–43, 549, 551; David A. Powell, *The Maps of Chickamauga: An Atlas of the Chickamauga Campaign, Including the Tullahoma Operations, June 22–September 23, 1863* (New York: Savas Beatie, 2009), 72–75; Cozzens, *This Terrible Sound*, 156–58.

10. OR, series 1, vol. 30, pt. 1, 539; Cozzens, *This Terrible Sound*, 186–87; Powell, *Maps of Chickamauga*, 80–81.

11. Dodge, *History of the Old Second Division*, 541–45; OR, series 1, vol. 30, pt. 1, 543.

12. OR, series 1, vol. 30, pt. 1, 545; *Willich at Chickamauga*, 3–4.

13. Dodge, *History of the Old Second Division*, 544–45; Villard, *Memoirs*, 2:122; *Willich at Chickamauga*, 4.

14. OR, series 1, vol. 30, pt. 1, 539.

15. Reinhart, *August Willich's Gallant Dutchmen*, 154.

16. Powell, *Maps of Chickamauga*, 128–29; Cozzens, *This Terrible Sound*, 191–95; *Willich at Chickamauga*, 4–5; Dodge, *History of the Old Second Division*, 545–47.

17. Powell, *Maps of Chickamauga*, 130–35; Cozzens, *This Terrible Sound*, 263–79.

18. OR, series 1, vol. 30, pt. 1, 539.

19. Dodge, *History of the Old Second Division*, 547–48.

20. Powell, *Maps of Chickamauga*, 136–37; Cope, *Fifteenth Ohio Volunteers*, 309–13; Villard, *Memoirs*, 2:122–25.

21. Dodge, *History of the Old Second Division*, 552.

22. Cozzens, *This Terrible Sound*, 294–97.

23. Willich, *Army*, 21.

24. *Harper's New Monthly Magazine* 49 (October 1874): 760. An anonymous Afton, Iowa correspondent claimed that Rosecrans threatened to arrest Willich the evening of September 19 for insubordination.

25. Cozzens, *This Terrible Sound*, 300–310.

26. Cozzens, *This Terrible Sound*, 317–43; Powell, *Maps of Chickamauga*, 152–53; Villard, *Memoirs*, 2:132.

27. OR, series 1, vol. 30, pt. 1, 535; Reinhart, *August Willich's Gallant Dutchmen*, 154–55.

28. OR, series 1, vol. 30, pt. 1, 540; Dodge, *History of the Old Second Division*, 556–58. Cozzens, *This Terrible Sound*, 353–56; Reinhart, *August Willich's Gallant Dutchmen*, 156.

29. Cozzens, *This Terrible Sound*, 357–67, 403–4.

30. Powell, *Maps of Chickamauga*, 200; Villard, *Memoirs*, 2:147–58.

31. Powell, *Maps of Chickamauga*, 224–25, 240–41.

32. Cozzens, *This Terrible Sound*, 497–98.

33. OR, series 1, vol. 30, pt. 1, 540.

34. Chesley A. Mosman, *The Rough Side of War: The Civil War Journal of Chesley A. Mosman, 1st Lieutenant, Company D, 59th Illinois Volunteer Infantry Regiment.* (Garden City, NY: Basin, 1987), 72.

35. *Willich at Chickamauga*, 7; Dodge, *History of the Old Second Division*, 558–61.

36. OR, series 1, vol. 30, pt. 1, 536; Dodge, *History of the Old Second Division*, 562–68.

37. OR, series 1, vol. 30, pt. 1, 544–45. Another eyewitness called Willich's command the "Iron Brigade." See *Willich at Chickamauga*, 8; Cope, *Fifteenth Ohio Volunteers*, 319–22; Villard, *Memoirs*, 2:161–62; Reinhart, *August Willich's Gallant Dutchmen*, 156–58.

38. *Belmont (OH) Chronicle*, October 20, 1863.

39. *OR*, series 1, vol. 30, pt. 1, 541; *Hancock (OH) Jeffersonian*, November 6; Mann, *Buckeye Vanguard*, 81–89.

40. *OR*, series 1, vol. 30, pt. 1, 536.

41. *OR*, series 1, vol. 30, pt. 1, 255.

42. *OR*, series 1, vol. 30, pt. 1, 554.

43. August Willich, biographical summary provided to George W. Childs, October 1863, Charles F. Gunther Collection, Chicago History Museum.

44. Willich, *Army*, 10, 18.

45. *OR*, series 1, vol. 30, pt. 1, 542.

46. *OR*, series 1, vol. 30, pt. 1, 541.

47. Peter Cozzens, *The Shipwreck of Their Hopes: The Battles for Chattanooga* (Chicago: University of Illinois Press, 1994), 1–7.

48. Peake, *Blood Shed in This War*, 39–40; August Willich to Oliver P. Morton, November 9, 1863, private collection.

49. Cozzens, *This Terrible Sound*, 223–24.

50. Ole Amundson Buslett, *The Fifteenth Wisconsin*, trans. by Barbara G. Scott (Ripon, WI: B. G. Scott, 1999), 684–85. Originally published in 1894.

51. Cozzens, *Shipwreck of Their Hopes*, 45–65.

52. Cozzens, *Shipwreck of Their Hopes*, 103–5, 124–25.

53. Cozzens, *Shipwreck of Their Hopes*, 126–30.

54. Hess, *Civil War Infantry Tactics*, 155–57.

55. Cozzens, *Shipwreck of Their Hopes*, 130–32; Wiley Sword, *Mountains Touched with Fire: Chattanooga Besieged, 1863* (New York: Saint Martin's, 1995), 175–85.

56. *OR*, series 1, vol. 31, pt. 2, 65–67, 263–64.

57. Cozzens, *Shipwreck of Their Hopes*, 137–41, 159–92.

58. Cozzens, *Shipwreck of Their Hopes*, 245–48.

59. Cozzens, *Shipwreck of Their Hopes*, 258–62.

60. *OR*, series 1, vol. 31, pt. 2, 253–61, 264, 268–83.

61. Cope, *Fifteenth Ohio Volunteers*, 385.

62. Jacob Glass to Fritz Glass, November 22, 1863, private collection.

63. *OR*, series 1, vol. 31, pt. 2, 264.

64. *New York Times*, January 26, February 20, 1876; *Cincinnati Gazette*, August 24, 1866.

65. Cope, *Fifteenth Ohio Volunteers*, 381.

66. Cope, *Fifteenth Ohio Volunteers*, 383; Mann, *Buckeye Vanguard*, 93–95.

67. *New York World*, December 4, 1863; Sword, *Mountains Touched with Fire*, 290–94; Reinhart, *August Willich's Gallant Dutchmen*, 160–64.

68. Cope, *Fifteenth Ohio Volunteers*, 382–83; Wiley Sword, *Mountains Touched with Fire*, 295.

69. *OR*, series 1, vol. 31, pt. 2, 265.

CHAPTER SIXTEEN

1. Peter Cozzens, *Shipwreck of Their Hopes*, 388.

2. Cozzens, *Shipwreck of Their Hopes*, 387.

3. Buslett, *Fifteenth Wisconsin*, 85–86.

4. Cope, *Fifteenth Ohio Volunteers*, 87; Reinhart, *August Willich's Gallant Dutchmen*, 167.

5. Cope, *Fifteenth Ohio Volunteers*, 424.

6. Cope, *Fifteenth Ohio Volunteers*, 418.

7. "Rocky Face Ridge," American Battlefield Trust, https://www.battlefields.org/learn/civil
-war/battles/rocky-face-ridge/.

8. "Rocky Face Ridge," American Battlefield Trust, https://www.battlefields.org/learn/civil
-war/battles/rocky-face-ridge/.

9. Buslett, *Fifteenth Wisconsin*, 91–92.

10. "Resaca," American Battlefield Trust, https://www.battlefields.org/learn/civil-war/battles
/resaca/.

11. *OR*, series 1, vol. 38, pt. 1, 390–91; Philip L. Secrist, *The Battle of Resaca: Atlanta Campaign 1864* (Macon, GA: Mercer University Press, 1998).

12. *OR*, series 1, vol. 38, pt. 1, 375.

13. Cope, *Fifteenth Ohio Volunteers*, 435.

14. August Willich Pension File No. 77658, Civil War Pension Files and Compiled Service Records, RG 94, National Archives, Washington, DC.

15. Cope, *Fifteenth Ohio Volunteers*, 435–36; *Cincinnati Examiner*, May 1,7 1864; Bigger, *Ohio's Silver-Tongued Orator*, 404. George S. Phillips to Sallie Phillips May 15, 1864, George S. Phillips Papers, Huntington Library, San Marino, California.

16. "Resaca," American Battlefield Trust, https://www.battlefields.org/learn/civil-war/battles
/resaca/.

17. *OR*, series 1, vol. 38, pt. 1, 400; Denslow Holton to Gilbert Durin, May 28, 1864, Durin Family Papers, Abraham Lincoln Presidential Library, Springfield, Illinois; Wallace McCloud Civil War Diary, McCloud Family Papers, Abraham Lincoln Presidential Library, Springfield, Illinois.

18. *OR*, series 1, vol. 38, pt. 1, 399–400.

19. Reinhart, *August Willich's Gallant Dutchmen*, 174–75.

20. *Milwaukee Sentinel*, June 8, 1864.

CHAPTER SEVENTEEN

1. *New York Times*, August 17, 1864.

2. Jerry Thompson, *The Life and Times of Major General Samuel P. Heintzelman* (College Station: Texas A&M Press, 2006).

3. *Roster and Record of Iowa Soldiers in the War of the Rebellion, together with Historical Sketches of Volunteer Organizations, 1861–1866* (Des Moines, IA: E. H. English, 1911), 5:741–43.

4. Frank Klement, *Copperheads in the Middle West* (Chicago: University of Chicago Press, 1960); Frank Klement, *Dark Lanterns: Secret Political Societies, Conspiracies, and Treason Trials in the Civil War* (Baton Rouge: Louisiana State University Press, 1984).

5. August Willich to C. H. Pettigrew, August 22, 1864, Letters Received by the Adjutant General, Main Series 1861–1870, National Archives, Washington, DC.

6. *Daily Ohio Statesman* (Columbus), August 29, 1864.

7. Felix Grundy Stidger, *Treason History of the Order of Sons of Liberty* (Chicago: Felix Stidger, 1903), 160–74.

8. "United States vs. Thomas Martin," Records of the Judge Advocate General, RG 153, National Archives, Washington, DC.

9. William M. Dickson, "The Last Confederate Victim of the War," *Century Illustrated Monthly Magazine* 35 (Apr. 1888): 961.

10. Walter H. Hebert, *Fighting Joe Hooker* (Lincoln: University of Nebraska Press, 1999).

11. Gen. Joseph Hooker to Gen. August Willich, May 1, 1865, Documents Relating to Civilians

Who Came Into Contact with the Army during the Civil War, Including Deserters, Thieves, and Spies, RG 109, National Archives, Washington, DC.

12. *Daily Sentinel* (Indianapolis), May 8, 1865.

13. Dickson, "Last Victim of the War," 961; Telegram from J. D. Taylor to O. H. Hart, May 4, 1865, telegram from George H. Pendleton to Gen. Joseph Hooker, May 5, 1865, Documents Relating to Civilians Who Came Into Contact with the Army during the Civil War.

14. Lieut. William Mahon to Capt. Charles A. Booth, May 3, 1865, Documents Relating to Civilians Who Came Into Contact with the Army during the Civil War.

15. *Daily Sentinel* (Indianapolis), May 8, 1865.

16. Telegram from Edwin J. Stanton to Gen. Joseph Hooker, May 5, 1865, Documents Relating to Civilians Who Came Into Contact with the Army during the Civil War.

17. *OR*, series 1, vol. 49, pt. 2, 679.

18. Gen. Joseph Hooker to Gen. August Willich, May 10, 1865, telegram from Edwin M. Stanton to Gen. Joseph Hooker, May 9, 1865, Documents Relating to Civilians Who Came Into Contact with the Army during the Civil War.

19. Samuel H. M. Byers, *Iowa in War Times* (Des Moines, IA: W. D. Condit, 1888), 559.

CHAPTER EIGHTEEN

1. William L. Richter, *The Army in Texas During Reconstruction, 1865–1870* (College Station: Texas A&M University Press, 1987), 15–18; Mann, *Buckeye Vanguard*, 143.

2. Cope, *Fifteenth Ohio Volunteers*, 716–21.

3. Joel Chambers, *War Fever Cured: The Civil War Diary of Private Joel R. Chambers, 1864–1865* (Memphis: W. R. Glasgow, 1980), 131–34; *OR*, series 1, vol. 49, pt. 2, 923, 965–66.

4. Cope, *Fifteenth Ohio Volunteers*, 725–32.

5. Cope, *Fifteenth Ohio Volunteers*, 744–48; Mann, *Buckeye Vanguard*, 144.

6. Cope, *Fifteenth Ohio Volunteers*, 750–55; Mann, *Buckeye Vanguard*, 145.

7. Cope, *Fifteenth Ohio Volunteers*, 758–60; Mann, *Buckeye Vanguard*, 145–47.

8. Cope, *Fifteenth Ohio Volunteers*, 759–62; Mann, *Buckeye Vanguard*, 147.

9. O.R., series 1, vol. 40, pt.2, 1168–69. Mann, *Buckeye Vanguard*, 147–48.

10. Cope, *Fifteenth Ohio Volunteers*, 762–68; Richter, *Army in Texas*, 25; Mann, *Buckeye Vanguard*, 148–49.

11. Cope, *Fifteenth Ohio Volunteers*, 766.

12. Cope, *Fifteenth Ohio Volunteers*, 779–81; Mann, *Buckeye Vanguard*, 149.

13. August Willich to Lorenzo Thomas, November 9, 1865, Willich pension file no 119,850, Civil War Pension Files and Compiled Service Records, RG 94, National Archives, Washington, DC.

14. Willich, *Army*, 3, 21.

15. Gian Gentile, Michael E. Linick, Michael Shurkin, *The Evolution of U.S. Military Policy from the Constitution to the Present* (Santa Monica, CA: Rand Corporation, 2017), iii, 2, 7–12, 24–25.

16. Gentile, Linick, and Shurkin, *Evolution of U.S. Military Policy*, 48.

17. Willich, *Army*, 21.

18. Willich, *Army*, 4, 21–22.

19. Willich, *Army*, 4–5.

20. Willich, *Army*, 4–5.

21. Willich, *Army*, 5.

22. Willich, *Army*, 7, 21.

23. Willich, *Army*, 23.

24. Gentile, Linick, and Shurkin, *Evolution of U.S. Military Policy*, 24.

CHAPTER NINETEEN

1. Barnett, "Vilification," 30; Application of August Willich for position in the regular army, Letters and Their Enclosures Received by the Commission Branch of the Adjutant General's Office, 1863–70, RG 94, National Archives, Washington, DC.

2. *Evansville (IN) Journal*, July 9, 1866.

3. Barnett, "Vilification," 32; *Ohio Statesman* (Columbus), July 30, 1866; *Evansville (IN) Journal*, August 2, 3, 15, 16, 1866.

4. Barnett, "Vilification," 32; *Evansville (IN) Journal*, August 23, 29, 1866.

5. Barnett, "Vilification," 32–33.

6. *Daily Empire* (Dayton, OH), September 7, 29, 1866; Carl F. Wittke "Friedrich Hassaurek: Cincinnati's Leading Forty-Eighter," *Ohio Historical Quarterly* 68 (1959): 1–17.

7. Efford, *German Immigrants*, 125–26.

8. Efford, *German Immigrants*, 14, 115–142.

9. *Cincinnati Enquirer*, June 27, 1868.

10. Barnett, "Vilification," 33–34.

11. *Cincinnati Enquirer*, February 7, 1869.

12. *Cincinnati Gazette*, March 12, 26, 30, 1869; *Cincinnati Enquirer*, August 25, 1868.

13. *Cincinnati Gazette*, April 8, 12, 1869.

14. Barnett, "Vilification," 35.

15. Barnett, "Vilification," 35; *Cincinnati Gazette*, May 17, 25, 27, 1869.

16. *Cincinnati Gazette*, June 2, 3, 1869.

17. Barnett, "Vilification," 36; *Cincinnati Gazette*, June 16, 19, 26, 1869.

18. *Cincinnati Commercial Times*, December 18, 1869.

19. Barnett, "Vilification," 36–37.

20. Barnett, "Vilification," 37.

21. Barnett, "Vilification," 37–38; Efford, *German Immigrants*, 225.

22. Barnett, "Vilification," 38–39; *Cincinnati Examiner*, June 17, 1870; *Cincinnati Gazette*, June 7, 20, 1870.

23. Michael E. Howard, *The Franco-Prussian War: The German Invasion of France 1870–1871* (New York: Routledge, 1991).

24. Charles D. Stewart, "A Bachelor General," *Wisconsin Magazine of History* 17, no. 2 (December 1933): 149; Easton, *Hegel's First American Followers*, 198–99. Easton errs in claiming that Willich left for Germany in May 1869. *Cincinnati Gazette*, March 12, 1869; *Cincinnati Gazette*, May 20, 1870; August Willich passport no. 6813, issued June 1, 1870, Selected Passports, National Archives, Washington, DC.

25. Howard, *Franco-Prussian War*, 32–60.

26. *Evansville (IN) Journal*, August 12, 1870.

27. Hugh Chisholm, ed., "Moltke, Helmuth Carl Bernhard," in *Encyclopedia Britannica* (New York: Cambridge University Press., 1911), 18:677–81.

28. Howard, *Franco-Prussian War*, 94–126.

29. *Chicago Republican*, August 11, 1870.

30. August Willich to Otto Metzner, March 2, 1872, private collection; Howard, *Franco-Prussian War*, 341–60.

31. Departure certificate of August Willich from Fredrich Wilhelm University, Berlin, March 31, 1871, attendance document from Royal Trade School, Berlin, May 2, 1871, H. A. Rattermann Collection, University of Illinois at Urbana–Champaign Library.

32. Passenger Lists of Vessels Arriving at New York, New York, 1820–1897, M237, Records

of the U.S. Customs Service, RG 36, Roll 349, National Archives, Washington, DC. *Cincinnati Gazette*, June 20, 1871; Minna Kinkel to Gottfried Kinkel, Sept. 7, 27, 1871, Papers of Gottfried and Johanna Kinkel, Bonn University Library, Bonn, Germany.

33. Easton, *Hegel's First American Followers*, 200; Efford, *German Immigrants*, 203.

CHAPTER TWENTY

1. Passenger Lists of Vessels Arriving at New York, New York, 1820–1897, M237, Records of the U.S. Customs Service, RG 36, Roll 349, National Archives, Washington, DC; Nadel, *Little Germany*, 17–26.

2. C. W. Williamson, *History of Western Ohio and Auglaize County* (Columbus, OH: W. M. Linn and Sons, 1905), 679–80; Earl J. Hess, *The Battle of Ezra Church and the Struggle for Atlanta* (Chapel Hill: University of North Carolina Press, 2015), 61.

3. Stewart, "Bachelor General," 149–51. Kraig Noble, "General August Willich," in *The St. Marys Anthology: Tales and Sketches from an American Small Town*, ed. Robert Howard (Saint Marys, OH, 2013), 36–44.

4. Gourevitch, *Slavery to the Cooperative Commonwealth*, 97–117; Levine, *Spirit of 1848*, 263–71.

5. Alison Clark Efford, "The Arms Scandal of 1870–1872: Immigrant Liberal Republicans and America's Place in the World," *Reconstruction in a Globalizing World*, ed. David Prior (New York: Fordham University Press, 2018), 94–120; Efford, *German Immigrants*, 143–70.

6. Efford, *German Immigrants*, 171–93.

7. Efford, *German Immigrants*, 194–98; Honeck, *We Are the Revolutionists*, 172–88.

8. Levine, *Spirit of 1848*, 266.

9. US Congress, *Congressional Globe, 42nd Congress, Third Session, Part 2* (Washington, DC, 1873), 725.

10. *Cincinnati Commercial*, October 3, 1873.

11. David T. Dixon, *The Lost Gettysburg Address: Charles Anderson's Civil War Odyssey* (Santa Barbara, CA: B-List History, 2015), 135–51.

12. *Holmes County (OH) Republican*, August 7, 1873.

13. *Daily Empire* (Dayton, OH), September 29, 1866.

14. *Cincinnati Commercial*, October 3, 1873; *Cincinnati Gazette*, April 8, 1869; *Macarthur (OH) Enquirer*, August 6, 1873.

15. Joseph Patterson Smith, *History of the Republican Party in Ohio* (Chicago: Lewis, 1898), 1:319.

16. *Humboldt (KS) Union*, September 30, 1876.

17. Levine, *Spirit of 1848*, 266, 269; E.L. Godkin, "A Great National Disgrace," *Nation* 25 (August 2, 1877), 68–69.

18. *Findlay (OH) Jeffersonian*, November 9, 1877.

19. Stewart, "Bachelor General," 150–53.

20. *St. Marys (OH) Argus*, January 26, 1878; *Wapakoneta (OH) Bee*, January 31, 1878.

21. *Cincinnati Commercial Times*, January 26, 1878; Tiffin (OH) Tribune, January 31, 1878.

22. *Cincinnati Commercial Times*, January 26, 1878; *Tiffin (OH) Tribune*, January 31, 1878.

23. *New York Times*, January 24, 1878.

24. Probate File of August Willich, Case no. 2534, Auglaize County, Ohio Probate Court, Wapakoneta.

CONCLUSION

1. Carl Schurz to Abraham Lincoln, April 23, 1862, Abraham Lincoln Papers, Library of Congress, Washington, DC.

2. Abraham Lincoln memorandum, January 17, 1865, Lincoln Signed Documents, Lincoln Financial Foundation Collection, Allen County Public Library, Fort Wayne, IN.

3. Engle, *Yankee Dutchman*; Trefousse, *Carl Schurz*; Townsend, *Yankee Warhorse*; Johann Stallo to John Sherman, 1864, Letters Received by the Commission Branch of the Adjutant General's Office, 1863–1870, National Archives, Washington, DC.

4. Carl von Clausewitz, *On War*, Edited and translated by Michael Howard and Peter Paret. New York: Alfred A. Knopf, 1993, 99–104. Originally published in 1832.

5. Reinhart, *August Willich's Gallant Dutchmen*, 15.

6. William L. Burton, *Melting Pot Soldiers: The Union's Ethnic Regiments* (New York: Fordham University Press, 1998); Christian B. Keller, *Chancellorsville and the Germans: Nativism, Ethnicity, and Civil War Memory* (New York: Fordham University Press, 2008); Helbich, "German-Born Union Soldiers: Motivation, Ethnicity, and Americanization," in *German-American Immigration and Ethnicity in Comparative Perspective*, ed. Wolfgang Helbich and Walter D. Kamphoefner (Madison: Max Kade Institute for German-American Studies, University of Wisconsin, 2004), 320.

7. Levine, *Spirit of 1848*; Wittke, *Refugees of Revolution*; Don Heinrich Tolzmann, ed., *The German Forty-Eighters, 1848–1998* (Indianapolis: Max Kade German-American Center, 1998).

8. Levine, *Spirit of 1848*, 256.

9. Eric Foner, "American Radicals and the Change We Could Believe In," *Nation*, December 14, 2016, https://www.thenation.com/article/teaching-the-history-of-radicalism-in-the-age-of-obama/.

10. Honeck, *We Are the Revolutionists*, 84. This nickname for Willich persisted in Europe and in the United States.

11. Easton, *Hegel's First American Followers*, 189.

12. Lause, *Free Labor*, viii–xvi, 1–27, 68–72, 172–74.

13. *Evansville (IN) Journal*, August 2, 1866.

14. Michael Drury, *Transatlantic Radicals and the Early American Republic* (Lawrence: University Press of Kansas, 1997).

15. Easton, *Hegel's First American Followers*, 166–67.

16. Max Weber, *Political Writings*, ed. Peter Lassman and Ronald Speirs (Cambridge: Cambridge University Press, 1994), 269.

17. My view of Willich as a skilled practitioner of the art of turning emotions into collective action is strongly influenced by sociologist James M. Jasper, *The Emotions of Protest* (Chicago: University of Chicago Press, 2018).

18. Jonathan Frankel, *Prophecy and Politics: Socialism, Nationalism, and the Russian Jews, 1862–1917* (Cambridge: Cambridge University Press, 1981), 19–21.

19. August Willich to Fritz Anneke, January 31, 1862, Fritz and Mathilde Anneke Papers, State Historical Society of Wisconsin, Madison.

Bibliography

MANUSCRIPT SOURCES

Abraham Lincoln Presidential Library, Springfield, IL
   Buck Family Papers
   Durin Family Papers
   Kays Family Papers
   McCloud Family Papers
Allen County Public Library, Fort Wayne, IN
   Lincoln Financial Foundation Collection
Bavarian State Library, Munich, Germany
Besançon Municipal Archives, Besançon, France
   Death Registers, 1848, 1849
Bonn University Library, Bonn, Germany
   Papers of Gottfried and Johanna Kinkel
Chicago History Museum
   Charles F. Gunther Collection
Cincinnati History Library and Archives
Filson Historical Society, Louisville, KY
Hoover Institution Archives, Stanford, CA
   Boris I. Nicolaevsky Collection
Huntington Library, San Marino,CA
   Diary of William McConnell
   George S. Phillips Papers, 1840–1904
Indiana Historical Society, Indianapolis
   James A. Little Civil War Diary, 1861–1862
   John Coburn Papers, 1870–1885
Indiana State Archives, Indianapolis
   Governor Morton Telegraph Books
   Oliver P. Morton Papers
International Institute for Social History, Amsterdam, Netherlands
   August Willich Papers, 1848–1850
Library of Congress, Washington, DC
   Abraham Lincoln Papers
   Liljenquist Family Collection
National Archives, College Park, MD
   Records of the Coast and Geodetic Survey, RG 23
National Archives, Washington, DC
   Civil War Pension Files
   Passenger Lists of Vessels Arriving at New York, New York, 1820–1897, M237
   Passport Applications, 1795–1905, M1371

Records of the Adjutant General's Office, 1762–1985, RG 94
Records of the Bureau of the Census, 1790–2010, RG 29
Records of the Judge Advocate General, RG 153
Records of the U.S. Customs Service, RG 36
National Library, Coburg, Germany
  Papers of Friedrich von Hoffman
Navarro College Archives, Corsicana, TX
  Gustavus Kunkler Papers
Newberry Library, Chicago
  Midwest Manuscripts Collection
Prussian Privy State Archives, Berlin
  Salary Compensation Commissions for the Eastern Provinces
State Historical Society of Wisconsin, Madison
  Fritz and Mathilde Anneke Papers
University of Illinois at Urbana–Champaign Library
  H. A. Rattermann Collection
University of Notre Dame, South Bend, IN
  Sherman Family Papers

NEWSPAPERS

Atlanta Intelligencer
Belletristisches Journal und New-Yorker Criminal-Zeitung
Belleviller Zeitung (Belleville, IL)
Belmont (OH) Chronicle
Boston Daily Bee
Cincinnati Commercial
Cincinnati Daily Press
Cincinnati Enquirer
Cincinnati Examiner
Cincinnati Gazette
Cincinnati Republikaner
Cincinnati Volksfreund
Daily Empire (Dayton, OH)
Daily Exchange (Baltimore)
Daily Ohio Statesman (Columbus)
Daily Sentinel (Indianapolis)
Daily Star (Cincinnati)
Daily Union (Washington, DC)
Der Deutsch Correspondent (Baltimore)
Der Nordstern (Saint Cloud, MN)
Easton (MD) Gazette
Evansville (IN) Journal
Findlay (OH) Jeffersonian
Harper's New Monthly Magazine
Holmes County (OH) Republican

Humboldt (KS) Union
Illinois Staats-Anzeiger
Indianapolis Journal
Macarthur (OH) Enquirer
Madison (IN) Daily Evening Courier
Miami Helmet (Piqua, OH)
Milwaukee Sentinel
Nashville Union
New York Staats-Zeitung
New York Times
New York World
Newark Daily Advertiser
Penny Press (Cincinnati)
Pittsburgh Daily Commercial
Portage (OH) Sentinel
Regensburg Zeitung (Bavaria)
Republican (Chicago)
Sociale Republik (New York)
St. Charles (IL) Chronicle
Sydney Morning Herald
Tifflin (OH) Tribune
Times (London)
United States Mechanics Own (Philadelphia)
Vorwärts! (Paris)
Wapakoneta (OH) Bee
Washington (DC) Union
Weekly Champion and Press (Atchison, KS)
Weekly Express (Chicago)
Western Reserve Chronicle (Warren, OH)

PUBLISHED PRIMARY SOURCES

Anneke, Friedrich. *Der Zweite Freiheitskampf der Vereignigten Staaten von Amerika.* Frankfurt am Main: J. D. Sauerlander, 1861.
———. *Ein ehrengerichtlichtler Proceß.* Leipzig, Germany: Otto Wigand, 1846.
———. *"Wäre ich auch zufällig ein Millionär geworden, meine Gesinnungen und Überzeugungen würden dadurch nicht gelitten haben . . .": Friedrich Annekes Briefe an Friedrich Hammacher, 1846–1859.* Wuppertal, Germany: Friedrich Engels Haus, 1998.
Anneke, Mathilde. *Memoiren einer Frau aus dem badisch-pfaelzischen Feldzuge.* Newark, NJ, 1853.
Becker, Johann Phillip, and Christian Essellen. *Geschihte der Süddeutschen Mai-Revolution.* Geneva, 1849.
Bishop, Judson W. *The Story of a Regiment, Being a Narrative of the Service of the Second Regiment, Minnesota Veteran Volunteer Infantry.* Saint Paul, MN, 1890.
Boernstein, Henry. *Memoirs of a Nobody: The Missouri Years of an Austrian Radical, 1849–1866.* Translated and edited by Steven Rowan. Saint Louis: Missouri Historical Society Press, 1997. Originally published in 1881.

Brant, Jefferson E. *History of the Eighty-Fifth Indiana Volunteer Infantry.* Bloomington, IN: Craven Brothers, 1902.

Bryant, William Cullen. *Poems by William Cullen Bryant.* New York: D. Appleton, 1855.

Buell, Don Carlos. "Shiloh Reviewed." In *Battles and Leaders of the Civil War,* edited by Robert U. Johnson and Clarence C. Buell, 1:487–536. New York: Century, 1887.

Burke, Edmund. *Reflections on the Revolution in France.* London: J. Dodsley, 1790.

Buslett, Ole Amundson. *The Fifteenth Wisconsin.* Translated by Barbara G. Scott. Ripon, WI: B. G. Scott, 1999. Originally published in 1894.

Byers, Samuel H. M. *Iowa in War Times.* Des Moines, IA: W. D. Condit, 1888.

Chambers, Joel. *War Fever Cured: The Civil War Diary of Private Joel R. Chambers, 1864–1865.* Memphis: W. R. Glasgow, 1980.

Cist, Charles. *Sketches and Statistics of Cincinnati in 1859.* Cincinnati, 1859.

Cist, Henry M. *The Army of the Cumberland.* New York: Scribner's, 1882.

Clausewitz, Carl von. *On War.* Edited and translated by Michael Howard and Peter Paret. New York: Alfred A. Knopf, 1993. Originally published in 1832.

Conway, Moncure D. *Autobiography, Memories and Experiences.* 2 vols. New York: Houghton and Mifflin, 1904.

———. *Thomas Paine: A Celebration.* Cincinnati: Dial, 1860.

Cope, Alexis. *The Fifteenth Ohio Volunteers and Its Campaigns.* Columbus, OH: Alexis Cope, 1916.

Corvin, Otto von. *Aus dem Leben eines Volkskämpfers.* Amsterdam: Binger, 1861.

Cox, Jacob D. "McClellan in West Virginia." In *Battles and Leaders of the Civil War,* edited by Robert U. Johnson and Clarence C. Buell, 1:131–37. New York: Century, 1887.

———. "War Preparations in the North." In *Battles and Leaders of the Civil War,* edited by Robert U. Johnson and Clarence C. Buell, 1:97–98. New York: Century, 1887.

Dickson, William M. "The Last Confederate Victim of the American Civil War." *Century* 35, no. 6 (April 1888): 961–62.

Dodge, William Sumner. *History of the Old Second Division, Army of the Cumberland.* Chicago: Church and Goodman, 1864.

Engels, Friedrich. "The Campaign for the Imperial German Constitution." In *Marx and Engels Collected Works,* 10:147–239. New York: International Publishers, 1978.

———. "Repudiation." In *Marx and Engels Collected Works,* 9:482–84. New York: International Publishers, 1977.

Feuerbach, Ludwig. *The Essence of Christianity.* Translated by Marian Evans. New York: Calvin Blanchard, 1855. Originally published in 1841.

Finnup, Frederick. *The Story of My Life.* Garden City, KS: Finnup Foundation, 1996.

Grant, Ulysses S. *Personal Memoirs of U. S. Grant.* New York: Charles L. Webster, 1885.

Great Britain. *Report of the Commissioners Appointed to Consider the Best Mode of Reorganizing the System for Training Officers for the Scientific Corps.* London: Eyre and Spottiswood, 1857.

Grebner, Constantin. *We Were the Ninth: A History of the Ninth Regiment, Ohio Volunteer Infantry, April 17, 1861 to June 7, 1864.* Translated and edited by Frederic Trautmann. Kent, OH: Kent State University Press, 1987. Originally published in 1897.

Grosh, Jere M. "His Last Contribution to *Buffalo, Rochester & Pittsburgh Employees Magazine.*" *Railway Life: Employees Magazine, Buffalo, Rochester & Pittsburgh Railway Co.,* 2, no. 3 (February 1914): 12–14.

Hecker, Friedrich. *Erhebung des Volkes in Baden für die deutsche Republik im Frühjahr 1848.* Basel, Switzerland, 1848.

Herzen, Alexander. *My Past and Thoughts.* Translated by Constance Garnett. 4 vols. New York: Knopf, 1968. Originally published in 1870.

Hess, Moses. *The Holy History of Mankind and Other Writings.* Translated and edited by Shlomo Avineri. Cambridge: Cambridge University Press, 2004. Originally published in 1837.

Hugo, Victor. *Les Miserables.* 4 vols. New York: Little, Brown, 1887. Originally published in 1862.

Johnson, Richard W. *A Soldier's Reminiscences in Peace and War.* Philadelphia: J. B. Lippincott, 1886.

Kamphoefner, Walter D., and Wolfbach Helbich, eds. *Germans in the Civil War: The Letters They Wrote Home.* Chapel Hill: University of North Carolina Press, 2006.

Kenny, D. J. *Illustrated Cincinnati, A Pictorial Hand-Book of the Queen City.* Cincinnati: Robert Clarke, 1875.

Kent, Will Parmiter. *The Story of Libby Prison, Also Some Perils and Sufferings of Certain of its Inmates.* Chicago: Libby Prison War Museum Association, 1890.

Koss, Rudolph. *Milwaukee.* Translated by Hans Ibsen. Milwaukee: Milwaukee *Herald*, 1871.

Koszyk, Kurt, and Karl Oberman, eds. *Zeitgenossen von Marx und Engels.* Amsterdam: Van Gorcum, 1975.

Leslie, C. *Instructions for the Application of Light Drill to Skirmishing in the Field: With Observations on Advanced and Rear Guards, and Flank Patrols.* Dublin: Pettigrew and Oulton, 1831.

Libby Chronicle, The. Devoted to Facts and Fun. A True Copy of the Libby Chronicle as Written by the Prisoners of Libby in 1863. Albany, NY: Louis N. Beaudry, 1889.

Liebknecht, Wilhelm. "Reminiscences of Marx." In *Reminiscences of Marx and Engels.* Translated by Ernest Untermann. Moscow: Foreign Language Publishing House, 1957. Originally published in 1896.

Lincoln, Abraham. *The Collected Works of Abraham Lincoln.* Edited by Roy Basler. 8 vols. New Brunswick, NJ: Rutgers University Press, 1953.

Logsdon, David R., ed. *Eyewitnesses at the Battle of Stones River.* Nashville: Kettle Mills Press, 2002.

Marx, Karl. *The Knight of Noble Consciousness.* In *Marx and Engels Collected Works*, 12:479. New York: International Publishers, 1979. Originally published in 1854.

Marx, Karl, and Friedrich Engels. *The Civil War in the United States.* Edited by Andrew Zimmerman. New York: International Publishers, 2016. Originally published in 1937.

———. "The Great Men of the Exile." In *Marx and Engels Collected Works*, 11:312–16. New York: International Publishers, 1979.

Mieroslawski, Ludwik. *Berichte des Generals Mieroslawski über den Feldzug in Baden.* Bern, Switzerland: Jenni, 1849.

Mögling, Theodor. *Briefe an seine Freunde.* Solothurn, Switzerland: J. Gassmann, 1858.

Moore, Frank, ed. *The Civil War in Song and Story.* New York: P. F. Collier, 1889.

Morris, Gouverneur. *The Diary and Letters of Gouverneur Morris, Minister of the United States to France; Member of the Constitutional Convention.* Edited by Anne Cary Morris. 2 vols. New York: Charles Scribner's Sons, 1888.

Mosman, Chesley A. *The Rough Side of War: The Civil War Journal of Chesley A. Mosman, 1st Lieutenant, Company D, 59th Illinois Volunteer Infantry Regiment.* Garden City, NY: Basin, 1987.

Newlin, W. H., David F. Lawler, and John W. Sherrick. *A History of the Seventy-Third Regiment of Illinois Infantry Volunteers.* Regimental Reunion Association of Survivors of the 73d Illinois Infantry Volunteers, 1890.

Otto, John Henry. *Memoirs of a Dutch Mudsill: The "War Memories" of John Henry Otto, Captain, Company D, 21st Regiment, Wisconsin Volunteer Infantry.* Edited by David Gould and James B. Kennedy. Kent, OH: Kent State University Press, 2004.

Paine, Thomas. *Common Sense.* Philadelphia: W. and T. Bradford, 1776.

———. *Rights of Man.* London: J. S. Jordan, 1791.

Reinhart, Joseph R., ed. *August Willich's Gallant Dutchmen: Civil War Letters from the 32nd Indiana Infantry.* Kent, OH: Kent State University Press, 2006.

Roster and Record of Iowa Soldiers in the War of the Rebellion, Together With Historical Sketches of Volunteer Organizations, 1861–1866. 6 vols. Des Moines, IA: E. H. English, 1911.

Rousseau, Jean-Jacques. *The Social Contract; or, The Principles of Political Rights.* New York: G. P. Putnam's Sons, 1893. Originally published in 1762.

Sallet, Friedrich von. *Gesammelte Gedichte.* 2 vols. Königsberg, Prussia: Im Verlage des Verfassers, 1843.

Schleiermacher, Friedrich. *Aus Schleiermacher's Leben in Briefen.* Berlin: Georg Reimer, 1858.

Schurz, Carl. *Intimate Letters of Carl Schurz, 1841–1869.* Edited and translated by Joseph Schafer. Madison, WI: State Historical Society of Wisconsin, 1928.

———. *The Reminiscences of Carl Schurz.* 3 vols. London: John Murray, 1909.

Scribner, Benjamin F. *How Soldiers Were Made; or, The War as I Saw It.* New Albany, IN: Benjamin F. Scribner, 1887.

Sheridan, Phillip H. *Personal Memoirs of P. H. Sheridan.* 2 vols. New York: Charles L. Webster, 1888.

Sherman, William T. *Memoirs of General William T. Sherman, Written by Himself.* 2 vols. New York: D. Appleton, 1875.

Society of the Army of the Cumberland: Twenty-First Reunion, Toledo, Ohio. Cincinnati: Robert Clarke, 1891.

Soldiers' and Patriots' Biographical Album Containing Biographies and Portraits of Soldiers and Loyal Citizens in the American Conflict, Together with the Great Commanders of the Union Army; Also a History of the Organizations Growing Out of the War [. . .]. Chicago: Union Veteran Publishing Company, 1892.

Staroste, Daniel. *Tagebuch über die Ereignisse in der Pfalz und Baden im Jahre 1849.* 2 vols. Potsdam, Germany: Riegel, 1853.

Struve, Gustav. *Geschichte der drei Volkserhebungen in Baden.* Bern, Switzerland: Verlag von Jenni, 1849.

Tafel, Gustav. *The Cincinnati Germans in the Civil War.* Edited and translated by Don Heinrich Tolzmann. Milford, OH: Little Miami, 2010.

Villard, Henry. *Memoirs of Henry Villard.* 2 vols. Boston: Houghton, Mifflin, 1904.

Wagner, Phillip. *Ein Achtundvierziger. Erlebtes und Gedachtes.* Leipzig, Germany: Otto Wigand, 1882.

Wallace, Lew. *An Autobiography.* 2 vols. New York: Harper and Brothers, 1906.

War of the Rebellion: A Compilation of the Official Records of the Union and Confederate Armies. 128 vols. Washington, DC: Government Printing Office, 1880–1901.

Weber, Max. *Political Writings.* Edited by Peter Lassman and Ronald Speirs. Cambridge: Cambridge University Press, 1994.

Whitney, Thomas R. *A Defence of the American Policy, as Opposed to the Encroachments of Foreign Influence.* New York: De Witt and Davenport, 1856.

Willich, August von. *Im preußischen Heere! Ein Disciplinarverfahren gegen Premier-Lieutenant v. Willich.* Mannheim, Germany: Verlag von Heinrich Hoff, 1848.

Willich, August. *The Army, Standing Army or National Army?* Cincinnati: A. Frey, 1866.

Woodward, James H. "General A. Mc D. McCook at Stone River." *A Paper Read Before the California Commandery of the Military Order of the Loyal Legion of the United States at Los Angeles, Cal., Feb. 22, 1892.* Los Angeles: Times-Mirror, 1892.

SECONDARY SOURCES

Andreas, A. T. *History of Chicago.* 2 vols. Chicago: A. T. Andreas, 1885.

Barnett, James. "August Willich, Soldier Extraordinary." *Bulletin of Historical and Philosophical Society of Ohio* 20, no. 1 (January 1962): 60–74.

———. "Germans in the Union Army." Typescript of speech to Cincinnati Civil War Round Table, March 21, 1963.

———. "The Vilification of August Willich." *Cincinnati Historical Society Bulletin* 24 (January 1966): 29–40.

———. "Willich's Thirty-Second Indiana Volunteers." *Cincinnati Historical Society Bulletin* 37 (Spring 1979): 48–70.

Bayly, C. A., and Eugenio F. Biagini, eds. *Giuseppe Mazzini and the Globalization of Democratic Nationalism, 1830–1920.* New York: Oxford University Press, 2009.

Becker, M. J. *The Germans of 1849 in America.* Mt. Vernon, OH: Republican Printing House, 1887.

Betham-Edwards, Mathilde. "Holidays in Eastern France." *Fraser's Magazine* 18 (September 1878): 636–41.

Bigger, David Dwight. *Ohio's Silver-Tongued Orator: Life and Speeches of General William H. Gibson.* Dayton, OH: United Brethren Publishing House, 1901.

Bradley, Michael R. *Tullahoma: The 1863 Campaign for the Control of Middle Tennessee.* Shippensburg, PA: Burd Street, 2000.

Breckman, Warren. *Marx, the Young Hegelians, and the Origins of Radical Social Theory: Dethroning the Self.* Cambridge: Cambridge University Press, 1999.

Burton, William L. *Melting Pot Soldiers: The Union's Ethnic Regiments.* New York: Fordham University Press, 1998.

Calkins, William Wirt. *The History of the One Hundred and Fourth Regiment of Illinois Volunteer Infantry.* Chicago: Donohue and Henneberry, 1895.

Carwardine, Richard. "'Simply a Theist': Herndon on Lincoln's Religion." *Journal of the Abraham Lincoln Association* 35, no. 2 (Summer 2014): 20–21.

Chisholm, Hugh, ed. "Moltke, Helmuth Carl Bernhard." In *Encyclopedia Britannica.* Vol. 18. New York: Cambridge University Press, 1911.

Chretien, Todd. "Marx and the Silesian Strikers." *SocialistWorker.org* (blog). *International Socialist Organization,* October 3, 2012. https://socialistworker.org/2012/10/03/marx-and-the-silesian-strikers/.

Conzen, Kathleen Neils. "German Americans and the Invention of Ethnicity." In *America and the Germans: An Assessment of a Three-Hundred-Year History,* edited by Frank Trommler and Joseph McVeigh, 1:131–47. Philadelphia: University of Pennsylvania Press, 1985.

———. *Immigrant Milwaukee.* Cambridge, MA: Harvard University Press, 1976.

Cooper, Edward S. *William Babcock Hazen: The Best Hated Man.* Madison, NJ: Farleigh Dickinson University Press, 2005.

Cornu, Auguste. "German Utopianism: 'True Socialism.'" *Science & Society* 12, no. 1 (Winter 1948): 97–112.

Cozzens, Peter. *No Better Place to Die.* Chicago: University of Illinois Press, 1990.

———. *The Shipwreck of Their Hopes: The Battles for Chattanooga*. Chicago: University of Illinois Press, 1994.

———. *This Terrible Sound: The Battle of Chickamauga*. Chicago: University of Illinois Press, 1994.

Cross, George. *The Theology of Schleiermacher*. Chicago: University of Chicago Press, 1911.

Dahlinger, Charles W. *The German Revolution of 1849*. New York: G. P. Putnam's Sons, 1903.

Daniel, Larry J. *Days of Glory: The Army of the Cumberland, 1861–1865*. Baton Rouge: Louisiana State University Press, 2004.

———. *Shiloh: The Battle That Changed the Civil War*. New York: Simon and Schuster, 1997.

De Jonge, Alfred. *Gottfried Kinkel as Political and Social Thinker*. New York: Columbia University Press, 1926.

DeVries, Dawn. "'Be Converted and Become as Little Children': Friedrich Schleiermacher on the Religious Significance of Childhood." In *The Child in Christian Thought*, edited by Marcia J. Bunge, 329–49. Grand Rapids, MI: William B. Eerdmans, 2001.

Diesbach, Alfred. "August von Willich." *Badische Heimat* 58 (1978): 481–98.

Dlubek, Rolf. "August Willich (1810–1878) Vom preußischen Offizier zum Streiter für die Arbeiteremanzipation auf zwei Kontinenten." In *Akteure eines Umbruchs. Männer und Frauen der Revolution von 1848/49*, edited by Helmut Bleiber, Walter Schmidt, and Susanne Schötz, 923–1003. Berlin: Trafo Verlag, 2003.

Dowe, Dieter, Heinz-Gerhard Haupt, Dieter Langewiesch,and Jonathan Sperber, eds. *Europe in 1848: Revolution and Reform*. Translated by David Higgins. New York: Berghahn Books, 2001.

Doyle, Don H. *The Cause of All Nations: An International History of the American Civil War*. New York: Basic Books, 2015.

Drury, Michael. *Transatlantic Radicals and the Early American Republic*. Lawrence: University Press of Kansas, 1997.

Dyer, Thomas G. *Secret Yankees: The Union Circle in Confederate Atlanta*. Baltimore: Johns Hopkins University Press, 1999.

Easton, Loyd D. "Hegelianism in Nineteenth-Century Ohio." *Journal of the History of Ideas* 23, no. 3, (July–September 1962): 355–78.

———. *Hegel's First American Followers*. Athens: Ohio University Press, 1966.

———. "Marx and 'The Knight of Noble Consciousness': August Willich." *Economies et Societies* 28, nos. 6–7 (June–July 1994): 169–80.

———. "Rutherford Hayes and August Willich: Union Generals and Social Reformers." In *Challenging Social Injustice: Essays on Socialism and the Devaluation of the Human Spirit*, edited by Russell L. Ensign and Louis M. Patsouras, 85–102. Lewiston, NY: Edwin Mellen Press, 1993.

Ecelbarger, Gary. "Before Cooper Union: Abraham Lincoln's 1859 Cincinnati Speech and Its Impact on His Nomination." *Journal of the Abraham Lincoln Association* 30, no. 1 (2009): 1–17.

Efford, Alison Clark. "Abraham Lincoln, German-Born Republicans, and American Citizenship." *Marquette Law Review* 93, no. 4 (Summer 2010): 1375–81.

———. "The Arms Scandal of 1870–1872: Immigrant Liberal Republicans and America's Place in the World," in *Reconstruction in a Globalizing World*, edited by David Prior, 94–120. New York: Fordham University Press, 2018.

———. *German Immigrants, Race, and Citizenship in the Civil War Era*. Cambridge: Cambridge University Press, 2013.

Engle, Stephen D. *Yankee Dutchman: The Life of Franz Sigel*. Baton Rouge: Louisiana State University Press, 1993.

Farzin, Sina. "Sallet, Friedrich von." *New German Biography* 22 (2005): 379–80.

Faust, Albert B. *The German Element in the United States*. Boston: Houghton Mifflin, 1909.

Felix, David. *Marx as Politician*. Carbondale: University of Southern Illinois Press, 1982.

Fleche, Andre M. *The Revolution of 1861: The American Civil War in the Age of Nationalist Conflict*. Chapel Hill: University of North Carolina Press, 2012.

Fleischmann, Otto. *Geschichte des Pfälzischen Aufstandes im Jahre 1849: Nach den zugänglichen Quellen geschildert*. Kaiserlautern, Germany: E. Thieme, 1899.

Frankel, Jonathan. *Prophecy and Politics: Socialism, Nationalism, and the Russian Jews, 1862–1917.* Cambridge: Cambridge University Press, 1981.

Freitag, Sabine, ed. *Exiles from European Revolutions: Refugees in Mid-Victorian England*. New York: Berghahn Books, 2003.

———. *Friedrich Hecker: Two Lives for Liberty*. Translated by Steven Rowan. Saint Louis: University of Missouri Press, 2006.

Fritsch, W. A. *History of Germans in Indiana*. New York: G. Steiger, 1896.

Gentile, Gian, Michael E. Linick, and Michael Shurkin. *The Evolution of U.S. Military Policy from the Constitution to the Present*. Santa Monica, CA: Rand Corporation, 2017.

Gienapp, William E. "Nativism and the Creation of a Republican Majority in the North before the Civil War." *Journal of American History* 72, no. 3 (December 1985): 529–59.

Gourevitch, Alex. *From Slavery to the Cooperative Commonwealth: Labor and Republican Liberty in the Nineteenth Century*. Cambridge: Cambridge University Press, 2014.

Greene, Lida L. "Hugh Forbes, Soldier of Fortune." *Annals of Iowa* 38 (1967): 610–11.

Hahn, Hans Joachim. *The 1848 Revolutions in German-Speaking Europe*. London: Longman, 2001.

Harper, Robert S. *Ohio Handbook of the Civil War*. Columbus: Ohio Historical Society, 1961.

Hebert, Walter H. *Fighting Joe Hooker*. Lincoln: University of Nebraska Press, 1999.

Helbich, Wolfgang. "German-Born Union Soldiers: Motivation, Ethnicity, and Americanization." In *German-American Immigration and Ethnicity in Comparative Perspective*, edited by Wolfgang Helbich and Walter D. Kamphoefner, 295–325. Madison: Max Kade Institute for German-American Studies, University of Wisconsin, 2004.

Hess, Earl J. *The Battle of Ezra Church and the Struggle for Atlanta*. Chapel Hill: University of North Carolina Press, 2015.

———. *Civil War Infantry Tactics: Training, Combat, and Small Unit Effectiveness*. Baton Rouge: Louisiana State University Press, 2015.

Honeck, Mischa. "Men of Principle: The German American War for the Union." Talk delivered May 4, 2012, at the US Capitol Historical Society Civil War Symposium.

———. *We Are the Revolutionists: German-Speaking Immigrants and American Abolitionists after 1848*. Athens: University of Georgia Press, 2011.

Howard, Michael E. *The Franco-Prussian War: The German Invasion of France, 1870–1871*. New York: Routledge, 1991.

Ingersoll, Robert J. "Thomas Paine." *North American Review* 155 (July 1892): 181–95.

Jasper, James M. *The Emotions of Protest*. Chicago: University of Chicago Press, 2018.

Kamenka, Eugene, and F. B. Smith, eds. *Intellectuals and Revolution: Socialism and the Experience of 1848*. New York: St. Martin's, 1979.

Kamman, William Frederic. *Socialism in German American Literature*. Philadelphia: Americana Germanica, 1917.

Kaye, Harvey J. *Thomas Paine: Firebrand of the Revolution*. New York: Oxford University Press, 2000.

Keil, Hartmut, ed. *German Workers' Culture in the United States, 1850 to 1920*. Washington, DC: Smithsonian Institution Press, 1988.

Keller, Christian B. *Chancellorsville and the Germans: Nativism, Ethnicity, and Civil War Memory.* New York: Fordham University Press, 2008.

Klement, Frank. *Copperheads in the Middle West.* Chicago: University of Chicago Press, 1960.

———. *Dark Lanterns: Secret Political Societies, Conspiracies, and Treason Trials in the Civil War.* Baton Rouge: Louisiana State University Press, 1984.

Kloss, Karen. "The Eccentric German General." *America's Civil War* 16 (September 2003): 46–54.

Kohut, Adolph. "Eine der ältesten und einflußreichen Familien Deutschlands." *Der Salon für Literatur, Kunst und Gesellschaft* (1890) no. 2, 129–136.

Langhoff, Helmut. "August von Willich in Wesel—Königlich Preußischer Offizier und 'Communist.'" *Wesel and Lower Rhine Historical Association* 6 (2018): 1–26. Reprint.

Lattek, Christine. *Revolutionary Refugees: German Socialism in Britain, 1840–1860.* London: Routledge, 2006.

Lause, Mark A. *Free Labor: The Civil War and the Making of an American Working Class.* Chicago: University of Illinois Press, 2015.

Le théâtre de Besançon: architecture de la musique #1. *Mediamus* (blog), October 18, 2007. https://mediamus.blogspot.com/2007/10/le-thtre-de-besanon-architecture-de-la.html/.

Levine, Bruce. *The Spirit of 1848: German Immigrants, Labor Conflict, and the Coming of the Civil War.* Chicago: University of Illinois Press, 1992.

———. "Who Were the Real Forty-Eighters in the United States?" In *Exiles from European Revolutions: Refugees in Mid-Victorian England,* edited by Sabine Freitag, 234–250. New York: Berghahn Books, 2003.

Luvaas, Jay, Stephen Bowman, and Leonard Fullenkamp, eds. *Guide to the Battle of Shiloh.* Lawrence: University Press of Kansas, 1996.

Mann, Richard F. *The Buckeye Vanguard: The Forty-Ninth Ohio Veteran Volunteer Infantry, 1861–1865.* Milford, OH: Little Miami, 2010.

McDaniel, W. Caleb. *The Problem of Democracy in the Age of Slavery: Garrisonian Abolitionists and Transatlantic Reform.* Baton Rouge: Louisiana State University Press, 2013.

McDonough, James L. *Shiloh–in Hell before Night.* Knoxville: University of Tennessee Press, 1977.

McLellan, David. *Karl Marx: His Life and Thought.* New York: Harper and Row, 1973.

McMurray, William J. *History of Auglaize County, Ohio.* 2 vols. Auglaize County, OH: Historical Publishing, 1923.

McMurtry, R. Gerald, ed. "Lincoln Visited by a German Delegation of Workingmen In Cincinnati, Ohio, February 12, 1861." *Lincoln Lore* 1575 (May 1969): 1–3.

McPherson, James M. *Abraham Lincoln and the Second American Revolution.* New York: Oxford University Press, 1991.

Moncure, James A. *Research Guide to European Historical Biography, 1450–Present.* 2 vols. Washington, DC: Beacham, 1992.

Mueller, Theodore. "Mathilde Franziska Anneke: Reformer, Suffragette, Author." *Historical Messenger of the Milwaukee County Historical Society* 23, no. 4 (December 1967): 125–30.

Nadel, Stanley. *Little Germany: Ethnicity, Religion, and Class in New York City, 1845–80.* Chicago: University of Illinois Press, 1990.

Nicolaevsky, Boris I. "August Willich, Ein Soldat der Revolution von 1848." *Der Abend* (Berlin), May 4 and 6, 1931.

Nicolaevsky, Boris I., and Otto Maenchen-Helfen. *Karl Marx: Man and Fighter.* Translated by Gwenda David and Eric Mosbocher. London: Methuen, 1936.

Noble, Kraig. "General August Willich." In *The St. Marys Anthology: Tales and Sketches from an American Small Town,* edited by Robert Howard, 36–44. Saint Marys, OH: Buzan, 2013.

Nosworthy, Brent. *The Bloody Crucible of Courage: Fighting Methods and Combat Experience of the Civil War.* New York: Carrol and Graf, 2003.

Oberman, Karl. *Joseph Weydemeyer: Pioneer of American Socialism.* New York: International Publishers, 1947.

O'Connell, Daniel F. "Letters Not Written in Blood: The Tullahoma Campaign." *Essential Civil War Curriculum* (blog). https://www.essentialcivilwarcurriculum.com/letters-not-written-in-blood-the-tullahomacampaign.html/.

Öfele, Martin W., *German-Speaking Officers in the U.S. Colored Troops, 1863–1867.* Gainesville: University Press of Florida, 2004.

———. *True Sons of the Republic: European Immigrants in the Union Army.* Westport, CT: Praeger, 2008.

Parkinson, Roger. *Clausewitz: A Biography.* New York: Cooper Square, 2002.

Peake, Michael A. *Blood Shed In This War: Civil War Illustrations by Captain Adolph Metzner, 32nd Indiana.* Indianapolis: Indiana Historical Society Press, 2010.

———. *Indiana's German Sons: A History of the 1st German 32nd Regiment Indiana Volunteer Infantry.* Indianapolis: Max Kade German-American Center, 1995.

Powell, David A. *The Maps of Chickamauga: An Atlas of the Chickamauga Campaign, Including the Tullahoma Operations, June 22–September 23, 1863.* New York: Savas Beatie, 2009.

Prokopowicz, Gerald J. *All for the Regiment: The Army of the Ohio, 1861–1862.* Chapel Hill: University of North Carolina Press, 2001.

Randers-Pehrson, Justine Davis. *Adolf Douai, 1819–1888: The Turbulent Life of a German Forty-Eighter in the Homeland and in the United States.* New York: Peter Lang, 2000.

———. *Germans and the Revolution of 1848–1849.* New York: Peter Lang, 2001

Rapport, Mike. *1848: Year of Revolution.* New York: Basic Books, 2008.

Ratterman, Heinrich A. "August Willich." *Der Deutsche Pionier* 9 (1878): 439–45.

Reiss, Ansgar. *Radikalismus und Exil: Gustav Struve und die Demokratie in Deutschland und Amerika.* Stuttgart, Germany: Steiner, 2004.

Reitz, Charles. "Socialist Turners of New York City, 1853: Archival Materials Warrant Further Research." *Yearbook of German-American Studies* 45 (2010): 95–106.

Richter, William L. *The Army in Texas during Reconstruction, 1865–1870.* College Station: Texas A&M University Press, 1987.

Roberts, Timothy Mason. *Distant Revolutions: 1848 and the Challenge to American Exceptionalism.* Charlottesville: University of Virginia Press, 2009.

Roche, Helen. "'Go Tell the Prussians . . .': The Spartan Paradigm in Prussian Military Thought during the Long Nineteenth Century." *New Voices in Classical Reception Studies* 7 (2012): 25–39.

Rude, Fernand. *Les Réfugiés Allemands a Besançon sous la Dexième République.* Besançon, France: Millot, 1939.

Schlicher, J. J. "Eduard Schroeter the Humanist." *Wisconsin Magazine of History* 28, no. 4 (March 1945): 307–24.

Secrist, Philip L. *The Battle of Resaca: Atlanta Campaign 1864.* Macon, GA: Mercer University Press, 1998.

Sellars, Roy W. "Fichte, Johann Gottlieb." In *The Encyclopedia Americana* vol. 11. New York: Encyclopedia Americana Corporation, 1919.

Shingleton, Royce, *High Seas Confederate: The Life and Times of John Newland Maffitt.* Columbia: University of South Carolina Press, 1994.

Smith, Timothy B. *Shiloh: Conquer or Perish.* Lawrence: University Press of Kansas, 2014.

Sperber, Jonathan. *The European Revolutions, 1848–1851*. Cambridge: Cambridge University Press, 1994.

———. *Karl Marx: A Nineteenth-Century Life*. New York: Liveright, 2013.

———. *Rhineland Radicals: The Democratic Movement and the Revolution of 1848–1849*. Princeton, NJ: Princeton University Press, 1991.

Stadelmann, Rudolph. *Social and Political History of the German 1848 Revolution*. Translated by James G. Chastain. Athens: Ohio University Press, 1975.

Stewart, Charles D. "A Bachelor General." *Wisconsin Magazine of History* 17, no.2 (December 1933): 131–54.

Stidger, Felix Grundy. *Treason History of the Order of Sons of Liberty*. Chicago: Felix Stidger, 1903.

Sword, Wiley. *Mountains Touched with Fire: Chattanooga Besieged, 1863*. New York: St. Martin's, 1995.

———. *Shiloh: Bloody April*. New York: William Morrow, 1974.

Taylor, Keith. *The Political Ideas of the Utopian Socialists*. London: Frank Cass, 1982.

Thompson, Jerry. *The Life and Times of Major General Samuel P. Heintzelman*. College Station: Texas A&M University Press, 2006.

Tolzmann, Don Heinrich. *German-Americana: Selected Essays*. Milford, OH: Little Miami, 2009.

———, ed. *The German Forty-Eighters, 1848–1998*. Indianapolis: Max Kade German-American Center, 1998.

———. *German Heritage Guide to the Greater Cincinnati Area*. Milford, OH: Little Miami, 2003.

———. *Over-the-Rhine Tour Guide*. Milford, OH: Little Miami, 2011.

Topham, Washington. "Northern Liberty Market." *Records of the Columbia Historical Society, Washington, D.C.* 24 (1922): 43–66.

Townsend, Mary Bobbitt. *Yankee Warhorse: A Biography of Major General Peter Osterhaus*. Columbia: University of Missouri Press, 2010.

Trefousse, Hans L. *Carl Schurz: A Biography*. Knoxville: University of Tennessee Press, 1982.

Valentin, Veit. *1848: Chapters of German History*. Translated by Ethel Scheffauer, London: George Allen and Unwin, 1940.

Walsh, Robert. "England's Last Fatal Duel." *Sword and Scale* (blog), June 6, 2015. http://swordandscale.com/englands-last-fatal-duel/.

White, Jr., Paul Richard. "A Decisive Level of Command: Brigade Leadership in the Army of the Cumberland, 1861–1864." Master's thesis, Middle Tennessee State University, 2014.

Williamson, C. W. *History of Western Ohio and Auglaize County*. Columbus, OH: W. M. Linn and Sons, 1905.

Wittke, Carl F. "Friedrich Hassaurek: Cincinnati's Leading Forty-Eighter." *Ohio Historical Quarterly* 68 (1959): 1–17.

———. *Refugees of Revolution: The German Forty-Eighters in America*. Philadelphia: University of Pennsylvania Press, 1952.

———*The Utopian Communist: A Biography of Wilhelm Weitling, Nineteenth Century Reformer*. Baton Rouge: Louisiana State University Press, 1950.

Woodworth, Steven E. *Six Armies in Tennessee: The Chickamauga and Chattanooga Campaigns*. Lincoln: University of Nebraska Press, 1998.

Wust, Klaus G. "German Immigrants and Their Newspapers in the District of Columbia." In *Thirtieth Report, Society for the History of the Germans in Maryland*, 36–65. Baltimore: Society for the History of the Germans in Maryland, 1959.

Zimmerman, Andrew. "From the Rhine to the Mississippi: Property, Democracy, and Socialism in the American Civil War." *Journal of the Civil War Era* 5, no. 1 (March 2015): 3–37.

Zimmermann, Felix. "Als die Lohnarbeit 'frei' wurde. Zum Verständnis der 'freien Arbeit' bei republikanischen und marxistischen Achtundvierzigern in den USA." *Arbeit—Bewegung—Geschichte. Zeitschrift für Historische Studien* no. 1 (2019): 94–110.

———. "A Different Republicanism: August Willich and the Trade Unions in Antebellum Cincinnati." Transcript of talk delivered April 1, 2017, at "The Legacy of 1848 through Today" conference, Northfield, MN.

Zucker, A. E., ed. *The Forty-Eighters: Political Refugees of the German Revolution of 1848.* New York: Columbia University Press, 1950.

Index